RE-IMAGINING DEMOCRACY
IN THE AGE OF REVOLUTIONS

Re-imagining Democracy in the Age of Revolutions charts a transformation in the way people thought about democracy in the North Atlantic region in the years between the American Revolution and the revolutions of 1848. In the mid-eighteenth century, 'democracy' was a word known only to the literate. It was associated primarily with the ancient world and had negative connotations: democracies were conceived to be unstable, warlike, and prone to mutate into despotisms. By the mid-nineteenth century, however, the word had passed into general use, although it was still not necessarily an approving term. In fact, there was much debate about whether democracy could achieve robust institutional form in advanced societies.

In this volume, a cast of internationally-renowned contributors shows how common trends developed throughout the United States, France, Britain, and Ireland, particularly focussing on the era of the American, French, and subsequent European revolutions. *Re-imagining Democracy in the Age of Revolutions* argues that 'modern democracy' was not invented in one place and then diffused elsewhere, but instead was the subject of parallel re-imaginings, as ancient ideas and examples were selectively invoked and reworked for modern use. The contributions significantly enhance our understanding of the diversity and complexity of our democratic inheritance.

Re-imagining Democracy in the Age of Revolutions

America, France, Britain, Ireland 1750–1850

Edited by
JOANNA INNES
and
MARK PHILP

OXFORD

UNIVERSITY PRESS

OXFORD
UNIVERSITY PRESS

Great Clarendon Street, Oxford, OX2 6DP,
United Kingdom

Oxford University Press is a department of the University of Oxford.
It furthers the University's objective of excellence in research, scholarship,
and education by publishing worldwide. Oxford is a registered trade mark of
Oxford University Press in the UK and in certain other countries

Published in the United States of America by Oxford University Press
198 Madison Avenue, New York, NY 10016, United States of America

British Library Cataloguing in Publication Data
Data available

Library of Congress Cataloging in Publication Data
Data available

ISBN 978–0–19–966915–8 (Hbk.)
ISBN 978–0–19–873881–7 (Pbk.)

Links to third party websites are provided by Oxford in good faith and
for information only. Oxford disclaims any responsibility for the materials
contained in any third party website referenced in this work.

Table of Contents

IV. IRELAND

Preface and Acknowledgements

This book represents the first significant fruit of a larger inquiry into the re-imagining of democracy in Europe and the Americas between the middle of the eighteenth and the middle of the nineteenth centuries. We first launched this inquiry almost ten years ago, when our friend Mariana Saad suggested to us that we find a topic on which we could collaborate 'with some French people'. Since then we have learnt a lot from many French people, more than the list of contributors to this volume might suggest.

We are especially grateful to François Jarrige, for having organized a number of Paris workshops for us, and brought French visitors to Oxford workshops. French scholars who have participated in our meetings have included: Serge Aberdam, Benoît Agnès, Sylvie Aprile, Fabrice Bensimon, Bertrand Binoche, Déborah Cohen, Laurent Colantonio, Michael Drolet, Geneviève Fraisse, Emmanuel Fureix, Maxime Kaci, Steve Kaplan, Anna Karla, Olivier Letrocquer, Gilles Malandain, Philippe Minard, the late Emile Perreau-Saussine, Nathalie Richard, Anne Simonin, Julien Vincent, and Sophie Wahnich.

We are also grateful to the many British and Irish scholars who have participated in our Oxford workshops—especially in the early days, when our thinking was inchoate and our sense of direction underdeveloped. They have included Richard Bourke, Chris Brooke, Malcolm Chase, Greg Claeys, Harry Dickinson, Oliver Dowlen, Carolyn Downs, John Dunn, Alex Franklin, Liz Frazer, Ultán Gillen, Kathryn Gleadle, Amanda Goodrich, Carl Griffin, Peter Gurney, Rachel Hammersley, Bob Harris, Gareth Stedman Jones, Jessica Kimpell (who kindly took notes on several occasions), Ray Lavertue, Jim Livesey, Philip Lockley, David Magee, Jon Mee, Katrina Navickas, Tadgh O Sullivan, Regina Poertner, Robert Poole, John Robertson, Helen Rogers, Philip Salmon, Philip Schofield, John Seed, Richard Sheldon, George Southcombe, and Richard Whatmore; also German scholars Thomas Biskup and Michael Schaich.

A lively and enjoyable American workshop was attended by several contributors to this book and also by Johannes Dillinger, Robin Einhorn, Eric Foner, Donald Ratcliffe, and Andrew Robertson.

Faramerz Dabhoiwala, Maurizio Isabella, Reidar Maliks, Eduardo Posada Carbo, Liz Potter, Rob Saunders, Nadia Urbinati, and John Watts kindly addressed our seminar. Repeat attenders at our reading group not already listed have included Tom Crook, Tom Cutterham, Graciela Iglesias Rogers, Shany Mor, Matthew Niblett, Anna Plassart, Frank Prochaska, Harry Smith, Tim Stuart-Buttle, and Laurence Whitehead. Nicholas Cole, Miriam Griffin, Andrew Lintott, Oswyn Murray, and Liz Potter helped us at a very illuminating reading-group session on ancient and modern democracy. Shany Mor and Graciela Iglesias Rogers also helped us to build up our ongoing group bibliography on Zotero (and thanks to Tim Hitchcock for alerting us to the existence of this website and software).

Among those speaking or otherwise helping at our June 2010 conference, the seedbed for this book, those who do not figure among contributors to this volume were Pierre Karila Cohen, Dan Feller, Eric Foner, Robert Gildea, Peter Grey, Peter Gurney; Louis Hincker, Gareth Stedman Jones, Alex Keyssar, Jim Livesey, Frank O'Gorman, Miles Taylor, and Sophie Wahnich.

It is perhaps appropriate that an inquiry into democracy should have been shaped by so many voices.

We are also grateful to Ben Jackson and David Leopold, to Emmanuel Fureix and Louis Hincker, to Stuart Jones, to Liz Frazer, to Rachel Foxley, and to Gareth Stedman Jones for giving us the opportunity to try out some of our ideas, and to learn from other participants in sessions that they organized; to Andreas Gestrich, Director of the German Historical Institute London, Michael Schaich, also of the GHIL, and Eckhart Hellmuth, then of the Ludwig Maximilian Universität Munich, for having helped us to organize an Anglo-German session; to Eduardo Posada Carbo and Samuel Valenzuela for having invited us to their pan-American conference at Notre Dame, Illinois; to Mauro Lenci for organizing two sessions in Pisa, and to Henk te Velde for his hospitality in Leiden. We hope that these interactions will bear fruit in future work.

Our initial meetings were financed by the Scientific and Technical Section of the French Embassy in London. The Oxford Faculty of History—and its offshoot the Modern European History Research Centre—and the Department of Politics and International Relations have repeatedly helped with small sums. The Oxford University John Fell Fund supported many of our workshops and our June 2010 conference with a major grant. Successive directors of the Maison Française d'Oxford have been helpful and generous. Nigel Bowles of the Rothermere American Institute Oxford very kindly hosted our 2010 conference. We would not have been able to sustain our varied programme of activities had many of our participants not paid their own way (with or without help from their institutions).

The Leverhulme Foundation has awarded us an international network grant to pursue our inquiry during 2012–15 through a series of workshops and conferences focusing on Mediterranean democracy. We greatly appreciate the help of Aileen Mooney, research officer of the Oxford History Faculty, with this and other funding applications.

We are grateful to Harry Smith for his assistance in the preparation of this volume, to Paul Slack, and to Stephanie Ireland and Christopher Wheeler of Oxford University Press for their interest and encouragement. Also to Cathryn Steele, Emma Barber, Richard Mason, Gail Eaton, and Megan James for their assistance at various stages in the production process.

Notes on Contributors

Laurent Colantonio is Maître de Conférences at the University of Poitiers. His initial research was dedicated to French political uses of O'Connell. He currently works on Irish national and popular movements. His research interests also include the writing of history and memory issues. He is the author of 'La Grande Famine en Irlande (1846–1851): objet d'histoire, enjeu de mémoire', *Revue historique* (2007); 'Exploring Daniel O'Connell's Political Ideology', in O. Coquelin et al. (eds), *Political Ideology in Ireland* (2009); and 'Mobilisation nationale, souveraineté populaire et normalisations en Irlande (années 1820–1840)', *Revue d'histoire du XIXe siècle* (2011). He is writing a biography of Daniel O'Connell.

S. J. Connolly is Professor of Irish History at the Queen's University, Belfast. The main focus of his research has been on different aspects of popular and elite politics, religion, and culture between the late seventeenth and nineteenth centuries. His books include *Priests and People in Pre-Famine Ireland 1780–1845* (1982); *Religion, Law and Power: The Making of Protestant Ireland* (1992); *Contested Island: Ireland 1460–1630* (2007); and *Divided Kingdom: Ireland 1630–1800* (2008). His current research is on civic culture in nineteenth-century Belfast.

Seth Cotlar is Professor of History at Willamette University in Salem, Oregon. His book, *Tom Paine's America: The Rise and Fall of Transatlantic Radicalism in the Early Republic* (2011), was awarded the James Broussard Best First Book Prize by the Society for Historians of the Early American Republic. His current project is a cultural history of nostalgia between the American Revolution and the Civil War.

Malcolm Crook is Emeritus Professor of French History at Keele University, where he has taught for the entirety of his career. He specializes in the eighteenth- and nineteenth-century history of France, with particular emphasis on the Revolutionary and Napoleonic periods. His books include a monograph on elections during the Revolution and a study of Napoleon's rise to power. He has recently stepped down as editor of the journal *French History* in order to complete a book on the development of electoral culture in France, entitled *How the French Learned to Vote*.

Michael Drolet teaches the History of Political Thought at the University of Oxford. His publications include *Tocqueville, Democracy and Social Reform* (2003), which was a *Choice Magazine* Outstanding Academic Title, and *The Postmodernism Reader: Foundational Texts* (2004). He has written extensively on nineteenth-century French liberalism and is currently writing an intellectual biography of Michel Chevalier.

Laura F. Edwards is Professor of History at Duke University. Her scholarship focuses on race, gender, labour, and the law in the nineteenth-century American South. Most recently, she was the author of *The People and Their Peace: Legal Culture and the Transformation of Inequality in the Post-Revolutionary South* (2009), which received the Littleton-Griswold prize for the best book on law and society and the Charles Sydnor prize for the best book on Southern history. She is working on a legal history of the Civil War and Reconstruction, for which she was awarded a Guggenheim Fellowship.

Ultán Gillen is Senior Lecturer in European (French) History at Teeside University. His research focuses on international revolution and counter-revolution during the age of revolutions. He has published on topics including the Enlightenment and Irish political culture, Irish counter-revolutionary constructions of history, and the relationship between French and Irish republicanism. He is currently completing a study of the political thought and legacy of the leading United Irishman Theobald Wolfe Tone, entitled *Theobald Wolfe Tone: Revolutionary Democrat*.

Joanna Innes is Fellow and Tutor in Modern History at Somerville College, Oxford. She works on government, society, and political culture, mainly in the British Isles circa 1688–1850. She co-edited with Arthur Burns *Rethinking the Age of Reform: Britain 1780–1850* (2003). Her book *Inferior Politics: Social Problems and Social Policies in Britain 1688–1800* (2009) brings together themes from several decades of her work. She has co-organized the Re-imagining Democracy project with Mark Philp since 2004.

Mark Philp is Professor of History and Politics at the University of Warwick. His research includes work on political thought and British history at the time of the French Revolution. Recent work includes *Reforming Ideas in Britain* (2013), and *Political Conduct* (2007). From 2007–2010 he directed the Leverhulme-funded research project editing William Godwin's diary, available at http://godwindiary.bodleian.ox.ac.uk/. He is co-organiser with Joanna Innes of the Re-imagining Democracy project.

Robert Saunders is Lecturer in History at Jesus College, Oxford, and Lecturer in Politics at Lincoln College, Oxford. His research interests include the history of democratic thought, the relationship between Britain and Europe, and the history of Thatcherism. He is the author of *Democracy and the Vote in British Politics, 1848–67: The Making of the Second Reform Act* (2011) and co-editor with Ben Jackson of *Making Thatcher's Britain* (2012).

Ruth Scurr is Fellow and Director of Studies in Politics at Gonville & Caius College, Cambridge. She teaches the History of Political Thought (1700–1890). Her book *Fatal Purity: Robespierre and the French Revolution* was published in 2006.

Adam I. P. Smith is Senior Lecturer in History at University College London. He is the author of several essays on US politics in the nineteenth century and of *No Party Now: Politics in the Civil War North* (2006). He is also a contributor and co-editor, with Nicola Miller and Axel Körner, of *America Imagined: Explaining the United States in Nineteenth-Century Europe and Latin America* (2012).

Abbreviations

Archives parlementaires	*Archives parlementaires de 1787 à 1860. Recueil des débats législatifs et politiques des Chambres françaises*, ed. Jérôme Mavidal and Emile Laurent (2eme série, 127 vols, Paris, 1867–1913).
Avalon Project	*The Avalon Project: Documents in Law, History and Diplomacy*, http://avalon.law.yale.edu
CJ	*House of Commons, Journals* (89 vols to 1834, London, 1803–34).
Hansard	[Hansard, publisher] *Parliamentary Debates*, 1st ser. (41 vols, London, 1803–20), 2nd ser. (24 vols, London, 1820–30).
NS	*Northern Star* (Leeds 1838–52).

Introduction

Joanna Innes and Mark Philp

In the middle of the eighteenth century, 'democracy' and 'democratic' were literate words, familiar to a broad educated public, but not in common use.[1] They connoted above all the ancient world: Greece and republican Rome. Yet Greek and Roman institutions differed: 'democracy' was accordingly not strongly associated with any specific institutional arrangement. In fact, many whose education gave them some familiarity with Greek and Roman history did not know a great deal about how ancient polities had been governed. 'Democracy' therefore connoted not so much a specific institutional order as a cluster of political phenomena: crowd activity; popular pressure on government; demagogues bidding for crowd support; impulsive politics; coercion or punishment of those who opposed the popular will; and in general tumult and instability—perhaps culminating in the emergence of a strong man who, either in the name of the people or in the name of order, might attempt to impose himself as an all-powerful leader, a tyrant or despot.[2] John Milton, in his epic poem *Paradise Regained*, evoked the 'fierce democracy' of the ancients. That phrase was endlessly recycled through the eighteenth and nineteenth centuries.[3]

It was possible to imagine democracy acquiring stable institutional form in the modern world. It was recognized that republics might be more or less democratic. And in Britain there developed from the seventeenth century a theory of 'mixed

---

[1] The anglophone magazine-reading public was expected to know the term and its cognates. Readers might have encountered Bolingbroke's much-reproduced *Craftsman* essays of the 1730s, which often invoked the mixed constitution; in the 1750s the terms figure in, for example, the *Gentleman's Magazine*, *Old Woman's Magazine*, *Scots Magazine*, and *Critical* and *Monthly Reviews*; see also Robert Dodsley, *The Preceptor* (London, 1758). In France at the same time, they occurred in *Le journal des savants* and in the publications of various royal and provincial academies; see also *Le précepteur* (1750).

[2] Jennifer Tolbert Roberts, *Athens on Trial: The Antidemocratic Tradition in Western Thought* (Princeton, NJ, 1994). For Rome as democracy, Richard Tuck, 'Hobbes and Democracy', in Annabel S. Brett et al. (eds), *Rethinking the Foundations of Modern Political Thought* (Cambridge, 2006), 180–3; Richard Bourke, 'Enlightenment, Revolution and Democracy', *Constellations* 15 (2008), 18–21; Ian McDaniel, 'Scottish Historians and Modern Revolutions', in Anke Fischer-Kattner et al. (eds), *Schleifspuren. Lesarten des 18 Jahrhunderts* (Munich, 2011), 75–84. M. N. S. Sellers, *American Republicanism: Roman Ideology in the United States Constitution* (Basingstoke, 1994), emphasizes fear of democracy in Roman tradition.

[3] John Milton, *Paradise Regained*, book 4, lines 267–70: 'Thence to the famous orators repair,/ Those ancients, whose resistless eloquence/Wielded at will that fierce democratie,/Shook the arsenal, and fulmin'd over Greece'. For instances, see chapter 2 by Adam I. P. Smith (p. 34) and chapter 11 by Laurent Colantonio (pp. 165 and 170) in this volume.

government'. In a blend of ideas deriving on the one hand from Aristotle sieved through Polybius, and on the other hand from the notion that the institutional apparatus should incorporate several 'estates', British government came to be conceptualized as combining monarchical, aristocratic, and democratic elements.[4] The virtue of democracy in this context was, however, thought to lie precisely in the mix, in its being balanced by other elements, so that none had the chance to become too powerful.

Unsurprisingly, in this context, neither American nor French revolutions were launched in the name of 'democracy'. Yet each threw up what educated contemporaries were quick to identify as democratic phenomena. And as each revolution unfolded, revolutionary leaders came under pressure to give more weight to democracy in government. This involved continuing the work of remodelling institutions that the revolutions had begun so as to give more effective voice to the mass of the people. Though 'democracy' retained problematic associations, and was often invoked to negative effect, in America and France at least the process of 're-imagining' democracy for modern times had begun—a process entailing change both in language and in practice.[5] Some observers in Britain and Ireland (and elsewhere) aspired to follow their example.[6]

Yet it was unclear how applicable American experiments were to the quite different European social and geopolitical environment. And French attempts to found democratic republics in France and other parts of Europe were discouraging, not least because, following the traditional script, the experiment gave rise first to tumult and then to Napoleonic despotism. In a European context, 'democracy' was substantially discredited by the unfolding of the French Revolution, and had to be re-imagined all over again, from the 1820s through the 1840s, to make possible the shift that crystallized during the revolutionary wave of 1848, when briefly, across Europe, many different contenders—from Marx to monarchs—quarrelled over whose cause was the most 'democratic'.[7]

Democracy at mid-century and for some decades after continued to connote insurrectionary movements, mass petitioning and crowd phenomena, as much as it did any particular institutional set-up. Still, by the mid-nineteenth century, a set of ideas had developed about the institutional form a modern democracy might be expected to take.[8] Above all (it had come to be supposed), for a polity to deserve

---

[4] Corinne Comstock Weston, *English Constitutional Theory and the House of Lords 1556–1832* (London, 1965). When German and French writers of the seventeenth and eighteenth centuries invoked ideas of mixed or balanced government, they commonly imagined monarchy as being tempered above all by aristocracy.

[5] See chapter 1 by Seth Cotlar and chapter 4 by Ruth Scurr in this volume.

[6] See chapter 7 by Mark Philp and chapter 10 by Ultán Gillen in this volume.

[7] Jens A. Christophersen, *The Meaning of 'Democracy' as Used in European Ideologies from the French to the Russian Revolution: An Historical Study in Political Language* (Oslo, 1966), esp. 118–57 (on Proudhon and Marx); Otto Brunner, Werner Conze, and Reinhardt Koselleck (eds), *Geschichtliche Grundbegriffe: Historisches Lexikon zur Politisch-Sozialen Sprache in Deutschland* (8 vols, Stuttgart, 1972–97), 1: 880 for monarchical democracy.

[8] Google Ngram (books.google.com/ngrams) suggests that in British English the phrase 'modern democracy' came into use in the 1790s, but for some decades following there were as many references to ancient as to modern democracy; only from the 1840s did the latter phrase forge ahead.

that title it should give prominence, among institutions of government, to a legislature whose members should be chosen by 'universal' (that is, adult male) suffrage. Yet few democrats thought that this sufficed. There remained much scope for debate about what else was entailed. Could a monarchy qualify as democratic, or was it necessary that the head of state also be elected? What other office-holders should be elected? Should they include judges? To what extent should the people's representatives themselves have originated from the common mass? Was it compatible with democracy that government should be centralized, or should the bulk of power be devolved? Was it necessary for all citizens to bear arms? What were the implications of democracy for women? Insofar as democracy connoted not only popular participation in government but also commitment to some form of social equality, could a polity rightly call itself 'democratic' when many who lived under its protection were enslaved? Did it suffice to make everyone (or all adult males) equal before the law—or was it necessary also to provide universal education? Or indeed, to ensure that all would-be independent adults had a chance to support themselves decently by their own exertions?[9]

Polities that call themselves democratic in the twenty-first century embody different answers to these questions. Some of these issues remain debating points. In the mid- nineteenth century, all were in contention. Moreover, at that time it was still unclear whether it was possible to give enduring institutional form to *any* full-blooded version of democracy: unclear that democracy was a realistic thing to hope for in the longer term. Many did not hope for it. A few thought that, though some form of 'pure democracy' (if that could be instituted) might have merit, by contrast representative democracy had been shown to be a sham. Some feared that instituting democracy would entail the triumph of narrow, self-seeking materialism. Some worried that it would bring vulgarity; that minority rights would be sacrificed to majority will, or that democratic politics would be emotional and impulse-driven, nationalistic and aggressive—and slide into rule by a strong leader (which in the early 1850s happened once again in France).[10]

By the middle of the nineteenth century, discourses about democracy had acquired some features that are familiar to us, but retained others that are less so. Institutional forms and practices that we equate with democracy had taken shape, yet these remained experimental and fluid, and notions about what more broadly constituted good democratic practice remained contentious. In 1848 probably more people were prepared to endorse democracy as an aspiration than at any time since the birth of Christ, yet many, for a wide range of reasons, did not aspire to it. Some instead placed their hopes in 'socialism', a term that had developed coevally with democracy's second re-imagining; others hoped that both democracy and socialism might yet be seen off, recognized as equally ill-fitted to the circumstances of the modern world.

[9] See chapters by Adam Smith (2), Michael Drolet (5), Innes, Philp, and Saunders (8), and Laurent Colantonio (11) in this volume.
[10] For critics, see Michael Drolet in this volume (chapter 5); Christophersen, *Meaning*, chs 3–9; Robert Saunders, 'Democracy', in David Craig and James Thompson (eds), *Languages of Politics in Modern British History* (Basingstoke, forthcoming 2013).

Our object in this book is to explore these early processes of 're-imagining democracy'. As we understand it and as we have sketched it above, this was partly a matter of reconceptualizing the reference of the word: giving 'democracy' richer modern content. But it also linked to social, political, and institutional change. Much of this change was autonomous—the world changed, for all kinds of reasons, and as a result it became possible to give such words as 'democracy' and 'democratic' new content. But some changes sprang from self-conscious attempts to give democratic aspiration purchase on the modern world; that is, from attempts to give sustainable meaning, under the rubric of 'democracy', to the idea that no one should be regarded as intrinsically more worthy than any other person, and that everyone should have a meaningful say in shaping the system of rules and obligations that makes it possible for human beings to live together—ideals that have ancient roots.

The first histories of democracy were composed in the later nineteenth century, and others have followed, though their number is not great. Historians from the past disagreed about how long democracy had been in the making, and how promising its prospects were.[11] More recent histories have—like this volume—been inclined to stress the open-ended or 'unfinished' nature of the journey.[12] Alongside general histories, a host of studies—sometimes general, sometimes focusing on particular states—have detailed institutional change, and the political contexts in which institutions were refashioned. During the past half-century, much new light has been shed on the social and cultural contexts of change: histories have been written from below and sideways. To a long-standing lineage of studies of significant thinkers, recent decades have also added studies of concepts and terminology, marking the influence of conceptual history and the linguistic turn. Interest in both past experience of and past talk about democracy has accelerated since the late 1980s, as a 'wave' of democratization has swept the territories of the former Soviet Union, South Africa, Latin America, and most recently parts of the Arab world. The 'Guide to Further Reading' at the end of this book provides an introduction to this rich and diverse body of work.

Yet, for all that has been done, there remains much to explore about the terrain covered here. It remains—for example—a challenge to bring our recently much-expanded knowledge of word use and debate into effective relationship with what we know about behaviour, practice, and the development of institutions. Many histories of words and ideas only lightly sketch their place within the social and

[11] Nahum Capen, *The History of Democracy; or, Political Progress Historically Illustrated, from the Earliest to the Latest Periods* (vol. publ., Hartford, CT, 1874), associated democracy with the Democratic Party, and was upbeat about both, whereas Jonathan Norcross, *The History of Democracy, Considered as a Party Name and as a Political Organization* (New York, 1883), was a republican diatribe against democracy and its 'captivating' leaders, from ancient Greece onwards. Thomas Erskine May, *Democracy in Europe. A History* (2 vols, London, 1877), was optimistic on balance. Sir Henry Sumner Maine, *Popular Government* (London, 1885), by contrast saw democracy as a recent and largely unsuccessful experiment.

[12] John Dunn (ed.), *Democracy: The Unfinished Journey, 508 BC to AD 1993* (Oxford, 1992); see also his *Setting the People Free: The Story of Democracy* (London, 2005); John Keane, *The Life and Death of Democracy* (London, 2009).

political world that speakers and writers tried to describe or affect. Conversely, histories of democratic institutions and practices still too often deploy modern ideas as to what is 'democratic' to characterize what they are charting—and consequently miss opportunities to explore ways in which past understandings shaped practice. Certain parts of the terrain that we explore have previously barely been penetrated: there has been surprisingly little work on patterns of talk about democracy in eighteenth- and nineteenth-century Britain and Ireland.[13] Moreover, the new reader, trying to make inroads into the field, will struggle to find accounts that pull together work on almost any aspect of the larger topic across different national historical traditions.

This book represents, at one and the same time, an introduction to the topic, an attempt to advance knowledge, and a bid to shape the research agenda. We have commissioned twelve experts in their fields to write chapters that chronicle and explore the first two waves in the re-imagining of democracy, as these took shape in the United States, France, Britain, and Ireland. (We have allocated separate chapters to Ireland although, formally, Britain and Ireland were sister kingdoms, and from 1801, were subject to a shared 'imperial parliament'. Yet, as our Irish chapters demonstrate, Irish experience of living in this shared polity was distinctive, and Irish language and practice developed in ways that were not only specific, but also had their own international impact. Irish experience accordingly merits separate treatment.)

Each region is the subject of three chapters. In each case, two focus primarily on language and ideas in each of the first two waves of 're-imagining', during the late eighteenth and mid-nineteenth centuries; a third chapter supplies broader social, political, and institutional context. The book represents a serious collaborative effort: some of the contributors have worked together over an extended period, and all attended a conference on the theme held in Oxford in the summer of 2010. As editors, we have tried to make sure the chapters cohere. But we have not required our contributors to write to a mechanical formula, nor to agree with one another on all interpretative points. Though conceived in a spirit of collaborative inquiry, the chapters display differences of emphasis and approach, and sometimes of judgement.

Readers may wonder why, in planning the book, we chose to commission separate chapters on language and ideas, on the one hand, and social, political, and institutional contexts on the other—the more so since we have argued that what the topic requires is attention to interactions between language and practice. It is not that we regard some of our authors as experts in language and others as experts in practice: on the contrary, all have an interest in both, and all the chapters that follow display, if in varying ways, an interest in contextualizing language and ideas. Our decision to separate the two—to encourage different contributors to adopt different emphases—has been essentially pragmatic. Precisely because we want to encourage attention to *interaction*, we have not wanted to run the risk of having the overall picture that the book presents dominated either by movement across

---

[13] Though see now Saunders, 'Democracy'.

6

Joanna Innes and Mark Philp

the varying objects to which democracy-related words have been applied at any given moment, or by too rigid a focus on particular institutions or practices, given that each of these was only occasionally central to what people thought about when they thought about 'democracy'. In effect we have adopted a bifocal approach in the hope that this will help readers to shift attention from one element of an interactive process to the other, and in this way grasp the complexities of the process of *bricolage* through which different visions and instantiations of democracy have been constructed.

To illustrate the scope for variation, consider the relationship between democracy and voting. In the early twenty-first century, letting all adult citizens vote for members of a legislature that wields significant powers is usually taken to be essential (though not sufficient) for a polity to qualify as 'democratic'. Yet, as we have noted (and as individual chapters illustrate more fully) at the start of our period, this association was not firmly established. Not even all 'democrats' initially favoured universal male suffrage (and hardly any positively advocated the enfranchisement of women); debates about 'democracy' were often debates about something quite different: for example, about how to constitute executive power, or what to do about street protest, or how to respond to demands for greater social equality. Over our period, democracy was increasingly associated with the establishment of powerful representative legislatures and the broad diffusion of voting rights; yet there remained great diversity in forms of practice: in the range of public officials who were subject to election, in how voting was carried out, and in beliefs as to whether holding an election necessarily entailed presenting voters with a meaningful choice, as opposed to giving them a symbolic opportunity to signify their membership of the political body and consent to the overall regime.

Differences in the importance attached to voting rights of course had much to do with differences in the forms that government took from place to place, also with differing ideas as to what an extension of voting rights was most likely to change. Differences in the form and character of rights bestowed when voting *was* extended had much to do with entrenched local habits and expectations, though also something to do with whatever it was that had prompted people to revise existing practices (perhaps partly under the inspiration of beliefs about practice elsewhere). Convergence—around an expectation that democracy would entail broad voting rights—in practice concealed substantial and continuing difference in terms of what voting involved and what (in various senses) it meant.[14]

Historical accounts that elide either differences in understandings of democracy or differences in the practices that implement an apparently shared concept obscure parts of what they should illuminate. The structure of our book reflects our attempt not to elide either form of difference.

Why the United States, France, Britain, and Ireland—and why have we organized the greater part of the book around local experiences, reserving only a final chapter for an inquiry into synergies between these? Commissioning specialists in

---

[14] See, with varying degrees of emphasis on this, chapters by Laura F. Edwards (3), Malcolm Crook (6), and Joanna Innes (9) in this volume.

the history of different regions to write different chapters provides a way of tapping into deep wells of scholarly expertise—given that so much historical practice is nation-focused. But our reason for making *this* choice has not primarily been pragmatic. On the contrary: a central argument of this book is that there can be no one history of the re-imagining of democracy; rather such a history must take the form of a series of adjacent (though interconnecting) local histories. This does not commit us to the view that in each case it is clear which local unit best frames study. Many polities were complex—like the kingdom of Great Britain and Ireland, and the federal republic of the United States: different costs and benefits flow from choosing one over another unit of analysis. What we are affirming is therefore only loosely specified. But there is something that we are rejecting: that is, a diffusionist model. We do not endorse the view that modern democracy was founded in any one place (America, France, Britain—or anywhere else one might propose) and thence diffused to other places. We think that the inquiries presented here suggest that this is not a good way of conceptualizing what happened—not least because, as we have already suggested and as the chapters that follow will further demonstrate, local experiences were in so many ways different. Democracy-related words were differently applied in different places, and acquired different connotations. Only at a high level of generality were the institutions and practices taken by contemporaries to embody 'democracy' the same from place to place.

There is a case, indeed, for suggesting that there was more of a shared democratic heritage across the European world—in Europe and New World colonies of settlement—at the start of our period, in 1750, than there was at the end, in 1850. What that initial shared heritage consisted in was a set of ideas about what 'democracy' meant that derived from the Greco-Roman world, and from the appropriation and reworking of Greco-Roman ideas by highly networked medieval and early-modern scholars. Once democracy began to be re-imagined in the age of revolutions—in political argument and through political experiment—that heritage fractured, splintering into very different forms in response to local circumstances, and subsequently undergoing reworking in the context of multifarious local disputes and power struggles. By the mid-nineteenth century, every nation had its own local history of encounters with the democratic challenge. Political leaders—old style and new style—had developed their own styles of response. The strategies that they devised helped to shape the way that their nations developed into the late nineteenth and twentieth centuries; traces of their differently directed efforts can be discerned today.

This is not of course to deny that there were interconnections. We explore these in our final chapter, 'Synergies'. When the thirteen British American colonies declared independence in 1776, and succeeded in establishing their independence in 1783, it was possible to dismiss this as a provincial occurrence, yet these events were in practice taken by many members of the reading public across Europe to be of world-historical significance.[15] Still greater was the shock and awe when the

---

[15] See, for example, the *Histoire des deux Indes*, published under the name of the Abbé Raynal in French (1770–81) and in English (1776–82); the section on the Revolution in America was also published independently in French and English in 1781.

greatest nation in Europe, France, fell to revolution six years later. The American example stirred interest in the future of the 'republic' as a political form in the modern world, and more broadly in ways in which 'the people' might wield political authority, and what might follow if they were allowed to do that. The French example set people talking about 'democracy', its possibilities and costs, as never before in modern times. In the early nineteenth century, the development of relatively orderly mass movements in Britain and Ireland provided yet more food for thought as to the possible forms of a modern democratic politics. In the early 1830s, the Frenchman Alexis de Tocqueville travelled to the United States, and, famously, recorded some of his observations and reflections in his widely translated *De la démocratie en Amérique*. Later in that decade, he visited Britain and Ireland and (as S. J. Connolly notes in chapter 12) reported on the forms he saw the democratic spirit taking within Ireland (with special attention to the role played by priests). Obviously notions about what democracy meant in the modern world, and what might be done about it, were informed by interest in what was happening elsewhere. Yet (as we argue in our final chapter) what in the end mattered in practice was what people did with what they knew (or thought they knew). In the end, local concerns and local circumstances carried most weight.

Why the United States, France, Britain, and Ireland? It follows from what we have just said that we have not chosen to focus on these places because we think that they represent a core from which democratic ideas and practices were disseminated. In subsequent work, we hope to show how, in other parts of Europe—northern, central, and Mediterranean Europe—people re-imagined democracy, over much the same period of years, by their own lights. Potentially, the British, French, and Americans could have transmitted ideas drawn from the Greco-Roman heritage to parts of the world which did not share that heritage—but implanting 'democracy' among non-European peoples was not a major policy objective for these powers at this time (this may need qualifying in respect of some individual emigrants from these polities—but probably not by much). If the United States and France were not sources from which democratic ideals and practice diffused, they were nonetheless certainly important reference points for those who thought about the role and prospects of democracy in the modern world, from the last quarter of the eighteenth century onwards. And particularly powerful interconnections between the United States, France, Britain, and Ireland—especially during the first wave of 're-imagining'—have persuaded us that there are advantages to be gained from studying them together. We do, however, hope in later work to set their experiences in broader comparative context. (It is not clear, incidentally, that our 'two waves' chronology works well in other parts of Europe. We reserve the right to revise it when we reflect—as we aim to do next—on Mediterranean experiences.)

In the title of our book, we frame the experiences that we are concerned with as elements of an 'age of revolutions'. This is partly shorthand: the phrase denotes a period of time. But to conclude this introduction, we will reflect on the relationship between the re-imagining of democracy and 'revolution' The years we are concerned with were marked by multiple revolutions—extra-legal regime changes—across Europe and the Americas: American and French revolutions; Spanish revolutionary resistance to Napoleon; Latin American revolutions; revolution in Spain in 1820—briefly echoed in Italy; Greek insurgence against the Ottomans; waves of revolution across western and southern and then across central and northern Europe in 1830 and 1848.[16] These were also—in ways that scholars explored intensively in the 1960s—years in which 'revolution' itself was re-imagined. It had connoted a sudden, unexpected turn of events, leading to change in who wielded power. It came—even before the American and French revolutions—to connote also (though these meanings were not necessarily bundled together) a change of epoch, a fundamental change in the nature of society. The American Revolution wrought change by building upon and re-invigorating a model provided by the British 'Glorious' Revolution of 1688; in this model, a 'revolution' was the work of a people reclaiming power from unworthy rulers, and instituting it anew. In its early years, what we term the French Revolution was often conceptualized (for good reason) as a series of revolutions; subsequently—introducing yet further connotations to the concept—these came to be conceptualized as episodes within a single, tumultuous revolutionary process, a process extraordinarily difficult to terminate.[17]

It is not necessary for a country actually to undergo a revolution for its rulers and politically active members to experience as profoundly challenging the reconciliation of people and government. Many forms of political tension and crisis have the potential to focus attention on that issue. But when the actions of hundreds of thousands of ordinary people make it difficult or impossible for a country's governors to continue the business of governing in the accustomed way, and limit the terms on which it is possible to conceive of re-stabilizing government, then questions about how the people's power can be aligned with the power of government become particularly compelling. So an age of revolutions is inherently likely to encourage imaginative attention to democracy (whether or not this word acquires a central role in discussion).

Still, what people are *doing* and *achieving* when they take to the streets is not self-evident: their actions are always open to a variety of constructions. Even if their actions do lead to reconstruction at the centre, these people do not have to be given credit for the outcome. They might alternatively be conceptualized as having acted as they did because government lost authority; their actions might be construed as merely disorderly. It might be concluded, not that they need to be enlisted to endorse a new regime, but rather that they should be dealt with sternly, put back in their place. So a popular revolution, a breakdown in order in which the people emerge as key legitimizers of new rulers or forms of rule, never just happens.

---

[16] Maurizio Isabella, *Risorgimento in Exile: Italian Emigrés and the Liberal International in the Post-Napoleonic Era* (Oxford, 2009), esp. part I; Clive H. Church, *Europe in 1830: Revolution and Political Change* (London, 1983); Dieter Dowe (ed.), *Europe in 1848: Revolution and Reform* (Oxford, 2001); Jonathan Sperber, *The European Revolutions, 1848–1851* (2nd edn, Cambridge, 2005).

[17] Keith Michael Baker, chapter 9 in his *Inventing the French Revolution* (Cambridge, 1990); Alain Rey, *Révolution: Histoire d'un mot* (Paris, 1989).

A revolution is a sequence of events that is conceptualized and responded to in a certain way, to which are attributed meanings that are not inherent.[18]

Whose imaginative work are we talking about, though? What those who contend for supreme power think and choose to state about what is happening matters, but what leaders who are thrown up from the people by the crisis itself, and what people in the crowd think is happening and represent themselves as doing, matters too. Their thoughts and actions may not suffice to determine the outcome of a revolution, but still they may open up certain possibilities and close down others. Revolutions which, however transiently, give power to the people take shape partly because some among the people think that this is within their scope: that it can and perhaps should fall to them to determine by whom and how they should be governed. In that sense, the 'age of revolutions' was surely the product as well as the cause of democratic ideas. Inasmuch as experience of democratic revolutions then shaped perceptions (leading among other things to the coinage of this very phrase, 'democratic revolution'),[19] these ideas recycled, and shaped subsequent behaviour and perceptions, bounding and rebounding to shape the character of this phase of European and American history.

[18] On this theme in a French context, see Colin Lucas, 'Talking About Urban Popular Violence in 1789', in Alan I. Forrest (ed.), *Reshaping France: Town, Country, and Region During the French Revolution* (Manchester, 1991); William Sewell, 'Historical Events as Transformations of Structures: Inventing Revolutions at the Bastille', in his *Logics of History: Social Theory and Social Transformation* (Chicago, IL, 2005).

[19] Edmund Burke was an influential early adopter; his reference to the 'death dance of Democratic Revolution' in his *Letter...to a Noble Lord* (London, 1796), 7, was much quoted. In France, the phrase occurs in print chiefly after 1800.

PART I
AMERICA

1

Languages of Democracy in America from the Revolution to the Election of 1800

Seth Cotlar

Neither the word 'democracy' nor any of its cognates appeared in Thomas Paine's *Common Sense* (1776), one of the most radically populist pamphlets of the Revolutionary era. The word 'democracy' surfaced occasionally in the debates over the Constitution in 1787–8, but usually with a negative connotation. Almost no one defended the Constitution as a democratic charter, and only a handful of the Constitution's most radical critics described their preferred alternatives as more democratic. A mere five years after the Constitutional Convention, however, Thomas Paine's *Rights of Man* (1792) lauded the new American political system as 'representation engrafted upon democracy' and cheered the triumph of democratic over aristocratic and monarchical principles around the globe. In 1793 the word 'democracy' appeared in American newspapers three times as often as it had the previous year, and in 1794 its usage doubled again.[1] By the year 1800 a slate of candidates who frequently identified themselves as Democrats (with Thomas Jefferson as their standard-bearer) gained control of the new nation's federal government. In the span of one generation and thanks in large part to the influence of the French Revolution, the word 'democracy' moved from the fringes of American public discourse into the centre—from a word used most frequently as a term of abuse in 1776 (and even 1787) to a term emblazoned upon the public banners of a successful, nationally coordinated political party.

This story is not simply one about the triumph of a coherent, unchanging democratic ideal that slowly won the hearts and minds of the American people between the imperial crisis and 1800. Rather, the language of democracy evolved significantly over those years. In the decades before independence, those few writers who used 'democracy' positively usually treated it as a synonym for 'republic', a much more commonly used term. When employed by their advocates, both 'republic' and 'democracy' referred to little more than the theoretical proposition that all legitimate political authority flowed up from the people and not down from their rulers. A far more common use of the term 'democracy' in the Revolutionary era,

---

[1] Based upon an analysis of the *Early American Newspaper Database*, http://www.readex.com/readex/index.cfm?content=362.

however, was as an epithet deployed by Loyalists and conservative Patriots to con-
demn the perceived threat of mob rule and excessive egalitarianism that they saw
emerging around them. While these fears were frequently overblown, there did
indeed develop in the 1770s and 1780s a segment of the Patriot movement that
began pushing the question of just how democratic the new American republics
should be. In their hands, democracy came to embody not just a theoretical understanding of where political authority came from, but a set of concrete prescriptions
for how political power should operate—who should have the right to vote, who
should hold office, and whose voices political authorities should heed. Put another
way, over the course of the Revolutionary crisis democracy ceased to be simply a
synonym for republic, and instead came to modify it. Tentatively during the debate
over the Constitution in 1787–8 and then with much greater intensity in the
1790s, a populist American opposition coalesced around the idea that American
republics at both the state and federal level should be less 'aristocratic' and more
'democratic', that is, their institutions and practices should be organized in such
a way as to render the polity more inclusive and participatory, more literally
self-governing.

The influence of the French Revolution in the early 1790s introduced two additional elements to the American language of democracy. First, the term 'democrat' came to describe a distinctive social type, the proudly assertive citizen who
rejected the social and political elitism of those American 'aristocrats' who were
unwilling to embrace the egalitarian implications of the French and American
revolutions. At first this usage did not have partisan meanings, but by the election
of 1796 the moniker democrat had become associated with support for a particular
slate of candidates. The most radical self-described democrats of the 1790s invested the term with a second and more utopian meaning. Democracy to them was
the great moral imperative of their revolutionary age. Its implications spilled far
beyond the boundaries of formal politics, calling upon citizens to work toward a
more just world marked by a rough degree of social and economic equality and
governed by a radically participatory and inclusive political system.

In the last half of the 1790s, in the context of a global reaction against the French
Revolution, these more radical connotations of the term 'democracy' came under
severe attack, putting American democrats on the defensive. Conservative Federalists associated the democratic aspirations of thinkers like Thomas Paine with every
form of unpalatable extremism imaginable—sexual libertinism, atheism, the redistribution of property, and mass murder to name but a few. Thus many proponents
of democracy—as an ideal and as the name for an emerging political coalition—
sought to distinguish themselves from the ultra-democratic, 'Jacobinical' menace
that supposedly threatened the nation. Through this process, America's language of
democracy became dissociated from the more radical implications that the term had
accrued during the heady days of the French Revolution. The genealogy of the
'Democratic Party' that triumphed in the election of 1800 thus included not only
the anti-aristocratic progressivism of the previous years, but also the conservative
anti-Jacobinism of the late 1790s. To be an American Democrat in 1800 meant that
one believed in equality and popular rule, but not *too* much.

THE LANGUAGE OF DEMOCRACY BEFORE 1776

Even though democracy did not become a widely used term in American public discourse until the early 1790s, the archive is dotted with occasional Anglo-American uses of the word in the century preceding the American Revolution. Most commonly, it appeared in learned discourse when scholars discussed the three types of government—monarchy, aristocracy, and democracy—that should be balanced against each other in an ideal political system, but which would devolve into tyranny if implemented in isolation. A second way in which colonists before the Revolution used the word 'democracy' was as a synonym for popular self-government, a more oppositional appropriation of the term that hearkened back to the radical republicanism of the English Civil War. It is in this context that Massachusetts Congregationalist John Wise, in a 1717 treatise on civil and ecclesiastical governance, spoke glowingly of democracy as 'a form of Government, which the Light of Nature does highly value'. Wise defined democracy as the ancient and simple idea that when men 'being Originally in condition of Natural Freedom and Equality' set up a government, they would 'be inclined to administer their common Affairs, by their common judgment'.[2] Wise used the word 'democracy' sparingly, and mostly as a way to laud New England's distinctive practices of church and town governance. All the same, his pamphlet marks the first time that an American publication deployed the term 'democracy' to characterize an aspect of colonial rule.

As the imperial crisis intensified during the 1760s and 1770s, positive uses of the word 'democracy' began to appear with greater frequency in Anglo-American political discourse. This change can be explained largely by the fact that the dispute between the colonies and Britain revolved around issues of taxation, and taxes were historically the province of the democratic elements of the British constitution. Thus it became commonplace for colonial writers to open their arguments, as Daniel Dulaney did in his 1765 pamphlet on the Stamp Act, by acknowledging that each of the three forms of government 'hath its peculiar Department, from which the other are excluded', and then reasserting the essential principle that the power to tax belonged solely to the 'Order of Democracy'.[3] As long as the political conversation revolved around taxation, kind words about the democratic aspects of the British constitution flowed from the pens of those asserting the rights of the colonists.

While there was nothing innovative about how colonists linked the democratic elements of the Constitution to taxation, a second shift in the use of the term 'democracy' harboured more radical implications. It is no coincidence that a group of Massachusetts Patriots reprinted John Wise's obscure 1717 pamphlet in the early 1770s. While his admirers did not identify him as a democrat, they recognized Wise as an early proponent of what we might call a literalist reading of Lockean

---

[2] John Wise, *A Vindication of the Government of New-England Churches* (Boston, 1717), 60, 47.
[3] Daniel Dulaney, *Considerations on the Propriety of Imposing Taxes in the British Colonies* (Annapolis, MD, 1765), 5, 8.

contract theory that gave democracy pride of place in the long-standing trinity of democracy, aristocracy, and monarchy. James Otis made a similar move in his influential 1764 pamphlet, *The Rights of the British Colonies Asserted*. Drawing on Locke's formulation of the state of nature, Otis identified 'a simple democracy, or government of all over all' as the world's original form of government. While he acknowledged that through 'express compact . . . the *individuals* of each society' could choose any form they saw fit, Otis implied (while stopping short of saying) that aristocracy and monarchy were artificial impositions layered upon a foundational democracy that both he and Wise identified as the most 'natural' and 'ancient' system.[4] This was a small but important step away from a theory of mixed government in which all three elements were understood to have their separate, yet equally important roles to play in the political order.

Otis and Wise gestured toward a question that would become important in the debate over independence—if democracy was the form of government that best reflected the original equality of all people, then shouldn't republics strive to be as democratic as possible? After July of 1776 this was no longer an abstract question. As colonists went about rewriting the political charters under which they lived, literally enacting the originating role of the people, the gap between the terms 'republic' and 'democracy' became more apparent. Lines of division emerged within many colonies over the question of just how democratic these new American republics should be. While there was widespread consensus that the new polities should all be republics that served the common good and derived their legitimacy from popular consent, the extent and nature of ordinary citizens' roles in these new governments was a source of great disagreement.

At the level of language, however, democracy was still a term most frequently imposed upon people by their opponents. Virtually every criticism of Paine's *Common Sense*, for example, echoed John Adams's charge that the text was 'so democratical, without any restraint' that it could only 'produce confusion and every evil work'.[5] Yet as generations of progressive scholarship has demonstrated, many Revolutionary-era Americans did not share Adams's belief that monarchical and aristocratic institutions were necessary to restrain the perceived dangers of democracy.[6] Works like *Common Sense* tapped into popular resentments and aspirations that had smouldered for years and were fanned by the mobilization that accompanied the War of Independence. Positive (though still sporadic) uses of the word 'democracy' can be found wherever the Patriot movement took on a particularly populist cast. In March of 1776, for example, one Pennsylvania pamphleteer lauded democracy as 'the plan of civil society wherein the community at large takes the care of its own welfare, and manages its concerns by representatives elected by the people out of their own body'. While those still shackled by 'political bigotry

[4] James Otis, *The Rights of the British Colonies Asserted and Proved* (Boston, MA, 1764), 11–12.
[5] John Adams, *Diary and Autobiography of John Adams*, ed. L. H. Butterfield et al. (4 vols, Cambridge, 1962), 3: 333.
[6] See, in the 'Guide to Further Reading', Young (1976 and 1993), Nash (2005), McDonnell (2010), Holton (2007), and Bouton (2007).

and prejudice' associated democracy with anarchy, this writer regarded it as an aspirational ideal.[7] Later that same year the citizens of rural Mecklenburg County, North Carolina, instructed their delegates to the state constitutional convention to 'oppose everything that leans to aristocracy or power in the hands of the rich and chief men exercised to the oppression of the poor'. The government they had in mind was 'a simple democracy, or as near it is possible'.[8] As these two examples suggest—one urban and one rural, 800 miles apart—the association of democracy with popular self-rule and an egalitarian social ethic had become a part of Anglo-American political culture by the time of the American Revolution.

The Pennsylvania Constitution of 1776 best epitomizes the high-water mark of democracy in the revolutionary era. Due to a unique set of political circumstances, a coalition of radical artisans, Enlightenment intellectuals, and populist farmers gained control of Pennsylvania's politics in 1776 at the time when the state rewrote its new charter.[9] The system they designed placed great power in the hands of ordinary citizens. Suffrage was extended to every taxpaying man over twenty-one. Representatives to the unicameral legislature were elected annually. No person could serve in the legislature more than four years out of any seven, thus ensuring wider participation in the government. Before any bill could pass into law, it had to be 'printed for the consideration of the people' and then voted on again in the next session of the assembly after a new election had intervened. The executive was comprised of an elected, twelve-man council, so as to avoid consolidating executive power in a single individual. Finally, an elected body called the Council of Censors was to meet every seven years to reassess the Constitution and determine whether it had been violated by any branch of the government. This document became a source of great contestation in Pennsylvania. To Loyalists and more moderate Patriots like John Adams, Pennsylvania's 1776 Constitution embodied the dangers of 'democratical' ideas like Paine's. While the Constitution's supporters rarely used the word 'democratic' to describe it, they proudly embraced the document as an experimental effort to create a republic shorn of the aristocratic and monarchical elements that they thought marred the vaunted British constitution.

1776–1789: DEMOCRACY AND THE DEBATES OVER THE NEW AMERICAN REPUBLICS

The political contestation over how democratic the new American republics should be continued in many states through the late 1770s and into the 1780s, but

[7] 'To the People of North-America on the Different Kinds of Government', in Peter Force (ed.), *American Archives* (4th ser., 6 vols, Washington DC, 1837–53), 5: 180–3.

[8] Cited in Merrill Jensen, 'Democracy and the American Revolution', *The Huntington Library Quarterly*, 20 (1957), 335. On back-country populism in North Carolina, see Marjoleine Kars, *Breaking Loose Together: The Regulator Rebellion in Pre-Revolutionary North Carolina* (Chapel Hill, NC, 2001).

[9] Gary Nash, 'Philadelphia's Radical Caucus that Propelled Pennsylvania to Independence and Democracy', in Gary Nash, Alfred Young, and Ray Raphael (eds), *Revolutionary Founders* (New York, 2011).

evidence from the newspapers and pamphlets of the era suggest that the language of democracy did not evolve significantly nor become a more prominent part of the nation's political dialogue.[10] The delegates to the Constitutional Convention of 1787 spoke of democracy much as the moderates and conservatives of 1776 had—as one of the three essential components of a properly mixed government, and also as a potentially anarchic force that needed to be kept in check by the new nation's political institutions. None of his fellow delegates argued with Elbridge Gerry's claim on the second day of the Convention that the nation's current crisis was the result of 'an excess of democracy', nor did they quibble with Alexander Hamilton's characterization of 'the amazing violence and turbulence of the democratic spirit'. With only a few exceptions, most of the framers shared Roger Sherman's sentiment that 'the people...should have [as] little to do...about the Government' as possible. The difficulty the delegates faced was figuring out how to craft a political system that could simultaneously counter the perceived dangers of democracy *and* win the support of a citizenry that harboured such a 'fondness for democrac[y]' and its attendant 'levelling spirit'.[11]

The framers and defenders of the Federal Constitution found two ways—one largely rhetorical and the other more substantive—to forge a link between democracy and the new Constitution, despite the significant extent to which that document differed from the more assertively democratic charters of the day like the Pennsylvania Constitution of 1776. In a speech delivered to his fellow Pennsylvanians very early in the ratification debates, James Wilson made the case that the Constitution was 'purely democratical' because the 'supreme power... [was] vested in the people'.[12] Even though senators served for six years and were not directly elected, even though the Constitution was very difficult to amend and was overseen not by an elected body but by appointed judges who served for life, and even though the House of Representatives was kept intentionally small so that only already prominent or wealthy men were likely to get elected; none of this was antidemocratic, according to Wilson, since every branch of the government ultimately, if often quite indirectly, drew its authority from the people. This attempt to equate democracy with a highly attenuated form of popular sovereignty seems to have fallen flat, for few Federalists repeated Wilson's attempt to depict the Constitution as democratic.

James Madison articulated a more sophisticated and convincing linkage between democracy and the Constitution. During the Constitutional Convention, Madison proposed that the creation of a large republic would provide 'the only defence

---

[10] This perhaps helps explain why a 500-page, award-winning study of the ratification debates does not include the word 'democracy' in the index. Pauline Maier, *Ratification: The People Debate the Constitution* (New York, 2010).

[11] Quotations all from Madison's 'Notes on the Debates of the Constitutional Convention', *Avalon Project*. This reading of the Constitutional Convention is informed by Alfred Young, 'Conservatives, the Constitution, and the "Genius of the People"', in Robert A. Goldwin and William A. Schambra (eds), *How Democratic Is the Constitution?* (Washington, DC, 1980).

[12] Cited in Richard Beeman, *Plain Honest Men: The Making of the American Constitution* (New York, 2009), 381.

against the inconveniences of democracy consistent with the democratic form of government'.[13] The primary inconvenience he had in mind was the problem of majority rule, the tendency of majority factions to form and then take over the machinery of government to the detriment of minorities. He expanded upon these ideas a year later in Federalist Papers numbers ten and fourteen,[14] where he introduced a new distinction between 'democracy', which he defined as the direct democracy of the ancient world, and a 'republic' characterized by the modern innovation of representation. Democracies had to be small because only then could citizens assemble as an entire group to deliberate and make laws. Republics, by contrast, could be large since citizens elected representatives to do the people's business. Even better, tyrannical majorities would be less likely to form in large republics because the diversity and geographical dispersion of the citizenry would prevent them from coordinating their efforts and consolidating their power. In the Federalist Papers, Madison abandoned his initial description of this innovation as 'consistent with the democratic form of government', instead referring to it as a 'republican remedy for the diseases most incident to republican government'. Madison's abandonment of any positive association between the Constitution and democracy is significant. Federalist numbers ten and fourteen depict democracy as an admirable but now obsolete relic from the Athenian past, and frame the new representative republic as the modern inheritor of that same spirit of republican self-rule. By positing such a bright line between old-fashioned democracies that by definition lacked representation and modern republics that had it, Madison sought to pre-empt the argument that the Constitution was insufficiently democratic. True democracy, Madison implied, belonged solely to the ancient past, not the republican future.

In the few years immediately following the Constitutional Convention, this effort to neutralize the language of democracy in American politics seems to have worked. The term 'democracy' appeared sporadically, but never systematically in the newspaper essays and pamphlets published during the ratification debates. Those critics of the Constitution who did deploy the language of democracy generally did so in a vague and largely rhetorical manner. In one of his opening statements against the Constitution at the Virginia ratifying Convention, for example, Patrick Henry described the obstacles that had been put in the way of amending the Constitution as a betrayal of 'the genius of democracy'.[15] Despite holding the floor for hours at a time during the ensuing three weeks of the Convention, Henry never developed his 'democratic critique' of the Constitution further. That same summer, a group of anti-Federalists gathered for a July 4th celebration in rural Pennsylvania and offered a toast to the hope that amendments should 'be speedily framed' so as to 'render the proposed Constitution . . . truly democratical'.[16] What exactly a truly democratical Constitution would look like, however, rarely became a topic of sustained discussion.

---

[13] Ralph Ketcham, *The Anti-Federalist Papers and the Constitutional Convention Debates* (New York, 2003), 51.

[14] The Federalist Papers, *The Avalon Project*: http://avalon.law.yale.edu/subject_menus/fed.asp

[15] Ketcham, *Anti-Federalist Papers*, 204–5.   [16] *Carlisle Gazette*, 9 July 1788.

In contrast to the minor role that the term 'democracy' played in the ratification debates, talk of 'aristocracy' abounded. The Constitution's critics derided the document as the 'most daring attempt to establish a despotic aristocracy among freemen that the world has ever witnessed'.[17] The fear was not that a hereditary aristocracy would be institutionalized in the new nation; rather, the charge of aristocratic intent was levied against those elite politicians who advocated for a less democratically accountable federal government that would be presided over by men demographically different from (and presumably superior to) ordinary citizens. Like Amos Singletary, an anti-Federalist delegate to the Massachusetts ratifying Convention, many ordinary citizens interpreted the Constitution as the work of a cabal of 'lawyers, and men of learning, and moneyed men, that talk so finely, and gloss over matters so smoothly, to make us poor illiterate people swallow down the pill'. The members of this new, American aristocracy, Singletary charged, 'expect to be the managers of this Constitution, and get all the power and all the money into their own hands, and then they will swallow up all us little folks . . . just as the whale swallowe'd up *Jonah*'.[18] In the final number of *The Federalist*, Alexander Hamilton derided such critics, claiming that their incessant talk of 'the wealthy, the well-born, and the great' deserved nothing but the 'disgust of all sensible men'.[19] Despite Hamilton's criticisms, charges of aristocratic intent clearly resonated with the significant number of citizens who mistrusted the nation's aspiring political and social elite.

The word 'aristocracy' encapsulated two key charges that anti-Federalists repeatedly levelled against the Constitution in 1787–8: 1. that control of the new Federal government would 'fall into the hands of the few and the great'; and 2. that its mechanisms were designed to 'deprive the people of a share in the government'.[20] These criticisms described fairly accurately, if uncharitably, the intent of most framers. Federal representatives were chosen from relatively large districts and senators were appointed by state legislatures because the framers assumed that such procedures would render more likely the selection of men 'distinguished for their rank in life and their weight of property'.[21] These 'natural aristocrats', it was thought, would govern with more wisdom than those from more humble walks of life.[22] Their independence from the fickleness of economic fortune and popular whims would stop the government from enacting foolishly short-sighted laws. According to most Federalists, the nation faced a fiscal and diplomatic crisis in 1787 precisely because the state governments had been too responsive to popular demands for debt relief. This is what Elbridge Gerry meant when he referred to the

[17] *Centinel* Number 1, 5 October 1787, in Ketcham, *Anti-Federalist Papers*, 231–2.
[18] Debates in the Convention of the Commonwealth of Massachusetts, on the Adoption of the Federal Constitution, http://www.constitution.org/rc/rat_ma.htm.
[19] *The Federalist*, no. 85, *Avalon Project*.
[20] Melancthon Smith, 21 June 1788 in Ketcham, *Anti-Federalist Papers*, 344–7.
[21] John Dickinson in Madison, *Notes on the Constitutional Convention*; Ketcham, *Anti-Federalist Papers*, 54.
[22] The hierarchical assumptions underpinning the Federalists' vision are discussed in Daniel Walker Howe, 'The Political Psychology of *The Federalist*', *William and Mary Quarterly*, 44 (1987), 485–509.

dangers of 'too much democracy'. Responsible legislation could only be expected from a government that was insulated from the passions of the people, and presided over by the sort of men who would honour the interests of the nation's wealthy creditors regardless of the short-term pain this might cause ordinary citizens. Federalists called this a sober, energetic government administered by those most suited to rule. Their opponents detected a plot to construct a new aristocracy of wealth and privilege. If the people consented to this 'complete Aristocracy', one anti-Federalist warned, then they would be subject to a governing class that would heed their voices as much as 'the whistling of the wind'.[23]

On the day New York ratified the Constitution in 1788, ensuring its success at the national level, a French observer who was well connected to New York City's commercial elite noted approvingly that 'the phantom of democracy which had seduced the people is about to disappear'.[24] Many leading Federalists privately shared this hope, but most knew better than to say it publicly. Ratification had been hard won, and the extent of popular scepticism about the Constitution suggested that a good portion of the people still adhered to a vision of politics far more egalitarian, localist, and participatory than that which the Federalists preferred. While this populist opposition had found common ground in their fears about the supposed aristocratic threat posed by the Constitution, their alternative did not yet have an agreed name. The gap between popular and elite politics that existed in 1787–8 took on a new meaning and discursive form in the early 1790s, when a French-inspired wave of political activism and optimism swept the Atlantic World. By 1794 those opposed to the aristocratic elements of the American polity and inspired by the French example had a name they could collectively embrace. They were now, unapologetically, democrats.

1790–1800: FROM DEMOCRATIC RADICALISM TO DEMOCRATIC RESPECTABILITY

Democracy, as a term with an unqualified, positive connotation, found its way into the American political lexicon between 1790 and 1794, largely through the efforts of a small but influential cohort of newspaper editors. Two of the leading democratic editors of the 1790s, Thomas Greenleaf of New York and Eleazar Oswald of Philadelphia, had cut their political teeth during the ratification debates when they opened their papers to anti-Federalist authors. As the French revolt against monarchy and aristocracy gathered steam and began to inspire similar movements in Britain and Ireland, Greenleaf and Oswald eagerly covered these developments and integrated them into their critical understanding of contemporary American politics. From the start, they identified events in France as a continuation of the

---

[23] John DeWitt in Ketcham, *Anti-Federalist Papers*, 313.
[24] Comte de Moustier to Comte de Montmorin, 2 August 1788, in Merrill Jensen, Robert A. Becker, and Gordon DenBoer (eds), *The Documentary History of the First Federal Elections, 1788–1790* (4 vols, Madison, WI, 1976–89), 1: 57.

American Revolution, the principles of which these editors began to describe retroactively as democratic. Indeed, pro-French Americans began offering a positive characterization of the French Revolution as democratic before the French themselves did. In 1790 Oswald applauded when the National Assembly abolished the nobility, thus 'democratically put[ting] an end to Prince, Duke, Marquis, &c.' and replacing these titles with the egalitarian term 'citizen'.[25] One year later Greenleaf published an account of the New York Tammany Society's celebration where a series of toasts were offered to the 'patriots of France' and the evening's festivities wrapped up with the wish that 'the baneful weeds of aristocracy [should] never be suffered to spring up in the garden of freedom'. The best way to check the encroachment of aristocracy in America, Greenleaf reminded his readers, was to 'nourish the democratic order among us'.[26] By early 1792, Greenleaf, Oswald, and a few other editors presided over opposition newspapers that were known to sympathetic as well as critical readers as democratic.

The outbreak of war in Europe and the accelerating pace of change in France transformed American political culture in 1793–4, making it more vibrantly expressive and deeply polarized than it had ever been. Americans revised their own lexicon, using the words 'democracy' or 'democrat' three times as often in their newspapers in 1793 as they had been in 1792, and their use doubled again in 1794. As 'democracy' became an increasingly central part of America's political language, the term accrued a host of new and intensely contested meanings. To those many Americans who invested great hopes in the success of the French Revolution, the world's political future seemed to hinge on the latest news from Europe. One British observer in Wilmington, Delaware, noted with astonishment in the summer of 1793 that 'Every time the newspapers arrive, the aristocrats and democrats' rushed into the streets to 'have a decent quarrel'.[27] French victories or losses seemed to involve much more than just incremental steps in a protracted military conflict; rather, each morsel of news was interpreted as part of the global struggle between democracy on the one hand and its monarchical and aristocratic enemies on the other. In most localities, one had little choice but to take sides. Foreign travellers noted the abundance of Americans wearing cockades expressing support for one side or the other. In over forty towns across the new nation, groups of the most ardent supporters of democracy abroad and at home formed political clubs (many of which identified themselves as 'Democratic Societies') that met regularly to discuss contemporary politics and theory. They issued numerous resolutions that were then printed in the nation's growing network of democratic newspapers. As the members of these societies saw it, they needed to coordinate their efforts on behalf of democracy because it was threatened by 'a powerful combination in Europe' *and* 'the growing establishment of pride, formality, [and] inequality…in these States'.[28] Within the span of just two years (1793–4), American supporters of

---

[25] *Independent Gazetteer* (Philadelphia), 28 August 1790.
[26] *New York Journal*, 24 February 1791.
[27] Huntington Library, MS22842, William Cobbett to James Mathieu, 19 July 1793.
[28] *New York Journal*, 8 March 1794.

the French Revolution pushed the term 'democracy' into the centre of the nation's political conversation.

This first generation of proud democrats, however, denied that they were up to something new. Democratic newspaper editors uncovered every positive use of the term 'democracy' or sentiments that sounded democratic from the Revolutionary era and reprinted them for their readers' delight. A few passages from John Adams's *Dissertation on the Canon and Feudal Law* (1765), for example, were reprinted multiple times in the 1790s as evidence of the democratic ideals that this founder had espoused during the revolution. Quoting passages where the Adams of 1765 called upon 'the rich' to make large contributions to support the education of the poor and urged his fellow citizens to 'demand' their rights and privileges 'against all the power and authority on earth' became an easy way to score points against the Adams of the 1790s who was rightly perceived as a critic of Francophile democrats.[29] Hence there arose a compelling, partisan narrative about the American Revolution that legitimated the democrats of the 1790s. As one writer in Greenleaf's *New York Journal* put it: 'What these states contended for during their struggle for independence, was then termed a free democratical government; and this was what the parties professed to advocate at the formation and adoption of the federal constitution.' Thus the author claimed that the contemporary innovators were not the democrats, but conservatives like John Adams who had betrayed the spirit of 1776 and 1787 by treating 'the term democracy...as something novel and frightful'.[30]

Though a growing cohort of democratic writers, newspaper editors, and readers eventually succeeded in inventing a genealogy for democracy that stretched back to the Revolutionary era, there was much disagreement within that community as to what it meant to espouse that ideal in contemporary America. The same author who denied there was anything novel about the term 'democracy', concluded his essay with quite a vague, even conservative, definition of it. Democracy, he argued, was simply another word for popular sovereignty, that is, for the ultimate grounding of legitimacy in the people, and it implied no structural critique of the nation's existing political system. This was the definition of democracy that James Wilson endorsed in 1787; it functioned in the 1790s as a way to parry the charge that democrats advocated something that departed from the nation's founding principles.

The problem with this strategy, however, was that it overlooked (or consciously repressed) the extent to which 1790s democrats did indeed have a critical relationship to the Constitutional order designed by the framers and presided over by conservative Federalists like Alexander Hamilton. The democrats of the 1790s were the inheritors of the anti-Federalist tradition that regarded the hierarchical and exclusionary political sociology that informed the Constitution as an aristocratic holdover. To be a democrat in 1794 meant that one was critical of those

---

[29] For one example of this appropriation of Adams's 1765 text, see *Independent Gazetteer* (Philadelphia), 28 August 1790.

[30] *New York Journal*, 5 July 1794.

members of the political elite who felt uniquely entitled to rule, as well as of privileged fellow citizens who felt that their opinions and interests deserved special attention from those in office. The Democratic Societies that formed in the mid 1790s opposed more than just the specific policies implemented by the Washington Administration; rather, they sought to push against what they perceived to be a political system that was closed to ordinary citizens like themselves. Inspired by the French example, they sought to democratize the new nation's political culture by building institutions like newspapers and political clubs that would help bring into existence a more assertive and astute citizenry. Democratization, they implied, was an unfinished process, and its opponents were legion. To a great extent, it was this idealistic vision of the political present that made the language of democracy so compelling to ordinary citizens in the mid 1790s.

The language of democracy had other experimental dimensions as well. Democracy had long been associated with 'levellerism' and agrarian laws, and most 1790s democrats were careful to distinguish themselves from those traditions. All the same, every time authors espoused policies designed to aid the poor or foster greater economic equality, they used the language of democracy to legitimize their claims. Democrats opposed virtually every one of Hamilton's actions as Treasury Secretary because they thought his policies disproportionately benefited those who were already wealthy. Democrats railed against land policies that sold public land to speculators in large parcels and denied easy access to ordinary citizens. They also criticized Hamilton's funding of the national debt because it favoured wealthy investors over the hundreds of thousands of ordinary citizens who had originally held the debt but sold it under duress for a pittance. These 'democratic' positions did not reflect an opposition to private property or the market; rather, they articulated a populist distrust of how well-connected elites tilted the political scales to benefit themselves. Hamilton's policies were dangerous, one author argued, because 'in every democratical government the laws ought to destroy, and prevent too great an inequality of condition among the citizens'.[31]

The *Democratic Songster* published in 1794 by George Keatinge, a United Irishman who had recently emigrated to Baltimore, Maryland, captures the diverse meanings that 'democracy' accrued in that decade. This collection contained a few 'French airs' like the Marseilles Hymn (in English and French), odes to American independence, an anti-slavery song, songs written in a sailor's voice decrying the horrors of impressment, and tavern favourites like 'There's Nothing Like Grog'. Keatinge's 36-page polyglot text brought together several strands of revolutionary sentiment under the heading of 'democracy'. Each piece validated the voice of the historically dispossessed or devalued—the slave stolen from Africa, the happily drunken sailor, the involuntary conscript into the British Navy, the newly empowered French peasant—and projected a 'democratic' future in which such figures would be given their due. When collected together and sold in the bookstore of a committed United Irishman, the text linked democracy with a world view that was

---

[31] *National Gazette* (Philadelphia), September 1793.

simultaneously revolutionary, plebeian, cosmopolitan, and assertively egalitarian. Thus, any reader encountering the article on slavery by 'A Consistent Democrat' in the 5 February 1796 edition of Greenleaf's *New York Journal* would have hardly been surprised that the piece advocated abolition.[32] While the Democrats would eventually become the party most dedicated to preserving slavery in the nineteenth century, it is nearly impossible to find the word 'democracy' associated with a defence of slavery in the 1790s. As one writer explained in a Philadelphia newspaper, 'The democratic prinnciples...teach that all men, of whatever nation, are brothers.'[33]

CONCLUSION

By 1795–6, thanks largely to the intensification of partisan conflict during the Jay Treaty crisis and the ensuing election cycle, talk of democracy became ubiquitous in American public life. For the first time newspapers begin printing detailed results of elections and identifying particular slates of candidates as democratic. Likewise, those years witnessed a significant increase in the number of personal letters ending with salutations like 'Your Friend & Fellow Democrat' or 'Remember me to all our democratical friends'.[34] When used sympathetically, the term had a host of different meanings. It could be associated with organizations that sought to create a more inclusive, participatory, and egalitarian political culture; a populist preference for rough economic equality; a belief in fundamental human equality that extended to a critique of racial slavery; or a more diffuse sympathy for the French cause and reflexive animosity toward anything redolent of aristocracy. The most radical democrats of the era embraced all of these meanings of the term, and some went further to embrace the critique of the Bible and organized religion that Paine offered in the *Age of Reason* (1795). Even though many self-described democrats rejected some or all of those positions in their more vehement forms, deep divisions amongst democrats did not emerge until after the election of 1800. In the last half of the 1790s, thanks to the term's generally positive and hopeful connotations, 'democracy' functioned effectively as a partisan label under which a diverse coalition of citizens gathered.

As more Americans began embracing the term 'democrat' as one of partisan affiliation, their political opponents initiated the nation's first explicitly anti-democratic print offensive. Inspired in part by their anti-Jacobin counterparts in Britain, Federalist printers in the United States churned out a host of texts that satirized the democrats in their midst—*The Democrat; or Intrigues and Adventures of Jean Le Noir* (1795); *A Bone to Gnaw, for the Democrats* (1795); and *The Guillotina, or a Democratic Dirge* (1796), to name just a few. Such texts offered a powerful

---

[32] *New York Journal*, 5 February 1796.
[33] *General Advertiser* (Philadelphia), 4 August 1794.
[34] Historical Society of Pennsylvania, Lea & Febiger Correspondence, Mason Weems to Matthew Carey, 24 October 1796, and John Page to Matthew Carey, 5 June 1797.

counter-narrative in which American democrats were not the beneficent and noble inheritors of the spirit of 1776, but rather cynical agents of a foreign conspiracy that sought to undermine the pillars of American society. According to their critics, democratic ideals led inevitably down the path toward the guillotine, the destruction of churches and families, inversions of the racial hierarchy, and the abolition of private property. These texts recapitulated the anti-democratic arguments of Revolutionary-era Loyalists and moderates, only this time fleshed out with lurid details from the French Terror.

As America and France hovered on the precipice of war in 1798, the attacks on the dangers of democracy drew additional ammunition from pseudo-journalistic reports that linked American democratic printers and activists to an international conspiracy aimed at overthrowing the American government. While in hindsight such charges seem ludicrous, they had a profound impact on American political culture in the summer of 1798, creating the climate in which the repressive Alien and Sedition Acts could be passed with significant public support. In an 1856 memoir that recounted his upbringing in a strongly Federalist family, Samuel Goodrich described the hyperbolic fears of democracy that circulated in 1798:

> We who are now familiar with democracy, can hardly comprehend the odium attached to it in those days, especially in the minds of the sober people of our neighborhood. They not only regarded it as hostile to good government, but as associated with infidelity in religion, radicalism in government, and licentiousness in society. It was considered a sort of monster, born of Tom Paine, the French Revolution, foreign *renegados*, and the great Father of Evil.[35]

In the summer of 1798 scores of Federalist militias organized to fight off a French-led democratic invasion, Federalist printers rushed into print with anti-French chapbooks aimed at young readers, and ministers admonished worshippers to resist the allure of democratic ideas that looked beneficent on the surface, but which masked sinister, Jacobinical intent.

As evidenced by the victory of the Jeffersonian Democrats in 1800, these attacks backfired politically. Nonetheless, they had a significant effect on the American language of democracy. In the run-up to the election of 1800, leading Democrats went to great lengths to distinguish their moderate, American form of democracy from that espoused by their more radical contemporaries at home and abroad. The Democrats of 1800 won the election, in part, by triangulating themselves against the Anglophile and aristocratic Federalists to their right, and the dangerous Jacobins to their left. The more experimental and radically egalitarian connotations of democracy that had suffused the language of democracy in the 1790s were pushed into the margins of American political discourse. If the American and French Revolutions had opened up analytical space between two eighteenth-century keywords, republicanism and democracy, the Jeffersonians of the early nineteenth century, also known as the Democratic-Republicans, did much to collapse the distinction between the two. At least at the level of language, the path toward a

---

[35] Samuel Goodrich, *Recollections of a Lifetime* (2 vols, New York, 1856), 1: 117–18.

more democratic nation was now presented as straightforward, involving little more than the election of Democrats into office.

Looking back from 1856, Samuel Goodrich marvelled at how 'the word democracy...changed its signification'. No longer a term of opprobrium, 'synonymous with Jacobinism', by the first decade of the 1800s democracy had 'put on clean linen, and affected respectability'.[36] The moderation of America's language of democracy in the nineteenth century did not go unchallenged. The struggle over the meaning of the term continued both within and outside the party that had successfully appropriated the name 'democrat' for itself. That said, the capture of this once oppositional concept by a political party had a long-lasting, moderating effect on the nation's language of democracy.

[36] Goodrich, *Recollections*, 1: 121.

2

The 'Fortunate Banner': Languages of Democracy in the United States, *c.*1848

Adam I. P. Smith

Over the years, historians have debated whether the antebellum United States, a society with both slavery and the widest franchise in the world, was really democratic. Most antebellum Americans had no doubts: democracy was the pre-eminent descriptor of their society and institutions. More than that: it encapsulated their vision of the future and described the world-historical function of their nation. Sometimes democracy was depicted as a Newtonian force: an unchanging, immutable fact of nature, operating according to universal laws. Sometimes it was imagined to be 'restless', 'turbulent', and 'unstoppable', a 'mighty energy' like a 'volcano' destroying hierarchy and privilege as it surged forward.[1] Whatever the imagery, it was the principle that guaranteed American freedom and the 'only true line of demarcation between republicanism and monarchy'.[2] Used adjectivally, terms like 'democratic manners' conveyed a social and cultural egalitarianism. This was the sense in which Alexis de Tocqueville used the term in his *De la démocratie en Amérique*, the first volume of which was published in Paris in 1835 and soon translated into English and disseminated in the United States. Despite his misgivings about the problems of majority rule, Tocqueville's identification of American society with democracy echoed the views of the Americans to whom he spoke on his travels. For them, democracy had a legitimizing function somewhat similar to 'civilization' in other cultures and places. It was a catch-all term that articulated and defined the character of the nation, the shorthand for those characteristics of American society and institutions that made it, in the minds of nineteenth-century Americans, exceptional.

One rough barometer of the era's most salient political vocabulary is provided by the titles of newspapers. Before 1820, very few journals in the newly United States were published under the name 'Democrat' and at least one was entitled the *Anti-Democrat*.[3] Between 1830 and 1860, the number of newspapers with the

---

[1] *Brooklyn Daily Eagle*, 7 November 1846; William Leggett, *A Collection of the Political Writings of William Leggett* (2 vols, New York, 1840), 1: 232, 277.

[2] *Pittsfield Sun* (Pittsfield, MA), 26 October 1848.

[3] The *Anti-Democrat* (Baltimore, MD) is listed in the Library of Congress catalogue as having been published 1802–3.

word 'Democrat' in the title substantially outnumbered other ideologically inflected alternatives such as 'Whig', 'Freeman', or even 'Republican'.[4] Republicanism continued to shape political culture profoundly, but by 1848 it had become substantially elided with democracy in popular usage. Democracy became shorthand for the basic republican principle of popular sovereignty. The 'democratic theory', explained one newspaper, 'is that the people's voice is the supreme law'.[5] Whether it was warnings of an over-mighty President Jackson ('King Andrew I'), or the 'hydra of corruption' that was the Bank of the United States, or fears of masonic or papal conspiracies, US political culture in the 1830s and 1840s often succumbed to what one historian has labelled the 'conspiracy paradigm'.[6] Yet in antebellum America this classical republican fear that power was encroaching on liberty was almost always described as a battle between democracy on the one hand and opponents of democracy on the other.

THE DEMOCRACY

The ubiquity of the word 'democracy', and its close identification with the nation, did not mean, however, that there was consensus over its political meaning. On the contrary, contests over the language of democracy were at the heart of politics at mid-century. In 1848 an Ohio politician, William Allen, gave a speech with such a poetic peroration that it was excerpted and reprinted in at least a dozen newspapers in the style that such newspapers usually reserved for biblical homilies. 'Democracy,' said Allen in a stylistic echo of St Paul's letter to the Corinthians, 'knows no baseness; it cowers to no danger; it oppresses no weakness. Fearless, generous, humane, it rebukes the arrogant, cherishes honor, and sympathises with the humble.... Destructive only of despotism, it is the sole conservator of liberty, labor and property. It is the sentiment of freedom, of equal obligations.'[7] This encomium presented democracy, like charity, as an emancipatory sentiment, but it was also rooted in a partisan political vision, that of the Democratic Party, or, as it was commonly referred to, especially by its supporters, '*the* Democracy'. In the midst of a hard-fought presidential election, Allen's lyricism was put to the service of the campaign of the Democracy's nominee, Lewis Cass.

---

[4] The Library of Congress online directory of newspapers lists 1,465 weekly, semi-weekly, or daily publications with the word 'Democrat' or 'Democratic' in the title published between 1830 and 1860. The second most popular title-word was 'Republican' with 1,039 titles in this period. In contrast, in the period between 1790 and 1820 there were 342 newspapers with 'Republican' in the title and only twenty-nine that contained 'Democrat'—and at least eight of these were compounds like 'Democratic Republican'. Of course, these statistics should be regarded as only roughly indicative. There is uncertainty about the precise publication dates of some of these newspapers. But the overall trend is clear. http://www.chroniclingamerica.loc.gov.

[5] *New York Evening Post*, cited in Mary P. Ryan, *Civic Wars: Democracy and Public Life in the American City During the Nineteenth Century* (Berkeley, CA, 1997), 112.

[6] Daniel Walker Howe, *The Political Culture of the American Whigs* (Chicago, IL, 1979), 80.

[7] *Wisconsin Democrat* (Madison, WI), 18 November 1848; *Pittsfield Sun* (Pittsfield, MA), 7 December 1848.

It followed that when the word 'democracy' appeared in newspapers and public prints, it most often referred directly to the Democratic Party.[8] Sometimes it appeared with a definite article and quotation marks (as in 'a portion of the "Democracy" of Reading, Pa. lately got together and nominated General Taylor for the Presidency').[9] At other times there was neither, as in a reference to 'this expounder of Democracy', even where the context made clear that what was meant was an exposition of the policies of the Democratic Party. The Democracy was the world's first mass political party, organizing an expanding electorate which by the 1830s included virtually all white men, through a system of ward and county committees, of sympathetic newspapers, and, above all, of regular public meetings and parades. But although the party of Andrew Jackson helped to formulate many of the enduring practices of mass politics, the Democracy did not conceptualize itself as one element in a pluralist party 'system' but as the organized manifestation of 'the people' and the sole guardian of the liberties won in the American Revolution.

Imagined in this way, the Democracy had performed a noble historical function as 'the instrument by which our institutions have been preserved in the progress of the nation'.[10] 'American Democracy', claimed one speaker, using the term in a way that elided the specific political referent and the historical movement, had 'done more, in fifty years, to elevate the moral and political condition of man than has been achieved by any other civil institution since the Christian era'.[11] In this double sense, democracy was an 'altar' at which Americans 'worshipped'. Like Christianity, democracy demanded devotion and a commitment to virtue. 'Moral courage' was required to keep the 'Democratic faith' against the machinations of its enemies.[12] One newspaper editor, who described himself as a democrat 'in the fullest and largest sense of the word', put the case succinctly: 'the principles of democracy are identical with the principles of human liberty'.[13]

If the dominant self-image of the Democratic Party was as the singular embodiment of the sovereign people, their enemies were a 'false, rotten, insubstantial, effete' elite, often rendered 'aristocrats' in shorthand. This struggle between the people and the aristocracy was ceaseless and universal. 'No matter how or when tried, democracy is ever the same', commented one editorial; wherever 'the *great interests of the country* are protected and advanced in all times and places', there could only be one force operating: it was 'the work of democracy—the people's will'.[14] In 1846 the poet and Democratic Party journalist Walt Whitman hailed Thomas Jefferson as 'the Columbus of our democratic faith', not primarily because he was the author of the Declaration of Independence, but as the victor of the

---

[8] Of the first five hundred matches for the word 'democracy' between 1845 and 1850 in the Readex American Historical Newspapers database (there were more than five thousand results in all), more than 95 per cent specifically referred to the party.

[9] *New Hampshire Sentinel* (Keene, NH), 6 January 1848.

[10] *United States Magazine and Democratic Review* (Washington, DC), May 1848.

[11] Samuel McRoberts, *To the Members of the General Assembly of Illinois* (Danville, IL, 1840), 7.

[12] *Brooklyn Daily Eagle*, 7 November 1846.   [13] Leggett, *Political Writings*, 1: 262, 7.

[14] *Pittsfield Sun* (Pittsfield, MA), 26 October 1848.

election of 1800 in which the machinations of the Anglophile, aristocratic Federalists had been defeated.[15]

This Democratic eschatology—pitting the people against a corrupt elite—was the framework through which many of the political issues of the 1830s and 1840s were seen. The Bank of the United States, the renewal of which President Jackson vetoed, symbolized the bloated monopolies of power that leached on the people's honest labour. Annexing Texas and war with Mexico, both jingoistically championed by supporters of President James K. Polk, were the fulfilment of democracy's (and the Democracy's) 'Manifest Destiny' and the means of securing to all white men the chance to own real property.[16] Historians have identified socio-economic and ethno-cultural factors underpinning Democratic Party ideology, but what is most striking is the way that policy questions were so often boiled down to fundamental constitutional and philosophical dispositions. Democrats were the believers in the 'unmediated', the 'unfettered', the 'direct' sovereignty of the people.

The antebellum Democratic Party did not have a singular or unchanging political identity. On the contrary, it was an unstable amalgam of often-warring factions riven by factional and policy divisions. But, for all those who adhered to the party, the word 'democracy' was talismanic. Democrats created a rhetorical community of 'stout, upright, moral common men', a 'hardy race of free men', the classes who formed the 'bone and sinew' of the country. Democrats sometimes referred to the people as the 'unterrified democracy'—or even the '*unbought, unterrified* democracy', intending to convey the image of a proud, manly, and incorruptible people.[17] Their candidates were 'fresh from the people'. Parades, which had at one time been organized to express differentiated 'orders' within society, became, in the hands of party managers, celebrations of an undifferentiated mass public; where once artisans paraded with symbols of their crafts, parties counted the numbers of people present as a marker of their claim to represent the 'great body of the people'.[18]

The Democratic vision of a polity defined by horizontal rather than vertical bonds was harshly exclusive as well as egalitarian since it defined democracy in terms of white men; but within the Democratic community egalitarian ideas were often pushed very hard. One significant radical faction in New York City was known as the Shirtless Democracy (a term presumably intended to evoke the *sans-culottes*). This movement of working-class men was led by Mike Walsh, a charismatic firebrand whose political power was based on muscle as much as oratory. The term 'shirtless', like so many political labels, was at first used disparagingly, but then adopted with pride. In a speech to the New York legislature after being elected a state representative in 1847, Walsh declared: 'I came here, though called in

[15] *Brooklyn Daily Eagle*, 7 November 1846.

[16] The phrase 'manifest destiny' was coined by John O'Sullivan, editor of the *Democratic Review*, the leading monthly journal of the Democratic Party. See *United States Magazine and Democratic Review* (Washington, DC), July–August 1845.

[17] *Wisconsin Democrat* (Madison, WI), 17 April 1847.

[18] For examples of this kind of language, see Marvin Meyers, *The Jacksonian Persuasion: Politics and Belief* (Stanford, CA, 1957), 19–24.

derision—and of that I am proud—the advocate of a houseless and shirtless democracy.'[19] The Shirtless Democracy took the anti-Bank rhetoric of Andrew Jackson several stages further and, arguing for a fairer distribution of property, attacked all concentrations of capital as fundamentally undemocratic. Even in this most egalitarian, anti-elitist form, the Democracy could not be described as anticapitalist, since it favoured small-scale entrepreneurialism; European social democratic ideas had more influence among reformist Whigs like Horace Greeley than among Democrats. But in the context of an industrializing economy in which relations of production were undergoing radical transformations, especially in the cities, the Shirtless Democracy held to a vision of society that represented a fundamental challenge to the existing economic order. Outside of the cities, land reformers not only argued for free access to western lands, but also campaigned against land monopoly in the east. In upstate New York an 'anti-rent' movement in the mid 1840s scored some successes in a campaign to break up the estates of large landholders. The language of democracy was at the core of the anti-renters' rhetorical case, linking self-government to a natural right to the land. Property ownership was the means to social mobility, and its availability—once 'cleared' of forest, Indians, and monopolistic landowners—the guarantor of American exceptionalism. Shirtless Democrats and radical anti-renters believed that inequality and exploitation were the result of reactionary and anti-democratic forces. The rising tide of democracy would sweep away forms of economic as well as political exploitation. They did not, unlike later socialists, believe in the necessity for a redistributive state. The abundance of resources in the United States would, they thought, naturally tend towards a state of material equality so long as democracy, in the co-dependent sense of the great body of the people and the principle of political equality, triumphed.

The great democratic heroes of the 1830s and 1840s typically had two characteristics in common: they were crusaders for the justice of the people against tyranny, fighting against overwhelming odds; and they were frontiersmen, embodying the pioneer spirit of the West which, in America, enabled democracy to be strongly linked to universal property ownership. The first celebrity actor in the United States, the physically powerful, bombastic Edwin B. Forrest, at the height of his popularity in 1848, made a career out of representing the quintessential democratic hero. In whatever part he was playing, his stage persona exemplified democratic manhood: like the imagined Thomas Jefferson, he was a strident redeemer of his people, burning with a lust for freedom; like Davy Crockett or Daniel Boone, a coonskin-wearing, fearless conqueror of the West; and, like Andrew Jackson, the embodiment of American nationalism, draped, literally and figuratively, in the stars and stripes. 'The Democracy' was brought to life in the boisterous, highly 'democratic' public space of the theatre, especially those in the big eastern cities where working-class men dominated the audiences.

---

[19] *The Subterranean* (New York), 30 January 1847.

CONTESTING DEMOCRACY

The problem for Democrats in 1848 was that the nature of the American community was more than usually in question. Immigration, contests over slavery, changing economic structures that undermined traditional artisan trades and created new forms of economic privilege: all these things raised difficult questions about self-government. Could such a highly differentiated society any longer claim to have a singular people, and, if not, what were the implications for what democracy meant? In 1848 the ubiquity of the language and the assertion of unity belied a sharp contest over the language of democracy between those who wanted to continue to harness it to the fundamentally egalitarian political project of 'the Democracy' and those who sought to attach it to alternative visions of political development. A writer in the *Christian Inquirer* observed in April 1849 that it was 'the *prestige* of that word [democracy] that more than anything else gives the ascendency to one party in this country', and it was this which explained 'the anxiety of the other[s] to get hold of the fortunate banner, or some shred of it'.[20] What this metaphor lacks as an evocation of the relationship between language and politics is recognition that the 'fortunate banner' could be not just seized but also redesigned, parodied, and paraded to different music, yet it does convey the growing challenge to the conflation of the term 'democracy' with the party of that name.

By mid-century, the Democracy had definitively lost any monopoly of the term it had once had. In January 1848 a Democratic Senator from Arkansas invoked Jefferson as 'the father of democracy, to whose church we all [including our opponents] now profess to belong'.[21] It is a measure of how far the word 'democracy' had become inseparable from the ways in which antebellum Americans imagined their society that when the Whigs won the 1840 presidential election they did so not only by adapting the techniques of mass mobilization but also by using the language of democracy. Indeed, Whigs first began to mimic their opponents' use of the language of democracy as early as the 'Bank War' of the 1830s. The Washington, DC, Whig organ, the *National Intelligencer*, describing the opposition to the re-charter of the bank as a power grab by a coterie of advisors around President Jackson, concluded that it was 'high time for the *true Democracy* of the Country to rise up and save the Republic'.[22] In New Orleans in 1837, opponents of the Jacksonians claimed 'the Whig Party is actually the Democratic Party'.[23] And by 1848 the *New York Tribune* was calling the public to meetings of the 'Democratic Whig Party'.[24] Democracy, noted a writer sympathetic to Whiggery in 1849, was 'so certain, settled predominating, overwhelming, that nothing is to be said about it—that one would as soon think of defending the solar system'.[25]

---

[20] *Christian Inquirer* (New York), 7 April 1849.
[21] Speech of Ambrose H. Sevier (Arkansas) in US Senate, *The Congressional Globe* (Washington, DC), 30th Congress, 1st Session, 26 January 1848, 235.
[22] *Daily National Intelligencer* (Washington, DC), 29 April 1834.
[23] *New Orleans Bee*, cited in Ryan, *Civil Wars*, 113.
[24] *New York Tribune*, 29 March 1848.
[25] *Christian Inquirer* (New York), 7 April 1849.

Whigs did not invoke a language of democracy as often or anything like as enthusiastically as their opponents and most retained a suspicion of 'unfettered' or 'pure' democracy. In 1839 the former Whig mayor of New York, Philip Hone, could still refer in his diary to the 'dunghill of Democracy', but by the 1850s even Hone was distinguishing between the 'fierce democracy' of which he disapproved and the 'good honest democracy' he did not.[26] The shift in language was unmistakeable. In 1849 a writer in the leading Unitarian weekly articulated both the continued discomfort of many middle-class Whigs with majoritarian language and also the supremacy of the language of democracy. On the one hand, he wrote, 'we are of this great, vaunted, flattered people, and we do not believe that we are half as wise as is said.... Individually we are full of errors, faults, and perils.... Can an aggregate of imperfections make perfection?' Yet on the other hand, there was no denying that 'in truth, we are *all* Democrats [now]. All parties bow to the people, ascribe everything to the people, not only all power but all wisdom.'[27]

Other political groups including anti-Masons, workingmen's parties, and anti-Catholic Nativists, also claimed to be 'fresh from the loins of the people' and often used majoritarian language. One of the most widely read anti-immigrant tracts of the antebellum era argued that 'our Democratic Constitution' was under assault from Catholic incomers.[28] Anti-slavery politicians were especially likely to use the language of democracy by 1848. Although enslaved people did not generally use democratic language—preferring instead the religious idea of the jubilee and the language of natural rights—their abolitionist allies worked hard to try to seize control of democratic discourse from the Democracy. Frederick Douglass, the prominent African-American abolitionist, consistently framed his struggle in terms of 'Free Labor against Slave Labor; Democracy against Serfdom.'[29] Anti-slavery campaigners challenged the legitimacy of the Democracy's appropriation of the term by highlighting the hypocritical inconsistency of advocating political equality for white men while also justifying human bondage. 'When will the people learn that the democrat, who will not carry his principles through to its legitimate application... is *no democrat at all*,' wrote the editor of a Boston abolitionist newspaper in 1848.[30] One anti-slavery writer from New England repeatedly taunted his opponents as the 'aristocratic democracy' because of their defence of 'the ruling Patriarchs of the South'.[31] Defenders of slavery, it was charged, were '*pseudo-democrats*' who 'trample the divine principles of true democracy under their unsanctified feet'.[32] Rejecting outright the exclusionary politics of the Democratic Party, abolitionists of various stripes developed instead a vision of democracy founded on the ideal of equal citizenship for all, a vision that came to be increasingly

---

[26] Philip Hone, *The Diary of Philip Hone* (2 vols, New York, 1889), 1: 384; 2: 693, 905.

[27] *Christian Inquirer* (New York), 7 April 1849.

[28] Anna Ella Carroll, *The Great American Battle; or the Contest Between Christianity and Political Romanism* (New York, 1856), 115.

[29] *The National Era* (Washington, DC), 20 April 1848.

[30] *Emancipator* (Boston, MA), 23 February 1848, 19 August 1846.

[31] *Semi-Weekly Eagle* (Brattleboro, VT), 17 April 1848.

[32] *The Liberator* (Boston, MA), 10 November 1848.

influential during and after the Civil War. This analysis denied that a society in which slavery was tolerated could be democratic at all.[33]

Aided by the anti-slavery campaigners' efforts to delegitimize the Democratic Party's ownership of the language, conservatives sought to reconcile democracy with moral and social order and the protection of property. The Whig leader Henry Clay led the effort to separate his political opponents from the 'fortunate banner' of democracy. The 'so-called' Democratic Party, argued Clay, had 'not the least just pretension [to that] denomination'.[34] Whereas their conservative predecessors might have denounced democracy, or fretted about how to 'balance' democracy with other elements, the new reconstitution of democratic discourse in the 1840s sought to appropriate this language, conscious that its great advantage is that it enables leaders to claim to speak for everyone. The Whig leaders who sought to re-engineer democracy sought to contrast a notion of ordered, constitutionally restrained democracy with 'excessive' democracy, by which they meant rioting, mob rule, demagoguery, and 'blind partisanship'. Only by linking democracy to the rule of law could democracy be made truly the guarantor of, rather than a threat to, liberty. At the heart of the shift was the effort to define democracy as a *system* not a *movement*. Whereas the Democracy Party understood the people to be a singular entity, the Whig democratic discourse of 1848 emphasized individual liberties guaranteed through a political system that rhetorically recognized the abstract principle of popular sovereignty even while taming the most challenging assertions of the political power of the masses. Opponents of the Democratic Party in 1848 America sought, in fact, to make democracy synonymous with something like the notion of 'representative government' shortly to become popular in Britain. In the long run, this effort to pluck the radical egalitarian sting from democratic discourse was as important for the development of the language of democracy in the US as has been the parallel effort to use democracy as a weapon to break down the barriers to inclusion in the political community.

MID-CENTURY CRISES

The 1848 Revolutions were critical to this conservative re-imagining of democracy. The events in Europe in that tumultuous year could be imagined as struggles to overcome despotism which therefore validated American democracy inasmuch as they attempted to import it into European monarchies. At the same time, the failure of the Revolutions seemed to underscore the impression that democratic impulses, if they were to create a stable polity, had to be balanced by institutions and a citizenry with the capacity for self-restraint. The idea that the French had proved themselves incapable of democracy was used to reinforce exceptionalist ideas about the United States. It also sharpened the perception of

---

[33] *Semi-Weekly Eagle* (Brattleboro, VT), 17 April 1848.

[34] Henry Clay, *Speech of Henry Clay; Delivered at the Great Barbecue at Lexington (Kentucky), June 9, 1842* (New York, 1842), 16.

many conservatives that American institutions were inherently fragile and susceptible to demagoguery and excesses of passion. In the 1790s the French Revolution had generated a powerful anti-democratic discourse in America. This did not happen after 1848. Even in the South, pro-slavery conservatives fearful of the spread of the revolutionary ideas from Europe only rarely framed their positions as anti-democratic. Instead, it became evident that an important watershed in the development of political language had been passed. Once, democracy had been the threat. Now, conservative journals presented American democratic government, duly constituted under law, to be a bulwark of stability and order in the face of 'communionist' and 'socialist' ideas emanating from Europe. On one level this was a continuation of the anxiety about Jacobinism that had haunted American politics for half a century, but the difference was that democracy no longer connoted the mob. In fact, the opposite was now true: the mob was a threat to democracy.

Opponents of the Democratic Party in 1848 represented a wide political spectrum from anti-slavery reformers to conservative Whigs. What they had in common was a conviction that democracy was not synonymous with 'the Democracy' and a tendency to talk about democracy as a form of government rather than as the undifferentiated 'people'. Some, like the influential *New York Tribune* editor Horace Greeley, embraced French social democratic ideas and continued to push them as a leading member of the Republican Party in the 1850s. For Greeley, what was instructive about the 1848 Revolution in France, at least in its early stages, was the articulation of a concept of democracy that depended on the harnessing of government power for progressive ends. If democracy represented the wave of the future, argued the *Tribune*, then it was a very different political project from that championed by the US Democratic Party whose 'cardinal tenets are a series of rigid and barren negatives'. In contrast *'true* Democrats' were those who did not just talk about protecting the people from imagined enemies, but who wanted to use the state to advance material progress.[35] In similar terms an editorial in the anti-slavery weekly, *The National Era*, commenting on events in Europe, enthused that democracy was the 'great idea of the world's future' and 'was sweeping all before it', but attacked the Democratic Party in the US for peddling 'false' or 'pretended' democracy.[36]

Two issues—the Dorr 'rebellion' and the Astor Place Riot—and the debates they prompted, illustrate the contested language of democracy at the end of the 1840s. In 1848 the Supreme Court heard arguments arising out of a bizarre political crisis in Rhode Island. In 1841 tiny Rhode Island was the only state still operating under a pre-Revolutionary Charter, one that retained a property qualification for voting and severely under-represented the more populous industrialized parts of the state. After failing to persuade the Charter government to reform, a 'people's movement' wrote a new Constitution and elected Thomas Dorr as its governor in defiance of the existing state government. The Dorrites justified their action as the practical expression of popular sovereignty and a manifestation of the rolling tide of

---

[35] *New York Tribune*, 24 April 1849.
[36] *The National Era* (Washington, DC), 20 April 1848.

democratization. The Charter government did not survive; but even while recognizing the political inevitability of having to compromise, the 'Law and Order Party' who were in control of the state wanted to make clear that Dorr's extra-legal actions were not acceptable: he was imprisoned at hard labour, although he was released a year later and in 1851 the state legislature restored his civil rights. The heart of the 'Rhode Island question' was whether popular sovereignty had been encoded in institutions or whether it remained possible for a majority of the people to alter or abolish their governments at will, outside the formal procedures laid down. This question focused attention on how the term 'democracy' was understood. The leading Jacksonian journal, the *Democratic Review*, accused Dorr's opponents of paying lip service to popular sovereignty while being horrified at the idea that sovereignty lay in the 'actual, real, living, flesh-and-blood People'.[37] To his opponents, Dorr's position tended to 'annihilate all government, and to destroy the peace of all society'.[38]

The Astor Place Riot, in May 1849, was a kind of bathetic echo of the June Days in Paris. Barricades were erected and twenty-five people were killed when the militia fired on a stone-throwing crowd. This bloody episode had its origins not in an attempted revolution, but in the politics of the theatre—specifically the effort of the partisans of Edwin B. Forrest to drive the English tragedian William Charles Macready from the stage and in the determination of the city authorities to allow Macready to perform. Among the interesting outcomes of this episode was that it catalyzed the distinction between the democratic discourse of the Democratic Party on the one hand and alternative appropriations of democracy on the other. Until the intervention of the militia at Astor Place, argued the *Democratic Review*, Americans had believed that 'the ballot-box was long since substituted for the bayonet'. Had the military now emerged as a 'permanent part of the government apparatus', as it was in 'European despotisms'? Were citizens to live under a daily regime of martial law, liable to be shot down in their daily pursuits 'if distant rioters provoke militia-men to fire through crowded streets?'[39]

In contrast, Whig newspapers vigorously defended the action of the authorities, notwithstanding the loss of life. For the Whig *Courier and Enquirer* the firm action of the militia had demonstrated to the world that democratic institutions did not equate to anarchy and that the killings were, in fact, 'an excellent advertisement to the Capitalists of the old world, that they might send their property to New York and rely upon the certainty that it would be safe from the clutches of red republicanism, or chartists, or communionists [*sic*] of any description'.[40] The work of the authorities in New York was, in effect, to cleanse democracy of its Jacobinical connotations. Democracy stood against the mob. Horace Greeley, who had also condemned Dorr, warned that the spirit of the anti-Macready mob was 'essentially the

---

[37] Quotations from Christian G. Fritz, *American Sovereigns: The People and America's Constitutional Tradition Before the Civil War* (New York, 2008), 275, 266.
[38] Clay, *Speech of Henry Clay*, 16.
[39] *United States Magazine and Democratic Review* (Washington, DC), June 1849.
[40] *Courier and Enquirer* (New York), 15 May 1849.

impulse of cowards'. Violence, he argued, was a legitimate democratic tool only when exercised by the state against those who would destroy the social order that guaranteed republican liberty. For Greeley, the blood 'poured out' would 'not have been shed in vain' if the authorities had learned 'to be uniformly stern and decided with mobs'.[41]

The defenders of the militia's actions in May 1849 in New York were arguing that democratic freedom depended on the vigorous implementation of the law and that popular politics should be restrained and formalized even in the one arena— the theatre—where a measure of riotous behaviour had been tolerated for the longest time. The attempt to impose a singular popular will through violence infringed the rights of an actor to earn his living by performing, as well as those of audience members who, in their political capacity not just as citizens but as consumers, had paid for the right to watch him. In a sermon on the Sunday after the killings, the Unitarian minister Henry W. Bellows told his congregation that an 'excess' of democracy must be combated through a moral reformation that would inculcate a new sense of duty to established authority. Democracy, he stressed, must be anchored by the fundamental principle of 'liberty under Law—whether of the Constitution or the Gospel'.[42] There had always been an undercurrent of anxiety about democracy's fragility. In the popular debating societies in which young men honed their oratorical skills, questions like 'Can democratic institutions be permanent?' were perennial favourites.[43] The heterogeneity of American society by 1848 made the task of making democracy safe for the world even more urgent. If the moral bonds that fastened society together were dissipating, the solution, for Bellows and like-minded bourgeois reformers, was to create new institutions that would inculcate a disciplined conception of national loyalty. Projects like New York's Central Park, which was built in the years following the Astor Place Riot, were quite self-consciously an effort to make democracy compatible with civilization, social order, and progress. Central Park, argued Bellows, was 'a royal work, undertaken and achieved by the Democracy'.[44] For those for whom one of the great questions of the antebellum decades was whether democracy could be sustained without degenerating into mobbism and anarchy, the lesson of the Dorr rebellion and the Astor Place Riot was that, if the authorities responded strongly, it could.

CONCLUSION

The contests over the meanings of democracy that were so visible in 1848 were intensified during the American Civil War (1861–5), which was fought by both

---

[41] *New York Tribune*, 15 May 1849.
[42] Henry W. Bellows, *A Sermon, occasioned by the late riot in New York, preached in the Church of the Divine Unity, on Sunday, May 13, 1849* (New York, 1849), 14.
[43] e.g. Delaware Historical Society Library, Minutes of the Wilmington Debating Society; *Boston Recorder*, 27 October 1848.
[44] Henry W. Bellows, 'Cities and Parks: With Special Reference to the New York Central Park', *Atlantic Monthly*, 7 (1861), 422.

sides using democracy as rallying cry. Northern wartime politics was characterized by the denigration of the Democratic Party by Whig-Republicans for its association with 'treason', while many northern Democrats opposed in the name of democracy what they saw as Lincoln's 'tyrannical' government. In July 1863 the New York City draft riots plus a rash of strikes and other evidence of civil disorder seemed, once again, to threaten social disintegration. There was a resurgence of attacks on the 'spurious', 'pretended', 'sham' democracy which, it was claimed, encouraged a culture of rioting and social disorder.[45] And Republicans added to their list of derogatory prefixes the term 'Tory Democracy', which carried the connotation of disloyalty. 'Who are your traitors, conspiring against the inalienable rights of men?' asked the abolitionist *Liberator* in 1863. 'Men, for shame, calling themselves "Democrats"!' The Democratic Party of the United States was, it argued, 'synonymous with the despotic party of Europe'. They had 'stolen the appellation "Democratic" to allure and beguile a class, mostly emigrants, that ... is not sufficiently cultured to distinguish names from principles'.[46]

The battle for the 'fortunate banner' of Democracy was not conclusively won by either side, but, from the 1840s onwards, the association of the word with the party that had adopted its name was always contested and was no longer the exclusive property of the party that marched under its banner. In the decades after 1848, the language of democracy in US political discourse became increasingly generalized and less specific in its application. But while elites gradually absorbed the term into the lexicon of patriotism, draining it of radical, egalitarian potential, less powerful groups continued to use it to legitimize their challenges to the status quo. Democracy was firmly established as the word that described the political journey, or the national aspirations, of nineteenth-century Americans. In that sense, the idealism of William Allen's 1848 peroration continued to resonate. Democracy, like America, was a work in progress. 'We have frequently printed the word democracy,' reflected Walt Whitman, the poet of democracy, 'yet I cannot too often repeat that it is a word the gist of which still sleeps ... notwithstanding the resonance and the many angry tempests out of which its syllables have come from pen or tongue.'[47] By the time Whitman wrote these words in *Democratic Vistas*, published after the Civil War, he had renounced his allegiance to the Democracy, but not, of course, to the ideal of democracy.

[45] e.g. *North American and United States Gazette* (Philadelphia, PA), 2 September 1863.
[46] *The Liberator* (Boston, MA), 30 January 1863; 26 June 1863.
[47] Walt Whitman, *Poetry and Prose*, ed. Justin Kaplan (New York, 1996), 984.

3

The Contradictions of Democracy in American Institutions and Practices

Laura F. Edwards

The American Revolution might best be described as a coalition of contradictions. It brought together a diverse array of groups with conflicting interests: merchants in the northern colonies who wanted to shed imperial policies that limited their economic opportunities; planters in the southern colonies who were economically tied to Britain, but who wanted more authority in that relationship; farmers and speculators who wanted to push into western lands closed to settlement by Britain; slaves who wanted freedom; working people who wanted to remake social, economic, and political arrangements in the colonies; and people whose attachments to the Revolution were so particular that they are now lost in the past. Further complicating this already unlikely coalition was the fact that entire families—women and children as well as adult men—identified with the Revolution and involved themselves in it. Some Patriots, as they called themselves, saw Britain as the problem and separation as the solution. Others saw the conflict in much broader terms, with Britain serving as a symbol for concerns about authority of all kinds. For these Patriots, the Revolution necessitated a fundamental remaking of the political system and social relations.

As this essay argues, the contradictory impulses that defined the American Revolution continued to shape American political institutions in the following decades. Specifically, those institutions embodied the tension between efforts to limit and to expand the people's participation in government. Post-Revolutionary political culture, characterized then and now as democratic, took shape through those contradictions. The extension of democracy for some not only came at the expense of others, but also constrained the Revolutionary era's most expansive notions of democracy.

REVOLUTIONARY FOUNDATIONS AND REVOLUTIONARY QUESTIONS

On 4 July 1776 the delegates to the Second Continental Congress issued the Declaration of Independence, which announced the colonies' intention to separate from Great Britain:

We hold these truths to be self-evident, that all men are created equal; that they are endowed by their Creator with certain unalienable rights; that among these are life, liberty, and the pursuit of happiness; that, to secure these rights, governments are instituted among men, deriving their just powers from the consent of the governed; that whenever any form of government becomes destructive of these ends, it is the right of the people to alter or to abolish it, and to institute new government, laying its foundation on such principles, and organizing its powers in such form, as to them shall seem most likely to effect their safety and happiness.[1]

The colonies' opposition to imperial rule was entwined with ideological currents that opened up questions about the source, form, and purpose of government. The Declaration of Independence distilled that heady ideological mix, with its strong base in natural-rights philosophy, overlaid with republican conceptions of virtue and independence, all tied together with the rhetorical strategies employed by pamphleteers, notably Tom Paine, to popularize these ideas. While inspiring, the Declaration's lofty rhetoric opened up a series of difficult institutional questions: What were the colonies now that they were no longer colonies? What form would their governments take? What was their political relationship to each other? The Declaration also complicated those questions by inviting multiple interpretations and providing little guidance in terms of practical application.

The Articles of Confederation, the closest thing to a national governing plan produced by the Second Continental Congress, deflected the most difficult of these issues. Drafted on the heels of the Declaration of Independence, the Articles affirmed the theoretical connection between the people and their government and then left the specifics of that relationship to the states. The document created 'the United States of America', but that entity was an association of states with extremely limited rights and duties; it was not a sovereign national government. Sovereignty lay with the states, which retained 'the sole and exclusive Regulation and Government of its internal police', a legal concept with deep roots in both English and Continental law and which covered virtually any issue that touched on the people's welfare. The framers hoped that locating governing authority in the states, and not in a strong national government, would promote the principles articulated in the Declaration of Independence, by keeping governing authority close to the people. The results, however, varied widely from state to state, depending on how political leaders defined 'the people'.[2]

Most of the thirteen colonies called conventions to write constitutions and reorganize themselves as states soon after the Declaration of Independence. The results captured the conflicting political currents contained within the Revolutionary cause. At one end were states that gave a narrow interpretation to Revolutionary principles. These constitutions were remarkable for their economy. They affirmed separation from Great Britain; spelled out the structures of state government,

---

[1] The Declaration of Independence (1776), from *Avalon Project*.
[2] Articles of Confederation (1781), *Avalon Project*; the Articles were drafted in 1776, agreed to by the Continental Congress in 1777, but not formally ratified until 1781.

which adhered closely to those that had existed under colonial rule; and studiously avoided reference to the democratic principles enshrined in the Declaration.[3]

The Constitution of South Carolina provides one of the most striking examples of this narrow vision of the people's relationship to government. South Carolina, North America's wealthiest colony, was controlled by a tight network of slaveholders. Their source of wealth—close commercial ties with Great Britain—was also the cause of their discontent: separation presented the opportunity to escape imperial regulations that these planters found so onerous. In their new state Constitution, the elite made it clear that political independence from Great Britain would secure their own hold on government. The Constitution made no mention of the people, their rights, or their relationship to government. It set property requirements for suffrage so high that only 10 per cent of the white male population qualified. Voting restrictions then combined with a skewed apportionment system to keep state government in the hands of the slaveholding elite. Little wonder that so many South Carolinians—free and enslaved—remained loyal to England: the Patriot cause in their state took particularly undemocratic forms.[4]

The constitutions of other states, by contrast, applied Revolutionary principles to political relationships at home. They often began with direct references to the Declaration of Independence, as did the Pennsylvania state Constitution, which declared that 'all men are born equally free and independent, and have certain natural, inherent, and inalienable rights, amongst which are, the enjoying and defending life and liberty, acquiring, possessing, and protecting property, and pursuing and obtaining happiness and safety'. The documents then gave concrete institutional forms to those principles. They established an array of individual rights, including freedom of religion, speech, and the press. They created decentralized governments that located law-making authority in representative, legislative bodies. They also made those legislative bodies responsible to a broader segment of the population through an expansion of suffrage. Pennsylvania, which produced one of the most democratic Revolutionary-era constitutions, created a unicameral legislature and granted suffrage to all free men over the age of twenty-one.[5]

Historians usually measure the realization of democratic principles in terms of the affirmation of civil rights and the extension of political rights. Yet these elements do not capture the most radical institutional innovations of these early constitutions, which linked sovereignty to 'the people' generally, not just those men who could vote or even those people who could claim civil rights. The New York Constitution, for instance, stated that 'no authority shall, on any presence whatever, be exercised over the people or members of this State but such as shall be derived from and granted by them'. Such statements conformed to contractual

---

[3] Constitutions of South Carolina (1776), New Hampshire (1776), New Jersey (1776), and Delaware (1776), *Avalon Project*.

[4] Constitution of South Carolina. Rachel N. Klein, *Unification of a Slave State: The Rise of the Planter Class in the South Carolina Backcountry, 1760–1808* (Chapel Hill, NC, 1990).

[5] Constitutions of Pennsylvania (1776), Maryland (1776), New York (1777), North Carolina (1776), Vermont (1777), and Virginia (1776), *Avalon Project*.

conceptions of sovereignty, which placed the emphasis on the people's consent to establish a government, not on their participation thereafter. A few states, however, went further, establishing a direct relationship between the people and the governing process. Pennsylvania's Constitution gave 'the people...the sole, exclusive and inherent right of governing and regulating the internal police'. So did Maryland, North Carolina, and Vermont. Internal police referred to the dynamics of governance at their most elemental form: the concept included *all* matters regarding the people's welfare at *all* levels of government. Such issues were decided in governing venues, such as local courts, where access did not depend on the vote or even the possession of individual rights. In fact, a great deal of routine public business was conducted in local courts at this time. If anything, Revolutionary state constitutions magnified the importance of those local governing arenas, by decentralizing state government and limiting the scope of its authority.[6]

Even the most radical state constitutions, however, suggest the institutional limits to democratic change. They were democratic in the sense that they located sovereignty in the people and gestured toward an inclusive rendering of that category. But these constitutions also affirmed existing hierarchies. Government might belong to the people in theory. In practice, however, Revolutionary-era constitutions did not address the fact that the vast majority of the population was constrained within status relationships—as a wife, a child, a servant, or a slave—which limited their civil and political rights and, as a result, constrained their access to the institutions of law and government. Only those men who qualified for suffrage could participate fully in governance. And only those people whose legal status allowed them to claim individual rights could enjoy the full benefit of the constitutions' legal protections. Those rights belonged to a small minority of the people, namely adult white men who owned property. Still, at a basic level, these state constitutions brought the Revolution home: in many of the new states, government belonged to the people in ways that it never had before.

Ultimately, it was neither state governments nor the federal government that nourished the seeds of institutional innovation. The federal government was, by design, too weak to provide effective leadership. State governments staggered under the burdens of war. Some all but collapsed, unable to sustain their most basic functions, let alone manage the endemic violence, economic dislocation, and social turmoil that marked daily life in so many states during the Revolution. Institutional uncertainty at the state and federal levels, however, allowed ordinary people to supply their own meanings to the Revolution's political principles. So did the nature of the Revolution, which relied on the support of a broad spectrum of people and which drew others into its vortex whether they wanted to be involved or not. That context encouraged a range of people to see themselves as members of 'the people' and to interpret their relationship to government in particularly expansive, democratic ways.

[6] Ibid.

THE REVOLUTION'S MANY MEANINGS

For many of those on society's margins, Revolutionary principles challenged entrenched hierarchies of wealth and status. People who were poor and illiterate were neither ignorant of the Revolution's guiding principles nor unaware of the implications for their own lives. The ideas in print culture circulated orally in taverns, country stores, fields, and workshops, acquiring new meanings as they passed from person to person. In these venues, notions of self-governance, natural rights, and independence supported a labour theory of value as well as strong critiques of inequality in a variety of forms. Rejection of imperial rule turned into a discussion about the form and meaning of government more generally, not only in its public manifestations at the national, state, and local levels, but also in its private iteration within households. These kinds of interpretations inspired urban workingmen—common labourers, sailors, journeymen, apprentices, and slaves—to join the Revolutionary cause. They also appealed to free blacks and enslaved African Americans, who used natural rights and republican conceptions of liberty to challenge racial inequality and slavery. All these people—enslaved and free, white and black—participated in the crowd actions that launched the Revolution and lent crucial support throughout the war, because they saw the cause in terms of broad social and political changes.[7]

Women in Patriot families also saw themselves as part of the Revolutionary cause, although they did not necessarily imagine an outcome in which they would achieve full civil and political equality. Rather, they identified with the notion of self-governance and rights for their heads of household, assuming that would benefit them and their families. A wide variety of women—white and black, rich and poor, free and enslaved—supported the effort. Wartime disruptions in trade meant that women had to produce items—notably textiles—that had previously been available for purchase. They kept farms and family business going, sometimes for years, while their menfolk served the war effort. Poorer women followed their male relatives into the army, scraping by while doing the domestic labour on which military operations depended. Women of all kinds also endured hardship and, often, violence as a result of the war.[8]

Wartime imagery and rhetoric acknowledged women's efforts. Stretching Revolutionary political ideology to accommodate women required conscious effort, because its underlying logic was profoundly gendered. The positive attributes of independence, reason, and virtue, deemed necessary to self-government, were portrayed as male characteristics, which took form in contrast to the negative, feminine traits of dependence, irrationality, and corruption. Within this framework, women were portrayed as so different from men that they could not claim the independence necessary for political participation nor pursue the natural rights that were, suppos-

---

[7] Alfred F. Young (ed.), *Beyond the American Revolution: Explorations in the History of American Radicalism* (DeKalb, IL, 1993); Gary B. Nash, *The Unknown American Revolution: The Unruly Birth of Democracy and the Struggle to Create America* (New York and London, 2005).

[8] Mary Beth Norton, *Liberty's Daughters: The Revolutionary Experience of American Women, 1750–1800* (Boston, MA, 1980).

edly, innate to all people. More than that, women actually posed a threat to the Revolutionary political project, because of the negative qualities associated with them. One famous cartoon ridiculed Patriot women in Edenton, North Carolina, by depicting them as women out of place and, therefore, out of control: they are physically grotesque, farcically self-absorbed, inappropriately sexual, and obviously incapable of comprehending weighty political issues. That Patriots produced positive portrayals of women takes on particular meaning in this context. One of the most iconic images depicted women as supporters of the political ideas that, in theory, their feminine nature threatened: the industrious Patriot woman at her spinning wheel, making homespun cloth to support her family's and her country's independence instead of buying imported goods from Great Britain. Popular imagery also depicted Liberty and other Revolutionary political principles as women. Yet even in the most positive renderings of women's wartime contributions, their relationship to the cause was mediated through men. Liberty might be depicted as a woman, but that only underscored the larger point: liberty, like women, was something that only men could possess and that men also needed to protect. Women, however, clearly considered the Revolution to be their political project too.[9]

Not everyone identified Revolutionary principles with the Patriot cause. Some people opposed the Revolution for the same reasons that others supported it: they saw themselves as part of the people, whose interests mattered and who should have a say in governance. In southern colonies, many in the back country remained loyal to Great Britain because they considered Patriot leaders as members of the tight, local elite who wanted to run government for their own benefit.[10] Enslaved African Americans had obvious reasons for distrusting a political movement led by slaveholders. During the war, tens of thousands of slaves fled to the British in hopes of achieving Revolutionary ideals—namely freedom—for themselves. The exodus began with the promise of Lord Dunmore, the Royal Governor of Virginia, to grant freedom to enslaved men who would join the Crown's forces. Issued in November 1775, he had three hundred volunteers just one month later. Lest the political implications were unclear, their uniforms had sashes that read 'Liberty to Slaves'. Patriot leaders inscribed their ire in the Declaration of Independence, listing efforts to 'inspire domestic insurrection' among the offences that justified separation. As the war dragged on, the problem of desertion became so acute that Patriot leaders responded in kind, promising freedom to enslaved men in exchange for military service. That so many enslaved people placed their faith in promises of freedom suggests how widely Revolutionary ideals circulated—and how profoundly they shaped the political sensibilities of all Americans.[11]

---

[9] Linda K. Kerber, *Women of the Republic: Intellect and Ideology in Revolutionary America* (Chapel Hill, NC, 1980); Carol Smith-Rosenberg, 'Dis-Covering the Subject of the "Great Constitutional Discussion", 1786–1789', *Journal of American History,* 79 (1992), 841–73.

[10] Klein, *Unification of a Slave State,* 79–108.

[11] Sylvia Frey, *Water from the Rock: Black Resistance in a Revolutionary Age* (Princeton, NJ, 1991); Woody Holton, *Forced Founders: Indians, Debtors, Slaves, and the Making of the American Revolution in Virginia* (Chapel Hill, NC, 1999).

All the various interpretations of the Revolution's political meanings acquired solidity through frequent use. Years of war, combined with weak governing structures, left an institutional vacuum in which people acted on their own political conceptions and planned futures framed in those terms. Those expectations did not sit well with many Patriot leaders, who did not anticipate such broad readings of Revolutionary ideology nor the conflicts that resulted. Neither the Revolution nor the war's outcome clarified the new republic's basic governing principles: Who were 'the people'? What was their actual relationship to government? What powers did government have over them? If anything the answers were less clear at the end of the war than they were at its outset.

Those ambiguities marked governing institutions in the new republic, as narrow readings of Revolutionary principles collided with broader, more democratic interpretations. Much of the historiography has been preoccupied with identifying the victor. Tellingly, however, no clear consensus has emerged: while some scholars portray the post-Revolutionary years in terms of the institutional limits on democracy, others emphasize the expansion of those principles, both within and outside the formal bounds of government. In fact, both interpretations describe the situation. Post-Revolutionary institutions communicated the political conflicts of the era. More than that, they actually joined restrictive and expansive visions of the people in a tight relationship, affirming both and weaving them together so that democracy for some often came at the expense of others.

THE CONTRADICTIONS OF THE
POST-REVOLUTIONARY ERA

Economic instability in the years following the Revolution exacerbated the tension between narrow and expansive interpretations of the people's relationship to government. During the war, states racked up debt, while disruptions in trade ravaged local economies. Afterward, political uncertainty magnified those economic problems, resulting in extremely tight credit markets, which made recovery more difficult. Creditors demanded that existing debts be paid and refused to extend further credit. In a world where currency was scarce and the resources of most households were tied up in land and productive property, basic economic transactions were impossible without credit. As state leaders scrambled to shore up confidence among creditors by raising revenue to pay off debts, many farmers and tradesmen struggled to pay their taxes and to finance their operations.

The resulting political conflicts pitted the people against their new state governments. While state legislators battled over the best means of handling debt, local communities took matters into their own hands, closing down courts and refusing to enforce laws unfavourable to debtors. Participants assumed the mantle of state authority even as they challenged it, invoking Revolutionary rhetoric, particularly conceptions of natural rights and the people's sovereignty, to explain themselves. In Pennsylvania, local communities constructed improvised barriers to keep judges from presiding at debt proceedings. Some unfortunate members of the judiciary found themselves trapped in manure-filled ditches that conveniently and inexplicably appeared on main arteries leading to court towns. Only when state authorities responded with a heavy hand did such situations escalate into violence. That happened with Shays' Rebellion in western Massachusetts, which received a good deal of attention by contemporaries and later historians, but was only the most dramatic of many such incidents.[12]

Insurgents expressed a popular view of democracy, in which notions of the people's sovereignty meant direct participation in government. Participation was not limited to the election of representatives. It took immediate forms: the idea was that people would come together and formulate rules that expressed their interests and needs. Such expectations tended to construe government as a series of highly localized institutions where decisions reflected the needs of particular communities. While state governments were necessary, their purview should be circumscribed to matters that local areas could not handle. It was an institutional vision at odds with that of many political leaders, who imagined larger, more coherent jurisdictional entities: states and, for some, a nation that tied those states together in an overarching political union.[13]

Local conflicts over debt solidified concerns among many of the republic's political leaders about the role of the people in government. Specifically, they feared that government institutions—at both the state and federal levels—were too weak to protect themselves from the people's expansive conceptions of their sovereignty, which would ultimately destroy the new republic's political experiment. Those concerns culminated in a convention, called by the Continental Congress in 1786, to propose changes to the current government. By the time the convention met, in 1787, its delegates—who had been appointed by their state legislatures—found themselves considering an altogether different government structure. That agenda reflected the efforts of nationalists—or Federalists—who wanted a stronger, national government and saw the convention as a means to create it. They arrived with a plan for the new Constitution, drafted by James Madison, and a strategy for capturing the convention's agenda, which was not straightforward because the Continental Congress had limited the convention's scope. Delegates were supposed to formulate recommendations to present to Congress, which would then decide whether and how to act on them, bearing in mind the interests of the sovereign states represented by that body. So how could this convention bypass that process and devise a new Constitution for the federal government? Madison supplied the answer, by elevating the people's sovereignty over that of the states. Delegates, he argued, could act in the name of the people, because sovereignty actually lay with them. The logic is enshrined in the preamble, 'We the People of

---

[12] Terry Bouton, *Taming Democracy: 'The People', the Founders, and the Troubled Ending of the American Revolution* (New York, 2007); Woody Holton, *Unruly Americans and the Origins of the Constitution* (New York, 2007).

[13] Willi Paul Adams, *The First American Constitutions: Republican Ideology and the Making of the State Constitution in the Revolutionary Era* (Lantham, MD, 2001); Steven Wilf, *Law's Imagined Republic: Popular Politics and Criminal Justice in Revolutionary America* (New York, 2010).

the United States, in Order to form a more perfect Union . . . do ordain and establish this Constitution for the United States of America.'[14]

The new Constitution replaced a confederacy of sovereign states with a sovereign federal government. The resulting structure, however, expressed a deep distrust of centralized authority. The Constitution distributed authority among the legislative, executive, and judicial branches, each with clearly defined duties and the responsibility of keeping the others in check. The legislative was further divided into two houses: The House of Representatives, which directly represented the people, and the Senate, which represented the states and which reflected the existing situation in which states were the sovereign units of government. The Constitution explicitly limited the new federal government's powers to certain areas: namely war and defence, relations with foreign nations, and commerce between the states. The states maintained authority over all other issues. The federal government exercised supremacy over the states, with its mandate to make laws 'necessary and proper' for the execution of its powers and the provision that made its enactments the 'supreme law of the land'. But it still shared sovereignty with the states and the people, a situation that generated confusion and conflicts—and that ultimately ended in the Civil War—because the division of authority among all these sovereign bodies was never as clear in practice as it was in theory.[15]

The preamble's invocation of the people did not translate into direct popular participation within the federal government. Federalists maintained that the new federal government would protect democratic *principles* by controlling the excesses of the democratic *processes*. Recent events, Federalists argued, only confirmed a point well established in the literature: direct participation subjected government to wild swings in public opinion that, ultimately, resulted in institutional collapse and the destruction of the people's rights and liberties. The new government's geographic distance from the people it served, its separation of powers, and its reliance on virtual representation—through elected representatives—insulated its workings from the emotions of the moment and allowed for reasoned deliberation. Geographic size would also serve as a stabilizing force. Where many political theorists had argued that only small states could sustain democratic governments, Federalists maintained that size actually tempered conflicts and minimized the dangers of factionalism by making it impossible for a minority to seize control.[16]

Delegates invoked the name of the people to legitimize their work, but they kept their deliberations secret. The American people knew nothing about the new Constitution until after the convention completed its work. Once the document was released, heated debate ensued. Anti-Federalists argued that centralized federal authority would, at best, fail to represent the people's interests and, at worst, devolve into despotism. The Constitution's architects responded in a series of newspaper essays, known collectively as the Federalist Papers, which addressed objections to the new government. The issues articulated in the press moved into

---

[14] Constitution of the United States (1787), *Avalon Project*; Jack Rakove, *Original Meanings: Politics and Ideas in the Making of the Constitution* (New York, 1996).
[15] Constitution of the United States.   [16] Ibid.

city streets and country byways, where ordinary people grappled with them in informal events and organized demonstrations. Opposition in many states was so strong that Federalists obtained ratification only with the promise of a Bill of Rights, a statement of basic rights intended to protect the people from encroachments of federal power. The minimum of nine states required for ratification was reached in June 1788, when New Hampshire approved the document. It was clear, however, that the new government needed the blessings of Virginia and New York, two of the largest, most populous, and politically influential states. Conventions there voted for ratification, but by narrow margins that signalled deep reservations about the proposed federal government. Nonetheless, the United States Constitution went into effect after the approval of Virginia and New York, although North Carolina refused to ratify it until after the Bill of Rights was proposed in 1789 and Rhode Island delayed until after passage of the Bill of Rights in 1791.

The US Constitution invoked the people, but it did not alter the status quo, in which states had jurisdiction over the public welfare and the people's rights. Deference to the states in these matters was most apparent in the Constitution's affirmation of slavery, notably the infamous clause that counted each slave as three-fifths of a person for purposes of apportionment in the House of Representatives. A compromise between states without slaves and those with large numbers of slaves, the three-fifths clause nonetheless recognized the legitimacy of slavery. Even the addition of the Bill of Rights had limited implications for most people. The enumerated rights include freedom of speech, the press, and religion, as well as dealing with procedural claims within the legal system. But the Constitution framed those rights in the negative, detailing what the federal government could not do, instead of articulating broad principles that the federal government would protect. The First Amendment, which protects religion, free speech, and assembly, is exemplary: 'Congress shall make no law respecting an establishment of religion, or prohibiting the free exercise thereof; or abridging the freedom of speech, or of the press; or the right of the people peaceably to assemble, and to petition the Government for a redress of grievances.' In practice, moreover, the Bill of Rights applied to matters that fell within the federal government's jurisdiction, a range of issues so narrow that they had little applicability in most people's lives.[17]

The Northwest Ordinance, by contrast, did articulate a clear vision of the people's relationship to government, largely because it dealt with the structure of states. Drafted in 1787 and approved by Congress in 1790, the Ordinance outlined the process by which new territory ceded by the Treaty of Paris—the area that is now Ohio, Indiana, Illinois, Wisconsin, Michigan, and Minnesota—would become sovereign states. In a broader sense, the Northwest Ordinance framed future expansion in a way that would allow the new republic to extend its borders across North America without altering its political institutions or principles. New territory would be divided into states that would enter the union on equal footing with the original states, once they acquired sufficient population and went through a

[17] Ibid.

period of political organization supervised by the US Congress. New states had to accept legal principles and political institutions compatible to those that already existed in other states. In particular, the Ordinance replicated established patterns in which local government maintained considerable responsibility for public safety, health, and welfare. But otherwise, people in the territories were allowed to frame their new state governments as they saw fit, a situation that resulted in considerable variation in legal rules and governing processes. Finally, the Ordinance provided the economic basis thought necessary to support democratic forms of government by providing for the sale of land to settlers in parcels of forty acres, an amount thought small enough to make ownership widely accessible. Underscoring the political importance attached to economic independence, the Ordinance also prohibited slavery in the Northwest Territory. This vision of the people's relationship to government was inscribed so deeply into the geography that it is still evident today in the neat checkerboard of farms that one sees when flying over the nation's vast midsection.[18]

To the extent that the Northwest Ordinance promoted democracy, it did so for some at the expense of others, a dynamic that characterized post-Revolutionary political culture more generally. Native tribes claimed land in the Northwest Territory, but they had not been included in negotiations at the Treaty of Paris. The Treaty turned their land over to the United States; the United States government, in turn, distributed it, as private property, to the people. Those 'people', moreover, were very particular kinds of Americans: they were white men who possessed the rights necessary to own property, the resources to purchase it, and the means to make it productive. Those men's economic and political independence rested on the exclusion of some, namely Indians, and the dependence of others, namely the wives, children, and hired hands whose labour was necessary to make the land productive. In this sense, the Ordinance represented a fundamental contradiction in the new republic's emerging political culture, which not only required but also reproduced hierarchies that were, in theory, inimical to it. Once embedded in the political structure of government, the resulting inequalities became more difficult to address, let alone abandon. To question them was to question the nation's democratic principles.[19]

Motivated by the same concerns that produced the US Constitution, state political leaders also moved to centralize the operations of state government. After the Revolution, some states revised their constitutions to place limits on democracy. The preamble of the second, 1790 Pennsylvania Constitution, for instance, read much like that of the US Constitution: 'We, the people of the commonwealth of Pennsylvania, ordain and establish this constitution for its government.' The document focused, primarily, on the structures of state government, which included clearly delineated executive, judicial, and legislative branches. A bill of rights placed limits on the state's power over the people. Conspicuously absent,

---

[18] Northwest Ordinance (1787), *Avalon Project*.
[19] Stephanie McCurry, *Masters of Small Worlds: Yeoman Households, Gender Relations, and the Political Culture of the Antebellum South Carolina Low Country* (New York, 1995).

however, was language that rooted sovereignty directly in the people. The same was true in other revised constitutions as well. In Pennsylvania and elsewhere, efforts to strengthen states also involved the subordination of local jurisdictions to state government by creating rationalized bodies of law that applied uniformly, regardless of local conditions. To these ends, state leaders collected and organized existing statutes, created appellate courts with the power to set precedent, and clearly elevated the state over local areas as the place where a uniform body of law was created and interpreted. All these changes were meant to regularize the operations of law and government, locating authority over the law at the state level. But they did so by distancing the people from the actual practice of governance.[20]

The power of states to define the people's relationship to governance is most apparent in questions of citizenship. The federal government determined who could be citizens; but the states determined what rights attached, if at all, to the people—be they citizens or not—within their borders. Most states determined rights and status based on considerations other than citizenship, with results that affirmed status relationships in much the same way as the Northwest Ordinance. In many instances, people who were not citizens enjoyed a wider range of rights than those who were. Women, for instance, could not claim full civil rights or political rights because of their status as wives or daughters or because of their gender. States and localities restricted the rights of free blacks because of race and the association with slavery. Similar concerns ultimately called the citizenship of free blacks into question as well; but lack of citizenship was not the reason for the restriction of rights. The expectation that citizenship would entail specific rights emerged only later in the nineteenth century, largely as a result of Constitutional Amendments enacted after the Civil War that extended federal authority over the legal status of citizens.

States also determined the handling of slavery. Legislatures began debating the abolition of slavery even before the end of the Revolutionary war, producing statutes that characterized slavery as antithetical to the new republic's basic principles. The preamble to the Pennsylvania statute, passed in 1780, cited the 'abhorrence of that condition to which the arms and tyranny of Great-Britain were exerted to reduce' and 'our duty ... to extend a portion of that freedom to others which hath been extended to us'. Just as liberty made bondage suspect, so natural rights overwhelmed the implications of racial difference: 'It is not for us to inquire, why, in the creation of mankind, the inhabitants of several parts of the earth were distinguished by a difference in feature or complexion. . . . It is sufficient to know, that all are the work of an Almighty Hand.' Legislatures considered abolition even in states where slavery was deeply entrenched, underscoring the tendency of Revolutionary political principles to migrate between questions about the structure of public institutions to those involving the exercise of authority generally and particularly in status relationships, such as that between master and slave. If government could deny natural rights to some, then what kept it from suspending the rights of others?

---

[20] Pennsylvania Constitution (1790), from the *Pennsylvania Constitution Web Page*, Duquesne University Law School, http://www.duq.edu/law/pa-constitution/constitutions/1790.cfm.

If tyranny produced political corruption, then what kept the tyranny of slavery from infecting the body politic? Those concerns ultimately ended slavery in the northern states between 1776 and 1804.[21]

The same political principles that enabled abolition, however, also provided the political rationale preserving the institutions and generating new measures to constrain free blacks. Southern states, where the vast majority of enslaved Americans lived, never abolished slavery. Instead, political leaders there embedded the institution deeply into the structures of government, through measures that acknowledged, defined, and regulated slavery as an essential component of the social order. Southern states also naturalized slavery by analogizing slaves to other household dependants, namely wives and children: race made people of African descent dependent, just as gender made women dependent and age made children dependent. By this logic, nature justified legal restrictions, not the recognition of rights, since people whose essential nature rendered them dependent could not exercise rights responsibly. Slavery, its defenders argued, would protect the republic by keeping this potentially disruptive population in check.[22] Similar concerns also limited the implications of abolition in the northern states. Statutes there made abolition gradual, based on the argument that people accustomed to bondage would require time to adjust to the responsibilities of freedom. In some northern states, abolition was so gradual that people were still legally enslaved into the 1850s. The same logic resulted in the denial of civil and political rights to free blacks and fuelled racial tensions. Racism took particularly insidious forms, characterizing black Americans as a threat to the new republic's political project and to the status of white Americans: the meaning of liberty would diminish if those of African ancestry exercised it.[23]

The authority that states had in theory, however, did not always accord with practice. Despite changes that centralized state authority, the states' sovereignty was still based in the people, even if only indirectly. Those people, who had their own ideas about what government should look like, acted as a check on state authority. In many states, local jurisdictions retained considerable authority throughout the first half of the nineteenth century: most questions about the public welfare were aired and decided there. The most visible of these venues were the circuit courts, which met on a regular schedule in county seats or court towns, which held jury trials and which dealt with a great deal of government business. But circuit courts were only the most conspicuous part of a system dominated by even more localized legal proceedings, including magistrates' hearings and trials, inquests, and other ad hoc legal forums that were intended to preserve the peace—the social order—as defined in local areas. Magistrates not only screened cases and tried minor offences, but also kept tabs on a range of matters involving markets and morals. In most legal matters, the interested parties collected evidence, gathered witnesses, and represented themselves. Cases were decided by

---

[21] 'An Act for the Gradual Abolition of Slavery', Pennsylvania (1780), *Avalon Project*.
[22] Lacy K. Ford, *Deliver Us from Evil: The Slavery Question in the Old South* (New York, 2009).
[23] Leslie M. Harris, *In the Shadow of Slavery: African Americans in New York City, 1626–1863* (Chicago, IL, 2003).

common law in its traditional sense as a flexible collection of principles rooted in local custom, but that also included an array of texts and principles as potential sources for authoritative legal principles. Each jurisdiction produced inconsistent rulings, aimed at resolving particular matters, rather than producing a uniform, comprehensive body of law. State legislatures and appellate courts deferred to localism, generating laws in public matters sporadically and haphazardly, often in response to local concerns and not always with the expectation that state law would supersede local practice.[24]

Localism was as much a conceptual approach to government as a description of its physical location. People of all kinds approached government, at all levels, with an air of proprietary familiarity. Putting Revolutionary conceptions of the people's sovereignty into practice, they expected government to respond to their problems and their conceptions of justice. Even people, such as free blacks, who had no reason to expect equitable treatment, still had faith that the government would work this way. Those expectations extended to state and national government as well. Individual requests for private acts, for instance, took up most of the state legislatures' business; in the post-Revolutionary decades, the volumes of public acts are slim by comparison. Such acts ranged as widely as the complaints brought to local magistrates, and included the incorporation of voluntary organizations, the chartering of businesses, grants of manumission, divorce, legitimization of children, and suspensions of existing laws in particular instances. They expressed both the legislatures' sovereign authority to make or modify law and the people's expectations that their legislatures would act on their behalf in personal matters in individualized ways.[25]

The consolidation of state authority over the first half of the nineteenth century, nonetheless, had profound implications for the people's relationship to government. As political leaders extended the reach of the state, they elaborated the rubric of individual rights that was prevalent in property law and extended it over a wide range of social relations, particularly domestic relations, that formerly had been handled locally through collective conceptions of 'the peace'. The logic inherent in the developing body of state law construed white men's patriarchal authority and civic participation as individual rights, akin to their already established property rights. White men's rights were increasingly asserted and protected at this level of government, solidifying their connection to it. These connections set the scene for the emergence of competitive political campaigns and the development of the first- and second-party system—whose dynamics shaped a distinctive political culture defined, at the time, as democratic. By the 1830s, political rhetoric commonly identified white men as 'freemen', that is, as legally recognized individuals who were paradigmatic citizens, at least within the realm of state and national government—for although the legal status of individuals was largely defined at the state level, the same political rhetoric characterized national politics as well. In parallel, the subordinate legal status of domestic dependants and slaves, defined by

---

[24] Laura F. Edwards, *The People and their Peace: Legal Culture and the Transformation of Inequality in the Post-Revolutionary South* (Chapel Hill, NC, 2009), 26–85.

[25] Ibid. 57–201.

their lack of rights, supplied a rationale for their exclusion from law and government. States defined them as altogether different categories of legal persons on the basis of the abstract categories of race, class, and/or gender. White women, African Americans, and the poor found it difficult to make themselves heard and their concerns visible within the body of state law, because they were excluded from the category of people with rights the state was designed to protect.[26]

The denial of rights to the vast majority of Americans and their exclusion from the polity masked even more profound inequalities within state and national government. White men were constituted as freemen through their rights *over* those without rights. In extending this legal framework, state leaders applied the precepts of liberal individualism to the existing patriarchal structure of law. They abstracted the authority white men already exercised in a social context, through their obligations to 'the peace' in localized law, and individualized both its privileges and restrictions. By the 1850s white men could claim rights not just in their property and their own labour, but also in the labour and bodies of their dependants and, through the abstractions of gender and race, over the lives of other subordinated people as well. Their authority extended over all black persons, slave or free, and no black person fully possessed his or her own body or the product of his or her labour.[27]

By the 1850s, democracy in America was simultaneously expansive and constrained for all the people. Political rhetoric placed a premium on the people's rights and their direct connection to government. That culture produced heated campaigns and the highest voter turnout in the nation's history. The political rhetoric, however, also depended on a series of oppositions: white men were free because they were not black, enslaved, or female. More than that, white men's freedom rested on their rights over those who were black, enslaved, and female. That rhetoric implied the presence of vital, participatory governing institutions. To be sure, most states dropped property requirements in the first half of the nineteenth century so that most free white men could vote. States also made more offices, including those of governors and judges, elective. The expansion of the electorate and of elective offices represented the expansion of democracy within governing institutions, at least for free white men who could vote. Even for them, however, democratic principles did not extend to governing institutions in an easy, direct way. In practice, state and national leaders' vision of democracy did not include fundamental changes in the economic or social structure that would put all white men on an equal footing. Legislators and jurists defined rights of freemen narrowly, so as to affirm existing inequalities and to protect the property interests of the wealthy, particularly slavery. They also defined the scope of government at these levels narrowly. By the 1850s freemen could look to state and national governments to uphold their rights, in abstract. But many of the white men included in this category could not count on those rights as a means to influence government institutions in meaningful ways or use them to define and address substantive questions of the public interest that affected their daily lives. Even for the nation's paradigmatic citizens, democracy came with constraints.

---

[26] Ibid. 220–85.
[27] Barbara Young Welke, *Law and the Borders of Belonging in the Long Nineteenth-Century United States* (New York and Cambridge, 2010).

PART II

FRANCE

4

Varieties of Democracy in the French Revolution

Ruth Scurr

INTRODUCTION

The French Revolution had a major impact on conceptions of 'democracy' inside and outside France, and continues to provide a key reference point in discussions of democracy's advent. Yet during the Revolution itself, especially in its early stages, the word and its cognates were not central to reforming or revolutionary discourse. At the beginning of the Revolution in 1789, democracy was a rarefied and rarely used term. When it was used, moreover, the word was applied in a variety of contexts—not all of them ones we might, in retrospect, expect.

One initial and fundamental distinction that needs to be drawn is between the terms 'democracy' (*démocratie*) and 'democrat' (*démocrate*), where 'democracy' refers primarily to a form of government, and 'democrat' is a badge or appellation of allegiance to revolutionary regime-change and the dismantling of a feudal or aristocratic past.[1] These terms converged when they were employed together in the establishment of representative government. When the term 'democracy' was contrasted with outmoded or pathological variants, and used to mean representative government, and the term 'democrat' was taken to identify a supporter or advocate of institutionalized power accountable to the sovereign people, the gap between 'democracy' and 'democrat' closed, even if temporarily and unstably.

In the course of the Revolution, the debate over forms of government shifted constantly in perspective. The most dramatic change took place between the conditions of 1789, when almost no one thought a republican government possible or desirable for France, and those of 1792, when there seemed no acceptable alternative.[2] A second dramatic change was less abrupt or synchronized. Edmund Burke foresaw it at the very outset of the Revolution, but others grasped it only after the Constitutional Monarchy collapsed in 1792, or even later, during the Terror itself.[3]

---

[1] Raymonde Monnier, 'Démocratie et révolution française', *Mots*, 59 (1999), 50.
[2] F. A. Aulard, *Histoire politique de la Révolution française. Origines et développement de la démocratie et de la République (1789–1804)* (Paris, 1901), 1.
[3] Edmund Burke, *Reflections on the Revolution in France* [1790], ed. J. G. A. Pocock (Indianapolis, IN, 1987).

It was a shift from viewing the coercive apparatus of government wielded by the *ancien régime* as something to dismantle or subject to the public interest, to a recognition that effective government might simply disappear under the pressure of efforts at rationalization. This moved the emphasis from the challenge of ensuring legitimate government to that of instituting and sustaining effective executive power. The idea that France's governors should be insulated from the nation that they governed shocked the revolutionaries of 1789, but under Thermidor and afterwards it became an explicit constitutional precept, all but universally accepted by theorists and politicians hoping to stabilize the republic.[4]

POPULAR SOVEREIGNTY, CONSTITUTING POWER, AND THE RIGHTS OF MAN

In his 1995 article on the history of the word 'democracy' in France, Pierre Rosanvallon drew attention to the fact that, for a long time, the term continued to be used only to designate an ancient and obsolete political system. For Rosanvallon, the ancient—almost technical—connotations of the word 'democracy' in the eighteenth century explain why it was absent from places where we might expect to find it in revolutionary discourse in 1789: the word 'democracy' was thus not used once in the debates on the right to vote between 1789 and 1791.[5]

This (retrospectively surprising) neglect was reinforced by the distinction drawn between popular sovereignty and the question of forms of government. In 1789 popular sovereignty was represented as society's right and opportunity to create its own rules and institutions by exercising its inalienable and historically unconstrained constituting power. This revolutionary definition of popular sovereignty marked a distinctive break with previous understandings of sovereignty as the exercise of power in the service, interests, or good of the people. According to the revolutionary definition, the good of the people could only be realized through the direct or represented action or agency of the people itself.[6]

In sharp contrast to this, democracy was, for the most part, defined narrowly as merely one of the technical ways of organizing government, and an obsolete and undesirable way at that. The distinction between popular sovereignty and the forms of government was prominent in the writings of both Montesquieu and Rousseau. For Montesquieu, the fundamental contrast lay between a democratic and an aristocratic republic: in the former, sovereignty was located in the people (*la peuple en corps a la souveraine puissance*); in the latter, it rested in the hands of a

---

[4] Cheryl B. Welch, *Liberty and Utility: The French Idéologues and the Transformation of Liberalism* (New York, 1984), 97–128; Sudhir Hazareesingh, *Intellectual Founders of the Republic: Five Studies in Nineteenth-Century French Republican Political Thought* (Oxford, 2001).

[5] Pierre Rosanvallon, 'The History of the Word "Democracy" in France', *Journal of Democracy*, 6 (1995), 143.

[6] Marcel Gauchet, *La Révolution des pouvoirs: la souveraineté, le peuple et la représentation, 1789–1799* (Paris, 1995).

part or section of the people (*entre les mains d'une parité du peuple*).[7] According to Montesquieu, it was a fundamental law of democracy that the people alone must make the laws; hence the integral connection, within democracy, between popular sovereignty and legislative power.[8]

Rosanvallon noted that 'it is little observed that in Rousseau's writings, the notion of democracy yields to that of popular sovereignty. For Rousseau, democracy is a form of government and a method of decision making, but does not constitute the essential thing: the very foundation of the social bond and the political order.'[9] The important commentaries on the *Social Contract* published in the *Bouche de fer* by the Abbé Fauchet between autumn 1790 and summer 1791 focused centrally on sovereignty: how best to make laws conform to the general interest; how to prevent representatives from losing touch with their constituents. The form of government was a secondary consideration, and the term 'democracy' relevant only to the issue of how best to organize executive power.

Interestingly, popular sovereignty as a political term appears very rarely in the influential writing of the Abbé Sieyès early in the Revolution. He asserted the right of the nation to sovereign power by a complex and indirect argument that relied upon a particular idea of constituting power. Constituting power, as Sieyès understood it, was the nation's inalienable right to legislate a Constitution for itself:

> Already in various parts of the kingdom there were forceful claims that it was high time to stop being cowardly victims of inveterate disorder. There have been appeals to the fundamental principles of the social order, and it has come now to be perceived that for any people the first and most important of all the laws of the social order is to have a good constitution. This is because only a good constitution can give and guarantee citizens the enjoyment of their natural and social rights, can confer stability on everything that may be done for the good, and can progressively extinguish all that has been done for the bad.[10]

Sieyès used the concept of constituting power in 1789 to suggest that the history of France should not be allowed to obstruct the possibility of the French nation expressing, constituting, and legitimately establishing itself for the first time ever. This was a radical repudiation of all forms of political thought and argument that tried to rationalize contemporary French public institutions by referring back to the distant past: the demise of Frankish power and the subsequent history of the Capetian and later Bourbon monarchy.

In his pre-Revolutionary pamphlet *On the Influence of the American Revolution on Europe* (1786), the Marquis de Condorcet drew on the discourse of rights, rather than the concepts of popular sovereignty or constituting power, to argue for a constitutional basis for enlightened government.[11] He characterized recent events

---

[7] Monnier, 'Démocratie', 51.

[8] Charles-Louis, Baron de Montesquieu, *De L'Esprit des loix* [1748], ed. J. Brethe de la Gressaye (4 vols, Paris, 1950–61), 1: 41.

[9] Rosanvallon, '"Democracy" in France', 142.

[10] *Sieyès: Political Writings, Including the Debate between Sieyès and Tom Paine in 1791*, ed. Michael Sonenscher (Indianapolis, IN, 2003), 5.

[11] *Condorcet: Selected Writings*, ed. K. M. Baker (Indianapolis, IN, 1976), 71–84.

in America as a sublime affirmation of the rights of man, and as a demonstration of the importance of a written declaration of those rights: 'The spectacle of a great people among whom the rights of man are respected is useful to all other peoples, despite the differences of climate, customs and constitutions.'[12] In the introduction to this work, Condorcet set out four basic rights of man:

1. Security of person, which includes the assurance that one will not be disturbed by any violence, either within one's family or in the use of one's faculties, the independent and free exercise of which must be preserved in everything which is not contrary to the rights of another.

2. Security and free enjoyment of property.

3. Since in society there are certain actions which must be subject to common rules; since it is necessary to establish punishments for violations by an individual of the rights of others (whether by violence or fraud), man also has the right to be subject in all these matters only to general laws extending to the entire body of citizens. The interpretation of these laws may not be arbitrary; and their execution must be entrusted to impartial hands.

4. Finally, the right to contribute, either directly or through representatives, to the making of the laws and to all actions taken in the name of society at large is a necessary consequence of the natural and primitive equality of man, and its equal enjoyment by each man using his reason must be regarded as the ultimate goal. Until this goal has been attained, it cannot be said that citizens enjoy this right in its entire extent.[13]

In 1786 Condorcet regarded the fourth of these rights as the least important and most problematic:

> Zealous republicans have regarded this right as the most fundamental of all. And it is certainly true that in an enlightened nation free from superstition, where it would really belong to every citizen who could or would exercise it, the enjoyment of this right would ensure the enjoyment of all the others. But it loses its most precious advantages if prejudices divert those who must exercise it from the narrow paths traced for them by the immutable laws of justice; and, in terms of public happiness, a republic with tyrannical laws can fall far short of a monarchy.[14]

It is thus clear that in 1786 Condorcet saw the example of America as helpful and relevant to the French, yet as not necessarily entailing regime-change. Indeed, he saw no reason why public happiness and rational government in accordance with justice and the rights of man could not be achieved under France's existing monarchical form of government. Early revolutionary debates and events caused Condorcet to change his mind dramatically. He lost faith in the new Constitution that the National Assembly was preparing for France; he lost faith above all in the character of the king and the role he might be expected to play inside a constitutional monarchy; and he progressively revised his view on the fourth of the fundamental

---

[12] Ibid. 77.   [13] Ibid. 73.   [14] Ibid. 74.

rights of man he had outlined in 1786, 'the right to contribute, either directly or through representatives, to the making of the laws'. After Louis XVI's flight to Varennes in 1791, Condorcet was one of the first to call openly for a republic: his focus was now sharply concentrated on the form of government best suited to Revolutionary France.[15]

REJECTING THE OLD REGIME

It followed from the primacy given to the concepts of popular sovereignty, constituting power, and the rights of man after 1789, that a political regime could only be considered properly legitimate if plausibly based on, or expressive of, the will of the people. What did this mean in the context of Revolutionary France? Unsurprisingly, it was easier to use the concept of popular sovereignty critically than it was to construct positive models of how constituting power might be used to establish a legitimate, accountable, and effective form of government compatible with the rights of man. Applied critically, the concept of popular sovereignty could be turned against all forms of privilege and the remnants of France's feudal past. It was in this context, as Rosanvallon has argued, that the term 'democrat' first became a badge of identity, coming into popular use as an antonym for 'aristocrat', a word that played a fundamental role in the sociopolitical terminology of the revolutionary period.[16] Up to 1791, 'democrat' designated not so much the partisan of a specific political regime (democracy) as an adversary of the *ancien régime* and a supporter of the revolutionary process. It meant 'attachment to the Revolution, to the popular cause'. But it was only one among many terms expressing political fidelity to the ideals of the Revolution; others including 'patriot', 'Jacobin', and 'sans-culotte'.

An interesting example is the reference to 'the democrat Robespierre' in the royalist press (*Journal de Louis XVI et de son peuple*) following his speech against the death penalty in May 1791.[17] Robespierre at this time was chiefly known for his passionate opposition to the plan to divide French citizens into two groups, active and passive, according to whether or not they paid a minimal amount of direct taxation, and to limit the franchise to the former. To his mind such a distinction between citizens had been outlawed by the Declaration of Rights. Similarly, he objected to the *marc d'agent*, a further qualification that the Assembly envisaged imposing on those who wished to stand for election; this would entail them paying taxes worth about fifty-three *livres*, well over ten times the amount of direct taxation necessary to become an active citizen. Robespierre also argued repeatedly for the rights of excluded groups like actors, Jews, and West Indians living under

[15] Keith M. Baker, *Cordorcet: From Natural Philosophy to Social Mathematics* (Chicago, IL, 1975), 304–6.

[16] Rosanvallon, '"Democracy" in France', 144.

[17] Maximilien Robespierre, *Oeuvres complètes de Maximilien Robespierre*, ed. E. Hamel (10 vols, Paris, 1910–67).

French colonial rule. With these protests, he began the campaign for radical extension of the suffrage. In retrospect, the appellation 'democrat' can be linked to his advocacy of widening voting rights—but at the time it was used sneeringly with negative connotations. In the spring of 1791 Robespierre was not yet an overt republican and there is no evidence that he had any constructive conception of how executive power could be made (and kept) accountable to popular sovereignty. Like other prominent revolutionaries, he could more easily identify what was not legitimate (anything perpetuating or replicating *ancien régime* privileges or inequalities) than solve the conundrum of modern government.[18]

The challenge of reconciling popular sovereignty with the organization of executive power was most sharply focused in the polemical exchange between Thomas Paine and the Abbé Sieyès in 1791, just after the king's flight to Varennes and the first public demands for a republic in France. When Paine declared himself against the 'Hell of monarchies', Sieyès responded by rejecting with equal vehemence the 'Hell of republics'.[19] In his later gloss on this exchange, Pierre-Louis Rœderer, Sieyès's friend and intellectual associate, claimed that Paine had meant to reject the hereditary, aristocratic monarchies in which the king was overwhelmingly powerful; whereas Sieyès, by contrast, had meant to reject democracy's disfunctional variants: demagogy, ochlocracy, and miarocracy (or government defiled with blood). Rœderer was of course reading the remark retrospectively (though not necessarily inaccurately), in the light of Sieyès's and his own concern to find a stable form of representative government once the first attempt at that had been derailed by the Terror.

DEMOCRACY AS A METHOD OF GOVERNMENT

To summarize: at the beginning of the Revolution, democracy was widely considered an outmoded, undesirable, and dangerous form of government. The distinction between legislative and executive power was prominent in the writings of Montesquieu and Rousseau, and a resource for those reflecting on constitutional design during the Revolution. In this context, when members of the National Assembly and Convention discussed (and more often than not dismissed) democracy as one form of government that could be conjoined with popular sovereignty, they focused primarily on the problem of executive power: how difficult it would be to organize, or even theorize, a democratic executive that would be both effective and accountable.

The distinction between legislative and executive power, however, made it possible to align the former with popular sovereignty, even while the latter remained the subject of extreme suspicion. Aligning legislative power with popular sovereignty led to elaborate reflection from 1789 onwards on the role of the people in

[18] Alfred Cobban, 'The Fundamental Ideas of Robespierre', in Cobban, *Aspects of the French Revolution* (London, 1971), 137–59.
[19] *Sieyès: Political Writings*, 167.

choosing and holding accountable members of the legislative branch of government. Although the Abbé Sieyès had distinguished between constituting and constituted power, in the National Assembly the two had become confused.[20] Preoccupation with legislative power resonated with the emphasis Rousseau had placed on it in the *Social Contract*. In strong contrast, the role that the people might play in choosing and holding accountable members of the executive branch was much less carefully theorized early in the Revolution. The awkward presence of Louis XVI at the centre of the executive branch of government was part of the problem, but the intrinsic difficulty of organizing any kind of effective executive power in a non-appropriative relation to popular sovereignty also played its part in undermining confidence in the 1791 Constitution.

Writing with hindsight in 1815, after the restoration of the monarchy, Rœderer claimed that:

> The Constitution of 1791, composed in accordance with national distrust, possessed no strength except against the royal power. Created with a view to setting the seal on the abolition of privileges, it was felt less necessary to found a truly monarchic institution [an effective system of one-man rule], than to prevent the king, the patron of privileges, from re-establishing them. More attention had been given to making the Constitution capable of overthrowing the king, than to making it capable of maintaining itself. It was basically a democratic republic with a phantom of royalty.[21]

Rœderer went on to date the advent of 'democracy' in France explicitly to 1792. With the deposition of the king, executive power also passed into the hands of the National Convention. But Rœderer referred not so much to this as to popular participation in the exercise of power more generally—and not only through the election of officials (a feature of revolutionary local government since 1790), but through direct action. As he wrote:

> The historians of the revolution, if there are any who merit the name, have attributed all the movements of the revolution to impulses coming from the national rostrum—a curious blunder! The orators on the national rostrum, however fiery and violent they may have been, were not the orators of the multitude. I repeat each popular assembly had its own, and one who stood out above all the others.... How shall I conclude? One saw at that time the realization, the revival of what happened in the revolution of 1648 in England. The writer Hobbes who defended, in his work *De Cive*, the monarchical system against the partisans of democracy, said to those who objected that a Caligula or a Nero might come to the throne under a monarchy: 'In a democracy there are as many Neros as there are orators whom the people adore. There are many under democracy and each day there are others, more base, that rise up from below.'[22]

Looking back on 1792—a year when, as head of the Department of Paris, he had been at the centre of events leading to the collapse of the Constitutional Monarchy—Rœderer argued that this had been a time of deep strife between the declining

[20] Ibid. 133–44.
[21] Pierre-Louis Rœderer, *The Spirit of the Revolution of 1789 and Other Writings of the Revolutionary Epoch [1789–1815]*, ed. Murray Forsyth (Aldershot, 1989), 68–9.
[22] Roederer, *Spirit of the Revolution*, 71.

monarchy and the growing force of democracy. He claimed that, between these two opposed powers, there had been a third party of moderate republicans who hoped to institute a form of government that would function as an elected aristocracy of merit. This third party, he argued, perished in the bitter strife between monarchy and democracy that culminated in the complete defeat of the former on 10 August 1792.

Rœderer insisted that France in 1792 had not been in a state of anarchy. There was not a complete absence of government, nor circumstances in which particular wills were substituted for the general will. Instead, there was a general and unanimous will, emanating from the people, alarming in both its content and extent. In an unpublished fragmentary note, he explained that his decision to translate Hobbes's *De Cive* during the Terror was motivated by his hope to understand the causes of instability that—in a healthy and active democracy—could be contained, but that had the potential to ruin a less healthy and vigorous democracy.[23] Hobbes, he argued, had provided a brilliant analysis of corrupt democracy, highlighting the potential dangers posed by rhetoric and eloquence inside this form of government. Was it a mistake to attribute the features of a corrupt democracy to all of its variants? As Rœderer saw it, the only conclusion that followed from Hobbes's analysis was that *all* democracies are in principle unstable. He pointed out that this argument could also be found in Rousseau's *Social Contract*—where it is claimed that democracy is a government without force in which prince, sovereign, and subjects are united in a single body,[24] therefore approximating to a non-government, lacking in unity and stability, more suited to gods than to men.

The model of a democratic republic that Rœderer set out in his lectures during the Terror, in 1793, was founded on what he believed to be agreed between Rousseau and Montesquieu and to be compatible with Hobbes's devastating analysis of the importance of political stability. By definition, a democratic government must divide power among a large number of the citizens, and for this reason the sentiment of equality must prevail. As a result, the people should be frugal, modest, and austere—free from the natural but corrupting influences of avarice and ambition. However, for a democracy to survive, it is also necessary for the majority of citizens to relish the exercise of power. This is only possible if individual citizens value and prioritize the public interest over their more personal interests. With regard to the relationship between the governed and their governors, Rœderer concluded, democratic government is unsuited to realizing the principles of the social order.[25]

The Abbé Sieyès had formulated a similar view earlier, as is evident from his claim that the problem of equality was at the heart of his disagreement with Paine in 1791 over the form of regime and government. Retrospectively, Sieyès thought that Paine had failed to respond to his sincere challenge to refute the claim that

---

[23] See his unpublished papers in the Archives Nationales, Paris, 29(AP)89.

[24] Jean-Jacques Rousseau, *The Political Writings of Jean Jacques Rousseau*, ed. C. E. Vaughan (2 vols, Oxford, 1962), 2: book 3, chapter 4.

[25] Pierre-Louis Rœderer, *Oeuvres du comte P.-L. Rœderer*, ed. A.-M. Rœderer (8 vols, Paris, 1853–9), 8: 298.

'there is more equality in *l'ordre social* than in *l'état de nature*, more in a representative monarchy than in any other government, than in a democracy above all'.[26]

REPRESENTATION AND SURVEILLANCE

In what ways could a legislature and executive be made expressive of popular will, if not through direct participation? Representation and what was termed at the time 'surveillance' represented two possible mechanisms, sometimes though not always linked to 'democracy'. Rosanvallon argued that:

> The Marquis d'Argenson [1694–1757] was quite alone among eighteenth-century writers in distinguishing between 'false' and 'legitimate' forms of democracy the first being fraught with danger, the second designating representative government. 'False democracy,' he wrote, 'soon collapses into anarchy. It is the government of the multitude; such is a people in revolt, insolently scorning law and reason. Its tyrannical despotism is obvious from the violence of its movements and the uncertainty of its deliberations. In *true democracy*, one acts through deputies, who are authorized by election; the mission of those elected by the people and the authority that such officials carry constitute the public power.' ... D'Argenson was the first to strip the word 'democracy' of its ancient and archaic referents and turn its technical meaning upside down (from the idea of direct self-government to that of representative government), an inversion that would take nearly a century to pass into ordinary usage in France.[27]

Sieyès (like Paine) distinguished between democracy and representation. In 1789 and afterwards, even as he consistently stressed the criterion of the size of the society, making representation merely a mechanism for accommodating a larger population, still he attributed a positive function to the representational process.

Yet in his attempts to think through a viable form of moderate republican government, Sieyès drew on the distinction between direct democracy and representative government to challenge the desirability of democracy: for him democracy (direct democracy) was a legitimate but unrefined and potentially unstable form of government, unsuited to the complexities of commercial society. By contrast, in August 1790, Condorcet used the term *démocraties représentatives* in opposition to the term *démocraties immédiates* when discussing the respect due to the law.[28] Condorcet was further developing his thoughts about what he had previously characterized as the fourth fundamental right of man: 'the right to contribute, either directly or through representatives, to the making of the laws'. Raymonde Monnier has pointed out that in the same month the writer and politician Louis-Charles de Lavicomterie used the term *démocratie représentée* in his tract *Du people et des rois*.[29]

---

[26] *Des Manuscripts de Sieyès, 1773–1799*, ed. Christine Fauré with Jacques Guilhaumou and Jacques Valier (Paris, 1999), 459.

[27] Rosanvallon, ' "Democracy" in France', 143.

[28] *Journal de la Société de 1789* (Paris, 1982), 10, 7 août 1789, 3.

[29] ' "Démocratie représentative" ou "république démocratique": de la querelle des mots (République) à la querelle des anciens et des modernes', *Annales historiques de la Révolution française*, 325 (2001), 3.

Here he argued that while Rousseau had shown that a *'véritable démocratie'* could never exist because of the impossibility of the people always assembling to govern themselves, this problem would disappear under a representative democracy.

Meanwhile, radicals who clustered around the Cordeliers group mobilized to defend the key concept of popular sovereignty, emphasizing the dangers of entrusting power to potentially corrupt public officials. Publications like Nicolas de Bonneville and Claude Fauchet's *Bouche de fer* and Pourcain Martel and Louis Fréron's *Orateur du peuple* neither employed the term 'democracy' nor invoked ideals of self-government when they denounced the manner in which deputies and administrators usurped the people's power.[30] Their watchword, as Rosanvallon has argued, was 'surveillance', and what they proposed above all was a procedure for the popular ratification of laws (which would have been prepared and voted on by the Chamber of Representatives). In December 1790, the radical lawyer François Robert treated the terms *république* and *démocratie* as synonyms, arguing that all citizens must contribute personally and individually to the making of the law.[31]

The disagreements between moderate republicans and the *parti démocratique* (as Rœderer called it) after August 1792 were not over whether or not a raw democracy (where the people would be both legislators and magistrates) could be instituted in France; neither thought that possible or desirable. Rather, they disagreed about the kind of representative regime that could or should be established. From the beginning of the Revolution, Robespierre had emphasized equality of right and social inclusion as the counterparts to popular sovereignty. In his speeches, as Rosanvallon has pointed out, the menacing archaism of democracy is evoked but at the same time relegated to the categories of 'pure' or 'absolute' democracy.[32] Robespierre speaks of organizing the republic 'in a manner equally removed from the tempests of absolute democracy and the perfidious tranquillity of representative despotism', and he inveighs against those who wish to establish 'pure democracy, and not that type of democracy which, for the sake of the general happiness, is tempered by laws'. (Though there were, in contrast, those who used the term *pure démocratie* to indicate an ideal of popular participation in government that they thought should be aimed for in 1793—Guyomar, for example).[33]

In his famous address of 10 May 1793, 'On Representative Government', Robespierre heaped scorn on functionaries and called for more direct involvement of the people in public affairs. Yet he never once used the word 'democracy'. In his speech of 5 February 1794, 'Concerning the Principles of Political Morality That Must Guide the National Convention in the Internal Administration of the Republic', by contrast, he insisted that democratic government and republican government were synonyms 'despite the abuses found in vulgar parlance'. 'Democracy,' he continued, 'is not a state where the people, continuously assembled, rules by itself over all public affairs... democracy is a state wherein the sovereign people,

---

[30] Rosanvallon, '"Democracy" in France', 144.
[31] François Robert, 'Le Républicanisme adapté à la France', in Marcel Dorigny (ed.), *Aux Origines de la république, 1789–1792*, (6 vols, Paris, 1991), vol. 2.
[32] Rosanvallon, '"Democracy" in France', 147. [33] Monnier, 'Démocratie', 56.

guided by laws of its own making, does all that it can do properly on its own while delegating to representatives all that the people cannot do itself'.[34] These 'representatives' might exercise either legislative or executive functions.

Robespierre and Saint-Just were to the fore in criticizing the independence of elected officials and other functionaries. They condemned not so much the principle of representation itself as the remoteness of the representatives. They dreamed instead, as Lucien Jaume has emphasized, of a 'regenerated representation'.[35] Their objective was to search out a way toward the identification of people and power, not to suggest the superiority of direct popular government. It was to evoke the former that they now used the word 'democracy'.

In his recent work on the *sans-culottes*, Michael Sonenscher has emphasized that the state of affairs that arose after the definitive collapse of the Constitutional Monarchy on 10 August 1792 was what contemporaries (such as Rœderer in 1793) referred to as a democratic republic.[36] There was a republic (because a republic had been declared after the official end of the monarchy), but there was no constitutionally specified system of republican government (because the National Convention, elected by universal suffrage to design such a government, had not yet had a chance to do so; and in fact even when it did, the proposed and ratified Constitution was indefinitely suspended). Therefore, drawing on the political thought of Rousseau, France could properly be described as a democracy in which there was no settled constitutional distinction between the citizens and magistrates. It was in these circumstances that Saint-Just argued that—under conditions in which every citizen was potentially a magistrate, and magistrates wielded substantial economic and political power through price controls and wartime requisitioning—'it was essential to maintain the integrity of the magistracy'.[37] Sonenscher suggests that the Terror was aimed in the first instance at the magistracy and 'was designed, by way of the panoply of measures adopted by the Convention, to ensure that they used their economic and political power in ways that were compatible with the *salus populi*'.[38]

CONCLUSION

By the time of Robespierre's death in July 1794 the idea of 'democracy', previously a problematic term, had acquired new negative associations, which the Thermidorians and later generations identified with the impotence of the short-lived constitutional monarchy that preceded the failure of the first French Republic, but above all with the pathological extremes of the Terror.[39]

[34] Robespierre, *Oeuvres complètes*.
[35] Lucien Jaume, *Le Discours jacobin et la démocratie* (Paris, 1989), 114–15.
[36] Michael Sonenscher in *H-France Forum* [issue devoted to a discussion of his book, *Sans-Culottes*], 4 (2009), 53. Access at http://www.h-france.net/forum/h-franceforumvol4.html.
[37] Ibid.   [38] Ibid.
[39] François-René, vicomte de Chateaubriand, *Essai sur les révolutions; Génie du Christianisme* (Paris, 2008); Benjamin Constant, *Constant: Political Writings*, ed. B. Fontana (Cambridge, 1988).

In 1794 Robespierre had distinguished himself as a rare advocate of democracy, arguing that:

> It is only under democracy, that the state is truly the homeland of all the individuals who compose it...the French are the first of the world's peoples to have established true democracy, by calling all men to equality and the fullness of rights proper to a citizen....Since the spirit of the Republic is virtue, or equality, and your end is to found, or consolidate, the Republic, it follows that the first rule of your political conduct must be to direct all your projects towards the maintenance of equality and the development of virtue: because the first concern of the legislator must be to fortify the principle of government.[40]

This definition of true (*véritable*) democracy emerged, as Monnier has argued, from combining the concepts associated with it by Montesquieu and Rousseau (*citoyenneté, égalité, souveraineté, vertu publique, amour de la patrie et de ses lois*).[41] Since 1789 the term 'democracy' had begun to carry connotations of equality and social inclusion, which were later revived in the nineteenth century, but more prominent and consequential to the intense disagreements of the 1790s was its deployment in debates over the design of the first French Republic and the shaping of legislative and executive power. The latter was to prove especially problematic, and to remain so, throughout the long struggle to stabilize subsequent French republics.

---

[40] Robespierre, *Oeuvres complètes*, 9: 557; 10: 350–4.
[41] Monnier, 'Démocratie', 51–2.

5

Democracy, Self, and the Problem of the General Will in Nineteenth-Century French Political Thought

Michael Drolet

In July 1850 the political and social theorist, historian, and statesman Alexis de Tocqueville (1805–1859) reflected on the condition of France. What he had to say was revealing:

> Our history from 1789 to 1830, viewed from a distance and as a whole, affords as it were the picture of a struggle to the death between the Ancien Régime, its traditions, memories, hopes, and men, as represented by the aristocracy, and the New France led by the Middle Class. The year 1830 closed the first period of our revolutions, or rather of our revolution: for there is but one, which has remained always the same in the face of varying fortunes, of which our fathers witnessed the beginning, and of which we, in all probability, shall not live to see the end.[1]

The revolution to which he referred was not that of 1789, but a hidden and more distant one whose roots lay in the deep past. It was the democratic revolution.[2] This revolution not only imprinted itself on the character of the French Revolution of 1789 but on the whole of nineteenth-century France's turbulent history.[3]

This chapter is about how France's nineteenth-century men of letters viewed democracy, thus broadly conceived. It does not focus on debates about institutional means of implementing democracy: about the merits or demerits of unicameralism versus bicameralism, or the value of plebiscites over elections, or on the struggles over the extension of the franchise, not just to all men but women too. Frenchmen and women debated these questions at length at the time. The form these debates took in 1789, 1830, and 1848 has been treated extensively in numerous works.[4] Rather this chapter focuses on debates about democracy conceived

[1] Alexis de Tocqueville, *Recollections*, trans. Alexander Teixeira de Mattos (London, 1948), 2.
[2] Tocqueville traced the origins of this revolution to 1270. Alexis de Tocqueville, *Democracy in America*, trans. George Lawrence (New York, 1969), 10.
[3] Alexis de Tocqueville, *Considérations sur la Révolution depuis son commencement jusqu'à la chute de l'Empire* in *Oeuvres* (3 vols, Paris, 2004), 3: 720–1.
[4] See, in particular, Pierre Rosanvallon, *La Démocratie inachevée: histoire de la souveraineté du peuple en France* (Paris, 2000).

above all as a social condition. Whether on the left of the political spectrum or on the right, French political thinkers understood democracy primarily as a form of society, defined by social equalization.[5] The dismantling of the caste barriers of *ancien régime* society was taken to have determined democracy's rise. French theorists directed their efforts to trying to make sense of the new social order.

Because it stressed the social form of democracy, nineteenth-century French social and political thought ascribed a privileged place to the investigation of social norms, outlooks, and manners.[6] But these considerations were tied to a deeper concern, which touched on a matter of profound philosophical meditation: the self.[7] Reflections on selfhood were central to the way French theorists made sense of democracy, though this topic has been largely neglected by intellectual historians. Thinkers like Tocqueville saw the equality of condition that defined democracy as tending to precipitate the development of socially divisive characteristics, in particular narrow individualism, or self-interestedness.[8]

Thus conceived, the rise of democracy in the late eighteenth century posed afresh an ancient problem: the conflict between individual self-interest and the common good. For liberals who studied with profit the works of the ancient anti-democrats Plato, Aristotle, and Thucydides—such as the historian and statesman François Guizot (1787–1874)—the impulse to an ever greater egalitarianism rendered democratic society factional and unstable. Guizot's views marked nineteenth-century French liberal thought profoundly. The disquiet of liberals motivated their attacks on socialist doctrines, for they saw in those a radical egalitarianism that profoundly altered people's dispositions, creating the conditions for enmity and strife. Section three of this chapter explores especially the liberals' views. But as we shall see in the fourth section, socialists were also preoccupied with questions of the self, and turned many of the elements of the liberals' critique of democracy back into a devastating critique of liberalism. But first, we need to set the scene by considering the foundational concepts of the common good and General Will.

COMMON GOOD AND GENERAL WILL

A striking feature of nineteenth-century French thought is the extent to which the problem of how to fulfil the age-old ambition of achieving a common good continued to be framed by the seventeenth- and eighteenth-century language of the General Will. Despite the widespread condemnation of Jean-Jacques Rousseau's thought, the fundamental problem with which he grappled—uniting narrow partisan interests into a coherent whole that expressed perfectly the general interest of all—remained central.

---

[5] André Tudesq, *La Démocratie en France depuis 1815* (Paris, 1971).

[6] See my 'Carrying the Banner of the Bourgeoisie: Democracy, Self and the Philosophical Foundations to François Guizot's Historical and Political Thought', *History of Political Thought*, 32 (2011), 645–90.

[7] The seminal study is Charles Taylor, *Sources of the Self* (Cambridge, 1989).

[8] Tocqueville, *Recollections*, 3.

Though preoccupation with the General Will was not exclusively French, it had, as Marcel Gauchet and Pierre Rosanvallon have shown, a far more important status within French political culture than in other national political traditions.[9] The seventeenth-century philosophers Antoine Arnauld (1560–1619), Blaise Pascal (1623–1662), Nicolas Malebranche (1638–1715), Pierre Bayle (1647–1706), and François Fénelon (1651–1715) all reflected at length on the idea of the General Will. Their considerations defined how, a century later, Montesquieu (1689–1755) and Rousseau (1712–1778) thought about it, and in turn how it was conceived in the nineteenth century when the development of democracy brought the issue into sharp focus.

Given that French liberals believed democratic society was prone to division, it is a paradox that they also believed that democracy made conceivable what, up to the middle of the eighteenth century, seemed a remote ideal: the achievement of a genuinely common good, one in which the mass of particular interests was united into a common whole.

Just how tantalizingly attainable this possibility seemed to have become was revealed by a statement made by Comte Lally-Tollendal in the summer of 1789. In the days before the storming of the Bastille he declared 'sovereignty resides only in the united whole' ('la souveraineté ne réside que dans le tout réuni'). Within a matter of weeks his pronouncement was accepted as a philosophical truism. The speed with which this declaration was accepted both as a self-evident truth, and as a statement of the founding principle of the new regime, was astonishing; it underscored the extent to which French manners and outlooks were changing. Tocqueville stressed the importance of this development in sketches for the chapters that were to make up his *Considération sur la Révolution depuis son commencement jusqu'à la chute de l'Empire*, a work he never completed.

Tocqueville observed that the Revolution spawned 'a moment when thousands of men became as it were insensible to their particular interests so that they could give thought to a common undertaking'.[10] Unity of will—he was suggesting—could be achieved within a democracy. When he also stressed the voluntary character of the impulse, he elevated it as defining the greatness of the Revolution, as demonstrating that liberty and democracy were compatible. However, he contrasted this ideal vision of free democracy with its tendency to factionalism. Tocqueville's observations on the politics of the Marquis de Condorcet (1743–1794) and the Abbé Sieyès (1748–1836) were designed to reveal how moderate and elevated ideas quickly gave way to narrow and incendiary doctrines. Somehow the Revolution's noble and universal character collapsed into a narrow particularism.

The Revolution revealed to nineteenth-century thinkers like Tocqueville that individual character could provide a basis for selfless action: identification with the collective whole. But equally democracy could narrow the individual's scope for collective engagement, and, as Tocqueville saw it, the conditions under which

---

[9] Marcel Gauchet, *L'Avènement de la démocratie*. vol. 1 *La Révolution moderne* (Paris, 2007); Pierre Rosanvallon, *Le Sacre du citoyen: histoire du suffrage universel en France* (Paris, 1992).
[10] Tocqueville, *Considérations sur la Révolution*, 504.

democratic society had been instituted in France had increasingly had that effect. He made this clear in his observations of the 1830 Revolution. Unlike 1789, 1830 revealed 'a government shorn of both virtue and greatness' and a population which in its 'egoism . . . thought much more of [its] private business than of public affairs; of [its] personal enjoyment than of the greatness of the nation'.[11]

This highlighted a further problem for Tocqueville. Democracy's tendency to division and factionalism could result in revolution but was, he thought, over time more likely to give rise to the managed removal of conflict: to a contrived and imposed collective unity. Self-interested individuals were naturally profoundly fearful of division and revolution, and this encouraged them to develop or submit to administrative centralization.[12]

The whole of Tocqueville's work can be understood as a prolonged engagement with the question of democracy's implications for the self. This was equally true of many of his contemporaries. They, like him, were engrossed by the prospect that, as the rise of equality of condition began to erode the barriers between classes and a mass society presented itself, there would be ever more hope of achieving a General Will. Yet they doubted that it was achievable. For since democratic society fostered individualism and narrow self-interest, and created the conditions for licence, division, and conflict, it made the achievement of a General Will impossible. If these destructive features were to be curbed, a profound exploration of character or self was needed. Curbing narrow self-interest and helping the individual to achieve a disciplined self-control were central preoccupations for Tocqueville and for many of his contemporaries.

LIBERALS, DEMOCRACY, AND THE SELF

Throughout much of the nineteenth century the majority of French liberal and conservative political philosophers adhered to a conception of democracy that was strikingly negative. François Guizot, for example, equated democracy with factionalism and division, with anarchy itself.[13] In *De la Démocratie en France*, written in the aftermath of the 1848 Revolution, he argued that the root of all of France's ills lay in the 'idolatry of Democracy'.[14] He declared that it served as 'the banner of all social hopes and ambitions of man,—pure and impure, noble and base, rational or irrational, possible or chimerical'. But this 'concealed' its real principle, which was 'chaos'.[15]

This idea had a long pedigree. It marked the reflections of most political thinkers throughout the eighteenth century, including Rousseau.[16] Its persistence into

---

[11] Tocqueville, *Recollections*, 3.
[12] Tocqueville noted that 'not only do men in democracies feel no natural inclination for revolutions, but they are afraid of them', *Democracy in America*, 2: part 3, chapter 21, 636.
[13] Guizot makes this point in his speech to the Chamber of Deputies of 29 December 1830. *Histoire parlementaire de France, recueil complet des discours prononcés dans la chambre de 1819 à 1848 par M. Guizot* (5 vols, Paris, 1863–4), 1: 178.
[14] François Guizot, *Democracy in France* (London, 1849), v.
[15] Guizot, *Democracy in France*, 3.
[16] Richard Bourke, 'Enlightenment, Revolution and Democracy', *Constellations*, 15 (2008), 10–32.

the nineteenth century owed much to the fact that it suggested a narrative about anarchy, revolution, and despotism that could explain why the French Revolution collapsed into the Terror and then into Napoleon Bonaparte's seizure of power in 1799. For Guizot and many others, including Tocqueville, the account had proved predictive because it was informed by an understanding of human character and its place within the natural scheme of things.

Two possible conditions of things were posited: on the one hand, a world in which politics mirrored a natural harmony; on the other, one in which politics was an unstable artifice constructed to maintain the legal domination of one group over another. Most nineteenth-century French theorists, including Guizot and Tocqueville, thought that achieving social peace depended on politics mirroring a natural harmony and thereby fostering an ideal state for man. Guizot conceived of this natural harmony as an inherent order that, in a neo-Platonic fashion, could be discovered by individuals with the requisite intellectual faculties. These faculties defined the 'citizen of ability' (*citoyen capacitaire*), who alone could be trusted to engage actively in politics.

Guizot's way of seeing politics as mirroring a natural harmony was shaped by his study of Plato and of the Common Sense philosophy of Thomas Reid (1710–1796). Other French liberals based their conceptions of social peace as mirroring natural harmony on very different epistemological foundations, chiefly deriving from John Locke's *An Essay Concerning Human Understanding* (1690). Accounts built on this alternative basis included the writings of the eighteenth-century *philosophes*, such as Jean d'Alembert (1717–1783), and those of Condorcet, whose ideas on mathematics and social organization shaped a group of nineteenth-century left-liberals, known collectively as the *Idéologues*. They included the philosopher and historian, Comte de Volney (1757–1820); the philosopher and political theorist, P. C. F. Daunou (1761–1840); the journalist and politician, Pierre-Louis Rœderer (1754–1835); and the philosopher, A.-L.-C. Destutt de Tracy (1754–1836), whose science of sensation, *idéologie*, gave its name to the group.

Yet other ways of conceptualizing the relationship between natural harmony and social peace could be found: in, for example, Auguste Comte's (1798–1857) positivism, one of the major currents of nineteenth-century thought, and in the economic liberalism of Charles Dunoyer (1786–1862), Frédéric Bastiat (1801–1850), and Joseph Garnier (1813–1881). These men subscribed to the idea *laissez-faire laissez-passer*, and saw politics as nothing more than an extension of economics and the underlying laws of nature that governed the market. Though resting on differing foundations, these competing types of French liberalism all shared a vision of politics that saw it as aiming to establish a social peace that reflected a natural harmony.

Political orders that did not mirror or express natural harmony did not merely fail to channel the General Will or deliver the good life. They also had the capacity to deform the individuals, the selves, whose good the polity should have advanced. In the aftermath of 1789, liberals and conservatives focused on the role of democracy and despotism in corrupting men's minds and sentiments, making the achievement of the General Will impossible.

It is remarkable that, over a wide ideological spectrum, nineteenth-century French political philosophers should have been united in tackling questions pertaining to the self. This involved directing their intellectual energies towards the discrete yet related domains of political economy, sociology, philosophy, and history. One of the most prominent groups of intellectuals to begin these intellectual peregrinations in the early nineteenth century was the group of moderate liberals known as the *Doctrinaires*. Called *Doctrinaires* because of their repeated references to 'principles', 'theories', and 'doctrines', this group comprised, amongst others, the philosopher and statesman Pierre-Paul Royer-Collard (1763–1845), the historian Prosper de Barante (1782–1866), the politician Hercule de Serre (1776–1824), the philosopher Philibert Damiron (1794–1862), and Guizot himself.[17]

The *Idéologues* also had intellectual heirs who sustained and developed their ideas into the nineteenth century. The best known of these was the philosopher Maine de Biran (1766–1824). Biran had fallen under Destutt de Tracy's spell as a young man, but soon charted his own intellectual course. His youthful moderate liberalism gave way to a fervent royalism. This shift of political conviction was intimately linked with a shift of philosophical belief. He moved from a theory of knowledge based on the psychology of Pierre Jean George Cabanis (1757–1808) to a distinctive epistemology that assigned a central place to the self. Biran's work was considered by many at the time to be the most profound of any philosopher of the century.[18] It challenged radically the philosophy of the *Idéologues* and their more faithful nineteenth-century heir, the philosopher Pierre Laromiguière (1756–1837) who taught at the École Normale. It also profoundly influenced the *Doctrinaires*, and would, through their work, filter down to Tocqueville. Biran was responsible for making Reidian Common Sense philosophy central to the *Doctrinaires*' understanding of self and society, and this directly affected their understanding of equality of condition, of democracy itself.

The *Doctrinaires* stressed a direct connection between what Royer-Collard called the 'inner state of society' and the inner life of the self.[19] Guizot illustrated the connection in many of his early works, including his unpublished *Principes de philosophie politique* (1821–3) and his *Histoire des origines du gouvernement représentatif en Europe* (1821).[20] The *Doctrinaire* philosopher Philibert Damiron showed the link with clarity in the introductory section to his 1828 *Essai sur l'histoire de la philoso-*

---

[17] For more on the *Doctrinaires*, see Aurelian Craiutu, *Liberalism Under Siege: The Political Thought of the French Doctrinaires* (Lanham, MD, 2003).

[18] Victor Cousin (1792–1867) declared him to be 'the first in France to have resurrected the glory of Descartes, almost entirely suppressed by the eighteenth century'. Victor Cousin, *Fragments philosophiques pour servir à l'histoire de la philosophie* (5 vols, Paris, 1865–6), 5: 315. Royer-Collard paid homage to his genius by asserting that 'c'était notre maître à tous!' Pierre Paul Royer-Collard, *Les Fragments philosophiques de Royer-Collard, réunis et publiés pour la première fois à part avec une introduction sur la philosophie écossaise et spiritualiste au XIXe siècle* (Paris, 1913), lxvii.

[19] Royer-Collard, 'Speech to the Chamber of Deputies 22 January 1822', *Archives parlementaires*, 31: 133.

[20] Guizot, *Principes de philosophie politique*, 367–8, and *History of Representative Government in Europe*, 288.

phie en France au dix-neuvième siècle, where he related human psychology and intellect to society's form and political institutions.[21]

In forging the link between the inner life of society and that of the self, the
Doctrinaires recast a number of older ideas. They revisited virtue, central to conceptions of the General Will, and offered a distinctive conception of political
sovereignty.

Doctrinaires such as Damiron worried that not only did equality of condition
create the foundations for the rise of the individual within society, but also that this
worked to particularly problematic effect when coupled with the materialist philosophy of the eighteenth-century *philosophes* and the growth of a materialist culture. These developments combined to produce a distorted and agitated self that
was neither tranquil nor had intellectual and psychological depth. The *Doctrinaires'* critique of democracy echoed not only that of Aristotle. With its repudiation of philosophical doctrines of sensationalism and attacks on materialism, it
bore a striking resemblance to Plato's disparaging analysis of sophistic and sceptic
philosophy and his critique of democracy. Like Plato, the *Doctrinaires* believed that
in the democratic order people were profoundly diminished. Being obsessed with
obtaining material possessions, they were forever restless. Having nothing more
than 'materialism as the goal of morality',[22] they lacked self-assurance and inner
peace; being subject to perpetual agitation they tended to fall into a profound state
of enervation. Damiron's neo-Platonic understanding of the proper self as that of
a person who enjoyed a kind of self-possession or was centred in himself led him
to see profound dangers in a materialist culture. This had a direct bearing on politics. For as Charles Taylor observed in his seminal study of the self, in the classic
view the 'capacities or potentialities' that defined the 'inner' self awaited a development which would realize them in the 'public world'.[23] Materialism fundamentally
altered that manifestation. It transformed politics in such a way that it was no
longer concerned with achieving what Guizot called the 'sovereignty of reason', but
was instead defined by force.

It was the establishment of the sovereignty of reason that defined the philosophical and political project of the *Doctrinaires*. They believed that only an elite
could avoid the corrupting powers of a materialist culture and rule according to
rational principles. This ideal regime was to be composed of citizens of ability who
stood out from the mass, who had privileged access to this realm of reason, and
could be trusted to rule in the interest of the common good.

For Guizot and the *Doctrinaires*, ability was inextricably linked to consciousness. Guizot's lectures on the *History of the Origins of Representative Government
in Europe* and *The History of Civilisation in Europe* (1828), lectures that shaped
a generation of aspiring young Frenchmen, showed that the development of free
and representative institutions took place within a wider twofold process: the

---

[21] Philibert Damiron, *Essai sur l'histoire de la philosophie en France au dix-neuvième siècle* (Paris,
1828), esp. ii and x–xi.
[22] Damiron, *Essai sur l'histoire de la philosophie*, xii.
[23] Taylor, *Sources of the Self*, 116.

rise of the middle classes, and the unveiling of a pre-existing rational order. In his lectures Guizot sought to make his auditors, whom he hoped might serve as the political vanguard of this class, aware of that class's historic destiny. Many of the *Doctrinaires* saw in the 1830 Revolution a sign of the successful awakening of a class's consciousness. After 1830, Guizot and other *Doctrinaires* moved from the corridors of academia to the halls of power. Their triumph was so complete that one of their number, the journalist Charles Rémusat (1797–1875), could boast that 'we are the government of the bourgeoisie'.[24] As if to emphasize just how elite the politics of the *Doctrinaires* was, the political franchise never crept above 3 per cent of the adult male population during the whole of the July Monarchy.

The observations of Guizot and the *Doctrinaires* on the growth of a materialist culture were not peculiar to liberals. They also pervaded the work of conservatives who did not share their beliefs in fundamental liberties and moderate constitutional monarchy, but preferred the world of the *ancien régime*. Thus they shaped the work of famous conservatives such as Joseph de Maistre (1753–1821) and Louis de Bonald (1754–1840), who raged against avarice and moral indifference.[25] But they also defined the work of lesser-known conservatives, such as Alban Villeneuve-Bargemont (1784–1850), whose *Économie politique chrétienne* attacked economic orthodoxy for fostering a culture of aggressive enrichment.

The critique of democracy offered by Guizot and other *Doctrinaires*, and their restriction of political power to citizens of ability, corresponded with a shift of power to a middle-class elite; conservatives drew on the same critique in order to affect a shift of power back to an absolute monarch—but this same critique was advanced by people more liberally inclined, such as Tocqueville, who believed that a wider political franchise was both inevitable and desirable.

What the *Doctrinaires* had to say about the self resonated with observations made by Tocqueville in his travels through America, the nation where equality of condition was most developed. Throughout his famous *De la démocratie en Amérique*, Tocqueville stressed the restiveness of democratic character. As he saw it, democratic society incited a pervasive and appetitive materialism. Individuals were always seeking to better their material condition, while being constantly fearful of losing what they had, and this generated an insatiable desire to acquire more. As he noted:

> The taste for physical pleasures must be regarded as the first cause of this secret restlessness betrayed by the actions of the Americans, and of the inconstancy of which they give daily examples. A man who has set his heart on nothing but the good things of the world is always in a hurry, for he has only a limited time in which to find them, get them, and enjoy them. Remembrance of the shortness of life continually goads him on. Apart from the goods he has, he thinks of a thousand others which death will prevent him from tasting if he does not hurry. This thought fills him with distress, fear,

[24] *Archives parlementaires*, 87: 438.
[25] Joseph de Maistre, *Considérations sur la France* (Bruxelles, 1988); Louis de Bonald, *Théorie du pouvoir politique et religieux dans la société civile, démontré par le raisonnement et par l'histoire*, in *Oeuvres complètes* (15 vols, Geneva, 1982), vol. 1.

and regret and keeps his mind continually in agitation, so that he is always changing his plans and his abode.[26]

Tocqueville observed that the desires of democratic man always exceeded his capabilities. In his words, the 'constant strife between the desires inspired by equality and the means it supplies to satisfy them harasses and wearies the mind'.[27] When coupled with the fact that each individual felt himself to be weak, pressures towards social conformity were overwhelming. At the same time, the pervasive love of material possessions rendered democratic society monotonous. Tocqueville believed that, paradoxically, democratic society was simultaneously agitated and monotonous. It was unreflective and lacking in intellectual and spiritual depth. The impact of this on the cultivation of the 'habits of the heart' was profound and disturbing.[28] Agitation and monotony conspired against the deepening of inner self-awareness and the gradual and unfolding apprehension of moral virtue. And this had profoundly deleterious consequences for the development of a conception of common good. Other French observers of American society, such as Michel Chevalier (1806–1879), came away with similar impressions.[29]

What Tocqueville along with Damiron and other *Doctrinaires* believed that they were observing was a kind of spiritual impoverishment intrinsic to democratic societies. But whereas the *Doctrinaires* believed this justified limiting political participation to a narrow elite, Tocqueville advocated multiplying instances in which individuals could engage in political and civic projects. He saw participation and deliberation as the means through which individuals would be raised above their immediate and petty concerns and made to feel part of some higher and noble collectivity. This was the impulse behind Tocqueville's advocacy of associative politics.

SOCIALISTS, DEMOCRACY, AND THE SELF

We have shown that liberal and conservatives were preoccupied with materialism, spiritual impoverishment, and social division, conditions they saw as to some extent springing from democracy, but also as worsening its effects. Republicans and socialists also saw these trends as characteristic of modern society, even though they contextualized them differently. They too were concerned with the state of individuals' psyches, but for socialists, those most adversely affected were the wealthy and educated. The vast majority suffered from a different problem: from being forced to live in an impoverished and brutalized state. Socialists identified spiritual corruption with the ruling classes, and then showed how this affected the social order more generally, exacerbating divisions in the polity.

---

[26] Tocqueville, *Democracy in America*, ch. 13, 537.
[27] Ibid. ch. 13, 537. See also ch. 21, 638.
[28] This was the object of part III, 'The Influence of Democracy on Mores Properly So Called', of the second volume of *Democracy in America*.
[29] Michel Chevalier, *Lettres sur l'Amérique du Nord* (2 vols, Brussels, 1837), 2: 118–19.

Leading socialists of this period argued that, while the development of industry had increased levels of productivity in France and French society had become more prosperous, this prosperity was not universally enjoyed; indeed, the vast majority of France's population lived in impoverished and desperate conditions. The fundamental problem facing France, they contended, was inequality. It was their engagement with the problem not of equality but of continuing inequality that marked the reflections of French socialists on democracy. From radical revolutionaries such as Auguste Blanqui (1805–1881), whose incendiary politics led to long periods of imprisonment, to utopian socialists such as Henri de Saint-Simon (1760–1825), who sought a peaceful transformation of France's society and polity, all socialists argued that those who enjoyed wealth and comfort at the expense of those who lacked these things had been morally corrupted. This was, for instance, the thesis of the anarchist and socialist Joseph Proudhon's famous *Qu'est-ce la propriété?*, which equated property with theft.[30] And it was a dominant theme of the work of one of the most influential socialists of the 1840s, Louis Blanc (1811–1882), whose renowned *Organisation du travail* (1839) showed how luxury and wealth corrupted France's governing class and rendered it blind to the sufferings of the poor.[31] Socialists not only equated inequality with moral corruption, they also challenged a common liberal and conservative assumption that equality was adverse to liberty, instead equating the absence of equality with the absence of liberty. For socialists, a whole class of individuals, those who worked with their hands for their daily bread, were slaves.[32] Governments that obtained their power from the rich and powerful, and exercised that power on their behalf, not only perpetuated the moral degradation of the wealthy, they also preserved a social order that was reliant on the slavery of the majority.[33] In the eyes of socialists, these governments were nothing more than oligarchies and despotisms.

Inequality was, in the minds of socialists, the source of all of society's ills, including the brutalization of the individual and the resulting profound disequilibrium of self—one of the root causes of suicide, according to Proudhon.[34] The inhumane conditions under which the labouring classes existed reflected profound disharmony arising from man's alienation from the natural order. In passing this judgement, French socialists did not depart fundamentally from the core thesis of Rousseau's *Discourse on the Origins of Inequality Among Men*, which was that inequality emerged out of human alienation and that the establishment of inequality in law strengthened its hold over men's minds and made consensual social unity impossible.

Among those who developed this argument was Filippo Buonarroti (1761–1837), whose 1828 description of Babeuf's 1796 Conspiracy of Equals achieved a wide readership in France during and after the 1830 Revolution. Buonarroti's *La Conspiration pour l'égalité dite de Babeuf* stressed how inequality was destructive to

---

[30] P.-J. Proudhon, *Qu'est-ce que la propriété?* (new edn, Paris, 1873), 13.
[31] Louis Blanc, *Organisation du travail* (5th edn, Paris, 1847), e.g. 8.
[32] Ibid. 4; Proudhon, *Qu'est-ce que la propriété?*, 13.
[33] Proudhon, *Qu'est-ce que la propriété?*, 182.   [34] Ibid. 2.

individuals and corrosive to public virtue. According to Buonarroti, the 'great majority of citizens were constantly subjected to toilsome labour, and condemned to languish in misery, ignorance and slavery'.[35] Inequality brought about a profound material and spiritual impoverishment that made the achievement of a General Will impossible.

Henri de Saint-Simon, who like Buonarroti had been an enthusiastic participant in the 1789 Revolution, described material and spiritual impoverishment in the language of a new 'social science'. In a series of articles and pamphlets written in the first two decades of the nineteenth century, he contended that humanity's spiritual impoverishment was the result of a failure of social organization, which itself was a direct consequence of persistently unequal property relations in which an idle and wealthy aristocracy ruled over the majority. Saint-Simon and his major disciples Olinde Rodrigues (1795–1851) and Prosper Enfantin (1796–1864) employed concepts developed by the *Idéologues*, characterizing society as divided between an industrious and impoverished majority and a wealthy but idle and parasitic aristocratic minority, whose form of government was usurpatory and despotic. Like the *Idéologues* before them, Saint-Simon and his followers sought a new form of social organization. But any resemblances to the *Idéologues* ended there. Saint-Simon's new social order of a triumvirate of scientists, artists, and industrialists (citizens of ability quite differently conceived from Guizot's) was to result in the improved material conditions of the poorest in society, the spiritual elevation of men, and social harmony.[36]

This was also the goal of Charles Fourier's (1772–1837) new industrial and social world. But whereas Saint-Simon aimed for the total reorganization of society, Fourier proposed to break with established oligarchies and despotisms and to create new ideal communities that he called *phalanges*. These communities, of between 1,600 and 2,000 individuals, were to be governed by a powerful spirit of association. The *phalanges* were committed to social and moral improvement. Though they were not socially egalitarian, their members ran them as direct democracies. The scheme drew on a particular understanding of human psychology, which portrayed individuals as driven by twelve passions; the *phalanges* would harness these passions to the best advantage of the individual and the community. Fourier believed that his discovery of what he thought was nature's mechanism of 'industrial attraction'—the underlying principle of the *phalanges*—would transform work into pleasure and guarantee a minimum income to all members of the community. Work would be shared and individuals' passions and talents stimulated as they moved between jobs during each day. With work transformed from a dull duty into an enjoyable and satisfying activity, social harmony would follow precisely because human character would cease to be brutalized and constrained in an antagonistic world of unrestrained competition and conflict.[37] This environ-

---

[35] Philippe Buonarroti, *La Conspiration pour l'égalité dite de Babeuf* (Paris, 1957 [1828]), 26–7.
[36] Henri de Saint-Simon, *Le nouveau Christianisme, et les écrits sur la religion* (Paris, 1969).
[37] Charles Fourier, *Le nouveau monde industriel et sociétaire* (Paris, 1973).

ment would offer psychological stimulation, mental equilibrium, personal fulfilment, and social harmony.

Though Saint-Simon and Fourier were not democrats, many of their followers
were. Fourier's leading disciple, the publicist Victor Considérant (1808–1893),
argued explicitly in favour of popular participation in politics. Others, such as
Etienne Cabet (1788–1856), not only stressed the centrality of equality of condition to justice, but also argued that universal and direct participation in politics
was integral to individual liberty. His highly popular *Voyage en Icarie* (1840), an
imaginary traveller's tale loosely modelled on Sir Thomas More's *Utopia* (1516),
embodied these ideas. It presented a community whose members were all citizens
and eligible for election to public office; where all work was communal and its
fruits equally shared; and where the solidarity and peace of the community took
precedence over the narrow demands of the individual.[38] Icarie was, for the book's
admirers, the representation of a perfect democratic republic. Though *Voyage en
Icarie* was a work of Cabet's imagination, he believed that it could serve as a model
for France. He thought this transformation should come about not by revolution,
which he totally rejected, but gradually, through the efforts of an enlightened
minority who would, over perhaps a hundred years, educate and persuade the
majority to the virtues of an Icarian life. Cabet's vision for France attracted a wide
following. *La Société pour fonder l'Icarie* had, at its height in 1844, about 100,000
members. But this was a short-lived movement and by the Revolution of 1848 its
membership had dwindled. Its attempts to set up utopian communities in America
collapsed in failure.

The ideal communities imagined by Cabet, Fourier, and their followers combined social and political equality. They were full deliberative and participatory
democracies. But none were realized in practice. Other socialists, including Proudhon and Blanc, had no faith in utopian communities. They directed their attention
to transforming the real world of France. They were passionately critical of the
'bourgeois' democracy that had emerged from the revolutions of 1789 and 1830,
seeing it as separating political concerns from fundamental economic considerations. This did not make them anti-democrats. However, Proudhon and Blanc gave
great weight to the social dimension of democracy, and stressed that only by achieving real social equality could political democracy be attained. This is what Proudhon
meant when he insisted that 'equality of condition is identical to equality of rights'.[39]
Blanc's 1839 *Organisation du travail* challenged economic orthodoxy fundamentally by asserting that market competition led to a 'frightening moral corruption':
the system of unfettered markets led to a lowering of wages, the deterioration
of working conditions, decrease in production, and loss of employment. These
losses brought increases in family strife, crime, and social collapse. It was nothing
less than a 'system of extermination'. Against conflict and chaos, he posited a right
to work. The 'moral and material amelioration' of the working classes that would
ensue would allow for the creation of genuine bonds of 'fraternal association'.[40]

---

[38] Etienne Cabet, *Voyage en Icarie* (Paris, 1845).
[39] Proudhon, *Qu'est-ce que la propriété?*, 16.   [40] Blanc, *Organisation du travail*, 827–8.

Recognition of the right to work was the first step toward a genuinely equal society. By this means brutalized men and women would be transformed into creative and spiritually fulfilled individuals. This could not be achieved overnight and until it was Blanc believed the polity would remain divided. In the absence of solidarity, for Blanc, there was no point in striving for more direct forms of democracy. Against the opinions of not only Considérant but also Proudhon, Blanc argued in favour of representation if those mandated to govern would do so in the interests of the unity of France. Though he argued in favour of popular sovereignty, for the present he thought that this should be mediated through representation by a political elite, a vanguard, that would turn the state, currently in the hands of the enemies of socialism, into an instrument that would further socialism's ends.

Blanc's socialism, with its stress on a vanguard class, contrasted with Proudhon's socialism, which emphasized the revolutionary activism of the masses—an activism whose functions was to make the proletariat aware of itself as a class emancipating itself from an oppressive bourgeois order—and at the same time mutualism, which involved workers attaining their own economic independence through various schemes of cooperation (although Proudhon's attempts at creating workers' cooperative banks, the '*banque d'échange*' and '*banque du peuple*', both failed). Throughout the whole of his work, Proudhon ascribed a central place to the individual within a free associative community. In a series of famous works—from *Système des contradictions économiques ou philosophie de la misère* to *Qu'est-ce que la propriété?*—he argued that society must cease to be defined by hierarchy and compulsion; once the veil of alienation was raised, it would conform instead to nature's 'organic law of humanity and the positive conception of order'.[41] A harmonious realm would result in which people would live equally and freely. The balance that defined society defined the character of all who inhabited it.

Though these types of socialism were different, they all engaged with the question of equality and its relation to the self. For the socialists, equality of condition, whilst defining the formal structure of society, its laws and constitutions, had yet to characterize the material conditions of people's lives. For some, like Considérant and Cabet, democracy, if pursued within the right framework, held out the promise of this more substantive equality and the full flourishing of the self. But for others, such as Proudhon and Blanc, only after questions pertaining to substantive equality were resolved could genuine political participation and associative bonds be achieved.

CONCLUSION

Two contrasting responses emerged from the concerns of liberals and socialists with how democracy shaped human character—in a way that opened up potential for achieving unity of will and yet threatened that very achievement. Guizot and

---

[41] P.-J. Proudhon, *Système des contradictions économiques ou philosophie de la misère*, in *Oeuvres complètes* (23 vols, Paris, 1923–74), 1: 89.

the *Doctrinaires* believed that democratic equality generated materialism and spiritual impoverishment; those ideas were central to their thoughts on the self, and the relation between individual character and politics. Fractured selves could never support more than a disordered and fractured polity. For this reason the *Doctrinaires*, along with some socialists such as Blanc, believed that a polity could (in the case of the *Doctrinaires*) only ever be governed by an intellectual elite or (in the case of Blanc) had to be governed by such an elite until a new, and egalitarian, order was established. For only through the wisdom of 'citizens of ability' could the common good be achieved. Conversely, for a liberal like Tocqueville, or a socialist such as Proudhon, this kind of elite politics could never achieve the generality of will that democracy held out as its tantalizing potential. Restricting participation would mean that individuals could never be raised beyond their petty concerns, and as a result the deep structure of the polity, and also the character of the individuals that composed it, would remain fractured. Only through active engagement and deliberation might individuals be raised to the level of a general unity.

That French political thought in the nineteenth century did not move fundamentally beyond those early reflections is a testament to the intellectual revolution that individuals such as Guizot, Tocqueville, Blanc, and Proudhon spawned.

6

Elections and Democracy
in France, 1789–1848

Malcolm Crook

Between the later eighteenth and mid-nineteenth centuries, the French sought to give power to the people. They did so within a social and institutional landscape that differed significantly from that prevailing in England—or indeed in Ireland or America, where English influence was powerful, though mediated by local circumstances. Distinctive features of their society and institutions helped to determine that the French agenda for change would be distinctive and that problems they identified were addressed in distinctive ways. Those same specificities also helped to ensure that, although before the Revolution *démocratie* and its derivatives possessed the same diverse range of associations in France as elsewhere, by the end of the period they had acquired particular resonance and meaning.[1]

The French Revolution began with a financial crisis. In order to stave off impending bankruptcy, the monarch was obliged to consult his subjects formally. Yet the summoning of the archaic Estates General, scheduled to meet in the spring of 1789, became the object of a deeply divisive argument about how this representative body should be organized. The issue was resolved only by the revolutionary merger of what were traditionally three separate chambers—representing the three Estates of clergy, nobles, and third estate (or commons)—into a single-chambered 'National Assembly' in June 1789. This development was the culmination of a wider debate about 'privilege' and its distorting effects on the social order in France. A series of royal ministers, from the 1760s onwards, had tried to reform some privileged institutions and practices, but the vital issue of voting at the Estates General prompted demands that went far beyond the removal of fiscal exemptions from Church and nobility. During the summer of 1789 popular upheaval in town and countryside forced deputies in the National Assembly to act on these matters and, on the heady night of 4 August 1789, the old regime ended. Prior to the Revolution, various

---

* I would like to thank Joanna Innes and Mark Philp for their helpful editorial assistance with this chapter.

[1] Pierre Rosanvallon, *La Démocratie inachevée: histoire de la souveraineté du peuple en France* (Paris, 2000), and 'The History of the Word "Democracy" in France', *Journal of Democracy*, 6 (1995), 140–54.

forms of privilege existed at all levels of society, enjoyed by individuals as well as corporate bodies; now they were comprehensively abolished.[2]

This process of stripping privilege out of society was celebrated at the time as an attempt to inject meaning into such values as 'liberty', 'equality', and 'fraternity', rather than institute 'democracy'. Personal as well as political rights were to be established. As Benjamin Constant later put it, this involved 'the right of each person to state his opinion, choose his line of work, dispose of his property ... to join with others to discuss common interests, worship as they please, or merely spend their time as they see fit'.[3] During the Restoration era, after 1814, the term 'democracy' was deployed to describe the post-Revolutionary social order: the 'levelled society'. Although peerages were reintroduced, few other forms of *ancien régime* privilege were restored. The decision not to attempt a counter-revolution in the social order—which proved much more durable than its changeable political superstructure—stimulated the search for an appropriate designation and 'democracy' was pressed into service for that purpose. As the historian Annelien de Dijn has recently suggested, the terms 'equal' and 'democratic' were used without distinction to describe this social condition.[4] Two decades later, the young nobleman Alexis de Tocqueville famously visited the United States, and reflected on what he had learned from that visit about the potential and tendencies of this social form in *De la démocratie en Amérique*.

From the outset of the Revolution of 1789, both within the National Assembly and beyond, the quest for a basis on which a new political order could found its legitimacy proved more contentious. As the nineteenth-century liberal essayist Lucien-Anatole Prévost-Paradol famously put it, 'The French Revolution established a society: it still seeks a government.'[5] Political authority, it was proclaimed in the 'Declaration of the Rights of Man and the Citizen', promulgated in August 1789, derived ultimately from the people (or, as it was expressed, from 'the nation'). This was a venerable notion, recently refurbished and given imaginative embodiment by British-American colonists in their revolution, though in the French case the nation subsumed the absolutism once enjoyed by the monarchy, now enhanced by the destruction of particularistic intermediary agencies. In France this core idea was subsequently translated into a phrase then also (as it happened) coming into occasional use in Britain: 'the sovereignty of the people'. This would remain a key phrase—sometimes approvingly, sometimes disapprovingly invoked—and it came to occupy some of the conceptual space that during the same era was encompassed in America (and, to a lesser extent, in Britain) by the concept of 'democracy'.[6]

---

[2] Michael Fitzsimmons, *The Night the Old Regime Ended: August 4 1789, and the French Revolution* (University Park, PA, 2003).

[3] Cited in Patrice Gueniffey, 'Democracy', in Edward Berenson et al. (eds), *The French Republic: History, Values, Debates* (Ithaca, NY, 2011), 119.

[4] Annelien de Dijn, *French Political Thought from Montesquieu to Tocqueville: Liberty in a Levelled Society?* (Cambridge, 2008), 83, 138.

[5] Cited in Jeremy Jennings, *Revolution and the Republic: A History of Political Thought in France since the Eighteenth Century* (Oxford, 2011), 192.

[6] For British usage: Pasi Ihalainen, *Agents of the People: Democracy and Popular Sovereignty in British and Swedish Parliamentary Debates* (Leiden, 2010).

In France, those who endorsed the principle of popular sovereignty often disagreed about how to embody it. Americans had addressed the task of building popular consent into the operation of government by invoking 'the people' in a variety of governmental contexts. They had set down rules for the conduct of government in the form of 'constitutions' drawn up by representatives, subsequently submitted for direct or indirect popular ratification. Then, as mandated by these constitutions, they entrusted many aspects of the work of government to elected (if often indirectly elected) officials. The French adopted many of the same devices, but in some respects they were more conservative, in others more radical, than their American counterparts. Their National Constituent Assembly did preserve one important link with the past after 1789, in so far as Louis XVI became 'king of the French people'. Yet, after considerable debate, he was awarded no more than a suspensive veto over legislation; the constitutional monarchy was so limited that some historians have described it as a republic *avant la lettre*. Moreover, the desire to repudiate the aristocratic past (noble titles were abolished in 1790) ensured that there was no place for a second chamber in the Constitution of 1791. Meanwhile an extraordinarily activist understanding of the forms that 'popular sovereignty' could properly take developed, an approach that was radical even by American standards, to the extent that spontaneous crowd activity and the *journées* of the Parisian sections were sometimes hailed as legitimately expressing the will of the people.

In 1792 the monarchical constitution was abrogated after less than a year in operation, and work on a new Constitution began. Against a background of war and internal rebellion, power became concentrated in the National Convention's 'Committee of Public Safety', which had to confront the huge challenge of mobilizing resources for a war against much of Europe while society was still being remade. Both the top-down and bottom-up excesses of this interlude, the Terror 1793–4, helped to give 'popular sovereignty' a mightily bad name. Yet this led in the years immediately following not to its renunciation, but rather to efforts to reinterpret it along less active lines. It was stressed that, while the people had a vital part to play in authorizing government—by endorsing constitutions, and helping elect local officials and national representatives—once they had discharged those duties their role was one of acquiescence. The Constitution of 1795 sought to balance an avowedly representative system between a bicameral legislature and an executive, five-man Directory. When Napoleon Bonaparte assumed control at the turn of the new century, and established a dictatorship, he certainly did not vaunt the principle of popular sovereignty, but he never explicitly rejected it either; he took care to secure formal expressions of consent to his regime.

Not until the Restoration was the principle of popular sovereignty officially overturned, as authority was once more vested in a monarch ruling under the dispensation of providence, who (notionally 'by his own choice') bestowed a 'Charter' upon his people in 1814. Despite the creation of a Chamber of Peers, there was no attempt to remove an element of representation, for the bicameral legislature was also endowed with a chamber of deputies, albeit one elected on a very narrow franchise. When the Crown sought further to restrict the independence of Parliament, by revising the electoral system in a still more regressive fashion, it provoked the Revolution of July 1830.

The 'three glorious days' could be regarded as a fresh expression of the sovereignty of the people. Even though monarchy was retained, and the franchise was not significantly extended, these events reinstated the concept in political debate. Defenders of the still relatively exclusive liberal regime, unable to deny the notion's intrinsic power, were obliged to rely on minimizing its practical significance.

Election had a historic role within French governmental processes, though in the eighteenth century its practice was somewhat desultory and confined to the local level. The summoning of the Estates General in 1789, which ignited the revolutionary process, stimulated a massive consultative exercise. From that time, elections have almost always played some part (even if, as under the two Napoleons, a largely residual and symbolic part) in legitimating and shaping the French political order.[7] Between the mid-eighteenth and mid-nineteenth centuries, the French did not associate the word 'democracy' primarily with elections, but more often—as the preceding sketch has suggested—with elements of popular sovereignty and, from 1815, with the 'levelled' social order. However, in parallel with developing usage elsewhere, they *sometimes* associated democracy with elections, and the right to vote. As Ruth Scurr has shown in chapter 4, some revolutionary thinkers and politicians suggested that the ancient tradition of direct or 'pure' democracy might somehow be made to inform representative institutions to forge a new hybrid, 'representative democracy'. In 1848 a refounded republic declared itself, in its Constitution, to be a 'democratic republic'.[8] Quite what that meant remained unclear. Still, if some took democracy to mean equality before the law, and others a more far-reaching form of social equality, it was generally agreed that universal (i.e. manhood) suffrage was both truly republican *and* truly democratic in ethos.

Given that it is not possible, in the space of a short essay, to review all the ways in which French society and polity were reordered—in the case of the polity, repeatedly reordered—during these turbulent years, as France became a sort of political laboratory, the remainder of this essay will focus on the changing role and character of elections. That is to say, it will focus on elements of 'democracy' that are central to present-day understandings of the concept: a broad franchise, freedom to vote, and regular elections. The French electoral tradition differed in many ways from the British and, as the French developed their own practices, they did not slavishly imitate either the British or the Americans in this regard. By drawing attention to distinctive features of French electoral culture, this essay contributes to one of the broader purposes of this volume: it underlines the diversity and contingency of democratic practices.

REPRESENTATION AND ELECTION TO 1789

In mid- and later eighteenth-century France, a variety of bodies presented themselves as in some sense 'representative' of the people or the nation. Not all of those bodies were elective. Representation did not traditionally connote election: it

---

[7] Pierre Rosanvallon, *Le Sacre du citoyen: histoire du suffrage universel en France* (Paris, 1992).
[8] François Luchaire, *Naissance d'une Constitution: 1848* (Paris, 1998).

meant rather the right or power to reflect or stand in for something or someone else. In that sense the monarch was the ultimate, and arguably the only lawful representative of the French nation: a point repeatedly made by royal apologists in early revolutionary debates.[9]

In the course of a series of political disputes during the eighteenth century certain other bodies laid claim to the right to represent the nation *to* the king and his ministers. Prominent among these were the *parlements*.[10] They were not elective bodies, but regional courts of law, staffed by magistrates who inherited or purchased their offices. When from the late 1760s the king and his ministers began to create elective regional assemblies, to serve as interlocutors on policy issues, the *parlements* quickly found themselves outflanked. Election was beginning to establish itself as the best way to legitimize representation, but no *national* assembly with any form of elective component met in France before the Revolution, as the Estates General had been dormant since 1614. However, there were some partially elective bodies that survived in frontier regions: in Brittany, Burgundy, and much of the Midi, for example. These were regional 'estates', representing different social orders (clergy, nobles, and commoners), which met sporadically and conducted much of their business in separate chambers.

In the later eighteenth century, a group of thinkers known as *économistes* or *physiocrates* began to argue that the French political order did not adequately reflect the natural form of the French social order. A.-R.-J. Turgot, a proponent of physiocratic ideas who attained ministerial rank in the mid-1770s, sketched out a plan for the establishment of a hierarchy of elective regional and local bodies. He did not intend them to constrain the exercise of governmental power, nor to fulfil a legislative function. Rather, their role was to align national policy with local human and material resources, to convey information about local circumstances, to inform monarchical policymaking, and to assist in carrying out the work of government. Although a few provincial assemblies were established in 1778, they were never introduced throughout the realm. Subsequent moves to establish additional provincial assemblies involved some interesting experimentation with election based on property ownership rather than social order, but proved equally limited in terms of geographical application. France remained an unwieldy administrative patchwork, with diverse concepts of representation coexisting uneasily.[11]

During the 1780s more or less self-appointed representatives of the nation and the public, like the *parlements*, continued to challenge and obstruct the implementation of royal policies. The king and his ministers accordingly experimented with a hand-picked 'Assembly of Notables', but this body proved unexpectedly difficult to manage and was quickly dissolved in 1787. The decision to summon a national

[9] Keith Michael Baker, 'Representation', in Keith Michael Baker et al. (eds), *The French Revolution and the Creation of Modern Political Culture* (4 vols, Oxford, 1987–94), 1: 469–72.

[10] William Doyle, 'The Parlements', in Baker et al. (eds), *The French Revolution*, 1: 157–67.

[11] Peter M. Jones, *Reform and Revolution in France: The Politics of Transition, 1774–1791* (Cambridge, 1995), 38–43.

assembly in the archaic form of the Estates General produced a means of escaping from this impasse. Though the basic intention was to proceed according to traditional forms—precisely those forms that had been followed when the Estates General had last been convoked in 1614—significant changes were made to the process for choosing deputies, chiefly as a result of pressure from those who felt disenfranchised. A massive, and in its own way highly 'democratic', consultative and electoral process was set in train.[12] The French people thus unconsciously embarked on an extended revolutionary adventure with an apprenticeship in modes of political conduct that differed markedly from those then prevailing either in Britain or America.

Although the number of deputies representing the Third Estate was doubled (to equal the two other orders combined), the demand for meeting in a single assembly in order to vote 'by head' rather than separately 'by order' was refused. In the spring of 1789 elections thus proceeded in three parallel streams: one for clergy, one for nobility, and one for commoners, in order to produce a tricameral assembly. All clergy and nobles had the right to attend their assemblies; the right to participate at parish or municipal level was accorded to all male commoners aged twenty-five or over, provided they were taxpayers (with some exceptions, such as Paris, where a higher fiscal threshold was set). However, clerical and noble deputies were usually elected after a single meeting, whereas for the (far more numerous) Third Estate the process passed through two, sometimes three, stages before reaching the *bailliage* level, at which the deputies who would sit in the Estates General were chosen. This process did not simply involve the election of delegates to meet at the next level, but also entailed the drafting of *cahiers de doléances*, which identified issues that the Estates General should consider. It has been estimated that some 3 million Frenchmen actually participated in this unprecedented electoral and deliberative process. Yet still it was a mediated process: it was not assumed that members of petty assemblies had the knowledge or judgement to choose national-level representatives themselves, and the final *cahiers*, which deputies took with them to Versailles as their mandates, were reduced to a single document per *bailliage*.

In fact, many expectations were confounded. The deputies' revolution at the Estates General, which secured the single National Assembly that commoners had demanded, led quickly to the abolition of orders altogether, and not merely for future elections and assemblies. Yet, other elements of this transitional electoral process, like the electoral assembly mechanism, survived through the revolutionary, into the imperial era and even beyond. Some practices would subsequently change—but not all changes brought France closer to either British or American norms—and, in any case, when developments did occur they were taken in the context of critical reflection on French practice, according to French values and ideas.

---

[12] Ran Halévi, 'La Monarchie et les élections: position des problèmes', in Baker et al. (eds), *The French Revolution*, 1: 387–402.

THE REVOLUTIONARY AND
IMPERIAL ERAS (1790–1815)

Throughout the Revolutionary era, the electoral process remained mediated, but broadly inclusive and multi-functional. The electoral assembly became a routine, regularly convoked, local institution, although the details of its operation and powers were subject to constant change as a result of the continuing upheaval.[13]

Revolutionary electoral geography mirrored revolutionary administrative geography, as the French National Assembly instituted an entirely uniform system of local government from top to bottom. In March 1790 former provinces were replaced by eighty-three *départements*, split into districts and *cantons*. At the base of this hierarchy were a multiplicity of *communes*, 40,000 of them in all, ranging in size from cities to villages, the former subdivided into *sections* (or voting wards) for electoral purposes. However, following the model of elections to the Estates General, elections to national assemblies were mediated or indirect: primary assemblies at the cantonal level chose delegates (called 'electors') to attend departmental assemblies, where the final choice of representatives was made. At the lower level, where election was direct, roughly 1 million posts (including Catholic clergy for a brief period) were to be filled by direct election and, indeed, frequently refilled. To be sure, elections virtually ceased during the Terror and, when they resumed after 1795, their remit was more restricted; the trend was towards decision-making and appointment at the centre.

The electoral process remained broadly inclusive, though quite how inclusive varied. In 1789 members of the National Assembly generally agreed that the right to vote should be limited to those exercising a degree of independence. The French nation was to comprise both 'active' and 'passive' citizens (terms coined by the Abbé Sieyès, whose aim was to distinguish between those who were in a position to participate politically from those who were not); only the former could vote. The 1791 Constitution set the age at which men became eligible for active citizenship at twenty-five, while to qualify they had also to pay annual taxes equivalent to three days' wages (the appropriate level being determined locally). Nonetheless, it has been calculated that two-thirds of the adult male population met these criteria. Only a few deputies, notably Maximilien Robespierre, initially challenged the exclusion of poorer males, while the passive status of women was vainly contested by rare advocates of female rights. The outbreak of war in 1792 necessitated the mobilization of a national army and those who were conscripted were promised full citizenship when their military service came to an end regardless of their fiscal circumstances. In 1793 a more radical, republican Constitution lowered the age threshold to twenty-one and established universal male suffrage, but it was never implemented due to the conflict. The 1795 Constitution subsequently reinstated fiscal qualifications, though it sufficed to pay any direct tax, however small the amount.

---

[13] Malcolm Crook, *Elections in the French Revolution: An Apprenticeship in Democracy, 1789–1799* (Cambridge, 1996) and Melvin Edelstein, *The French Revolution and the Birth of Electoral Democracy* (Farnham, 2014).

The real restriction on citizenship was imposed at the secondary level of the departmental assemblies, where national deputies were chosen. As Patrice Gueniffey has put it, 'numbers would be balanced by reason', as some 50,000 second-degree electors were entrusted with making the crucial choices in 1791.[14] These individuals had to meet a more stringent tax qualification, equivalent to the value of ten days' local wages, though the need to travel to the *chef-lieu* of the department, besides spending some time there, ensured that it was generally men of more significant means than that who were chosen to attend. During the radical phase of the Revolution, in 1792, the removal of the fiscal requirement made precious little difference to this emergent elective 'aristocracy'.

In England and America, elections were organized by the local authorities. In France after 1789 the electoral assembly was more autonomous: it was the constitutive body from which other elements in government derived their sanction. Proceedings therefore began with the choice of supervisory officials (president, secretary, and scrutineers). Moreover, three rounds of voting might be needed before anyone achieved the necessary fraction of votes (an absolute majority was needed for a name to be carried during either of the first two rounds of voting). Since different categories—mayors and councillors, for example—were elected separately, the process would normally take a few days; in the bigger cities it might take more than a week. Given that candidatures were not (formally) declared, there was no distinction between opposed and unopposed elections so that elections had to take place whenever the time came to fill offices. These time-consuming complexities generally limited participation at the primary level to less than 30 per cent of those eligible to vote.

After 1789, assemblies ceased to be asked to draw up *cahiers de doléances*. However, in practice, electoral assemblies provided opportunities for discussion, as voters waited their turn to vote (in strict alphabetical order), or to learn the outcome of their efforts. Indeed, in and around the assemblies a good deal of informal 'party-formation' took place, as voters met one another, exchanged ideas, and weighed up allegiances after the first- and second-round results were announced. It was but a short step from casual debate to the more formal drafting of resolutions. In December 1789, as part of its municipal legislation, the National Assembly explicitly permitted citizens to gather in order to draw up collective petitions even outside the electoral cycle, provided they secured the support of a certain number of registered voters. In the bigger cities, where political associations, chief among them the Jacobin clubs, were already active, this facility was frequently exploited. Until the autumn of 1793, when the latitude for convening meetings was gradually reduced, it was not only petitions that emerged from this milieu. The sections launched the great Parisian insurrection of August 1792, while the urban revolts of the following summer originated in a similar fashion.

A proposal to refer the 1791 Constitution for ratification by the people was rejected, but when the National Convention met in 1792 it immediately announced

---

[14] Patrice Gueniffey, *Le Nombre et la raison: La Révolution française et les élections* (Paris, 1993), 98–105 and 404–28.

that a new republican Constitution would be put to a popular vote. In July 1793 this promise was duly fulfilled and discussion as well as voting took place in the primary assemblies. A whole series of observations were recorded, mostly related to the constitutional text, or to the revised Declaration of the Rights of Man that prefaced the document (which now proclaimed the right to education and public assistance, besides the notorious right to insurrection). Participants also took the opportunity to raise more general issues, such as the need for testamentary legislation or price controls. The Constitution of 1793 was overwhelmingly approved, but shelved for the duration of the war in which the Republic was engaged. After the fall of Robespierre, in Thermidor 1794, a chastened Convention drafted a more moderate Constitution, and again presented it to the people for approval. Once more a great deal of discussion took place in the assemblies and the views that were expressed included extraneous remarks as well as more relevant observations.

However, the Thermidorians believed that the preceding period had seen an excess of 'democracy'—in the sense of mob rule. They remained republicans, and elaborated the modern republican principle of representative government, but they firmly believed that political power should mirror the natural structures of the post-Revolutionary social order.[15] One of those responsible for drafting the new Constitution of 1795, Boissy d'Anglas, boldly stated: 'We must be ruled by the best'; according to him, they were to be found among the wealthy. Attempts were made to institute checks and balances at the centre of government, as well as to constrain active popular participation at lower levels. Since the establishment of the National Assembly in 1789, all legislatures had been unicameral, but now proposals from a Council of Five Hundred were subject to approval by a smaller Council of Elders. Elections to these legislative bodies were to be annual, but partial, in an effort to encourage gradual rather than sudden changes of direction. Membership of the departmental electoral colleges was reduced from 50,000 to 30,000, while the total number of elective posts was drastically diminished, not least at municipal level where smaller communes were grouped into cantonal municipalities. Yet the system was plagued with instability and, when elections produced Councils hostile to the executive Directory in 1797 and 1798, many deputies were simply expelled. Not surprisingly, interest in voting waned.

Napoleon came to power with the support of those who wished to see further strengthening of the executive. He consistently acted with that end in view, yet he continued to try to demonstrate that his regime was based on the consent of the people, while minimizing opportunities for the formation of any kind of collective popular will. The Constitution of 1799, which established the Consulate, declared baldly that the 'government has been invested in three consuls', named for ten years; it dispensed with the now customary Declaration of Rights. All 'males aged over twenty-one who had resided in the Republic for a year' were to be registered to vote (though in practice servants and paupers were excluded). The term 'universal

[15] Andrew Jainchill, *Reimagining Politics after the Terror: The Republican Origins of French Liberalism* (Ithaca, NY, 2008).

suffrage' was introduced at this time, apparently from Britain though, in the classic judgement of Alphonse Aulard, 'while pretending to re-establish universal suffrage... Bonaparte actually destroyed it'.[16]

Like the two previous constitutions, that of 1799 was subjected to popular ratification, but it was not submitted for the approval of electoral assemblies; instead, individuals were invited to sign public registers indicating assent or dissent, a process ultimately termed a 'plebiscite'. That procedure was repeated after the Constitution was revised in 1802 and again in 1804 (when the hereditary empire was established). This may not have deterred a few individuals from expressing dissent, nor inhibited more of them from adding reservations to their affirmations. However, in the absence of any mechanism of control, there was nothing to prevent local mayors, who kept the registers, from inscribing the names of those who had not voted. Recent research has also demonstrated conclusively that the figures were deliberately massaged so as to indicate support for the regime, especially on the first occasion, when a total of some 1 million favourable votes was more than doubled.[17]

The system of Revolutionary assemblies and departmental electoral colleges was reinstated for ordinary electoral purposes in 1802 and operated until Napoleon's fall from power a decade or so later.[18] However, the primary assemblies met only every five years. They could choose delegates to the departmental colleges (with a total membership of roughly 60,000, in what was now an expanded Republic) only from among the 600 most highly taxed individuals in each department, whom Napoleon referred to as his 'bedrock of granite'. These second-degree electors sat for life and were entrusted merely with the task of nominating candidates for the legislature, among whom the Senate made the final choice. At the local level, elections ceased, save in the case of justices of the peace, and municipal councillors in towns of more than 5,000 inhabitants, though voters only proposed names; all other officials were appointed.

At the establishment of the hereditary empire in 1804 it was declared that 'the government of the Republic is invested in an emperor who will be called Emperor of the French people'. Napoleon indeed swore to uphold equality of rights as well as political and civil liberties, but the return of a full-blown court, not to mention the creation of an imperial nobility and Napoleon's penchant for members of the old ruling class, underlined the extent to which he had abandoned the more egalitarian aspirations of the Revolution. To the extent that these survived, it was chiefly in the form of the 'career open to talents' (and even here in practice, emphasis focused above all on rallying the talented from various powerful and propertied social strata, not on promoting mobility from the lower echelons). Napoleon's waning reputation was partially salvaged by the Hundred Days of 1815, when he

---

[16] Alphonse Aulard, *Histoire politique de la Révolution française: Origines et développement de la démocratie et de la République (1789–1804)* (4th edn, Paris, 1909), 706–9.

[17] Malcolm Crook, '"Confiance d'en bas, manipulation d'en haut": la pratique plébiscitaire sous Napoléon (1799–1815)', in Philippe Bourdin et al. (eds), *L'Incident électoral de la Révolution à la Ve République* (Clermont-Ferrand, 2002).

[18] Jean-Yves Coppolani, *Les Elections en France à l'époque napoléonienne* (Paris, 1980).

briefly returned to power in the guise of the people's choice, '*empereur par la volonté du peuple*', and was consecrated by a final plebiscite.[19]

THE RESTORED AND LIBERAL
MONARCHIES (1814–48)

Though the restored Louis XVIII issued a Charter, graciously bestowing certain political rights upon his people, the restored Bourbon monarchy formally contracted political rights, and the liberal Orleanist monarchy only marginally extended them. The *Charte* established a bicameral legislature, with an appointed House of Peers and an elected Chamber of Deputies.[20] The right to initiate all legislation was vested in the Crown, and legislative proposals were introduced with ostentatious royal endorsement, making it difficult to oppose them without apparent disloyalty, as 'ultra-royalists' like Chateaubriand protested.

The electoral infrastructure was narrowed by the simple expedient of shearing away the primary layer. Henceforth, elections to national assemblies were direct, not mediated, but the right to vote in them was severely restricted. Under the Restoration, electors were required to be at least thirty years of age, and to pay 300 francs a year in direct taxation. The number of those who met these criteria was somewhat larger than the number who had formerly staffed departmental colleges: some 100,000 men enjoyed the right to elect deputies under the restored monarchy, as compared to 30,000–60,000 members of departmental colleges in the Revolutionary and Imperial eras. This limited suffrage was strongly advocated by newly emergent liberals, whose object was to find a fourth way in politics—not replicating *ancien régime* monarchical despotism, nor Revolutionary popular republicanism, nor yet new-fangled imperial despotism. They argued that executive power should be genuinely counterweighted, by a legislature representing educated 'public opinion'. Primary assemblies, as they saw it, contributed nothing of value, and might be detrimental to good government if they in any way compromised the considered choice of intelligent men of property. Benjamin Constant thus stoutly defended the so-called *loi Lainé* of 1817 (named after the minister of the interior who introduced this electoral project) on the grounds that 'It is better to award to 100,000 men a direct, active and real participation . . . than to give to 4,000,000 an indirect, passive and chimerical involvement, which is always restricted to an empty ceremony.'[21]

Interestingly, in the extensive parliamentary debate that accompanied the franchise question, some dissident royalists (often as much a thorn in the side of monarchical government as the liberals) argued for the retention of a broad, first-degree electorate. The comte de la Bourdonnaye did so in such extreme terms as to earn the sobriquet 'le Jacobin blanc'. 'The proposed electoral law,' he argued,

---

[19] Malcolm Crook, '"Ma volonté est celle du peuple": Voting in the Plebiscite and Parliamentary Elections during Napoleon's Hundred Days, April–May 1815', *French Historical Studies*, 32 (2009), 619–45.
[20] Jacques Godechot, *Les Constitutions de la France* (Paris, 1970), 217–24.
[21] *Le Mercure de France* (Paris), 18 January 1817.

'divides this immense majority of the nation into two classes...you are degrading all citizens. You are forcing the whole population to bow down before the golden calf, before the aristocracy of wealth, the harshest and most unyielding of all aristocracies.'[22] Sentiments of this sort, however, predicated a traditional two-tier electoral process, which was expected to vest effective power in the hands of a propertied elite. The comte de Castelbajac gave the game away when he commented that 'the indirect electoral method was not so bad, since it was at once more popular and also more aristocratic...the people were able to exercise their rights, but there was a guarantee against them abusing it'.[23]

The French electorate of the period 1814–48 was much smaller than the contemporary British electorate (whereas the Revolutionary electorate had been much larger—insofar as these two very different kinds of electorate can be meaningfully compared in terms of scale). Yet, as in Britain, so in France, elections were public affairs, involving the participation of more than just formally qualified voters, especially in the *chefs-lieux* where they assembled.[24] In France, as in Britain, elections took place over several days and generated a festival atmosphere as several hundred electors came to town and remained there for the duration of the electoral assembly. The resulting atmosphere was certainly boisterous, as canvassing took place and successive rounds of voting were conducted. Indeed, the carnival might threaten to turn into a charivari, but generally the celebrations were noisy rather than disorderly. Pamphlets and caricatures were produced, while processions, illuminations, and banquets were commonplace, with songs composed especially for the occasion and often sung in the local language. Non-voters clearly felt they had a stake in the proceedings, 'demonstrating the desires, hopes and fears of the nation', as one observer put it in 1830.

By the late 1820s, some royalists had begun to argue that the Restoration suffrage was too generous: it offered too much latitude to determined opponents of monarchy. A proposal to give still more weight to wealthier voters, who already enjoyed a 'double vote', served only to provoke the downfall of the Bourbon regime. Yet the franchise was not dramatically extended under the Orleanist successor, Louis-Philippe, designated 'king of the French people' under a modified Charter—though a small number of those endowed with intellectual or professional *capacités* (academics or retired military officers) who failed to fulfil the fiscal criterion were nonetheless awarded the parliamentary vote. At the same time, allowing the assemblies to begin operations by choosing their own presidents constituted a symbolic recognition of citizen sovereignty. Since the Revolution the government had used its right of nomination to the presidency to put forward individuals whom it wished to see elected as deputies—as these individuals invariably were. In 1830 a lowering of the tax requirement to 200 francs, and a reduction of the voting age to twenty-five, still gave only 170,000 individuals the right to vote.

---

[22] *Archives parlementaires*, 17: 737.   [23] Ibid. 17: 704.

[24] Malcolm Crook, 'Suffrage et citoyenneté sous la Restauration', in Michel Pertué (ed.), *Suffrage, citoyenneté et révolutions* (Paris, 2002), and James Vernon, *Politics and the People: A Study in English Political Culture, c.1815–1867* (Cambridge, 1993).

The liberal monarchy did not merely rest on a narrow electoral base: it also failed to establish the legitimacy of its proceedings in the eyes of many French people.[25] Its nervousness in the face of criticism made the monarchy too ready to constrain civil liberties, especially the liberty of the press. Its *dirigisme* offended those who thought that local inhabitants should have more say in local affairs. By contrast, the monarchy's determined adherence to certain 'free-market' values, such as its refusal to acknowledge workers' right to organize, and the brutal repression of strikes and other forms of collective action, together with its failure to organize welfare schemes, alienated not only workers and the poor, but also those of higher status who reckoned these problems needed more effective solutions. The Orleanist monarchy came to be regarded as corrupt and introverted, insensitive to the needs and aspirations of the people at large. As a result the case for broadening the electorate was more widely accepted.

Growing wealth was gradually increasing the numbers who crossed the tax threshold, so that by the mid-1840s the total number of voters had risen to 240,000, but a wider franchise was ruled out by the prime minister, François Guizot. In an eve-of-poll speech in 1846 he stated: 'It is, no doubt, tempting providence to use the words "once and for all", but I think I can be so bold as to state that the current state of affairs will not be seriously challenged.'[26] He duly obtained an overwhelming victory in the ensuing general election. In March 1847 he remained unresponsive to demands—supported by a significant campaign—for a modest extension of the vote (a reduction of the fiscal requirement to 100 francs and additional *capacités*). He reiterated in the Chamber of Deputies that 'the day of universal suffrage will never dawn; there will never be a time when all human beings, no matter who they are, will be invited to exercise political rights'.[27] Less than a year later, a revolution implemented universal male suffrage and inscribed it in the republican Constitution of 1848.

THE REVOLUTION OF 1848 AND ITS AFTERMATH

Universal male suffrage was instituted by a decree of the provisional government of the newly founded Second Republic on 5 March 1848. Though by that time common enough in the Americas, this was still a daring innovation in a European context—the more so because, in contrast to previous French practice even in the most radical phase of the Revolutionary era, all members of this massive electorate voted directly for their parliamentary representatives. Not only in France, but also in states influenced by the celebrated Spanish 'Cadiz' Constitution of 1812, most earlier experiments with a broad suffrage had operated through a mediated electoral process.

In a French context, universal suffrage could be understood as the reinstatement of a Revolutionary practice. It was also a symbol of social inclusion; it was hoped

---

[25] Pierre Rosanvallon, *La Monarchie impossible. Les chartes de 1814 et de 1830* (Paris, 1994), 149–81.
[26] *Le Moniteur Universel* (Paris), 4 August 1846.   [27] Ibid. 27 March 1847.

that it would inaugurate an era of more harmonious social relations.[28] Yet there had been little or no discussion of the consequences, political or practical, of suddenly enfranchising so vast an electorate (holding the elections just six weeks later was a significant feat in itself). Universal male suffrage had not been deemed a realistic prospect during the preceding regime: critics had instead focused on modest electoral reform. A much broader franchise had, to be sure, been introduced for elections in towns and villages in 1831, so that some 3 million Frenchmen had recently enjoyed the opportunity to vote at this level, besides electing officers in the National Guard militia.[29] The primary stage of the electoral system had thus been reconstituted in a local context. Still, the award of full political rights to all adult males in 1848 was a huge leap in the dark. When elections took place to create a Constituent Assembly, in April 1848, some 9 million Frenchmen had the opportunity to choose national representatives and over 80 per cent of them actually did so. They went on to choose local councils during the summer, then a president of the Republic in December. This latter election once again attracted a massive turnout, though it resulted in an overwhelming victory for Louis-Napoleon, nephew of Napoleon Bonaparte.

The Constitution of 1848 (which was not subjected to popular ratification) provided for a unicameral assembly, and enshrined direct universal male voting rights. It also proclaimed that 'all noble titles...were abolished for ever'; it affirmed equality before the law and general eligibility for public office.[30] It promised to put a basic education within 'everyone's reach' and to ensure the existence of needy citizens, either by procuring employment or by offering assistance (though the latter assurance was expressed much more guardedly than it had been in 1793). Nonetheless, the Constitution also included safeguards against what many members of the Constituent Assembly clearly regarded as the excesses of the most radical phase of the first revolution. It was clearly spelled out in the Constitution that 'members of the National Assembly were representatives' not simply of the department electing them, but 'of France as a whole', and that they 'could not be given any specific mandate whatsoever'. Although polling stations might still be called *assemblées*, traditional primary assemblies came to an end in 1848. Electoral officials were now appointed from among local mayors and councillors. Because the electorate was so vast, voters were instructed to prepare their ballot papers in advance, submit their *bulletins* to designated officials, then immediately retire. Any discussion would result in annulment of the proceedings, though deliberation continued to occupy a place in the French electoral imagination, even if the Constitution repudiated the idea of direct democracy.

The electoral sociability surrounding the old assemblies was displaced onto public meetings and embryonic political parties, not to mention a burgeoning press—all of which profited, at least temporarily, from an extension of civil liberties,

---

[28] Raymond Huard, *Le Suffrage universel en France, 1848–1946* (Paris, 1991), 30–4.

[29] Christine Guionnet, *L'Apprentissage de la politique moderne: Les élections municipales sous la Monarchie de Juillet* (Paris, 1997).

[30] Godechot, *Les Constitutions de la France*, 263–77.

not to speak of the heightened interest in politics that accompanied the Revolution. Its outbreak in 1848 had prompted the creation of a multitude of political clubs, not least in Paris, where some 200 emerged virtually overnight and attracted up to 100,000 members.[31] Like their predecessors in the 1790s they served as schools for citizenship, and now also as electoral organizations (all the more necessary under the new system of direct elections in which there was still no obligation to declare a candidature and voters remained free to nominate whomsoever they wished). However, these new rights would soon be overridden when the short-lived Second Republic came to an abrupt end in 1851.

The year 1848 rhetorically sealed the bond between republicanism and democracy, which had not been enduringly forged during the earlier Republic. Though the Second Republic did not experience difficulties to the same extent as the First, it too proved disappointing. The experiment with a directly elected presidency played into the hands of Bonapartists, as Louis-Napoleon exploited the first Napoleon's populist legacy to triumph in the presidential election of December 1848. He overthrew the Republic three years later and restored universal male suffrage after conservatives had restricted the franchise afresh in 1850, by imposing lengthy residence requirements on voters. However, like his uncle, Louis-Napoleon took steps to restrict the effective power of the electorate and employed plebiscites as a means of securing approval for the foundation of a Second Empire. Yet if 1848 revealed the tendency of democracy to threaten anarchy, then mutate into despotism, as many had feared, it did enshrine the principle of universal suffrage and thus laid the basis for a much more enduring democratic republican regime after 1870.

---

[31] Peter Amann, *Revolution and Mass Democracy: The Paris Club Movement of 1848* (Princeton, NJ, 1975), 34–5.

PART III
BRITAIN

7

Talking about Democracy:
Britain in the 1790s

Mark Philp

'Democracy' was used with a variety of references in Britain in the eighteenth century. Adam Smith associated it with primitive forms of government, and that idea was linked to the characterization of America as 'democratical' in form in its early years. It was used to refer, following Plato and Aristotle, to a range of ancient city states and their unruly political orders, with an emphasis placed on the tumultuous and inconstant character of democratic rule and its tendency to degenerate, through the rise of demagogues, into tyrannies. For many it denoted a type of small-scale republic, as sketched in the work of Montesquieu, with whom they shared the proviso that the *moeurs*, principles, and institutions of such states were simply not transferable to the more substantial commercial states of Britain and France or to the huge tracts of land covered by the American states. Finally, but for many most significantly, the term 'democracy' had an important place in the triptych of British politics by forming one element, alongside monarchy and aristocracy, in a theory of mixed government that dates back at least as far as the Greek historian Polybius and that, by the eighteenth century, had come to express a broad consensus of opinion on the character of the constitutional settlement following the Glorious Revolution of 1688.

Only in the last of these senses was there much positive value attached to the term, and even here what was lacking was any clear conception or affirmation of a democratic principle as such. It may seem unsurprising that 'democracy' was not boldly or widely affirmed, given the lack of any strong practical commitment to empowering the people, and that few sought to promote practical political equality—as witness the slow process by which the terms of popular participation came to be contested in the eighteenth and early nineteenth centuries. The dramatically restricted franchise, the domination of many seats by aristocratic interests, and the infrequency of contested elections, were challenged at various times on various grounds. But though there were a variety of ways of underpinning claims for an equal representation of the people's voice, a wider suffrage, or for free, fair, and frequent elections, still none of these appealed to a fundamental democratic principle.

In part, this was because of the dominance of the negative legacy of ancient characterizations of democracy. But it was also because voting, apportionment, and representation were identified as elements in a constitutional compromise that could be justified historically and consequentially, in terms of tradition, stability, and expedience within a framework of mixed government and the constitutional settlement of 1688. This meant that while recurrent debates—about the role of the people in the state, the relationship between the ends of the state, the public good, and the popular will, and the claims made for and against the popular basis of government—throughout the eighteenth century might include some reference to democracy, they did not accord it a prominent, independent role or value. Over time, it is possible to identify an emerging conception of something like the sovereignty of the people, but invoking this did not entail demanding direct popular participation in government. Rather, what was in question was the long-standing notion that all lawful power had its *origins* in the consent of the people, and should be exercised in such a way as to promote their interests. Construed in this way, popular sovereignty provided a reference point to which to appeal when attacking or supporting the conduct of government.

From 1780 a demand for 'parliamentary reform' also emerged, but this was framed by readings of the constitutional consensus and the fear that this had become unbalanced by the power of the Crown and by the corruption of representation within the Commons.[1] Even the more radical supporters of the movement, such as Major John Cartwright, who called for universal manhood suffrage and annual parliaments, continued to work largely within a model of mixed government. His pithy *Declaration of the Rights of Englishmen* (1784) starts with the traditional reference to 'King, Lords of Parliament, and Representatives of *the whole Body* of the Freemen of this Realm' and concludes by following William Blackstone, Matthew Hale, and Montesquieu in thinking that the greatest danger lies in the corruption of the representatives, and to admonish the people of England 'to keep vigilant watch over the acts of their Representatives'. This emphasis on securing the relationship between the people and their representatives to ensure the independence of the popular component of the constitution began a refocusing of debates about the Constitution that was further developed in subsequent decades. It also created an agenda for parliamentary and political reform that endorsed the mobilization of groups both inside and outside Parliament in pursuit of these objectives, giving a new impetus to political organization and setting the scene for the emergence of a more vigorous struggle over reform in the 1790s. Cartwright and his associates nonetheless did not see themselves as pursuing 'democracy', which he identified as a form of government suitable only for small and simple states.[2]

---

[1] Pasi Ihalainen's useful and very detailed study, focusing on parliamentary language, *Agents of the People: Democracy and Popular Sovereignty in British and Swedish Parliamentary and Public Debates 1734–1800* (Leiden, 2010), tends to see changes in expression in the light of what might then follow, rather than seeing them, as I do here, as variations around a common set of themes.

[2] John Cartwright, *The Legislative Rights of the Commonalty Vindicated, or Take Your Choice!* (London, 1777), 6. For his endorsement of democracy later in his career: Naomi C. Miller, 'John Cartwright and Radical Parliamentary Reform, 1808–1819', *English Historical Review*, 83 (1968), 705–28, and Rachel Eckersley, 'Of Radical Design: John Cartwright and the Redesign of the Reform Campaign, c.1800–1811', *History*, 89 (2004), 560–80.

In a few cases 'democracy' was invoked as something like a value, or as something to which value attached. Catherine Macaulay's discussion in 1767 of a 'democratic republican' constitution for Corsica (drawn largely from the model of the Roman Republic) was one clear but isolated case.[3] Moreover, Corsica (like Switzerland) was a small city state whose institutions were of dubious relevance to large commercial societies. In William Young's 1786 examination of ancient Greece there was the beginning of a recognition of the complex character of the Athenian *polis* and its democracy.[4] Yet Young needs careful reading: he was distinctive in resisting the equation of democracy with disorder, and in finding elements of the Athenian practice worthy of praise; he saw it as a political form that realized a number of distinct values. But, while this was one step to an accommodation with the example of ancient Greece (and a step further than his contemporaries took until the opening decades of the nineteenth century when there was a systematic re-evaluation of Athenian democracy and of Aristotle's account of it), praise for Ancient Greece was not taken to imply that its institutions should be adopted in the modern world.[5] And while Imperial Rome was seen as having parallels with Britain and its empire, it could hardly be said that such parallels were a source of reassurance—since the empire was associated with the destruction of the republic and the rise of autocracy. There was a complex set of debates about the exact causes of Rome's decline, and their relevance to Britain, but in these it was not suggested that the concept of 'democracy' had much to add. And these debates were not popular—they were aimed at the highly literate. On the rare occasions on which the term 'democracy' was used positively, its exact referent was often obscure, and what was offered rarely went beyond a positive reading of Montesquieu's classification of ancient republics, with the application restricted to small states or other states that could bear ancient *moeurs*—and thus, specifically not to commercial societies that valorized private over public liberty.

Indeed, if there was a standard vocabulary other than that of the mixed Constitution with which to express the demands for more popular participation it was that of 'republic' or 'commonwealth' (Catherine Macaulay was known as a republican, not as a democrat). When John Adams, who was a supporter of the British model and its constitutional thinking, discussed types of states in his *Defence of the Constitutions of Government of the United States of America* (1787, published in Britain in 1794), he commented that: 'There is...a peculiar sense in which the words *republic, commonwealth, popular state*, are used by English and French writers: who mean by them a democracy, or rather a representative democracy; a

---

[3] Catherine Macaulay, *Loose Remarks on Certain Positions to be found in Mr. Hobbes's 'Philosophical Rudiments of Government and Society', with a Short Sketch of a Democratical Form of Government, In a Letter to Signor Paoli* (London, 1767).

[4] William Young, *The Spirit of Athens* (London, 1777); in 2nd and 3rd edns, *The History of Athens; Including a Commentary on the Principles, Policy, and Practice, or Republican Government...* (London, 1786, 1804); Peter Liddel, 'William Young and the Spirit of Athens', in J. Moore, I. Macgregor Morris, and A. J. Bayliss (eds), *Reinventing History: The Enlightenment Origins of Ancient History* (London, 2008).

[5] Young's *The Rights of Englishmen; or the British Constitution of Government, Compared with that of a Democratic Republic* (London, 1793) was more critical.

government in one centre, and that centre the nation; that is to say, that centre a single assembly, chosen at stated periods by the people, and invested with the whole sovereignty; the whole legislative, executive, and judicial power to be exercised in a body, or by committees, as they shall think proper.'[6] This was the sense, Adams said, in which these words were used by the seventeenth-century republican Marchamont Nedham, who certainly did not gloss them in terms of 'democracy'. Adams was effectively trying to map seventeenth- and eighteenth-century discussions on to an emergent typology derived from other sources: on the one hand, from the classical world, on the other, from American experience.

Just as there was a place for 'democracy' within mixed government, so too was there a place for 'aristocracy'. Montesquieu's classification of republics had distinguished between democratic and aristocratic republics; he saw the latter as, on the whole, more stable.[7] Only in the 1790s, following the outbreak of the French Revolution, did the two terms come to be treated as antithetical, and only then did the terms 'democrat' and 'aristocrat' become widely used terms of contrastive description. I will suggest that these words—'democrat' in particular—gained currency some time before the concept of democracy itself attained new salience. Rather than intense subjective identification with democracy or democratic government leading people to subscribe themselves as 'democrats', the process unfolded in reverse: 'democrat' was forged primarily as a term to denigrate and attack those proposing reform; some of those attacked subsequently appropriated the term as a rhetorical strategy of resistance to their detractors, and some of these (but by no means all), in doing so, articulated new elements of the conceptual potential of the term.

THE REACTION AGAINST FRANCE

In February 1790, in reaction to the opening months of the French Revolution, the leading Whig politician and philosopher, Edmund Burke, used his *Speech on the Army Estimates* to denounce French innovations. He followed up his comments in his *Reflections on the Revolution in France* in November of that year. Burke insisted that the French Revolutionaries were introducing democracy into the state, while destroying the other orders of rule. He turned the rather learned discussions of democracy, and the more general sense of its lack of relevance to contemporary European states prior to 1790, into a systematic part of his invective against French and English reformers. In doing so, he raised the denigration of democracy to a new pitch: 'a perfect democracy is therefore the most shameless

---

[6] *A Defence of the Constitutions of Government of the United States of America* (3 vols, London, 1794), 3: 160–1. Adams started by taking 'republic' in its widest possible sense—'If, indeed, a republic signifies nothing but public affairs, it is equally applicable to all nations; and every kind of government, despotisms, monarchies, aristocracies, democracies, and every possible or imaginable composition of them are all republics.' If narrowed to 'define a republic as a government of more than one' this would rule out only despotisms, since monarchs rule through others. We might narrow it further to signify a government in which all are 'equally subject to the laws' (3: 159)—which Adams regarded as the true meaning.

[7] Charles-Louis, Baron de Montesquieu, *L'Esprit des Lois* (Paris, 1748), books 3 and 5.

thing in the world'; France 'affects to be a pure democracy', yet 'an absolute democracy, no more than an absolute monarchy', can be 'reckoned among the legitimate forms of government':

> ... in a democracy, the majority of the citizens is capable of exercising the most cruel oppressions upon the minority, whenever strong divisions prevail ... and the oppression of the minority will extend to far greater numbers and will be carried on with much greater fury than can ever be feared from a single sceptre.

France has preferred 'a despotic democracy to a government of reciprocal controul. The triumph of the victorious party was over the principles of the British Constitution':[8]

> Our present danger from the example of a people, whose character knows no medium, is, with regard to government, a danger from anarchy; a danger of being led through an admiration of successful fraud and violence, to an imitation of the excesses of an irrational, unprincipled, proscribing, confiscating, plundering, ferocious, bloody, and tyrannical democracy.[9]

These charges and Burke's response to France were met with some puzzlement, since neither the French nor the English who welcomed the events in France conceived of their activity or their objectives in terms of democracy. Thomas Paine, who had returned to Europe after making his reputation in the American Revolution, responded to Burke in his *Rights of Man* by following the American route and denying that democracy was a relevant term: 'original simple democracy ... is incapable of extension, not from principle, but from the inconvenience of its form; and monarchy and aristocracy from their incapacity'. But Burke's remarks also prompted Paine to refine some of his claims about the nature of the relationship between the people and their governments, and in doing so he came to advocate not democracy, but (in its place) a system of representation:

> the representative system naturally [remedies] at once the defects of the simple democracy as to form, and the incapacity of the other two (aristocracy and monarchy) with respect to knowledge.... By ingrafting representation upon democracy, we arrive at a system of embracing and confederating all the various interests and every extent of territory and population.... The American government ... is representation ingrafted upon democracy.... It is the easiest of all forms of government to be understood, and the most eligible in practice; and excludes at once the ignorance and insecurity of the hereditary mode, and the inconvenience of the simple democracy.[10]

What that 'ingrafting' meant, what role representation had with respect to the executive branch, what the suffrage should be, and on what basis representatives should act (according to their personal consciences or their electors' preferences), all remained to be spelled out. Paine's writings were sketchy on a great many such matters; indeed,

[8] Edmund Burke, *Reflections on the Revolution in France* (London, 1790), 139, 185, 186, 201.
[9] 'Speech on the Army Estimates', in *The Works of the Right Honourable Edmund Burke* (8 vols, London, 1808), 5: 9.
[10] Thomas Paine, *Rights of Man, Common Sense and other Political Writings*, ed. Mark Philp (Oxford, 1995), 232–3. The quotations are from the second part of *Rights of Man* (1792).

though he was canonized as 'the famous democrat' by Friedrich Engels, his claim to that title by the standards of Engels' own day is shaky: neither part of his *Rights of Man* (1791 and 1792) made a case for universal manhood suffrage (which first appeared in his *Letter Addressed to the Addressers*, 1792).[11] Forty years later William Carpenter's *The Political Text Book* (1833) put together a series of quotations from Paine to turn him into a 'democrat', in a way that involved a retrospective reinterpretation of Paine's position in 1790–2; this provided a foretaste of most modern treatments of him.

Burke's use of 'democracy' to discredit the French and their supporters in Britain was strikingly successful in the short term. Paine did not challenge him on democracy in the first part of *Rights of Man* (1791); he did not insist on its value, nor did he use the term 'democracy' to designate his preferred mode of government in the second part published the following year. Moreover, there was little positive use of the term 'democracy' even among the supporters of events in France in 1791 and 1792. The phrase 'representative democracy'—which is how we might now characterize what Paine supported—was used only rarely (most frequently by Americans such as John Adams and, in 1799, Joel Barlow,[12] and by Frenchmen acquainted with America, such as Brissot de Warville,[13] although there was some Irish use at the end of the 1790s).[14] 'Representative government' was in more common use (not before 1789 but with rapidly increasing intensity in the early 1790s, also under the influence of Barlow and France), but in and of itself it usually had little that we would regard as a specifically democratic content, and few at the time linked it to 'democracy'. One tactic in debates introduced by supporters of the government involved accusing those who argued for representative government of seeking the elimination of all other elements of the Constitution. Thomas Hardy, the founder of the London Corresponding Society and a defendant in the 1794 Treason Trials, was accused of looking 'for the speedy accomplishment of all his wishes—and these must be the annihilation of all ranks, of a king, of the nobles— and the establishment of a representative government'.[15] Representative government was seen as the precise name for what he sought, not democracy. When the Parliamentary Committee on Secrecy reported on the reformers in 1799, it accused them of seeking the 'substitution of a representative government, founded on the new doctrine of the Rights of Man; and uniting, in one body, all the legislative and executive powers of the state'. They were not accused of advocating democracy.[16]

---

[11] Friedrich Engels, *The Condition of the Working Class in England*, ed. David McLellan (Oxford, 1993), 25.

[12] Joel Barlow, *To his Fellow Citizens of the United States: Letter II, on Certain Political Measures Proposed to their Constitution* (Paris, 1799).

[13] Jacques-Pierre Brissot de Warville, *New Travels in the United States of America performed in 1788* (London, 1794).

[14] Thomas Addis Emmet, *Memoire, or Detailed Statement of the Origins and Progress of the Irish Union* (Dublin, [1800?]).

[15] *Bell's Reports of the State Trials for High Treason: The Arraignment* (London, 1794), 102. This was, indeed, the upshot of Barlow's position in *Advice to the Privileged Orders* (London, 1791). Yet Barlow referred to democracy only once, and then obliquely; what he did not do was to link democracy to representative government.

[16] *Report of the Committee of Secrecy of the House of Commons of Great Britain* (Dublin, 1799), 15.

When Charles James Fox, the leader of those Whigs not overtly hostile to reform, avowed supporting representative government, he did so with reference, and in opposition, to what he saw as a false conception of that form: 'I do not mean a Representative Government in the sense that some invidious persons are ready to impute to me, but a true Representation of the People in this House.'[17] The political philosopher William Godwin, while featuring a measured and often positive discussion of democracy in his visionary *An Enquiry Concerning Political Justice* (1793), linked it to 'representative government' only when he made alterations in the third edition of 1798, and even then his discussion was not extensive.

DEMOCRATS

Those agitating for political reform in the beginning of the 1790s clearly wanted reform to strengthen the popular part of the Constitution so as to mitigate the corruption of the legislature by the Crown and the Lords and to ensure that representatives acted with due respect for those to whom they were ultimately accountable, but they did not see themselves as advocating 'democracy'. Over time, however, many did come to see themselves as 'democrats'—and some came to see their opponents as 'aristocrats'. They did so because Burke's invective had an infectious influence, supplying one of the central terms loyalists used to castigate those advocating reform. Indeed, the spectre of democracy stalked the pages of the press and loyalist writing. Paine was denounced as a democrat as early as March 1792 in the *Morning Herald*,[18] and from 1791 *The Times* used 'democrat' to describe a French 'type' and to disparage aspects of French radicalism. There was a similar pattern of reference in other newspapers. The Loyalist 'Creed of the democrat' was forcibly expressed in April 1792:

> I BELIEVE in Mobs....I BELIEVE that NATIONS are like INDIVIDUALS and that everything was born to be undone . . .; I BELIEVE – Mr THOMAS PAINE the greatest creature that ever was or ever will be....I BELIEVE the said THOMAS PAINE to be a *most disinterested man*, because he is very poor, and proposes taking away from the rich what they have, which cannot affect himself. This is the true faith – the CA IRA of an honest man.[19]

George Woodward provided an even-handed critique of a range of political types in his *Elements of Bacchus or, Toasts and Sentiments given by Distinguished Characters* (1792); a caricature of 'The Democrat' as a slightly tipsy man, Tom Terrible, wearing a French cockade and accompanied by a long description of his miserable character, was followed immediately by an equally unappealing 'Lord SLASH' the aristocrat.[20] The neatest instance of an attempt to brand reformers by association

---

[17] *Speech of the Right Honourable Charles-James Fox...Friday, the 4th January, 1798, on the Assessed-Tax Bill* (London, 1798), 34.

[18] *Morning Herald* (London), 21 March 1792.   [19] *World (1787)* (London), 12 April 1792.

[20] G. M. Woodward, *Elements of Bacchus or, Toasts and Sentiments given by Distinguished Characters* (London, 1792).

entailed a report that the Electorate of Bavaria had prohibited the translation of Homer's *Iliad* on the ground that it abounded in democratic principles. 'This is pushing precaution to a ridiculous excess, for *Thersites* is the only democrat in that *chef d'oeuvre* of epic poetry; and he is a liar, a bully and a coward.'[21] The first *Times* use of 'democrat' to describe an individual in England was to 'Mr Thelwall, the Democrat', but this was as late at 1794.

We can also document the use of anti-democratic language in practical contexts. When the renowned writer and headmaster of Tonbridge School, Vicesimus Knox, went to preach a sermon in Brighton in August 1793, he found himself physically attacked and hounded out of the hall by opponents who shouted him down: 'I heard myself called, in the first instance, *a democratical scoundrel that deserved to be hanged.* "A Democrat, a Democrat, a d_____d Democrat. Out with the Democrat—no Democrats".'[22] And the loyalist and evangelical writer Hannah More used her cheap tract *Village Politics* to rehearse a conversation she hoped would be widely repeated among her popular audience: Tom asks his fellow labourer Jack what 'dost thou take a *Democrat* to be?'—and Jack's unhesitating reply is 'One who likes to be governed by a thousand tyrants, and yet can't bear a king.'[23]

Nonetheless, even as democrats were stigmatized, some embraced that identity and used it as an affirmative language of self-description. In Britain, there were several ambiguous avowals of identity. On 1 April 1791 a Sir St John Mildmay had a horse 'democrat' running at Winchester;[24] and the signature 'A staunch Democrat' was on a list of subscribers to a fund to provide support for the aged, infirm, and the children of *refugees from France* on 2 October 1792.[25] But within a relatively short time the terminology began to be positively and provocatively sported by some of the radical press—often in contrast to another character type: the aristocrat. The radical newspaper editor Sampson Perry used his *Argus* in February 1792 to comment that, while 'An Aristocrat is one who wishes the bulk of mankind to be depressed and degraded for the partial advantage and splendour of certain privileged orders. A Democrat is one who wishes well to human kind in general and only requires (to use a boxing metaphor) a clear stage and no favour.'[26] Charlotte Smith's heroine Geraldine in her novel *Desmond* (1792) remarked of her husband: 'I determine never to think on any article...like Mr Verney; and therefore, as he is, he knows not why, a very furious aristocrat; that I, with no better reason, become democrat.'[27] The anonymous *A Political Dictionary for the*

---

[21] *The Times*, 20 August 1791; 18 September 1792; 23 October 1792; 4 April 1793; 23 September 1793; 25 December 1793; the Thelwall reference is in 16 May 1794 (after Thelwall's arrest); on Homer, 15 August 1798.

[22] Vicesimus Knox, *A Narrative of Transactions relative to a Sermon preached August 18, 1793* (2nd edn, London, 1793), 30.

[23] Hannah More, *Village Politics* (5th edn, London, 1793), 19.

[24] *The Star* (London), 6 April 1791.

[25] *Morning Chronicle* (London), 2 October 1792.

[26] *Argus of the Constitution* (London), 29 February 1792.

[27] Charlotte Smith, *Desmond* [1792], ed. A. Blank and J. Todd (New York, 2001), 327.

Guinea-less Pigs, or a Glossary of Emphatical Words... (*c.*1795) defined 'aristocrat' as 'lately, one who without respect to Capacity, or Probity, wou'd lodge all power, in the hands of the Nobility', whereas a Democrat 'favours that form of *Government, wherein the supreme Power is lodged with the people, who exercise the same by persons of their own Order, deputed for that purpose.*' The scurrilous writer Charles Pigott, in his *Political Dictionary,* defined an 'aristocrat' as—'a fool, or scoundrel, generally both, a monster of rapacity, and an enemy to mankind', whereas a democrat is 'one who maintains the rights of the people; an enemy to the privileged orders, and all monarchical encroachments, the advocate of peace, economy and reform'.[28]

John Gale Jones, one of the leading radicals who maintained the cause of reform after the Treason Trials of 1794, on his tour around the Thames ports of 'Rochester, Chatham, Maidstone, Gravesend etc' in 1795–6 (that is, a tour around key defensive ports against the power of France), claimed to have met a range of people whom he embraced as fellow democrats: 'I here met a most intelligent person, a farmer from Gillingham...he was a strong Democrat and, I doubt, something more than a Reformer'; he then breakfasted with a medical friend, 'I found him an intelligent man, and I need not, therefore add, a Democrat'; and his farmer friend offered to introduce him to an officer connected with the Prison ships for French captives 'who was an excellent Democrat, but who, from the nature of his situation, was prevented from avowing his principles'.[29]

One of the more charming instances occurs in 1795, when the young novelist Amelia Alderson, writing with characteristic flirtatiousness to William Godwin in the wake of his even-handed criticism of the government and the reform organizations in his *Considerations on Lord Grenville's and Mr Pitt's Bills, concerning Treasonable Practices and Unlawful Assemblies,* reported: 'I read your "considerations" with delight, but alas I fear my admiration of them has deprived me in the opinion of many of all claims to the honourable title of Democrat. I am afraid I must never show my face at certain political lectures again, unless I chuse to run the risk of being pointed out as a spy.'[30] The pleasantry relied on a pattern of reference that both valorized the term 'democrat' (Godwin did, after all defend democracy as the only legitimate form of government in his *Enquiry Concerning Political Justice*), while retaining an arch distance from it, implicitly acknowledging it as a term used for hostile description that has segued into a positive self-description for many.

Moreover, the letter suggests that in their private discourse people may have been more inclined to adopt and experiment with democratic terminology, developing a use that conveyed a distinctive sense of shared identity. John Thelwall's wife, in a letter written immediately after the Royal Proclamation Against Seditious Writings in May 1792, noted 'Fox's speech, which I suppose you have read, & which is bolder & more explicit, has put us poor democrats a little in heart again'.[31]

---

[28] *A Political Dictionary for the Guinea-less pigs, or a Glossary of Emphatical Words* (London, *c.*1795), 3; Charles Pigott, *Political Dictionary* (London, 1795), 3, 14.

[29] John Gale Jones, *Sketch of a Political Tour through...* (London, 1796), 32, 41, 42.

[30] Bodleian Library, Abinger Papers, Dep b. 210.5–6.

[31] Stella Thelwall to her brother, Jack Vellum, National Archives, London, TS 11/953.

And Kathryn Gleadle has noted references in the Gurney and Galton family archives to these families' attempts to educate their children in 'democratic manners', and her forthcoming work on family diaries suggests that the terminology was liberally distributed in the private lives and papers of those with reformist and often dissenting leanings, although, as in the case of Alderson, there may also be a certain frisson and sport associated with such use.[32]

The invective against democracy did not in any way diminish in the 1790s, although some of those so stigmatized did come to see it as a badge of honour, signifying a personal commitment to equality, mutual respect, and candour, and others used it as a form of rhetorical play to infuriate their opponents. But opponents remained powerful and vocal. In the House of Lords in July 1797, the Bishop of Rochester, speaking on a Bill relating to the constitution of Company of Surgeons, signalled the continuing negative power of the terminology: 'He thought Democracy a monster that ought to be unkenneled from its lurking places, and hunted down wherever it could be found: it was a monster which, in these times, ought to be extinguished at birth.'[33]

One important feature of the political debates of the second half of the eighteenth century is that there was no strong sense of entailment between the idea that the people were in some ways the ultimate source of legitimacy for government and demands for active participation. The people were seen by many as the basis and proper object for government, but it did not follow that they should direct it (in Joseph Priestley's *Essay on the First Principles of Government*, (1771), for example he underlines the place of the people and their interests as the true foundation for government, but does not see this as entailing that they should play an active part in government).[34] The proliferation of associations and petitioning in the 1780s[35] does suggest that there was a growing sense that legitimate political rule had to be in the interests of the people, broadly understood.[36] And these methods were seen increasingly as part of a process of holding power broadly accountable, but without accountability amounting to direction, and without it requiring extensive participation. One could toast the 'majesty of the people' (as the Duke of Norfolk did to his cost); or argue 'by what right did the glorious and immortal King William the Third, . . . come to the throne of these realms, if not by that of the sovereignty of the people'—but in neither case did this invocation of the people imply that they should be practically involved in political rule. Moreover, even if one did hold that they should have more involvement, it did not follow that one would conceive of this as advocating democracy.[37]

---

[32] Kathryn Gleadle, ' "Opinions Deliver'd in Conversation": Conversation, Politics, and Gender in the Late Eighteenth Century', in José Harris (ed.), *Civil Society in British History: Ideas, Identities, Institutions* (Oxford, 2003), 77; and (forthcoming) 'The Juvenile Enlightenment: British Children and the French Revolution'.

[33] *Parliamentary Register, 1796–1802* (18 vols, London, 1797–1802), 3: 230.

[34] Joseph Priestley, *Essay . . . in Political Writings*, ed. Peter Miller (Cambridge, 1993), 11.

[35] See Joanna Innes's chapter 9.

[36] T. M. Parssinen, 'Association, Convention and Anti-Parliament in British Radical Politics, 1771–1848', *English Historical Review*, 88 (1973), 503–44.

[37] Georgina Green, ' "The Majesty of the People" and Radical Writing in the 1790s' (unpublished D.Phil. thesis, Oxford, 2009), 18.

Paine did try to give the people a more substantial role by advocating the kind of conventionism for Britain that he saw as characterizing the American founding experience, and which in France was associated (in particular in the work of Abbé Sieyès) with the distinction between constituent and constituted power. But Paine's discussion of conventionism was divorced from his comments on representation and representative democracy. Rather than seeing them as connected, his account of political participation through conventionism recalled John Locke's idea that in certain circumstances power returned to the people. Accordingly, Paine insisted only that there 'ought to be, in the constitution of every country, a mode of referring back, on any extraordinary occasion, to the sovereign and original constituent power, which is the nation itself'.[38] This thought added fuel to the reform movement and focused attempts in 1793–4 to establish a British Convention—a project undertaken with some idea of the ultimate rights of the people and driven by a sense of the urgency of creating conditions for the establishment of a properly representative Parliament. But the move to convoke a convention was not undertaken in the name of democracy. Moreover, many who supported that movement did so less from Painite sympathies and more on the basis of a conviction in the indefeasible rights of free-born Englishmen. And while they linked those claims to rights to representation within the democratic part of the constitution, they did not represent these claims as entailing a right to a democracy. What being a 'democrat' seemed to represent for those who came to claim the title in the 1790s was support for a set of values—for some ideal of equality, for the importance of public debate and criticism and of unlimited participation in this debate, and also, perhaps, some sense that open, candid, and politically engaged conduct was desirable.

FINDING A CONTENT FOR THE WORD

During the 1790s, many reformers thus showed a willingness to take on the despised identity of 'democrat' and to turn it to positive use—spurred on by the attractions of being against aristocracy as a principle (conceived of variously in terms of arbitrary power, rapaciousness, unwarranted privilege, and idleness and corruption). The content that people were endorsing when they described themselves as 'democrats' was partly reactive—something that was the opposite of aristocracy and arbitrary rule—but also implied support for regulated and accountable power, equality before the law, respect for talents, and morality. Beyond that, there operated a profound equivocation between two strikingly dissimilar senses of the term that many radicals played on in their writing and thinking in the highly charged times of the 1790s. On the one hand, there was an already established tradition of political reform that had emerged in the 1780s, which argued for the strengthening of the popular part of the British constitution and the limitation of royal and aristocratic influence in the House of Commons. On the other hand,

---

[38] Paine, *Rights of Man*, 375.

several radicals, especially those with strong roots in the new extra-parliamentary movement for reform, at least toyed with the prospect of a constitution that would eliminate any distinct role for an aristocracy or even a monarchy. But the difficulty of breaking free of the constitutionalist idiom of Major Cartwright, with its adherence to the established ideal of the mixed constitution, is evident even in the work of John Thelwall, one of the most outspoken 'democrats' of his generation.[39] Writing in 1796 in his periodical *The Tribune*, Thelwall suggested that there were two meanings of 'democracy': 'if we look back to the real meaning of the term we shall find it to be government by the great body of the people'. But that 'describes a republic without any intermediate order, such as we now call a representative assembly...[and] a democracy, purely and simply considered, can never exist, save, only, in a small country....Nor even in such a state can this species of government exist long, without occasional tumult and disorder. Modern legislators, therefore, have invented what is called a representative democracy....' But he went on to say that strictly speaking this is no democracy at all 'if the representatives are vested with the complete and full powers of the state', since that is justly called an aristocracy (since this meant rule by the wisest few). Nonetheless, the 'Commons in parliament assembled' stands for 'the democracy of the country, who by their representatives are (ought to be I mean) represented in the commons house of parliament'. So democracy is the 'basis of our government' with the admission 'of some mixture of aristocracy in its legislature, and adopting an hereditary chief magistrate to be responsible for the execution of the laws and who is called the *King*'. According to Thelwall, we ought to call a government of this kind 'a *limited* or *restrained democracy*; the theory and the maxims of our government teaching us, that it is for the sake of the democracy (that is the great body of the people) that all our laws and institutions are made; and that all constituted functionaries are...subordinate to the grand object, the welfare of that great *body from whom all power is derived, and for whom all power should be exercised*'.[40] Thelwall also borrowed Paine's earlier definition of the term 'republic'—which Paine may have derived from James Madison: 'by republic we now mean a government so constituted and organized that the whole body of the people may convey their will to the heart and centre of government and by means of representatives and properly appointed officers, conduct the business of the country according to the general voice of the people'.[41]

Thelwall remained broadly in a mixed government tradition, perhaps for prudential reasons, but more probably because he did not find it easy to say what a pure representative democracy demanded, or to say whether what it demanded was what he and his fellow reformers should aspire to. Such ambivalence (and prudence) was widespread: even those who identified with reform and change were

[39] John Cartwright, *A Letter to the High Sheriff of the County of Lincoln, respecting the Bills of Lord Grenville and Mr Pitt* (London, 1795), 10, 98, 103, 106.
[40] John Thelwall, *The Tribune* (3 vols, London, 1795–6), 2: 210, 212, 213, 217.
[41] Thelwall, *Tribune*, 3: 196; Paine, *Rights of Man*, 230–1. Cf. Paine's 'Letter to the Abbé Sieyès', where he wrote that by republicanism 'I understand simply a government by representation—a government founded upon the principles of the Declaration of Rights', *The Complete Writings of Thomas Paine*, ed. Philip S. Foner (2 vols, Secaucus, NJ, 1945), 2: 520.

uncertain about what was possible, in principle or in practice, in terms of institutional innovation. Even the 'great democrat' Thomas Paine delivered relatively little of interest in detailed matters of institutional and constitutional design either for France or elsewhere, despite the opportunities he had to engage with such matters. His belief was that there would be lots of experiments and that many forms might be appropriate, but he retained his resistance to 'democracy' as the appropriate terminology throughout, being content with the term 'republic' as he had redefined it.

CONCLUSION

There is a clear message from this survey of usages of the term 'democracy' and 'democrat' in late eighteenth-century England. The former was largely a 'literate' term—it was a term used in the classification of states, and one that was part of a relatively sophisticated literary inheritance. It was not for the most part a term in general circulation prior to 1790, and even in the 1790s it did not quite become a popular *concept* or *principle*. It acquired currency—or 'democrat' did—in some contexts, for example among radical reformers to goad their opponents, but it lacked a determinate content. It referenced the people, and some degree of equality, and it validated the popular in some form. But, except when advanced in relatively sophisticated contexts, as in the arguments of Thelwall and Cartwright about the balance of the British constitution, it lacked precise intellectual content. In debates about the nature of legitimate government, of which there were many, the word 'democracy', and the institutional traditions associated with that word, played at best a minor role.

In the 1790s 'democrat' became a badge of identity—perhaps more widely embraced than 'Jacobin', since not so tied to French associations, but similarly rhetorical and polemical in form. It did not specify a distinct programme, set of demands, or conception of the nature of popular institutions. It was a 'fighting word' in the ideological contestation of the 1790s. Those who adopted it did so because they knew what they were against—'aristocracy'. But to be against one thing is not to be in favour of a single other thing. 'Democracy' and cognate terms stood for a number of indistinct and muddled references and meanings, and with the collapse of the reform societies in the later part of the decade, the term faded from view. When popular pressures for reform revived in the 1810s, they drew on the language of constitutionalism and reform, and rather more rarely that of Painite republicanism, for their rallying cries, rather than on the terminology of democracy.

8

The Rise of Democratic Discourse in the Reform Era: Britain in the 1830s and 1840s

Joanna Innes, Mark Philp, and Robert Saunders

'Democracy' entered the nineteenth century in Britain with a great deal of negative baggage. Some of this had long attached to it, deriving from the experience of ancient republics; other elements were more novel, stemming from the French Revolution, American politics, or Irish insurgency. Conservative Britons gave the United States credit for its stand against Revolutionary France, but continued to worry about the subgroup of Americans called 'democrats'. In the early nineteenth century, French democracy gave way to military despotism (fulfilling one story about democracy's impact), American democrats were cast as villains in the 1812–15 British-American War, and the Catholic leader Daniel O'Connell started welding the Irish 'democracy' into a disciplined political force. Though democracy did not loom so large in the British dystopian imagination as it had in the 1790s, it continued to figure as a bogey, and 'democrat' remained a favourite term of abuse. Whigs and radicals sometimes responded that this rhetoric was overplayed for partisan purposes; democracy no longer was (if it ever had been) the greatest challenge facing Britain. Yet though radicals (at least) were happy to rail against 'aristocrats', neither opposition grouping made a sustained effort to salvage 'democracy' or its cognates as terms of approbation. Those who positively endorsed these concepts were either eccentrics or operated in exceptional circumstances.[1]

Attitudes softened in the 1820s, with changes in the global context, and the falling away of British radical fervour after its bloody suppression during the Peterloo Massacre, Manchester, in August 1819.[2] More profound change was wrought by the Reform Bill debates of 1831–2, and the subsequent remodelling of the representative system. By denouncing the Whigs' plans as 'democratic' (not how the Whigs themselves presented them), the Tories forced debate about the character and merits of democracy in a contemporary British setting. This ensured that the implementation of Reform was widely seen as, for better or worse, a move

---

[1] See Troy Bickham, *The Weight of Vengeance: The United States, the British Empire and the War of 1812* (Oxford, 2012), esp. chapter 2. For Whigs and radicals, see e.g. *Morning Chronicle* (London), 11 March 1812, 22 January 1825; *Examiner*, 28 July 1822; *Political Register*, 25 June 1808.

[2] Arthur Burns and Joanna Innes, 'Introduction' to Burns and Innes (eds), *Rethinking the Age of Reform, Britain, 1780–1850* (Cambridge, 2003).

towards democracy. Although older associations continued to be exploited, and both Tory hostility to democracy and Whig ambivalence about it endured, the ground of debate shifted.

Probably the most striking effect was the emergence of the language of democracy in popular radical discourse. Radical publicists began to argue that, insofar as the Reform Acts had retained a wealth-related franchise, they had not instituted democracy—and that the post-Reform policy record showed this to be a significant failure. 'Democracy' and cognate terms wove through the speeches and writings of the Chartists as they had not through those of earlier reformers, not even during the 1790s. As older ideas about democracy in the ancient world and during the French Revolution were reworked, and new ideas accumulated about democracy and its fortunes in contemporary Europe and the Americas, use of this language gave Chartists a way of positioning themselves within a broader and still unfolding historical story.[3]

THE IMPACT OF THE REFORM BILL

'Democracy' continued throughout this period to be a generic term, denoting the people's exercise of power in public affairs; 'popular government' remained a common synonym. This broad term encompassed many variants. 'Pure democracy' connoted the direct exercise of popular power, as opposed to representative democracy. 'The democracy' meant either the people at large, as opposed to king and nobility, or the common people, the 'mobocracy'. Democracy was often represented as one element in a trinity, along with monarchy and aristocracy (the three together defining a mixed constitution), but also as the antonym of one or other of these terms: opposing positions could be described as democratic versus aristocratic, or the democratic principle contrasted with the monarchical principle. In the 1790s (as Mark Philp argues in chapter 7) a 'democrat' was not necessarily someone who favoured 'democracy': democracy had too little specific content (at least, too little specific positive content) to serve as an object of aspiration. As 'democracy' acquired more positive content during the early nineteenth century, the words became more closely aligned. By the 1840s, a British 'democrat' probably did favour 'democracy' (though might still reject 'pure democracy').

Though the range of ways in which the words were applied was broad enough to make it possible to speak positively of 'democracy' without entirely denying its negative associations, neither Whigs nor most radicals pushed the concept to the fore. Even a radical Whig like MP Samuel Whitbread took care to distance himself from 'democracy', 'a form of government which I abhor; violent, uncomfortable, ungrateful, cruel, unjust, only to be surpassed in wickedness by a savage, rooted,

---

[3] Peter Gurney presented interesting material in this connection at our conference, which was to have appeared in this volume, but he has preferred to publish in the *Journal of Modern History*. His 'The Democratic Idiom: Languages of Democracy in the Chartist Movement' should appear there in 2014. We gratefully acknowledge sight of his conference paper. We have not seen the final published version.

and confirmed despotism'.[4] It is unclear how far the term had ever taken root in popular radical circles, but in any case two leading early nineteenth-century popular leaders, William Cobbett and Henry Hunt, had been anti-Jacobins in the 1790s. Their instinct was to appropriate loyalist tropes to the radical cause: they presented radical reform as patriotic and constitutional, as well as building on an older discourse calling for the reform of corruption and abuse. Though they championed 'the cause of the people', they seem to have seen no advantage in characterizing that cause as 'democratic'.[5]

Some radical reformers endorsed the term. The constitutional philosopher Jeremy Bentham concluded that democracy was the best form of government, because best calculated to promote the greatest happiness of the greatest number. Bentham was influential among a small coterie, had an impressive range of international contacts and links with both Whigs and popular radicals, but those who admired him rarely shared his love of neologisms. Those who did were among the more intellectual, and less immediately influential of his followers (though they gained influence in the world of letters during the 1820s).[6] The appearance of a periodical named *The Democratic Recorder* in 1819 looks like a response to exceptional circumstances. Thomas Dolby, its publisher, was at this time publisher to both Cobbett and Hunt, neither of whom (as we have noted) favoured this vocabulary. But in 1819, after a long series of pro-reform petitions had failed to make a mark, frustrated radicals engaged in ever more dramatic gestures of defiance. This periodical's title probably aimed to conjure with Tory fears. Its masthead asked rhetorically 'Are the Masters of Kings! The Creators of Kings!! The Transporters of Kings!!! The Executors of Kings!!!! to submit to a vile Faction?'[7] Clearly this was not meant to ingratiate.

In 1831 the new, predominantly Whig ministry—the first since 1806–7—introduced a Reform Bill for England and Wales, followed by analogous bills for Scotland and Ireland. These proposed more swingeing changes than had been expected—disfranchising many small boroughs and enfranchising numerous large towns; and standardizing voting qualifications across towns in ways that were predicted to double the English electorate (it was on England that most debate focused).[8] The Whigs did not present their measures as democratizing in intent, but their critics did, developing several linked charges. The measures would radically expand the power of the House of Commons (the democratic element within the constitution), at the expense

---

[4] Hansard 1st ser., 13: 705 (Commons, 17 March 1809).

[5] James Vernon (ed.), *Re-reading the Constitution: New Narratives in the Political History of England's Long Nineteenth Century* (Cambridge, 1996). Few reform petitions used 'democratic' terminology, though some did: the *Commons Journals* give two instances from 1817, one each from 1821 and 1822; two instances from 1831 both opposed reform: *CJ* 72: 169, 424; 76: 268; 77: 29; 86: 310, 424.

[6] Philip Schofield, *Utility and Democracy: The Political Thought of Jeremy Bentham* (Oxford, 2006).

[7] John Belchem, *'Orator' Hunt: Henry Hunt and English Working-Class Radicalism* (Oxford, 1985), 81, 122, 137, 140–1, 161.

[8] Michael Brock, *The Great Reform Act* (London, 1973); Philip Salmon, 'The English Reform Legislation', in D. R. Fisher (ed.), *The History of Parliament: the House of Commons 1820–1832* (7 vols, Oxford, 2009), also on the History of Parliament website at http://www.historyofparliamentonline.org/volume/1820–1832/survey/ix-english-reform-legislation.

of king and Lords; they would make the House of Commons over-dependent on 'the democracy', that is, to dictation from without; and they would set in train a 'democratic revolution', beginning a process of change which would escape Whig control, just as reform had escaped control in France after 1789. As in France, the British democratic revolution would (it was predicted) bring down king, nobility, and Church, and probably also entail assaults on property.[9]

Ministerial Whigs followed their established line, not endorsing democracy, but arguing that it was not as black as it was painted, and even had some positive features. Lord John Russell, who introduced the English bill, for example warned that 'there was a fallacy in the word democratic, which it seemed was made to imply an association of democrats, whose wish was, to overturn the House of Lords and the Crown. He [Russell] denied altogether that the measure would have the effect of rendering that House a democratic assemblage, *in that sense of the word* [our emphasis].' Supporters of the bill outside the House—such as those assembled in political unions—also did not push 'democracy' to the fore, though they gave it the occasional sympathetic mention. Mainly they talked about the oppressiveness of 'boroughmongers', and the need to reclaim rights. At a meeting of Essex Reform Committees in the aftermath of victory, the chairman assured his audience: 'Democracy cannot exist in this country...It is the mere phantom of the Anti-Reformers' brains.' He equated democracy with 'perfect equalisation...no division of property; it means that no man shall be able to command his fellow men by superiority of intellect or fortune'.[10]

Phantom of the brain or not, throughout the reform debates, anti-reformers in Parliament and the press insisted that what was at issue was 'democracy'. Their insistence forced the term forwards; it loomed much larger in the closing than it had in the opening stages of debate.[11] Traditional arguments for and against democracy were in this context thrashed out, and—more interestingly—generalities were given contemporary content. Reformers claimed that an unrepresentative oligarchy had dragged Britain into a series of unnecessary, bloody, and expensive wars, which had bequeathed a crippling load of debt. A system more responsive to the will of the people would, they alleged, avoid war. This was roundly challenged: 'Is all history then a fable?' Democracies, on the contrary, were notoriously warlike—and the people, far from lamenting Britain's part in the war against Revolutionary France, had heartily supported it.[12] Were democracies unstable? American experience was adduced to the contrary. Recently, numerous American states had revised their constitutions, but the states whose constitutions had been most democratic (such as Connecticut) had not needed to change.[13] Would a shift towards democ-

---

[9] Speakers reported in Hansard to this effect include party leaders the Duke of Wellington and Sir Robert Peel; the Tory man of business John Wilson Croker; the moderate Earl of Harrowby, the ultra Sir Robert Inglis; the populist Michael Sadler; and the Carlist-sympathizer Viscount Porchester.

[10] Hansard 2nd ser., 3: 310; 7: 462 (Commons, 9 March, 21 September 1831); Nancy LoPatin, *Political Unions, Popular Politics and the Great Reform Act of 1832* (Basingstoke, 1999); *Morning Chronicle* (London), 10 October 1832.

[11] It was especially prominent in March–April 1832.

[12] Hansard 2nd ser., 7: 429 (Lord Althorp, Commons, 21 September 1831), 1154–5 (Earl of Harrowby, Lords, 4 October 1831).

[13] Hansard 2nd ser., 7: 287 (Col Maberley, Commons, 20 September 1831).

racy inevitably lead to the destruction of monarchy and confiscation of property? Whig spokesmen argued that nothing about the current state of society supported that claim, whatever might have been the case in other places and at other times (and whatever, in the worst scenario, might come to pass in Britain if king and Lords proved entirely insensitive to public opinion).[14]

When Tories fantasized about the democratic implications of reform, what worried them most concretely was not that the people at large might acquire more power, but rather that power might accrue to a particular subset of the people: shopkeepers and tradesmen in large towns, a category of person the Reform Bills did indeed aim to enfranchise in greater numbers, and to whom the reconstruction of constituencies did indeed promise to give more power. Tories may genuinely have believed that such men had it in them to metamorphose into the sans-culottes of their nightmares. They did have grounds for believing that some were abrasive, ungenteel in their manners, happy to mock established institutions, and especially the Church of England's privileges. Tory complaints shifted uneasily between predictions of apocalypse and worries that MPs serving for this kind of constituency might lower the tone of the House.[15] To balance such voters, they argued, it was important to preserve the rights of freemen, freeholders and the like, in boroughs where they had traditionally voted. Moreover, they sought to extend the county vote to one set of non-property owner—tenants with holdings worth £50 per annum or more, however insecure their tenure. Whigs asked whether these were not odd demands from sworn foes of democracy.[16] The Tory impulse was in part opportunistic: they hoped to win the support of these categories of voter, not least by claiming to have secured them their votes. But they also developed a principled position, based on a series of connected arguments. First, they claimed that a uniform borough franchise would privilege certain sections of the community. Second, they alleged that these voters were 'democratic' in outlook: hostile to established institutions and levelling by instinct. A larger electorate, though poorer, might be more 'aristocratic' in its preferences. The Democracy—it became clear—connoted to them not just 'the common people', but (most strongly) a subset of the people with particularly alarming attitudes. In the last analysis, if the weight of the putatively democratically inclined could be curbed, Tories were grudgingly willing to accept change.[17]

After long and fierce debate, and an unnerving display of brinkmanship by the House of Lords, all three Reform Bills were carried—considerably amended, but not so as to reduce the scale of popular enfranchisement. Indeed, a wider range of

---

[14] Hansard 2nd ser., 2: 1296–7 (Sir John Cam Hobhouse, Commons, 3 March 1831); 3: 744 (Thomas Wyse, Commons, 2 March 1831).

[15] e.g. Hansard 2nd ser., 5: 689 (Sir Charles Wetherell, Commons, 3 August 1831); 6: 564 (Edward Sugden, Commons, 24 August 1831); 13: 20 (Lord Wharncliffe, Lords, 24 May 1832). For this bogey made flesh, see James Williamson Brook, *The Democrats of Marylebone* (London, 1839).

[16] Hansard 2nd ser., 6: 557 (Sjt. Wilde, Commons, 24 August 1831); 12: 731–2 (Earl Grey, Lords, 7 May 1832).

[17] Hansard 2nd ser., 12: 727–31 (Lord Ellenborough, Lords, 7 May 1832). Freemen were subsequently encouraged to join 'Operative Conservative Association'. Tenants-at-will proved unexpectedly independent, helping to make post-Reform rural electorates too 'democratical' for some tastes.

people ultimately retained or gained the vote than had initially been proposed, though the amended constituency scheme shifted less power to new voters than had the original proposal. The Tories' line of attack helped ensure that what ensued was widely represented as, for better or worse, a shift towards democracy. Now the challenge of governing this new polity had to be faced. This gave new salience to accounts of democracy elsewhere: Tories were especially drawn to Fisher Ames' jaundiced account of democracy in America; Whigs and intellectual radicals, to Alexis de Tocqueville's more nuanced reflections.[18]

Among Tory responses to this challenge, Benjamin Disraeli's was exceptional. At this time a foppish and eccentric young man, still striving for a parliamentary seat, Disraeli was not yet identifiable as a prime minister in the making. His view at this juncture was that the Tories' best way forwards lay in an anti-Whig alliance with radicals. To this end, he propagated a Tory form of democratic ideology, which he aired in the four urban constituencies that he contested during the early 1830s. As between aristocratic and democratic principles, he proclaimed, 'I feel it absolutely necessary to advance to the new or democratic principle.' By this he meant, first, allowing individuals to advance on merit. He also associated democracy with 'national' and 'popular' institutions. The Church of England, the monarchy, and the House of Lords were all in this sense 'democratic', because they acted on behalf of the people and enjoyed their support. 'The Tory party,' Disraeli insisted, 'is the really democratic party in England'—while the established Church, because par excellence an institution open to talent, was 'the most democratic institution in the country... [though] this is the institution the Radicals are ever menacing and decrying.'[19]

Most Tories responded differently. Though they strove to master the technical and other requirements of the new political game, most did not abandon their rhetorically anti-democratic stance. On the contrary, they clearly calculated that a refurbished anti-democratic discourse retained potential. It could provide tropes around which to rally local social leaders; it accordingly figured prominently in after-dinner speeches at meetings of new county Conservative Associations.[20] Moreover the rhetoric could be deployed more widely—so long as it was made clear that attacks on 'democracy' were not attacks on the people as such, but only particularly obnoxious subsets of people. Irish Catholics—the Irish 'democracy'—were demonized in this context. Growing numbers of Irish immigrants to Britain had thrown up adherents of radical politics; the Whigs had

---

[18] For Tocqueville's reception, see Synergies, n.31; [Fisher Ames], *The Influence of Democracy on Liberty, Property and the Happiness of Society Considered* (London, 1835), sympathetically reviewed in the Tory *Quarterly Review*, 58 (1835), 548–73.

[19] Jens Andreas Christophersen, *The Meaning of 'Democracy' as Used in European Ideologies from the French to the Russian Revolution: An Historical Study in Political Language* (Oslo, 1966), 56–60; Robert Saunders, *Democracy and the Vote in British Politics, 1848–1867: The Making of the Second Reform Act* (Farnham, 2011), 68–73.

[20] Philip Salmon, *Electoral Reform at Work: Local Politics and National Parties, 1832–1841* (Woodbridge, 2002); e.g. dinners in North Staffordshire, South Lincolnshire, and Norwich, reported in the *Morning Post* on 6, 12, and 14 August 1831. Also the satirical account of a dinner in Lancashire in the *Examiner*, 7 September 1834.

shown themselves ready to reform the Irish established Church, and, especially after 1835, looked to the support of the Irish MP Daniel O'Connell and his following to sustain themselves in Parliament. Given this, there was some basis for equating democracy with Popery. Accordingly (to give one example), voters in Shrewsbury during the election of 1837 were urged to combat 'the Demon of Democracy and Papal Tyranny'.[21]

Whig ministers continued to face Tory charges that they were too democratic, and had to defend further reform measures (notably, the Municipal Corporations Act) from that charge. But from 1835 they additionally found themselves assailed by an enlarged parliamentary Radical group for being insufficiently democratic. During the reform debates, Daniel O'Connell had been the Commons' most forthright proponent of democracy; from mid-decade, his advocacy was echoed by British Radical MPs John Roebuck, Thomas Wakley, and Thomas Slingsby Duncombe. Whigs, who had never warmly embraced the democratic cause, thenceforth increasingly surrendered this rhetoric to radicals in and out of Parliament, though this left them vulnerable to the Tory charge that they had initiated the slide to democracy and were now—as predicted—powerless to arrest it.[22]

A few radicals outside Parliament were quick to challenge the Whig version of reform. Among them, the cheap-print publisher Henry Hetherington and his editors Thomas Mayhew and Bronterre O'Brien sustained the case post-Reform in a new periodical, *The Poor Man's Guardian* (sold cheaply and semi-clandestinely, because Hetherington refused in principle to pay stamp duties). The periodical's title indicated its intent: to guard poor men against Whig deception. It maintained that Whigs were no democrats. Early issues emphasized (with supporting quotations) that, though the Whig press had suggested otherwise, Whigs in Parliament had explicitly rejected 'democracy' and indeed any substantive extension to the power of the people at large. Yet, the *PMG* argued, democracy was a good thing; the people should want it. O'Brien combined these urgings with an attempt to rehabilitate the 'democratic' phase of the French Revolution (previously excoriated as an era of Terror): he praised Maximilien Robespierre's exalted character, and celebrated Babeuf's conspiracy for equality.[23] In subsequent years, as popular discontent with Reform policies grew (in response, above all, to the 1834 Poor Law Amendment Act), and as more came over to the view that

---

[21] *Remarks on the Anti-Protestant and Democratic Tendency of the Reform Bill* (Bristol, 1831); for Shrewsbury, John A. Phillips, *The Great Reform Bill in the Boroughs: English Electoral Behaviour, 1818–1841* (Oxford, 1992), 153.

[22] Hansard 2nd ser., 22: 720 (Daniel O'Connell, Commons, 18 February 1830); 30: 1,164 (John Roebuck, Commons, 31 August 1835); 36: 28–39 (John Roebuck, Commons, 31 January 1837); 36: 429–30 (Thomas Wakley, Commons, 10 February 1837).

[23] Patricia Hollis, *The Pauper Press: A Study in Working-Class Radicalism of the 1830s* (Oxford, 1970), for the *Poor Man's Guardian* and its milieu. For the Reform Bill (which did not much interest Hollis), *Poor Man's Guardian*, 3 October, 15 December 1831; editorial comment 27 October 1832. For French Revolutionary democracy, e.g. 3 November, 22 December 1832, 27 April 1833; *Buonarroti's History of Babeuf's Conspiracy for Equality* ed. and trans. [James] Bronterre O'Brien (London, 1836).

Reform had been an act of class treachery, 'democracy' was for the first time widely endorsed as an appropriate target for popular aspiration.

CHARTISM

From 1837 to 1848 popular radicalism was dominated by the campaign for 'the People's Charter': a programme of reforms including universal male suffrage, secret voting, and equal electoral districts. The language of democracy was central to the utterances of Chartists. Some among them had employed it earlier—including, as we have just seen, John Roebuck, a follower of Bentham and friend of John Stuart Mill who helped devise the Charter. In his *Pamphlets for the People* (1835), Roebuck stated that: 'if good government is to be hoped for on earth, it must be the off-spring of democracy . . .' This followed from the Whigs' evident shortcomings: 'We have tried long enough the blessings of an aristocracy. We have seen that good government is wholly incompatible with aristocratic rule. We are driven to democracy as an experiment, whether we will or not.'[24] George Julian Harney, once Hetherington's shop-boy, like O'Brien a supporter of the French democratic revolution, revered Jean-Paul Marat and borrowed his *nom de plume*, 'L'ami du peuple'.[25] Harney founded the East London Democratic Association in 1837 (subsequently the London Democratic Association)—whose title was echoed by the Marylebone Democratic Association, the London Female Democratic Association (both 1839), and by societies in Leeds, Nottingham, Norwich, and parts of Scotland. Harney became an active Chartist, and as such was associated with the *London Democrat* (1839) and *The Democratic Review of British and Foreign Politics, History, and Literature* (1849).

'Democratic' was sometimes used to signal difference from Owenite organizations, which invested less hope in politics, and foregrounded their members' identity as working men, but the need to differentiate quickly faded. Robert Owen's opposition waned, many of his followers and sympathizers developed links with Chartism, and Chartist evocations of 'democracy' blurred in focus.[26] Enthusiasm for democracy became general, as the Chartist press made clear: when the radical orator Henry Vincent addressed a meeting in White Conduit House in 1839, 'as "citizens of the British democracy"', the meeting gave 'three tremendous cheers'.[27]

The language of democracy was ubiquitous in the *Northern Star*, established at the end of 1837. The organ of the Irish-born Feargus O'Connor, this was the best-selling, longest-enduring Chartist paper. Though it represented above all O'Connor's

---

[24] John Roebuck, *Pamphlets for the People* (London, 1835), 1: 6–8.
[25] A. R. Schoyen, *The Chartist Challenge: A Portrait of George Julian Harney* (London, 1958).
[26] Jennifer Bennett, 'The London Democratic Association', in James Epstein and Dorothy Thompson, *The Chartist Experience* (London, 1982), 111. For Owen and Chartism, see Gregory Claeys, *Citizens and Saints: Politics and Anti-Politics in Early British Socialism* (Cambridge, 1989), 91–3, 239–50.
[27] *The Chartist* (London), 16 February 1839.

version of Chartism, it reported a wide range of Chartist events, and thus provides insight into the broader movement. A word search finds about fifty references per year to both 'democracy' and 'democratic' in the first three years of the paper, rising to 300–400 for 'democracy' and over 700 for 'democratic' in 1841 and 1842, then to between 150 and 600 until its end in June 1852. The peaks were 1841–2, 1847, and 1849–50 (a pattern paralleled by the less common 'democrat'). Similar patterns obtained for 'republican', 'sovereignty', and 'sovereignty of the people'. Though uses varied, there were common tropes: there was frequent reference to 'the coming triumph of democracy' (6 January 1838), or 'the triumph of democracy...hastening forward' (7 July 1838); it was said that 'the standard of Democracy has been unfurled' (18 May 1839). Other Chartist papers used similar phrases—the *Chartist Circular* referred to 'the steady and gigantic strides of Democracy' (5 December 1840), and claimed that 'democracy though slow in its progress, is sure, and...must ultimately triumph'. *The Chartist* perceived in a meeting 'the deep breathing of that strong democracy' (16 February 1839). Democracy was invoked across a range of entries: editorials, reports of speeches, and in correspondence to the press—not least in the way that people signed off their letters: 'In the fraternity of Democracy' (12 October 1839); 'Yours in democracy' (16 November 1839); 'In the cause of democracy and justice' (2 May 1840); 'Yours in the cause of Democracy' (23 May 1840).

The words opened up a larger realm of discourse. 'The democracy' meant the people—above all the right of the people as a whole to have a say in their government. It was frequently stated that 'The people are the source of all power'[28]; 'By democracy you will understand the right of every society to choose its own governors'.[29] Aristocracy and democracy were seen as clashing because one represented a small, self-serving group, the other the people as a whole. Democracy was linked with the sovereign power of the people, as when the prospect was invoked of 'the sovereignty of the people [being] established by the victorious triumph of the great principles of democracy'.[30] Chartists William Lovett and John Collins, writing from Warwick Gaol in 1840, acknowledged criticisms of democracy arising from the experience of the ancient world, but countered by noting the 'peculiar feature of modern democracy...*popular representation*. By this great improvement in legislation numerous evils which were felt in ancient democracies are avoided; for while every man can exercise influence over his representative, to effect his political desires, the passions and the prejudices of the multitude are kept back from the deliberations of legislation, or the decisions of justice.'[31] Harney drew together the ideas of equality, self-government, and popular sovereignty in speaking to an audience in Bedlington, Northumberland: 'The only form of freedom is that of democracy. In a democracy the community is its

---

[28] *Northern Star* (Leeds), 15 February 1840 [henceforth *NS*]; but also variants, including most frequently 'the people the source of all legitimate power' or 'the legitimate source of all power' in over one hundred issues of the *NS*.

[29] *Chartist Circular* (Glasgow), 4 September 1841.

[30] *NS*, 21 July 1838; 31 March 1838.

[31] William Lovett and John Collins, *Chartism: A New Organisation of the People...* (1840), in G. Claeys (ed.), *The Chartist Movement in Britain* (London, 2001), 214.

own master. The will of the people is the sovereign power. In this form alone is truly recognised the sovereignty of the people. Democracy is the universal diffusion of power—a system that recognises the political equality of men, and a right to every man to a participation in the Government of his country.'[32]

The connection between modern democracy and suffrage was axiomatic; for Chartists, 'the temple of Democracy [was] based on Universal Suffrage'.[33] The other five principles of the Charter—annual Parliaments, equal representation, secret ballot, no property qualification, and payment for representatives—were seen not as defining components of democracy but rather as the means for realizing democracy. Democracy in turn was strongly associated with equality. The London Democratic Association's first objective was to avail itself 'of every opportunity in the progress of society, for practically establishing the principles of Social, Political and Universal Equality'.[34] Universal suffrage was 'democratic' not only because it empowered the people but also because it distributed political power equally.[35] 'Democracy is... giving to *all* equal political privileges, and equal guarantees for the enjoyment of social happiness.'[36] Political equality was seen as demanding legal equality and cultural, social, and educational equality. Equality functioned as a fundamental premise, deriving from God having made men equal, or from 'the first great principle of nature', the equality of men.[37]

Equality was represented as a force at work in modern history. Chartists identified the working 'throughout society of a mighty though invisible agent... that is the fruit of knowledge—opening the eyes of the masses... of their being entitled to equal rights as men and equal rights as citizens. The strife that is now going on is between the new and the old... between mind on the one hand and wealth and hereditary privilege on the other.'[38] Equality functioned as both premise and prediction: as society made progress, equality would increase, because privilege and monopoly would be eradicated, and because people would be better educated and more enlightened. Social and economic equality were identified both as conditions for political democracy and as obtainable only through it: 'None could value education more than we do.... you may educate [the people] in the exercise and enjoyment of manhood's highest attribute, perfect freedom of thought, speech, and of action... [but this] *can only be attained where the people are politically equal.*' The end, then, was 'an enlightened democracy—a system of Government according to which, every member of society shall be considered a man, and nothing more'.[39]

The sources for this positive affirmation of democracy were sometimes in tension. Harney and O'Brien, both admirers of the French republic of 1793, advocated 'physical force' to achieve reform in the 1830s, and were denounced by some for doing so.[40] Under their influence, the *Poor Man's Guardian* dismissed Paine, seeing him as a supporter of the French Constitution of 1791 and an enemy to its

[32] *NS*, 6 July 1839.   [33] *NS*, 3 March 1838; 19 May 1838.   [34] *NS*, 21 July 1838.

[35] John Alfred Langford, *English Democracy: Its History and Principles* (London, 1853).

[36] *NS*, 27 April 1844.   [37] *NS*, 17 March 1838; 8 July 1843; 7 April 1838.

[38] *NS*, 5 October 1839.   [39] *NS*, 11 July 1846; *Chartist Circular* (Glasgow), 19.12.40.

[40] *Chartist* (London),16 March 1839.

democratic successor of 1793.[41] Other sections of the movement took a different line. When Feargus O'Connor called upon the people 'to rally round the standard of democracy in the NATIONAL ASSOCIATION', he quoted Paine's endorsement of the Marquis of Lafayette's adage: 'FOR A NATION TO BE FREE IT IS SUFFICIENT THAT SHE WILLS IT' (1 August 1840).[42] Harney clearly recognized the value of common reference points and therefore did not demur when his own East London Democratic Association endorsed Paine's principles, even establishing its annual meeting on his birthday. The centenary of Paine's birth was indeed widely celebrated and his works were republished and circulated[43]—with the *Dissertation on First Principles of Government* (1795), in which the case for manhood suffrage was most clearly articulated, playing a prominent role.[44] The Paine that Chartists joined in celebrating stood for equal rights and popular sovereignty: for the principle that the people could and should govern themselves through representatives, elected on the basis of universal suffrage and then held to account.

'Republicanism' was less axiomatic. In 1838 Bronterre O'Brien sought to set aside the question of a Republic: 'any attempts to mix up the question of a *Republic* (than which nothing can be more vague), with that of *Universal Suffrage* (which is a well-understood thing,) can have no other effect than to sow division in our ranks and to dissolve our organisation'.[45] Nonetheless, in several debates reference was made to the Charter 'restoring republicanism'.[46] A leader in the *Northern Star* stated that:

It cannot be denied that *there is a strong tendency towards republicanism throughout Europe and America*; the reverential awe once felt for monarchical rule is gradually falling away; the connection between the aristocracy and the people every day becomes weaker and weaker; the democracy in every civilised country is gaining a giant's strength; it has rapidly progressed in intellectual, moral, social and political power, while the laws, the maxims of rulers, and the minds of the titled orders, have not kept pace with this advancement.

Yet the *Star* was not anti-monarchical: 'It is not of the monarch that we complain.... It is of the substitution of an oligarchy for the nation ...'[47] The monarchy was described as a relatively inexpensive comet, compared to the luxurious trail of oligarchy that attended it and corrupted it. Nonetheless O'Connor remained

---

[41] *Poor Man's Guardian* (London), 8 December 1832; 14 February 1835.

[42] Thomas Paine, *Rights of Man, Common Sense*, ed. Mark Philp (Oxford, 1995), 172; W. J. Linton, *James Watson: A Memoir* (Manchester, 1879) 7, 11, 12, 25; *NS*, 15 May 1847: 'Westminster Debating Society'.

[43] Schoyen, *The Chartist Challenge*, 14. For dinners, toasts, and recommendations of his works in 1837 alone: *Champion and Weekly Herald* (London), 5 February 1837; *London Dispatch and People's Political and Social Reformer*, 5 February, 12 February, 20 February, 26 March, 9 April, 30 April, 12 November 1837; *Bradford Observer*, 19 January 1837; *Morning Post* (London), 21 February 1837.

[44] 'Dr Campbell against the Chartists', *NS*, 12 February 1848, in which Paine's *Rights of Man* is identified as core to the movement, and *Age of Reason* is rejected; *Chartist Circular* (Glasgow), 28 September 1839.

[45] *NS*, 1 September 1838.

[46] *NS*, 6 July 1839, 19 September 1840. The term was much more widely used in *The Chartist Circular* (Glasgow), e.g. 28 December 1839 *et seq.* for 'Republican Aphorisms'.

[47] *NS*, 2 January 1841.

sceptical about republicanism: 'a mere talisman to rouse the mind to action for a change, leaving to the successful party the task of saying what the change should be'.[48]

From the 1830s, and still more during the 1840s, 'democrat' emerged as a pan-European category of identity. Self-proclaimed democrats across Europe expected to be able to establish solidarity with democrats elsewhere. British radicals had expressed solidarity with their European counterparts in the Restoration era; Chartists continued to take an interest in continental developments during the more liberal 1830s and 1840s, aligning themselves with emergent 'democrats'. Most closely tied to the Chartists were the 'Fraternal Democrats', who emerged in 1845 under Harney's leadership, and who sought to build 'an assemblage for useful information' with émigré reformers in the capital.[49] As a result of European influence both republicanism and social democracy attracted more notice from 1848. In C. G. Harding's *The Republican* (to which Giuseppe Mazzini's friend, the poet and engraver, William Linton, contributed extensively) republicanism and democracy were effectively equated: 'Our definition of Republicanism is simply this, self-government; the right of every individual to govern himself, either in person or by representation.'[50] Harney's *Democratic Review* enlisted contributions from Mazzini, 'Charles Marx', and Louis Blanc. Frederick Engels published with him, as did Helen Macfarlane, an admirer of Marx and Engels and translator of their *Communist Manifesto* (1848), which was serialised in Harney's *Red Republican* in 1850.[51] This new title indexed both revolutionary activity on the continent and Harney's now solid conviction (which he persuaded the National Charter Association to endorse) that democratic rights and social rights were indissoluble objectives. 'Henceforth Chartism is *Démocratique et Sociale*.'[52] Between 1848 and 1850 the colour of the Chartist flag changed both literally and metaphorically from green to red.[53]

If democracy was the goal, did the means to that goal also need to be democratic? And what might that entail? Any form of mobilization of the people could loosely be characterized as 'democratic', an insurrection as much as a public meeting or a structured organization. The historian Malcolm Chase says of the 1838 Chartist Convention that 'there was very little critical comment on matters of internal governance'.[54] Yet a critical discourse was slowly emerging, in which 'democratic principles' were identified and accorded weight, courses of action being approved, for example, when they did not entail 'any departure from democratic principles'. Inconsistencies between people's behaviour and principles were sometimes identified—as in the case of Robert Philp in Bath,

---

[48] *NS*, 19 October 1844.

[49] Malcolm Chase, *Chartism: A New History* (Manchester, 2007), 286–7; Schoyen, *Chartist Challenge*, 136–40.

[50] *The Republican: A Magazine* (London), November 1848, 141–2.

[51] Schoyen, *Chartist Challenge*, 203–4. For Mazzini, see Salvadori Mastellone, 'Mazzini's International League and the Politics of the London Democratic Manifestos 1837–1850', in C. A. Bayly and Eugenio F. Biagini, *Giuseppe Mazzini and the Globalisation of Democratic Nationalism 1830–1920* (Oxford, 2008), and *La Nascita della Democrazia in Europa* (Florence, 2009).

[52] Schoyen, *Chartist Challenge*, 209, citing Harney and paraphrasing *The Times*, 22 April 1851.

[53] Schoyen, *Chartist Challenge*, 198.   [54] Chase, *Chartism*, 35–6.

who 'claims independence of thought *and of action*', while denying to others a like claim. 'Pretty consistent in an advocate of democratic principles!'[55]

'Democratic Organisation', when invoked by 'Howard Morton' (possibly a pseudonym for Helen Macfarlane), conveyed 'the fusion of all the different sections of Social Reformers . . . into *one whole*': it referenced personnel, not practice.[56] By contrast, Lovett's London Working Men's Association aimed to be 'as democratic in its workings as the principles of it are in their nature'. In fact, it has been argued, local organizations of Chartists did not follow the most accountable models available—trade unions and friendly societies, which held frequent general meetings—but were more like parish vestries, with quarterly meetings operating as a final source of authority, but meeting chiefly to elect an executive committee to conduct business, a practice that inevitably favoured those with more personal independence.[57] It proved difficult to translate democratic local practice into a national form, especially since organizational options were also constrained by the Corresponding Societies Act (1799), the Seditious Meetings Act (1817), and the 'Gagging Act' (1848).[58] We should perhaps see the new procedural applications of democratic terminology as reflecting difficulties born of this context.

Critical terms included 'anti-democratic' and, a newer coinage, 'undemocratic'. The terms were not clearly distinguished. Both were used to refer to policies that rode roughshod over the people, as in the case of the 'abhorrent, most undemocratic, most despotic' New Poor Law, or to problematic conduct, such as the 'undemocratic' behaviour of 'the Sturge party' who proposed their own bill for reform, rather than listening to proposals from the Chartist Convention.[59] Both terms were turned against the Executive Committees of the local branches, and applied at times to the National Convention—because of the 'self-constituted' character of the executive of the Chartist Association or to challenge the consistency of Chartist decisions with Chartist organizational principles.[60] They were also applied to refer to obstructionism or physical force interruptions of Chartist or other meetings.[61]

The mainstream press frequently wrote of democratic principles or forces operating on a global scale, and Chartists equally saw democracy at work in many contexts; their press referred to both ancient and modern examples, using them to

[55] *NS*, 26 March 1842. Other instances include: one in relation to Sunderland, *NS*, 4 February 1843; with respect to 'Mr Cooper's Despotism', *NS*, 17 January 1845; and to the selling on of plots of land under the land scheme, *NS*, 15 May 1847.

[56] Schoyen, *Chartist Challenge*, 204.

[57] Eileen Yeo, 'Some Practices and Problems of Chartist Democracy', in Epstein and Thompson, *Chartist Experience*, 347, 353–4. As Yeo points out, the inclusion of women in the movement, including their holding office, was seen by many as integral to its democratic character.

[58] Yeo, 'Some Practices and Problems', 360.

[59] *The London Dispatch and People's Political and Social Reformer*, 25 June 1837. For Sturge as 'anti-democratic', *NS*, 29 October 1842.

[60] 'Anti-democratic' in *Morning Chronicle* (London), 16 July 1837 and 17 July 1840; *The Examiner* (London), 29 September 1839, 8 January 1840; *NS*, 6 August 1842, *et seq*. 'Undemocratic' in *NS*, 6, 13, 20 December 1851; *Lloyds Weekly London Newspaper*, 22 December 1844. The term was not commonplace in newspapers until the 1890s.

[61] *NS*, 8 February 1845; *Lloyds Weekly London Newspaper*, 9 February 1845.

explore the strengths and weaknesses of past and present institutions. Athens, for example, exemplified the collective virtue of the people, the dangers of a 'decay of democratic energy' and of demagogues, and the importance of honouring public benefactors.[62] 'Ancient Rome, its democracy and public virtues, with their decay and corruption', the 'corrupt laws of rotting Rome', the Roman principle that military service freed a man, examples of Roman tyranny, and the Gracchi and their commitment to the people's right to land—all stimulated comment and reflection.[63] The French Republic of 1792, and the institutions of the United States, Switzerland, and Norway (under its 1814 Constitution) were cited as examples of modern democratic practice.[64] The image of America, at one stage a beacon for British radicals and reformers, was, however, increasingly tarnished. The persistence of slavery, American 'lust for military rapine', their violent politics, lack of sympathy for the struggles of their English working-class brethren, and tolerance of 'banker-craft, lawyer-craft, and the thousand and one schemes of profit-craft', allowing wealth to be concentrated in a few hands, were all denounced.[65] As early as 1834, the *Poor Man's Guardian* denounced America as an exploitative economic order because of 'the progress of middle-class despotism'.[66] Some Chartists, though, attributed American defects to an insufficiency of democracy. 'In the Southern States,' Harney insisted, 'Democracy does not exist.'[67]

The forces of 'democracy' were often identified, by both friends and critics, as vigorously in play in Ireland in this period. Chartists were, however, ambivalent about O'Connell's political tactics which, they suggested, had allowed the Whigs to create dissension 'between the English and the Irish democracy'.[68] O'Connell's alliance with the Whigs in 1835 earned him widespread distrust; his relationship with the Irish-born British Chartist O'Connor was never better than strained. Chartists and O'Connellite Repealers (advocates of the repeal of the Act of Union) each had doubts about the other's programme, although there was more sympathy for and welcome given to 'Irish democrats' from 1848, following O'Connell's death and the onset of the Irish famine.[69]

During the mid-twentieth century, historians characteristically represented Chartism as weakened by internal divisions. More recently, such divisions have been downplayed. All organizations experience internal division; more striking is the extent to which Chartists managed to maintain unity, despite their many differences over both tactics and the form a good society should take. Chartist writing equally

---

[62] *Chartist Circular* (Glasgow), 18 January 1840; 29 August 1840; 17 July 1841; 12 December 1840.
[63] *Chartist* (London), 23 February 1839; *NS*, 28 November 1840; 27 November 1841; 19 July 1845; 6 July 1844.
[64] *NS*, 22 September 1838.
[65] 20 April 1844; see also 22 June 1844, 6 July 1844.
[66] *Poor Man's Guardian* (London), 1 November 1834; Gregory Claeys, 'The Example of America a Warning to England? The Transformation of America in British Radicalism and Socialism, 1790–1850', in Ian Dyck and Malcolm Chase (eds), *Living and Learning: Essays in Honour of J. F. C. Harrison* (Aldershot, 1996), 66–80.
[67] *NS*, 27 April 1844.
[68] *NS*, 10 February 1848.
[69] Dorothy Thompson, 'Ireland and the Irish in English Radicalism', in Epstein and Thompson, *Chartist Experience*, 146; *NS*, 13 April 1850.

displays a high degree of consensus in identifying democracy as a point of reference, and about its chief components: the ineluctable rise of the people and the role they could now properly claim in controlling government and legislation.

The Chartists' adoption of the language of democracy had little impact on elite political usage, other than to fix the term more firmly in the lexicon of British politics, and to strengthen the notion that the natural target of democratic aspiration was the franchise. For although Chartism was in many ways an innovative political movement—a multifaceted political and social experiment—this was not how most propertied and educated contemporaries saw it. To them it crystallized and sharpened long-standing ideas about how democracy was likely to present itself. Chartism was not the democracy of the elites' worst nightmares, but it met standard, negative expectations of democracy nonetheless: being vulgar, tumultuous, whipped on by demagogues, and despotic in its pretensions. In elite circles, even those who saw some seeds of hope in Chartism tended to think that it demonstrated how much the people still needed to improve, and how imperative it was that they acquire better leaders. Chartism probably hardened the aversion of the traditional political classes to democracy and their preference for the further development of Britain's mixed-constitutional heritage. The aftermath of European experiences in 1848—which saw would-be democratic experiments founder and, in the case of France, give way to a Bonapartist revival—provided confirmation for those who thought that Britain had found a better course.[70]

[70] Jonathan Parry, *The Politics of Patriotism: English Liberalism, National Identity and Europe, 1830–1886* (London, 1993); Saunders, *Democracy and the Vote.*

9

People and Power in British Politics to 1850

Joanna Innes

This chapter explores three ways in which the British people participated in politics during the eighteenth and early nineteenth centuries: through voting, petitioning, and joining political clubs. Voting and petitioning were venerable practices; political clubs entered the political scene from the later seventeenth century. The form, function, and meanings of all these activities varied by context as well as changing over time. All were employed by diverse people for diverse purposes, yet all had the potential to serve as vehicles for large-scale mobilization for political ends.

According to a tradition of thinking about 'mixed monarchy' that crystallized in the seventeenth century and remained powerful throughout our period, the House of Commons represented the democratic element in the constitution.[1] Alongside the monarch, in whose hands lay supreme executive power, and the 'aristocratic' House of Lords, the Commons embodied democracy by giving representatives of the people a voice at the heart of government. Indeed, it was arguably *only* through the Commons that the people could, within the terms of the constitution, claim a voice. Still, the Commons had this role by virtue of representing the people and attending to their grievances. Insofar as it could be charged with failing to do these things, there was a case for its reform.

Classically educated contemporaries also understood democracy *relationally*, as a form of political culture in which politicians vied for power as self-proclaimed champions of the people. When British political life was described in the later eighteenth century as becoming more (usually, worryingly more) democratic, this was illustrated by citing appeals made to public opinion on questions of government, rude attacks on men in power, and the sacrifice of ministers to appease popular discontent. Proposals by the young prime minister, William Pitt the younger, to increase the representation of populous constituencies, in the early 1780s, were objected to on the grounds that this would make the constitution 'too democratic'—probably meaning that it would encourage politicians to court popular favour.[2]

---

[1] Corinne Comstock Weston, *English Constitutional Theory and the House of Lords, 1556–1832* (London, 1965).

[2] e.g. *Gentleman's Magazine*, 27 (1757), 311; *Town and Country Magazine*, 8 (1776), 134; *The R–l Register*, 6 (1781), 127; Francis Osborne, Duke of Leeds, *An Address to the Independent Members of*

Politicians who breached political norms by orienting themselves to opinion 'out of doors' were sometimes called 'demagogues' (a word borrowed, like 'democracy', from the Greek political lexicon). That term was applied to critics of the exceptionally powerful prime minister Robert Walpole (1721–42). At mid-century, it was also applied to William Pitt the elder, who claimed to have been called to office 'by the voice of the people'; at the century's end, to Charles James Fox, who, at a time when most of his fellows gave priority to the security of king and constitution, continued to advertise popular grievances. In the early nineteenth century, by contrast, the term 'demagogue' came to be applied to leaders who operated wholly out of doors, to 'mob orators' such as Henry Hunt and William Cobbett, who built up a following through publication and by addressing mass meetings; later to Chartist leaders, especially to those, such as Feargus O'Connor, who relished the rough-and-tumble of mass politics.[3]

What was reflected here was a shift in perceptions of the people's role in politics. Over our period, the people increasingly came to be conceptualized as independent actors, throwing up their own leaders, pressing upon governmental institutions from without, trying to impose their own, distinct agendas upon the political classes. This chapter attempts to sketch the working out of this process of change *within* broadly traditional institutions and practices.

Throughout the period there were people who called for the British political system to be reconstructed from the ground up, rejecting the tradition of mixed government. They included in the late seventeenth century James Harrington; in the mid-eighteenth-century various 'commonwealthmen' (as chronicled by Caroline Robbins); and, later, Thomas Paine, James Mill, and late-Chartist 'red republicans'. Yet these people challenged an order which most of their contemporaries saw as providing room for manoeuvre. The period saw older forms of elite political conduct change under pressure. Those who called for more profound structural change failed to press their case home.[4]

VOTING

The idea that English government comprised monarchic, aristocratic, and democratic elements was first formulated in the mid-seventeenth century. The Glorious Revolution of 1688 consolidated that tradition. It established Parliament as both in principle and in practice necessary to government; Parliament's annual votes of

---

both Houses of Parliament (London, 1782), 11; *Remembrancer*, 2 (1783), 354 (all these magazines published in London).

[3] Jennifer Tolbert Roberts, *Athens on Trial: The Antidemocratic Tradition in Western Thought* (Princeton, NJ, 1994); 'Theophilus Thorn' [William Falconer], *The Demagogue* (London, 1766); *Tomahawk Or Censor General* (London), Saturday, 2 January 1796; *Sun* (London), Tuesday, 15 January 1799; *The Morning Post* (London), Friday, 26 June 1818; James Epstein, *The Lion of Freedom: Feargus O'Connor and the Chartist Movement, 1832–1842* (London, 1982), esp. 90–3.

[4] Caroline Robbins, *The Eighteenth-Century Commonwealthman* (Cambridge, MA, 1959); F. K. Prochaska, *The Republic of Britain, 1760–2000* (London, 2000).

revenue thereafter played a vital part in sustaining the fiscal-military state. In 1707 the Westminster Parliament subsumed the once distinct Scottish Parliament, and in 1801 the Irish Parliament. Thus it became, step by step, central to the government first of Britain, then of the British Isles.

During the seventeenth century managing Parliament came to be recognized as a key task for the king's ministers. When its power was consolidated, that confirmed the requirement. The demands of business elongated sessions, and made Parliament a site in which issues of concern to the political classes could be aired, and ministerial policies tested. In the early eighteenth century, monarchs came to accept that ministers were best recruited from among those who had proved themselves in party struggle and on the debating floor—and if possible, from among members of the House of Commons, since it was there that financial business was chiefly transacted. Parliamentary politics were not entirely public: not only was there much manoeuvring behind the scenes, but press reporting of debates was limited and intermittent until Parliament decided to sanction it in the 1770s. Yet long before that, abridged reports of debates reached the public through various written and oral channels.[5]

These developments combined to enhance the significance of elections.[6] Following the Revolution of 1688, it was initially agreed that new general elections should be held at least every three years, though—partly because of the trouble and expense occasioned—this was revised, in 1716, to at least once every seven years. The representative system had evolved over time, and had numerous idiosyncratic features that later reformers attacked as anomalies. MPs represented either counties or boroughs. By any criterion, small boroughs were over-represented—the result of past lobbying by patrons to win representation for towns within their sphere of influence. In the fifty-two counties of England and Wales and perhaps half of the two hundred or so parliamentary boroughs, electorates were quite large and diverse. In the counties, ownership of land worth forty shillings a year (a late medieval qualification, made nugatory by inflation) qualified a man to vote; in sixteen towns that had the status of counties, the same qualification applied. Otherwise, in the more open boroughs, it might suffice to be a freeman (a qualification that could be obtained by completing an apprenticeship) or a ratepayer. Yet even such broadly drawn requirements excluded the majority of adult males (as well as all women and children). In the other half—the more closed half—of English and Welsh boroughs, voters were few; in a couple of dozen cases, only members of corporate governing bodies had the vote

[5] David Hayton, 'Contested Kingdoms, 1688–1756', in Paul Langford (ed.), *Short Oxford History of the British Isles: The Eighteenth Century* (Oxford, 2002). See also David Hayton, 'Introductory Survey, 1690–1715', D. Hayton, E. Cruickshanks, and S. Handley (eds), *The History of Parliament: the House of Commons, 1690–1715* (Cambridge, 2002), also on the History of Parliament website at http://www.historyofparliamentonline.org/research/surveys/surveys-1690–1715.

[6] Mark Knights, *Representation and Misrepresentation in Late Stuart Britain: Partisanship and Political Culture* (Oxford, 2004); Frank O'Gorman, *Voters, Patrons and Parties: The Unreformed Electoral System of Hanoverian England, 1734–1832* (Oxford, 1989), and subsequent discussion between Derek Beales and O'Gorman in *Parliamentary History*, 11 (1992), 139–50, and 12 (1993), 171–83.

(and these men were not usually themselves elected, but co-opted by their fellows). All Scottish county and borough franchises were narrowly drawn.

It has been estimated that under these rules perhaps 3–5 per cent of the English and Welsh population (12–20 per cent of adult males) were qualified to vote; many fewer in Scotland. Proportions trended downwards over time because, while population grew, property ownership remained constricted, and numbers of free-men in urban populations shrank. However, national averages elide local diversity. In counties and large boroughs, the electorate spanned a wide social range, from huge landowners down to small farmers, from wealthy merchants to artisans and even labourers. Numbering in the hundreds or thousands, such electorates were too large to be easily controlled. Though patrons—major local landowners and public figures—might maintain ascendancy, their hold was never uncontested; public issues were routinely canvassed, and sometimes carried the day. Elsewhere, candidates had to worry only about winning over members of the corporation, or a few dozen voters. Even in the largest constituencies, some votes were mobilized through promises of favour: favours candidates could offer as local landowners or employers, or by recommending clients for government jobs. What varied was the weight such factors carried in the balance. There were finally a dozen or two hyper-popular small-town constituencies where bribery ran rife, as a multitude of poor voters traded votes for cash.

The skewed distribution of constituencies, restrictions on who qualified to vote, and the means exerted to influence results limited the scope for elections to serve as channels for public sentiment. Though they provided some indication of the will of the people, their function (in practice) was to affirm the position of whatever ministers the monarch had last appointed. Only once in the eighteenth century (in 1741) did an election precipitate a change of ministry; this did not happen again until 1830. This reflected in part ministers' success in trimming their policies to keep voters happy, but more the fact that many voters saw an advantage in sup-porting those already in royal favour; this seemed the most likely way to endear oneself to government, and thus to gain sympathetic attention or access to patron-age. The combination of opinion-based and opportunistic support was almost always enough to see a ministry home. Support from small constituencies, where opportunism was common, disproportionately favoured sitting ministers.

Not only were elections before 1830 not in practice contests for control of gov-ernment, but also, at any given election, only a minority of seats were contested, meaning most voters had no chance to vote. County contests were particularly troublesome and expensive, though sometimes seats changed hands without a formal vote—perhaps because of what door-to-door canvassing suggested would be the outcome.

All this said, opposition groups normally behaved as if something significant were at stake in general elections. They may have hoped to strengthen their hand within Parliament by showing ministers that they could stir the people; perhaps they hoped to prepare the ground for a shift in power within the lifetime of a par-liament. Whatever exactly they thought, they routinely took advantage of elections to air contentious issues. Insofar as they did this within Parliament and this was reported, or insofar as they propagandized in print, echoes of this contention might touch any literate person anywhere in the country. The effect was that, for all their limitations, elections helped to sustain a contentious political culture.

Emphasis on the contentiousness of early and mid-eighteenth-century political life has emerged in recent decades, challenging previous characterizations of this period as somnolent. Now it is argued that divisions ran deep, cutting through social classes, and interacting with local conflicts—such as, in towns, animosities between pro- and anti-corporation parties. In the early eighteenth century, differences of opinion arose from the Glorious Revolution and its aftermath: from disputes about the succession to the throne; the privileges of the Church of England, and Britain's involvement in European wars. Opinion clustered around rival 'Whig' and 'Tory' poles. The accession of a new line of Hanoverian kings in 1714 tilted royal favour towards the Whigs. But opposition from Tories and Whig dissidents continued. They claimed that ministerial influence was undermining the democratic part of the constitution, though they did not commit themselves to any particular recipe for redressing this. Shifting patterns of conflict played out against a background of longer-term change, notably, in the dissemination of political information by an expanding press. Not only reports of debates but also reports generated for or by Parliament increasingly entered the public domain. Parliament's decision to relax its objections to the reporting of debates from the 1770s can be seen as a step in a slowly evolving relationship.[7]

Granting all this, yet there remains a case for identifying the early years of the third Hanoverian king (George III) as marking a watershed in patterns of public engagement. This was partly because when the young king came to the throne in 1760 he broke the mould of politics. He shattered Whig hegemony, bouncing an important subset of formerly dominant Whigs into long-term opposition. The political temperature rose; patterns of political life became, for a while, less predictable. There was much to compete for, and little certainty about what form victory might take.[8]

Also important in effecting change were Britain's deteriorating relations with her American colonies, which through the 1760s protested about tax and other policies, and in the 1770s formally rebelled. The American example suggested new strategies for political opposition and renewal. At first, the power of this example was counteracted by concern about just how shockingly far the rebels were prepared to go. The conflict had its greatest domestic impact only in 1780, as it became apparent that Britain was losing the war—in which France and Spain had joined, hoping to prise away other colonies—while the economy went into recession and taxes soared. This crystallized discontent with what was now identified as a pattern of mismanagement and stimulated both tactical experiments and shifts in thinking.[9]

---

[7] Knights, *Representation*; Kathleen Wilson, *The Sense of the People: Politics, Culture and Imperialism in England, 1715–85* (Cambridge, 1995); H. T. Dickinson, *The Politics of the People in Eighteenth-Century Britain* (Basingstoke, 1996).

[8] John Brewer, *Party Ideology and Popular Politics at the Accession of George III* (Cambridge, 1976).

[9] Stephen Conway, *The British Isles and the War of American Independence* (Oxford, 2000).

Building on recent initiatives (further discussed in the next section), action was channelled initially into petitioning Parliament, soliciting reforms in public administration. Some who supported this campaign tried to institutionalize it, solidifying their constituency organizations into 'associations', which corresponded, and then assembled via representatives in what the king termed a 'congress' (with the American example evidently in mind). Though opposition politicians influenced this movement, they were unable wholly to control it. Independency started to cohere into a semi-autonomous third force.[10]

Linked with these changes in patterns of action were changes in ideas. Some argued that the problem was not just that ministers had too much influence over supposedly representative institutions. Still worse (they argued) were deficiencies in the representative system: a result of skewed constituency geography and limited access to the vote. The key failure, on this account, was not that ministers influenced Parliament too much but that the people influenced it too little. The solution: parliamentary reform (a new slogan, coined at this juncture).[11] The 1770s saw a revival of interest in older forms of analysis demonstrating the poor fit between constituencies and the distribution of wealth (and presumably also population, though data on that was lacking). Thereafter, this empirical critique was extended to show how borough representation had evolved through time, how qualifications for voting varied, and which magnates controlled what election outcomes. Enquiries such as these informed all later critiques of the representative system (and all historians' accounts of it).[12]

These findings did not prove that the system needed change. It could be argued—and was for several decades successfully argued—that, whatever their idiosyncrasies, existing arrangements delivered good results. Still, once the anomalies had been exposed, the system had to be defended as viable *despite* them. Moreover, thenceforth, when public policies proved especially controversial, critics could argue that the problem lay in Parliament's imperfect mapping of society. Parliamentary reform would remain a *leitmotif* of British politics into the early twentieth century (until women were granted the vote).

The American crisis thus stimulated new forms of political initiative, and crystallized a reformulated political critique. It also generated a new political polarity, between moderate and 'radical' reformers. The moderate advocated change in the distribution of constituencies, perhaps coupled with more frequent elections and some recalibration of voting rights. Radicals started from first principles, usually from the premise that all adult males were equally entitled to their say. The radical programme—first promulgated in the City of Westminster (a populous, ratepayer constituency)—urged, in addition to this moderate agenda, universal (manhood) suffrage, universal eligibility for election and payment for MPs. 'Radicalism' formed a distinctive strand in British politics for a century thereafter. Though

---

[10] John Cannon, *Parliamentary Reform, 1640–1832* (Cambridge, 1972); Eugene Charlton Black, *The Association: British Extraparliamentary Political Organization, 1769–1793* (Cambridge, MA, 1963).

[11] Joanna Innes, '"Reform" in English Public Life: The Fortunes of a Word', in Arthur Burns and Joanna Innes (eds), *Rethinking the Age of Reform, Britain, 1780–1850* (Cambridge, 2003).

[12] Black, *Association*, 283–8.

radicals gained some seats in Parliament, they were always especially associated with what I have termed the third-force approach to politics (though they never monopolized that).[13]

From this point onwards, more and less radical versions of reform analysis were sustained by the inherent power of these ideas, a variable cast of reform champions (some of them MPs, many not), and a sequence of often short-lived societies and associations. Occasional petitioning campaigns thrust the cause on public notice and drew in recruits. The cause was subject to redefinition, and supporting organization was always fluid. In the early nineteenth century such loose assemblages of occasionally activated public feeling came to be termed 'movements'. What the American crisis generated was not called a movement at the time, but in retrospect it has seemed natural to term it that.

The argument that there was something fundamentally awry in relations between Parliament and people did not quickly win over MPs. During the 1780s, amidst fall-out from the loss of the American colonies, political rivals Pitt the younger and Charles James Fox both flirted with schemes for parliamentary reform, but made little headway. Throughout the later eighteenth and early nineteenth centuries, MPs showed themselves ready to endorse some kinds of reform, but in their own fashion, generally focusing on the reduction of ministerial influence. As early as 1770—against the background of public turbulence, it is true, but not in response to a specific campaign—Parliament had agreed to Grenville's Election Act, which aimed to ensure that when local election results were disputed, the dispute would be resolved not in whatever way best suited the prime minister of the day, but with principled respect for rules. Thereafter, in a handful of cases in which *post mortems* found that a particular constituency had been deeply corrupt, Parliament ordered its boundaries redrawn, so as to increase numbers of voters.

Parliament also displayed a recurrent appetite for attacking what was represented as the overblown and excessively costly apparatus of executive government. The American War (among much else) precipitated a review of the structure of public administration, aimed both at cutting costs and at reducing influence. MPs took up that task again, against the background of public clamour but with their own brand of reforming zeal, during the Napoleonic Wars. By that point standards in public life were changing. Ministers increasingly accepted the need to be seen to found their power on un-bought consent. By 1830, the cumulative pruning of patronage and restlessness among voters reduced ministers' advantage to the point that general elections had the potential to function as serious assessments of their performance.[14]

Some MPs did convert to the cause of moderate parliamentary reform: they came to see a need to reduce anomalies, and better to match structures of power

---

[13] For terminology, Innes, '"Reform" in English Public Life', 86–7, 91–2; for the later days of radicalism as a parliamentary movement, Miles Taylor, *The Decline of British Radicalism, 1847–60* (Cambridge, 1995).

[14] Philip Harling, *The Waning of 'Old Corruption': The Politics of Economical Reform in Britain, 1779–1846* (Oxford, 1996).

in society. The radical cause by contrast gained little parliamentary support, and indeed only fluctuating support outside Parliament. Many people continued, throughout our period, to doubt the wisdom of extending the vote to all men. They questioned whether the rambunctiousness that marked popular contests should be made general, and worried—partly with the experience of corrupt, hyper-popular small-town constituencies in mind—that poorer voters would be no more than pawns in the hands of the wealthy: expanding the electorate might increase, not diminish influence. During the early nineteenth century, as economic disruption arising from war and post-war adjustment ran alongside both industrialization and changes in public policy informed by political economy, it became evident that there were problems with the traditional proposition that a Parliament elected on a restricted franchise *could* effectively express the whole range of public sentiments. At this point the radical reform cause, though retaining a principled and moral character, also began to assume a class colouring. In response, opponents of reform added a new argument to their armoury: working men could not be trusted with the vote because they would inevitably use it to attack sound economic principles. Yet it remained possible to present the reform cause in ways that did not divide people along class lines. In the later 1820s, when the heirs of Pitt (now dubbed Tories) had alienated various sections of the public, new reform organizations, so-called Political Unions, made a virtue of their cross-class character.[15]

The 1830 election revealed the sitting Tory ministry's unsustainably narrow base of support, and brought the Whigs to power after seventy years of only occasionally punctuated opposition. They could hope as a party to benefit from a measure of parliamentary reform, not least because many borough corporations had come to identify their interests with Toryism. Since the corporations' record in urban affairs was controversial, an assault on them could be expected to work to Whig advantage. The Reform Bill that the Whigs now floated was swingeing enough to generate both excitement and alarm, though it was essentially moderate in conception, being concerned to make the House of Commons better reflect the natural balance of power in society.[16]

To this end, the Whigs proposed—and after much heated argument persuaded Parliament to agree—to reconstruct the grid of constituencies, and redistribute MPs across them. They retained the basic distinction between county and borough seats, but abolished the smallest urban constituencies, and left others with one instead of the traditional two MPs. They placed additional MPs in the largest counties, and founded new constituencies in the largest unrepresented towns and also in the metropolis. Their plan to increase the representation of Scotland

---

[15] E. P Thompson, *The Making of the English Working Class* (rev. edn, Harmondsworth, 1968); Nancy D. LoPatin, *Political Unions, Popular Politics and the Great Reform Act of 1832* (Basingstoke, 1999).

[16] Michael Brock, *The Great Reform Act* (London, 1973); Philip Salmon, 'The English Reform Legislation', in D. R. Fisher (ed.), *The History of Parliament: The House of Commons, 1820–1832* (Cambridge, 2009), also on the History of Parliament website at http://www.historyofparliamentonline.org/volume/1820–1832/survey/ix-english-reform-legislation.

and Ireland at the expense of relatively over-represented England was (by contrast) successfully fought off by English rearguard action.[17]

They also sought more consistently to represent the interests of property by extending voting rights: not downwards, to social groups traditionally excluded, but laterally, to draw in more of a 'middle class' of people. The forms of small property-interest entitling people to vote in English county constituencies were diversified, and in Scotland redefined to match English norms. All borough constituencies were opened up to male inhabitant householders, provided that the assessed value of the property they occupied passed a minimum threshold (they did not need to own the property). The 'middle class' enfranchised by this means was not a clearly bounded social group. Though *relatively* middle, and intended to exclude the poor and transient, it included many artisans.

It has recently been stressed that, in absolute terms, the electorate had mushroomed in preceding decades, as population boomed. The Reform Act extended that trend of growth, increasing numbers of voters by about 45 per cent (though the decision to insist that town voters be resident also led to disqualifications; in some towns, voter numbers shrank). The effect of reform on *proportions* of people voting across England and Wales was less impressive: proportions of voters grew, but perhaps not enough to match early eighteenth-century levels. Modern estimates suggest that less than 5 per cent of the population could claim the reformed franchise, under 20 per cent of adult males.[18] Yet to emphasize only limited change in proportions would be distorting. Within a rapidly growing population, the Act created a larger-than-ever electorate, with very large numbers of first-time voters. Moreover, averages elide local diversity. The Act made most difference in Scotland, and in previously corporation-dominated English boroughs, which it opened up to public contest; also to the three dozen brand-new urban constituencies. The Reform struggle boosted Whig fortunes, and though in England Toryism soon bounced back (as voters old and new distributed themselves across the political spectrum), thenceforth neither party established lasting hegemony. Contests became more frequent. More MPs represented lively, independent-minded electorates, and were stimulated to assert themselves in the Commons. Both the Commons and the electorate became harder for ministers to manage. Monarchs found their choice of minister seriously constrained by election results. In all these ways, the democratic part of the constitution became more democratic, more responsive to the will of the people, as expressed in elections, and as a result public opinion pressed harder upon the executive.[19]

Still, the Reform Act did not fulfil radical aspirations. Indeed, to those who upheld the right of all men to vote, it was a slap in the face. For whereas previously the mass of the population had been excluded by tradition in a system riddled with

[17] Miles Taylor, 'Empire and Parliamentary Reform: The 1832 Reform Act Revisited', in Burns and Innes, *Rethinking the Age of Reform*.

[18] O'Gorman, *Voters, Patrons*, 178–9.

[19] Philip Salmon, *Electoral Reform at Work: Local Politics and National Parties, 1832–41* (Woodbridge, 2002); Taylor, *Decline of British Radicalism*.

anomalies, now the poorer were excluded by design—on such grounds as that they did not have a sufficient stake in the country, and were not capable of forming rational political views.

Deprived by the enactment of moderate reform of the chance to build significant cross-class alliances, lower middle-class and working-class reformers and their occasional higher-status sympathizers were forced to regroup. Their growing distaste for policies pursued by the Reform ministry—their stringent, cost-cutting welfare policies, their half-hearted regulation of factory working conditions, and their persistence in coercing Ireland—supplied impetus for doing that. The centrepiece of the new organizational effort, the People's Charter, restated the by now time-hallowed radical programme: it called for universal (manhood) suffrage, equal electoral districts, annual parliaments, and so forth. But arguments for this programme had now to meet the new case for exclusion. There was ever more reason to stress the worthiness, the upright personal qualities of the ordinary working man. It was argued too that Whig reformers—though they had attacked the power of borough corporations and some other forms of privilege and monopoly—had not done enough on this score. So long as political rights and power were unevenly distributed, those with privileged access to power would have the means of advantaging themselves. Without political justice, no social justice.[20]

PETITIONING

Though symbolically and increasingly practically important, elections never provided the only channel by which people could approach Parliament. Much popular political activity focused on attempts directly to influence what Parliament did.

Throughout our period, Parliament dealt with a variety of business. It passed a raft of fiscal and other measures at the behest of ministers, and addressed other public matters at the behest of other MPs. It also processed local and private applications, from communities and individuals. It broke entails and granted divorces; it empowered groups of landowners to reorganize and enclose landholdings; it endorsed road-building; and empowered townspeople to tax themselves to introduce 'improvements'. All such private and local applications were initiated by petition. Parliament also recognized the right of those affected by public legislation to make representations: thus, economic interest groups had the right to petition, and might be granted permission to be heard in person or by counsel when legislation adversely affected them.[21]

Until the later eighteenth century, Parliament was much less ready to accept the public's right to petition on issues affecting Church or State: that was seen as potentially calling Parliament's own rights into question. A 1661 act against tumultuous petitioning recognized a right to petition king or Parliament on such matters—but only insofar as this was done in properly convened county meetings,

---

[20] Malcolm Chase, *Chartism: A New History* (Manchester, 2007).
[21] Paul Langford, *Public Life and the Propertied Englishman, 1689–1798* (Oxford, 1991).

or by the City of London. Though some petitions and addresses were brought to public meetings, circulated for signing, and dispatched to king or Parliament in the early eighteenth century—and moreover, printed, or reported on in the press, so as to reach a wider public—the practice was contested. In 1701 Parliament notoriously ordered the imprisonment of members of a Kent Grand Jury who dared to challenge its foreign policy. Those who wished to organize critical expressions of public sentiment thereafter proceeded carefully, so as not to inflame constitutional sensibilities. Sometimes they called meetings to 'instruct' MPs; sometimes they sent congratulatory addresses or other tokens of esteem to favoured politicians.[22]

One of the most striking changes in popular political practice in the 1760s was the assertive resumption of the practice of petitioning king or Parliament on public matters. Precisely what inspired this is unclear. Catherine Macaulay's *History of England* (1763–83) may have directed attention to seventeenth-century precedents. Affirmation of the right to petition in the 1689 Bill of Rights may have supplied inspiration. American petitions against new forms of taxation must have encouraged interest in the approach. The first wave of English public petitions (in 1769) issued from meetings summoned in some counties and a handful of towns; they addressed the king, and made generally conceived complaints about ministerial mismanagement. The new Whig opposition both encouraged and struggled to control these initiatives. They failed to ride to power on the back of them (as they may have hoped), but government took no robust action against petitioners, contenting itself with suggesting to its supporters that they discourage local meetings. Emboldened, opponents of government added the device to their repertoire.[23]

Petitioning played a vital part in enabling the development of a movement with some autonomy from conventional party politics; from 1780, petitioning and the cause of radical parliamentary reform became symbiotic. But petitioning, having demonstrated its potential as a rallying and agenda-setting device, was soon adopted for other ends too. Within a few years, petitions promoted religious and moral ends: making the case against concessions to Catholics, for concessions to Dissenters, and against the slave trade. These campaigns made their own contributions to expanding petitioning's reach. Religious and moral issues could be argued to be everyone's business. Anti-Catholic campaigners scattered petitions around parish vestries, and some gathered signatures from women as well as men. Anti-slavery campaigners encouraged even small towns to participate, on this basis eliciting over five hundred petitions—dwarfing the few dozen from counties and substantial towns which the first political petitioners had been content to elicit.[24]

---

[22] Mark Knights, *Representation*, chapter 3, and 'Participation and Representation before Democracy: Petitions and Addresses in Pre-Modern Britain', in Ian Shapiro et al. (eds), *Political Representation* (Cambridge, 2009).

[23] Colin Leys, 'Petitioning in the Nineteenth and Twentieth Centuries', *Political Studies*, 3 (1955), 45–64; George Rudé, *Wilkes and Liberty: A Social Study of 1763 to 1774* (Oxford, 1962), chapters 7–8.

[24] Joanna Innes, 'Legislation and Public Participation, 1760–1830', in David Lemmings (ed.), *The British and their Laws in the Eighteenth Century* (Woodbridge, 2005), chapter 5; Ian Haywood and John Seed (eds), *The Gordon Riots: Politics, Culture and Insurrection in Late Eighteenth-Century Britain* (Cambridge, 2012), chapters 2–3.

These new approaches also affected practices of *private* petitioning. In the 1780s manufacturers protesting against tax policies encouraged workers in their thousands to endorse their petitions. By the 1790s petitions emanating from workers—not a novelty in themselves—drew thousands of signatures. In 1804 thousands of signatures to a cotton weavers' petition relating to arbitration and wage settlements were collected within days across several counties by organizers who were described as running from house to house in weaving districts, prevailing on women and children to sign.

The 1810s saw new records set in terms of numbers of petitions addressing a single issue. What is striking is the wide front across which this applied: political, religious, and economic. A broad reshaping of political culture was in train. Activists could potentially access multiple platforms: the radical leader Henry Hunt tirelessly (and tiresomely) attended meetings on all kinds of subjects, urging parliamentary reform as the answer to all problems.[25]

Petitioning served to involve people in politics but it was not necessarily gratifying. Many petitions failed, including workers' petitions seeking either to protect traditional forms of economic regulation or to promote new ones. Petitions for peace, drawn up in the depths of wartime misery, likewise failed to move Parliament or king. Already in the 1760s it had been argued that if the authorities proved obdurate, more vigorous steps might be taken; if these failed, power returned to the people. Theories like this—whether informed by reading or pragmatically improvised by increasingly desperate protesters—seem to have shaped much popular action in the 1790s and early post-war years: petitioning alternated with marches, demonstrations of force, threats, arson, and even assassination.[26] The same notion—that petitioning was only one element in a repertoire, whose more forceful parts might need to be deployed if that failed—informed especially early Chartist thinking.

Yet some campaigns were crowned with stunning victories, sometimes after years of effort. Catholics gained the right to sit in Parliament after more than two decades of petitioning across Britain and Ireland (in the face of many counter-petitions). Petitions provided support for the Whigs' 1832 Reform Bill—if constitutionally ambiguous support, in that the argument that petitioners might graduate to the use of force was wielded to daunt Lords and king. Though petitioning sometimes had threatening undertones, it offered a vent for popular feeling and a mode of influencing politics that could be seen as reducing the likelihood of revolution. The development within Britain of this highly orchestrated and largely peaceful form of democratic politics was by this point attracting comment from other quarters. In France, both Catholic campaigners and people keen to see an extension of the franchise experimented with petitioning, though nowhere did this practice become as routine a part of political life as in the British Isles.[27]

---

[25] John Belchem, *'Orator' Hunt: Henry Hunt and English Working-Class Radicalism* (Oxford, 1985), 173, 176, 177, 184, 186, 192, 193, 202.

[26] Steven Poole, *The Politics of Regicide in England, 1760–1850* (Manchester, 2000).

[27] Benoît Agnès, 'L'Appel au pouvoir. Essai sur le petitionnement auprès des chambres legislatives et électives en France et au Royaume Uni entre 1814 et 1848' (unpublished doctoral thesis, Paris I, 2009), 311–44: 'Imiter l'Angleterre: les français et l'agitation britannique'.

ASSOCIATION

'Clubs' and 'societies' first proliferated in seventeenth-century Britain. Most lacked any legal identity (though some appointed trustees to safeguard their resources). It must have helped that governments and parliaments largely accepted their existence. In the wake of the Toleration Act of 1689, even voluntary religious societies enjoyed some protection. In an increasingly prosperous consumer society, tolerance seemed to be all that voluntary associations needed to flourish. Their purposes included promotion of piety, mutual aid, philanthropy, the pursuit of common material interests (for example, trade regulation) and of shared leisure interests (including drinking and chatting).[28]

Early political clubs ranged from MPs' dining societies (like the Whigs' Kit Kat Club) to local constituency associations (like Bristol's White Lion club, or the Westminster Society of Independent Electors), through to neighbourhood social clubs whose members shared a political sensibility. Such clubs both expressed and nurtured political identity. They might perform organizational functions: for example, serve as nodes to mobilize voters in elections. Some were formed to coordinate particular political initiatives—like the 1760s Society of Supporters of the Bill of Rights, first formed to pay the debts of the beleaguered patriot hero, John Wilkes, later an organizing centre for other Wilkite (proto-radical) initiatives. Societies that performed various functions for a group with common concerns might among other things coordinate political interventions. The London-based Protestant Dissenting Deputies, which brought metropolitan ministers together to discuss common concerns, monitored legislation affecting Dissenters, and made representations on their behalf.[29] In the later eighteenth century, middle- and working-class mutual-aid societies made representations to Parliament about what was and was not acceptable to them in the way of regulation. Societies expressed their initial members' existing political interests, but might draw in and politicize others. They facilitated the development of a participatory political culture by encouraging people to see their views about public matters as of more than personal significance.

Their polymorphous character favoured hybridization: cross-fertilization between existing types. Petitioning campaigns had the potential to subsume existing associational nodes and give them new meaning, as well as spawning new nodes to meet their own requirements. The anti-Catholic petitioning campaign of 1780 recruited parishes as organizational units; they often functioned as such in later religiously or morally inflected petitioning campaigns. Workers' petitioning campaigns concerned with the regulation of employment relationships were often generated in the first instance out of existing trade-club networks, which were then expanded to raise funds (petitioning Parliament could be an expensive business, entailing both logistical costs and fees).

---

[28] Peter Clark, *British Clubs and Societies, 1580–1800: The Origins of an Associational World* (Oxford, 2000).

[29] Graham Wootton, *Pressure Groups in Britain, 1720–1970* (London, 1975).

Even when consciously instrumental, political clubs played a part in shaping and sustaining identities. They could do this without being partisan. From the 1780s, debating societies became fashionable in the metropolis.[30] They met during the London season—the winter months, when people sought indoor entertainment. They did not debate explicitly party-political questions, and often focused on social and moral issues, but they explored issues of political conduct, and some public-policy issues (including the merits of the slave trade and the significance of the French Revolution). Provincial 'Literary and Philosophical Societies', though more scholarly and less commercial, were in some ways parallel. Radical 'corresponding societies', which spread through major towns in the 1790s, drew on the example of these societies (and their French equivalents); several managers of debating societies figured among leaders of the London Corresponding Society. Societies of both kinds encouraged the view that marginal professionals, shopkeepers, and artisans had a right not just to form but publicly to express political opinions, and as such promoted members' personal development. Associational life also generated its own ideology, which in the early nineteenth century was often encapsulated in the formula 'union is strength'.

Societies—charitable societies, for example—often drew support from both men and women, though their organizing committees were usually single-sex. There were women-only societies: charitable societies wholly run by women were in operation by the later eighteenth century; working women's mutual-aid societies likewise. Women were increasingly given a place in political displays during the 1810s: by the 1830s there were Female Political Unions and Female Radical Associations supportive of Chartism. These aimed not to obtain votes for women but to register their active membership of local communities and demonstrate the breadth of support for change.[31]

For those lacking personal power in eighteenth- and early nineteenth-century British society, associational life offered a chance to interact with mainstream politics on their own terms. It is difficult to be sure how patterns changed over time, but the historical record gives the impression that societies both proliferated and ramified, as more people gained confidence in their ability collectively to shape aspects of their lives.[32] Associational activity also seems increasingly to have been coloured by self-improving themes, either in religious or in enlightenment mode. Well-developed habits of self-organization gave early nineteenth-century popular political culture resilience and resourcefulness. Had it not been for this dense infrastructure of associational solidarity, and practical organizational experience, it is hard to see how Chartism—self-consciously a movement of the marginalized—could ever have got off the ground.

---

[30] Mary Thale, 'London Debating Societies in the 1790s', *Historical Journal*, 32 (1989), 57–86.
[31] Helen Rogers, *Women and the People: Authority, Authorship and the Radical Tradition in Nineteenth-Century England* (Aldershot, 2000), chapters 1–3.
[32] Joanna Innes and Arthur Burns, 'Introduction', in Burns and Innes, *Rethinking the Age of Reform*, 23.

CONJUNCTURES

There is a danger that emphasis on trends over time may blur the specificity of particular moments. This final section focuses on two periods highlighted in this book, the 1790s and 1840s. Both periods saw petitioning campaigns requesting extension of the right to vote. But to understand *why*, in each decade, some people sought to make Parliament more responsive, and what place this activity had among other forms of political engagement, we need to attend to the specificities of these conjunctures.

In the 1790s the cause of parliamentary reform, first identified as a campaign goal in the closing years of the American War, was reanimated. But much had happened in the interim to shape ideas and conduct, even before the outbreak of revolution in France. Britain formally acknowledged the loss of her American colonies in 1783. Though people disagreed about what had gone wrong, it was widely agreed that something had. Those who had waged war were discredited. The most credible leaders remaining—Pitt and Fox—each presented himself as a friend to reform, including parliamentary reform but not only that. Though public appetite for constitutional change waned with the war's end, there remained an appetite for other reform initiatives. The public agenda was enriched by a variety of what we might term 'enlightened' causes, such as extension of religious liberty and educational opportunity, penal reform, the reduction of barriers to commerce and labour mobility, and abolition of the slave trade. Meanwhile, evangelical forms of Christianity, which likewise emphasized humans' capacity (with God's help) to change not only themselves but the wider society, exhibited proselytizing zeal and gained recruits, ranging from prominent members of the political class to poor, illiterate men and women. In this context, ordinary people were increasingly accorded at least rhetorical respect: they were hailed as beings whose happiness mattered; whose interests and views politicians should heed; whose latent desire to better their own condition (material or spiritual) deserved nurturing, not least because it had the potential to drive forward the progress of 'civilization' (a concept then gaining ground).[33]

In this context, enlightened aspects of the French Revolutionary agenda struck a powerful chord. Moreover, the distinctively British constitutional project of reforming Parliament took on new meanings. More emphasis was given to its existential aspect: to the idea that what was at stake was recognition of common human capacities. Promoting parliamentary reform remained an important focus for radical activity, but this increasingly took its place alongside other self- and society-improving endeavours. Some—such as the radical moral theorist and novelist William Godwin—thought that priority should be given to personal improvement and experiments in living, since unless individuals reformed themselves, collective action would achieve little. The politics of virtue was not exclusively a politics of the excluded: it appealed to men, women, and children from varying social milieus, though it had special appeal for those who thought

---

[33] Innes and Burns, 'Introduction', 4–10.

that they were undervalued because of their political or religious affiliations, gender, race, social status, or some combination of these.[34]

Yet as the 1790s unfolded, those who were interested in reforming both themselves and society, and had therefore responded positively to French example, came under tremendous pressure: official, social, and psychological. As the French Revolution radicalized, Louis XVI was executed, and France and Britain went to war, those who still called for reform were assailed as would-be revolutionaries and traitors—the more so insofar as it was feared that they might win a broader popular following (though it is unclear how far they ever did). Government, Parliament, local authorities, and patriotic zealots combined to demobilize and discredit them. Some emigrated, others suffered transportation, imprisonment, and even execution; some went underground; some withdrew into private life; others broke under pressure and converted to loyalism. After Thermidor, as something like a regular government was re-established in France, and yet the French seemed determined on reshaping Europe in their own image, many erstwhile reformers probably genuinely reassessed the needs of the moment, agreeing that, as things stood, Britain and her constitution merited defending, even if they hoped later to resume the work of reform.[35]

Though reformers saw themselves as 'the friends of the people', they were never the only ones to do that. The prime minister, Pitt, and some of the more conservative Whigs who from 1792 rallied to his support, had in preceding years played a part in encouraging new forms of popular mobilization. In that context we should not be surprised to find them making unwontedly vigorous efforts to mobilize the people *behind* king and constitution, not only by such means as the much-studied ritual burnings of Thomas Paine's effigy in response to the second, republican part of his *Rights of Man*, but also through more routine local celebrations. It became common, for example, for parades to be staged assembling military volunteers, members of friendly societies (recently sanctioned by legislation), and Sunday School children to exhibit approved forms of civic virtue. Though government certainly feared the possible effects of 'Jacobin' contagion, they did—if with some qualms—sanction the arming of home-defence 'volunteer' forces, from 1794. When the threat of French invasion peaked in 1803, vast swathes of the adult male population were enlisted into one or another armed force.[36] The government was never sufficiently worried about public opinion to try to postpone elections, and when radicals pitched their hats into the ring in some popular constituencies, ministers were content to let the battle for hearts and minds play out.[37]

---

[34] For a flavour, see Penelope J. Corfield and Chris Evans (eds), *Youth and Revolution in the 1790s: Letters of William Pattisson, Thomas Amyot and Henry Crabb Robinson* (Stroud, 1996).

[35] J. E. Cookson, *The Friends of Peace: Anti-War Liberalism in England, 1793–1815* (Cambridge, 1982), chapter 5.

[36] Austin Gee, *The British Volunteer Movement, 1794–1814* (Oxford, 2003).

[37] R. G. Thorne, 'The Constituencies', in Thorne (ed.), *The History of Parliament: The House of Commons, 1790–1820* (London, 1996), also on the History of Parliament website at http://www. historyofparliamentonline.org/volume/1790–1820/survey/i-constituencies.

There has been much debate among historians about the mindset of rank-and-file respondents to loyalist initiatives. Given the numbers who served as volunteers, some must have gone on to support renascent radicalism, as new leaders helped to jettison its anti-patriotic image early in the new century. In fact the political classes were never entirely confident that, in encouraging popular loyalism, they had not taken a tiger by the tail. References to the dangers of 'democracy' at the turn of the century often relate to the dangers inherent in 'military democracy' in the form of volunteers.[38]

Renascent popular reformism in the early nineteenth century stood in a complex relationship to precursor movements. It often presented itself as ardently patriotic and 'constitutionalist'—though radical versions of constitutionalism were unusually emphatic about the primeval rights of Saxon invaders, subsequently eroded by 'feudal' and other forms of tyranny. So long as the Napoleonic Wars lasted, it was difficult for radicals to do much with the heritage of French-inflected reform politics, though with the war's end, new possibilities emerged; the French Revolutionary tradition also acquired more promising resonance once it offered an alternative to the monarchical legitimism of Restoration Europe. The liberty cap again became a symbol of radical aspiration. William Cobbett, anti-Jacobin turned radical journalist, having decamped to America to avoid prosecution for his radical views, returned two years later, in 1819, with Thomas Paine's bones. Subsequent French revolutions (1830, 1848) encouraged reclamation of the previous generations' heroes and ideals, encouraging British liberal as well as radical identification with aspects of this history.[39]

Socially, the early nineteenth-century reform movement was heterogeneous. The most nationally prominent new leaders in the century's opening years were radical gentlemen (though some, like Cobbett, were decidedly middling, small-landowning, and business 'gentlemen'). Radicalism acquired an intellectual wing from around 1810, in the form of the briefless barrister Jeremy Bentham and his circle. But, compared to the 'Association movement' of 1780, which had enjoyed significant support in the counties, the movement now had a lower centre of gravity. As radical reformers recruited to their cause masses of small shopkeepers, artisans, and industrial workers, and the culture of the movement acquired a more plebeian flavour, it became harder for those of higher rank wholly to identify with it. The very word 'radical' took on plebeian connotations. At the same time, the balance of population shifted markedly towards historically less developed 'manufacturing districts'—accordingly less densely equipped with urban and other governmental institutions, such that people were thrown more on to their own devices in terms of devising infrastructure for political engagement. In this context, parishes and trade unions gained importance as political sites, while book clubs, newspaper reading rooms, Methodist meetings, Dissenting and heterodox

[38] Gee, *British Volunteer Movement*, chapter 7.
[39] James Epstein, 'Understanding the Cap of Liberty: Symbolic Practice and Social Conflict in Early Nineteenth-Century England', *Past and Present*, 122 (1989), 75–118; J. R. Dinwiddy, 'English Radicals and the French Revolution, 1800–50', in Dinwiddy, *Radicalism and Reform in Britain, 1780–1850* (London, 1992).

chapels, and mutual-aid societies provided venues for politicized sociability and training grounds for leadership. Activists' consciousness was often forged through multiple forms of collective and public engagement. In this context, there was always scope for uncertainty or debate about which should be given priority, as well as about the modes of action appropriate in any given case.[40]

The political culture of Chartism was coloured by all these developments. Chartists employed a plethora of traditional modes of action, including petitioning, threats (and the occasional eruption) of armed struggle, and the summoning of conventions (which the government now permitted to meet for the first time since the 1780s). Chartist newspapers, above all the *Northern Star*, helped dispersed adherents to conceive of themselves as joined in a larger cause—building on a strand of publishing that had first taken off at the end of the Napoleonic Wars. More novel was the threat to launch a general strike, or 'national holiday'. If the Chartist repertoire was largely a familiar one, Chartism yet had a specific character deriving from its critical engagement with the version of 'reform' promulgated by Whig ministries between 1830 and 1842. These ministries saw themselves as dismantling monopoly and privilege, as rationalizing rule. To those they had excluded from the vote—industrial workers struggling with the boom-bust cycles of the global economy; underpaid agricultural labourers; millions who knew that at least part of their lives would be spent striving hopelessly to make ends meet—they could however seem to have little to offer, for they refused to 'interfere' with the market, or to demoralize people by encouraging them to look to government for assistance. In this context, Chartism was a strategy as much as it was a cause: a device for rallying into a single movement, whose members could take heart from one another, all those alienated by the rigour and parsimony of this version of reform, to whom it made sense to attribute disappointed hopes at least in part to lack of a political voice.

Chartists failed to achieve the constitutional changes they sought, and in the face of repeated failure the movement ultimately fragmented. But it fragmented rather than died.[41] Individual Chartists often continued to pursue, by other means, the ends they had for a time pursued under the Chartist banner: cultivating self-respect and mutual confidence among men and women of the 'working class', and staking a claim for the rights of such people to have their needs and views attended to, to be recognized as having the right to be heard.

[40] For the politicization of many institutions, Derek Fraser, *Urban Politics in Victorian England: The Structure of Politics in Victorian Cities* (Leicester, 1976). For the infrastructure of working-class politics, Thompson, *Making*, esp. chapters 12 and 16.
[41] Chase, *Chartism*, chapter 11.

PART IV

IRELAND

10

Constructing Democratic Thought in Ireland in the Age of Revolution, 1775–1800

Ultán Gillen

DEMOCRACY: IRELAND'S FUTURE RE-IMAGINED

On 17 March 1792 the *Northern Star*, the newspaper of the recently founded Society of United Irishmen, sought to improve the public's understanding of democracy:

> The terms *Aristocrat* and *Democrat* are not yet thoroughly understood by the people of this country. Did they know that the *former* signifies a man who wishes the bulk of the Nation to be kept down for the partial advantage of a few privileged individuals, and that the *latter* means one, who only desires fair play and equal protection for all, could they hesitate a moment which to prefer?[1]

This particular piece of democratic propaganda used simple language for its target audience, the lower orders. Examining the implications of the words used reveals much about the political languages employed to construct a distinctly Irish form of the revolutionary democratic politics sweeping the Atlantic world. The *Northern Star*'s choice of words alluded to those aspects of government and society that shaped the contours of Irish democratic thought. According to this newspaper, democracy was a system of government that enshrined the principle of equality. In Ireland, this meant especially equality for all denominations, and therefore the transformation of Ireland's confessional state which secured political power for the adherents of the Anglican Established Church of Ireland, only 10 per cent of the population. Democracy, it was implied, would also mean the end of unfair taxation and of the concentration of government patronage in the hands of a narrow elite—'a few privileged individuals'—who, in United Irish eyes, sold their votes to a British minister. As they saw it, Britain corrupted the Irish Parliament, a situation requiring at the least urgent reform or, for the more militant, separation. The antithesis that they constructed was therefore as follows: aristocracy meant an Ireland where the nation's rights were violated by Britain; where government did not truly represent the people; where heavy taxes paid for the corruption that denied the people their rights; where they were kept divided along religious lines

---

[1] *Northern Star* (Belfast), 17 March 1792.

in the interests of the local elite and Britain; and where the denial of their rights impoverished the people. Democracy, by contrast, would mean the Irish nation gaining possession of all its rights; an end to sectarian division; the people's interests being pursued without aristocratic or British interference; and laws and taxes that instead of oppressing and impoverishing the people would make the country rich. Democracy, in short, was the opposite of aristocracy. In United Irish eyes, democracy would mean a united, free, and prosperous Irish people.

The French Revolution, claimed the leading United Irishman Theobald Wolfe Tone, split Ireland into 'two great parties, the *Aristocrats* and the *Democrats* (epithets borrowed from France)', a division he also found in the American and Batavian republics.[2] William Drennan, one of Ireland's most prominent pamphleteers of the 1780s and 1790s and with Tone the man most responsible for constructing United Irish ideology in the early 1790s, also believed that every man had to choose between the two parties, though he regarded himself as unusual in being 'democratic without being popular'.[3] The unfortunate Thomas Russell, another prominent United Irish leader, informed by the love of his life that her father would never consent to her marrying a democrat, could only wonder how she had learnt of his politics.[4] Conservatives like Russell's prospective father-in-law believed that democracy was a dangerous force long before the United Irish alliance with Revolutionary France, and they dwelt at length on the perceived faults of democracy and its adherents. Their opponents did the same for aristocracy and aristocrats. Despite (or perhaps because of) the prominence of 'democrat' and 'aristocrat' as terms of abuse, explicit discussions of democracy and its meaning by those generally regarded as democrats were surprisingly few. Thomas Addis Emmet, another key United Irish leader, later attributed this to repression. 'The utterance of opinions, favourable to reform and democracy, was prevented in the upper and middling ranks, by the coercion they experienced, and by the outcries that were raised against France, against her principles, and from them against liberty itself.'[5] A pattern of government action against dissident opinion did emerge from the late 1780s, accelerating after war with France began, but the United Irishmen chose to focus their propaganda on practical measures rather than conceptual discussions of democracy, partly because it was aimed at the lower orders, and partly to avoid alienating potential support. The reluctance of those who avowed themselves democrats, either publicly or privately, to discuss concepts of democracy extensively, and a preference for other political labels such as 'republican' or 'patriot', makes reconstructing Irish understandings of democracy problematic.

This chapter argues that Irish democrats developed a vision of a secular, democratic, and commercial republic that would transform government, economy, and society in the interests of the middle and lower orders. It argues that the most

---

[2] Theobald Wolfe Tone, *The Writings of Theobald Wolfe Tone, 1763–98*, ed. T. W. Moody, R. B. McDowel, and C. J. Woods (3 vols, Oxford, 1998–2007), 2: 295.

[3] *The Drennan—McTier Letters*, ed. Jean Agnew (3 vols, Dublin, 1998–9), 2: 86; 1: 559.

[4] *Journals and Memoirs of Thomas Russell, 1791–5*, ed. C. J. Woods (Belfast, 1991), 155.

[5] W. J. MacNeven, *Pieces of Irish History* (New York, 1807), 70–1.

prominent political languages used to construct Irish democracy were claims of right (both natural rights and the rights of man, applied to individuals and the nation as a whole), classical republicanism, Enlightenment toleration and political economy, egalitarianism, and revolutionary internationalism. This model both echoes and differs from those offered by Ian McBride and Stephen Small. McBride, discussing Irish nationalism and republicanism in the 1790s, stated that radical vocabularies drew on 'the myth of an ancient constitution, classical republicanism, natural rights theory, Enlightenment rationalism and the rights of man'. Small argued that Irish radicalism, patriotism, and republicanism were 'largely constructed out of five key political languages: Protestant superiority, ancient constitutionalism, commercial grievance, classical republicanism, and natural rights'.[6] The differences from these models here reflect the narrower focus of this chapter, but also its argument that while the political languages of democrats had much in common with the rest of political culture, their rejection of the constitution of king, Lords and Commons and the British connection means that the similarities are deceptive, obscuring the revolutionary nature of democratic political and social thought.

THE RIGHTS OF THE PEOPLE OF IRELAND, THE AMERICAN REVOLUTION, AND REFORM

Certain inescapable structural facets of Irish life shaped democratic thought, which in many senses sought to overcome them. Primary amongst them was the connection with Britain, closely followed by the confessional state and religious division. These factors complicated the questions—such as political strategy or who should be enfranchised—facing democrats everywhere. The enormous significance of these issues, their perceived responsibility for other problems, and their seeming intractability within even a reformed status quo pushed some radicals in the 1790s to embrace an independent, secular democratic republic. The concept of Irish democracy was not elaborated until the 1790s, but its origins lie in the era of the American Revolution.

The most prominent language used to construct democratic thought was claims of right for the nation and the individual—though such claims, whether made in the language of natural rights or the rights of man, did not necessarily entail a commitment to political rights for all. The withdrawal of troops for use in America precipitated the formation of a Volunteer army that grew to 40,000-strong. The Volunteers elected their officers, but, initially at least, excluded Catholics and the poor from their ranks. Originally founded for national defence, they soon turned their attention to redressing political and commercial grievances. Allied with patriot politicians, the press, and wider public opinion, they secured (i.e. extorted) a series of concessions from Westminster. This political role was perfectly in line with the Volunteers' classical republican view of themselves as

---

[6] Ian McBride, 'The Harp without the Crown: Nationalism and Republicanism in the 1790s', in S. J. Connolly (ed.), *Political Ideas in Eighteenth-Century Ireland* (Dublin, 2000), 159; Stephen Small, *Political Thought in Ireland, 1776–1798: Republicanism, Patriotism and Radicalism* (Oxford, 2002), 1–2.

citizen-soldiers stepping forward to aid their country in its time of need. In response to those who argued that under the constitution bodies of armed men ought not to be passing political resolutions, the Ulster Volunteer Convention held in Dungannon on 15 February 1782 unanimously declared that 'a citizen, by learning the use of arms, does not abandon any of his civil rights'. Ireland's right to trade with the colonies ('free trade') was recognized in 1779, so attention shifted to legislative independence. The Dungannon Convention stated that 'a claim of any body of men, other than the King, Lords and Commons of Ireland, to make laws to bind this kingdom, is unconstitutional, illegal, and a *grievance*'.[7] Charles Francis Sheridan, a Whig and no democrat, in 1779 grounded his influential argument for legislative independence in the language of natural rights. He had a distinctive understanding of what natural rights were. He argued that there were four natural rights, the fourth being the right to defend the other three. The fourth natural right was an act of power, and was the duty of government. Because Westminster politicians were not drawn from the Irish nation, their legislating for Ireland was a '*usurpation of the fourth natural right of mankind*'.[8] Sheridan's particular formulation of natural rights was not widely shared, but the idea that England legislating for Ireland violated the rights of the kingdom as a whole, and of Irishmen as individuals, motivated the constitutional agitation that culminated in legislative independence in 1782. Subsequently, even those loyal to the British government who had initially opposed legislative independence came to endorse it.

The failure of 1782 to produce either parliamentary reform or genuine freedom from British control forced the most radical by the 1790s to seek different means to achieve what they perceived as truly representative government, thus feeding into the construction of democratic thought. Radicals, forced by these failures to interrogate their assumptions, stretched their political principles in new directions. The French Revolution ensured that this process led many to embrace the democratic cause. Still, important moves in this direction had come earlier. In 1783 a parliamentary reform campaign was mounted by many of the remaining Volunteers. They met fierce resistance not just from London, but also from the majority of the local political elite who now saw them not as virtuous patriots but as an armed force attempting to overawe Parliament, the legitimate representative of the Irish nation. Some conservatives detected 'an armed and unbridled Democracy' in the Volunteers, with each unit 'a little independent republic...perfectly democratic'.[9] In the first of these remarks, democracy was still implicitly viewed as an element in the constitution, whereas the second identified democracy with republicanism. Riven with divisions over class and religion, the reform campaign collapsed fairly quickly. Ideologically, however, this proved an innovative time, in which important steps were taken towards the elaboration of a theory of democratic politics.

---

[7] C. H. Wilson, *A Compleat Collection of the Resolutions of the Volunteers, Grand Juries, &c. of Ireland, which Followed the Celebrated Dungannon Diet* (2 vols, Dublin, 1782), 1: 1.

[8] *Observations on the Doctrine laid down by Sir William Blackstone respecting the extent of the power of the British Parliament, Particularly in relation to Ireland* (Dublin, 1779), 56.

[9] *Thoughts on the Conduct and Continuation of the Volunteers of Ireland* (Dublin, 1783), 3; *Seasonable Advice to the People of Ireland, during the Present Recess of Parliament* (Dublin, 1783), 4.

William Drennan's *Letters of Orellana, an Irish Helot* appeared in the *Belfast Newsletter* in 1784, and in pamphlet form in 1785, published by the Constitutional Society of Dublin so that it could be distributed gratis. Each beginning 'Fellow Slaves', the *Letters* were shockingly blunt in their dismissal of 1782. Despite their few years in martial garb, Irishmen could not legitimately call themselves patriots or freemen. The problem was simple, and 1782 had not addressed it: '*the democratic spirit of the constitution is no more!*'[10] This was not the common argument that corruption had upset the balance of monarchy, aristocracy, and democracy within the constitution. Such a balance was an illusion. Liberty could be guaranteed only by a political system based on what Drennan termed constitutional rights, 'those rights respecting life, liberty, and property, without which we cannot be free'. A constitution and laws could only be judged by whether they flowed from these rights, and whether they were enforced by the 'controuling energy and momentum of that mighty mass to which those rights belong'.[11] Liberty required a virtuous and vigilant population. Drennan defined constitutional rights—the right not to be taxed without representation for example—as 'the rights of human nature'.[12] The people's rights were clearly violated by Ireland's current system of representation. Drennan therefore constructed an argument for democracy—as a political system as opposed to an element in the constitution—from the traditional political languages of classical republicanism and natural rights. He also, however, used a new political language, which is termed here revolutionary internationalism. This involved using the example of America or France to bolster the case for democracy in Ireland. Drennan drew on the US Declaration of Independence to identify constitutional rights and asked 'what is the distance between an Irishman and a Freeman? Not less than three thousand miles.'[13] A republic with a democratic spirit, Drennan implied, was the best form of government for Ireland. The *Letters* made Drennan's literary reputation and proved highly popular and influential into the 1790s even though, as S. J. Connolly has noted, Drennan himself pulled back from some of the more radical implications of his own argument in other parts of the *Letters*.[14]

THE FRENCH REVOLUTION, THE CHALLENGE TO THE SOCIAL ORDER, AND DEVELOPING VISIONS OF DEMOCRACY

After the failure of the Volunteers' parliamentary reform campaign, the radicals went into decline, though they played a prominent role in mobilizing public opinion against Pitt's Commercial Propositions of 1785 and during the Regency Crisis of 1788–9. Both these crises were interpreted as attacks on the rights established in 1782.

[10] [William Drennan], *The Letters of Orellana, an Irish Helot* (Dublin, 1785), 11.
[11] Ibid. 12, 13.   [12] Ibid. 13.   [13] Ibid. 14.
[14] S. J. Connolly, 'Precedent and Principle: The Patriots and their Critics', in Connolly (ed.), *Political Ideas*, 146.

They contributed to the refining of claims of right among radicals that fed into the creation of a new political vision. Combined with the absence of reform and continued British influence over the Irish Parliament, they sapped faith in 1782—for example, Ireland's most popular newspaper in the late 1780s, the *Dublin Evening Post*, frequently referred to 1782 as a sham. The Regency Crisis produced the formation of the Irish Whig Club, and allied clubs such as the more radical 'Whigs of the Capital'. The 1790 election brought an alliance of Whigs and radical reformers some success, thus they won both seats for the city of Dublin. The liberal and radical opposition to government was further invigorated by the example of France. Shortly after the Bastille fell (14–15 July 1789) one newspaper asked, 'When the people of Ireland see that a nation, which was lately immersed in slavery, are now ably contending for the rights of man, will the Irish, who are cajoled with the idea that they are free while restricted in their commerce, sit idle?'[15] The idea that the French nation had successfully recovered its rights was celebrated across the Irish political spectrum in the initial stages of the Revolution, but it was only some liberals and radicals who argued that aspects of the French example were worth copying in Ireland; the language of the rights of man was shared by all when it could be interpreted in moderate terms, but revolutionary internationalism was not.

Irish usage of the language of revolutionary internationalism overwhelmingly centred on France. Calls to imitate the spirit of the French reformers appeared before the Bastille fell. Interest in the potential implications for Ireland of the French Revolution shaped Irish politics in the 1790s, especially once invasion aided by a popular United Irish uprising became likely. In many respects, democracy became synonymous with Revolutionary France. The fact that the Revolution itself was not static but went through several radically different phases was reflected in Irish conceptions of democracy, among both its adherents and its opponents.

Opponents of democracy countered revolutionary internationalism by using the example of France to try to discredit democracy. John Fitzgibbon, the most reactionary and powerful figure in the Irish government, in 1793 attacked Whig reform plans as inevitably producing a pure democracy like France, and with it 'a state of frantic and savage despotism'.[16] Joseph Pollock, a leading radical at the Volunteer Convention of 1782 and in 1793 a Whig, condemned a party dedicated to establishing a 'real democracy' that would bring civil war as it had in France. Supporting his claim that democrats were 'not contemptible in numbers or industry', someone placed placards warning against aristocrats (i.e. Whigs like him) at the Volunteer Convention in 1793; the opponents of aristocracy carried the day on most motions.[17] Innumerable examples could be drawn from the utterances of both moderate Whigs and conservatives linking democracy, France, and Irish radicals to violence, tyranny, and anarchy. This was a central plank in anti-democratic strategy, and seemed to have some effect on bourgeois radicals in 1798, contributing to the poor turnout of United Irishmen in some areas.

---

[15] *Morning Post; or Dublin Courant*, 15 August 1789.
[16] *The Speech of the Right Honourable John Lord Baron Fitzgibbon, March 13th 1793* (Dublin, 1793), 25.
[17] Joseph Pollock, *Letters to the Inhabitants of the Town and Lordship of Newry* (Dublin, 1793), 197.

The fullest example of radical propaganda using the language of revolutionary internationalism appeared in August 1790, when the 'Whigs of the Capital' produced a fake *Address from the National Assembly of France to the People of Ireland*. The Whigs of the Capital—who included Napper Tandy and other prominent radicals from the Volunteer reform campaign—later produced the first cheap edition of Tom Paine's *Rights of Man, Part I* (1791), and many members later played crucial roles in the United Irishmen in both their open and clandestine manifestations. The *Address* was a remarkable document, in its criticisms of the constitution, its hostile attitude towards Britain, and attacks on the three pillars of *ancien régime* Europe: monarchy, aristocracy, and state religion. It appeared in a context where conservative propagandists had already begun labelling radicals in Ireland and France as democrats.[18] The Whigs of the Capital had already been denounced for filling the streets of Dublin with 'the ensign of French Democracy'.[19] For some conservatives, then, 'French principles' already meant democracy. The *Address* was about France, but pre-Revolutionary France also stood for Ireland. The *Address* deployed revolutionary internationalism, claims of right, and egalitarianism to argue the case for change. Elements of certain types of Enlightenment thinking, about the economy and war for example, can also be discerned. The *Address* did not advocate democracy for Ireland, and nor it did describe France as a democracy. However, its themes, especially the attack on aristocracy, would prove fundamental to ideas of democracy as they developed in the 1790s. Given its source, its date of publication, and its themes, the *Address* provides a particularly valuable insight into the ideological resources that were available to those seeking to construct a new conception of politics in the years after 1789.

The *Address* rejected the fundamental assumptions of Irish politics, comparing its failures with the political rights and equality provided by Revolutionary France. The Declaration of Rights of Man and Citizen, 'an eternal declaration of war' against mankind's oppressors, was 'a law to legislators themselves'.[20] The French had declared that any state not guaranteeing civic rights to all 'has NO CONSTITUTION; and from that moment, the jealousy of nations free by reputation, has arisen against us'.[21] In other words, a confessional state like Ireland or Britain offered a false freedom to all its people, and not just the victims of discrimination. When a constitution had become so corrupted that effectively there was none, there was only one choice. The French had made it. Rebuilding 'from the very foundation', they discovered 'the hollowness and instability of those artificial principles on which some nations so fondly rest. Political abuses must be overturned completely and at once, or not at all—A slow and partial reform always ends where it begun.'[22] At a stroke, the British constitutional reforming tradition was dismissed as an inevitable failure. Only revolutionary change placing sovereignty firmly in the hands of the people could guarantee liberty and equality.

---

[18] For example, *A Letter Addressed to James Napper Tandy* (Dublin, 1790), 2, 16.
[19] *Observations on the Vindication of the Whig Club* (Dublin, 1790), 9.
[20] *Address from the National Assembly of France to the People of Ireland* (Dublin, 1790), 14.
[21] Ibid. 9.   [22] Ibid. 13.

The *Address* viewed the world in Manichean terms. The forces of liberty, France and her supporters, were arrayed against the forces of despotism and the 'aristocracies of the earth'. Kings and aristocrats, it claimed, understood all too well the threat posed by the rights of man as practised in France. Having abolished feudalism, made the law the expression of the general will through genuinely representative government, and introduced meritocracy, the French 'did not leave [themselves] a single friend, from Russia down to Sardinia, in the cabinet of Kings'.[23] The *Address* predicted that an international counter-revolutionary crusade would soon be launched against France. Leading it would be a nation 'whose grand object is to keep the great majority of the people in eternal ignorance, and eternal servitude . . . to say such as thou *wert*, centuries ago, continue *to be* for centuries to come, and that Nation calls itself free'.[24] This nation was of course Britain, which stood accused of denying its own people freedom and of seeking to deny it to others, namely, inhabitants of Ireland. Revolutionary internationalism grew naturally in the age of revolution, but its attractiveness in Ireland stemmed from the desire for an ally able to counteract British power. In this sense, it functioned as an updated version of the tradition of looking to the Crown's enemies abroad for aid. Once the war with France began, an alliance between Irish and French democrats became the great fear of Irish conservatives. When the alliance was formed, it became the great hope of the United Irishmen, being perhaps the strongest card they had to play in the violent, polarized atmosphere that developed after 1793.

Monarchy and aristocracy, the *Address* claimed, offered only the prospect of war; the 'Assembly' offered the 'brotherhood of humanity', 'a republic of free kingdoms' bound together by commerce.[25] The French wanted a 'great federal republic', a 'confederation in *favour* of human rights', that would 'guarantee the liberties of each and all; [and] substitute a balance of freedom in place of a balance of power'.[26] The *Address* stressed the suffering of the poor, blaming it on the demands of kings, aristocrats, and clerics. The peace and prosperity brought about by revolutionary change would greatly improve their lot. This language fit perfectly into Enlightenment discussions of peace, war, and commerce (as recently outlined by David Bell), as well as into Irish concerns with economic development and the impact of Anglo-Irish relations upon this.[27] The language of international revolution served a very direct instrumental purpose given Ireland's geopolitical situation, but simultaneously reflected a genuine ideological commitment to a different Ireland and a different world. Irish separatists viewed their struggle within an internationalist framework; to describe them as simply 'nationalist' is to miss this central part of their world view.

The languages of rights, equality, and revolutionary internationalism were prominent well before the publication of Paine's *Rights of Man*, although its appearance clarified and intensified their usage. Irish revolutionary thought was not simply Paineite, not just something created by and adapted from his work. The justification offered by the *Address* for the French National Assembly's introduction

---

[23] Ibid. 7–8.   [24] Ibid. 30.   [25] Ibid. 3–4.   [26] Ibid. 21–2.
[27] David A. Bell, *The First Total War* (London, 2007), chapter 2.

of the distinction between active and passive citizens (i.e. excluding from the franchise many of the poor), and the fact that the United Irish press referred to Directorial France (which had re-introduced property qualifications for political rights) as democratic, remind us of the fluid nature of political ideas, and that democracy was widely conceived as a social as well as political ideology. An anti-aristocratic egalitarian spirit rather than a particular set of political arrangements defined democracy for some.

CONCEPTIONS OF EQUALITY, HOPES OF MATERIAL GAIN, AND UNDERSTANDINGS OF DEMOCRACY

Three different types of equality existed within Irish revolutionary thought. Most prominent was religious equality, followed by political equality, with social equality increasingly important as the United Irishmen and Defenders sought to build an organization capable of effecting revolution. Although there were some people, like Sir Edward Newenham, who wanted radical reform that excluded Catholics, they did not describe themselves as democrats. Nor did the Whig reformers, like Henry Grattan, who, despite wishing to see Catholics granted equal political rights, explicitly rejected democracy. Not everyone who believed in religious equality avowed themselves a democrat, but those who avowed themselves democrats commonly believed in religious equality, although some from the lower orders associated revolution, and possibly democracy, with Catholic *revanche*.

A major change between the eras of the American and French Revolutions was in attitudes towards equality. Religious and political equality were much more assertively propagated in the 1790s. Some radicals embraced them during the reform campaign of 1783–4 by making Catholics and the poor Volunteers, and providing them with arms, one of the most important marks of citizenship. However, these were still a minority at the time the movement collapsed. By the 1790s, the language of Enlightenment had grown much more powerful within political culture, helping create an atmosphere conducive to increased toleration, if not equality. Arguments for greater toleration using Enlightened language appeared before the French Revolution, but multiplied rapidly after it, when arguments for full religious equality became commonplace. The Presbyterian Reverend Samuel Barber summed this mood up well. 'Science enlarges the Mind, ascertains the Rights of Men, and before Science sooner or later all Tyranny must fall.'[28] Even the *Freeman's Journal*, at this point Ireland's most reactionary newspaper, could be found calling for extended religious toleration 'in this enlightened age'.[29]

Full religious equality was central to the founding Declaration and Resolutions of the United Irishmen in October 1791. In an era 'when the rights of men are

[28] Presbyterian Historical Society of Ireland. Barber MSS, S. Barber, Sermons. Some conservatives attributed Presbyterian radicalism to Presbyterianism's supposedly democratic principles, e.g. *A Representation of the Present Critical State of Affairs in Ireland* (Dublin, 1791), 37.
[29] *Freeman's Journal* (Dublin), 19 January 1790.

ascertained in theory and that theory substantiated by practice', the United
Irishmen sought a 'NATIONAL GOVERNMENT' (replacing one under Britain's
control). 'That great measure essential to the prosperity and freedom of Ireland,
AN EQUAL REPRESENTATION OF ALL THE PEOPLE IN PARLIAMENT'
would bring this about. The newly founded United Irish society ignored the issue
of property qualifications for the franchise, but made clear that it sought to abolish
religious distinctions, not just in politics but in the minds of the people. Only 'the
equal distribution of the rights of man through all sects and all denominations of
Irishmen' could solve the structural problems of British influence, religious division, and poverty.[30] Unlike religious equality, universal manhood suffrage was open
to question, and it was only after great debate that the Dublin United Irishmen
approved it for their plan of reform in 1793. However, the Dublin Society was
socially atypical, being wealthier, a point picked up by the United Irishman-turned-
government-informer W. P. Carey who justified his actions by asserting that 'Our
Democracy here is unworthy of the name... a contemptible aristocracy in dis-
guise'.[31] Many United Irishmen, especially in the north, unambiguously embraced
the French model and radical versions of equality along with it. The founding of
the Irish Jacobins as a front for the Belfast United Irishmen is one indication of this
fact. The christening of a child near Belfast as 'Dumouriez' after the Republic's
leading general is perhaps another. Praise for the power, strength, happiness, and
virtue enjoyed by inhabitants of the new French Republic in radical propaganda
served to promote the democratic cause at home. The conservative Thomas Blac-
quiere blamed the American and French Revolutions for making democracy and
equality 'the favourite topics of discussion among the lower classes of people, particularly in the north of Ireland'.[32] The egalitarian message being discussed by the
lower orders was constantly promoted through newspapers, pamphlets, poetry,
songs, oaths, and toasts. For example, the highly influential United Irish song-
book, *Paddy's Resource*, included toasts to 'Liberty and Equality', 'The well founded
claims of the Catholics of Ireland; and may no religious distinctions rob citizens of
their rights', and 'A speedy divorce to Church and State'.[33] Equality was a simple
language that the popular classes could embrace, and, as in France, interpret for
themselves in socially radical ways.

United Irish propaganda increasingly suggested that revolution would bring
material benefits. The propaganda of the United Irishmen and their allies, and
popular expectations reported to government, referred to wage increases, a reduction in (and sometimes abolition of) rents and taxes, and the abolition of tithes.
The Union Doctrine, or Poor Man's Catechism gave an example of how advocacy of
social equality within the framework of political rights became an important means
of mobilizing support for the United Irishmen. 'I believe in a revolution founded
on the rights of man, in the natural and imprescriptible rights of *all* citizens to the

[30] Tone, *Writings*, 1: 140–1.
[31] Cited in Michael Durey, 'The Dublin Society of United Irishmen and the Politics of the Carey-
Drennan Dispute, 1792–1794', *Historical Journal*, 37 (1994), 108.
[32] Thomas Blaquiere, *General Observations on the State of Affairs in Ireland, and its Defence against
an Invasion* (Dublin, 1797), 17.
[33] *Paddy's Resource* (Dublin, 1795), 95–6.

land. I believe the soil, nor any part of it, cannot be transferred without the consent of the people, or their representatives, convened and authorized, by the votes of every man having arrived at the age of twenty one.'[34] The *Catechism* spoke of 'a fair division of the land' that would guarantee everyone a comfortable living once the land had been reclaimed from the nobility.[35] The *Manifesto of the Provisional Government* for the abortive United Irish rebellion of 1803 promised the redistribution of property belonging to the Established Church, English interests, and counter-revolutionaries. There were, unsurprisingly, limits to the social radicalism of the United Irishmen, as attested by their actions against strikers in the early 1790s and the desire of some of their leaders for French help to protect the social order. Nevertheless, their willingness to address the social and economic concerns of the lower orders to secure support for establishing the republic places them firmly in the Jacobin tradition of 1793–4.

The poor were not the only people expecting material benefit from political change. Stephen Small has rightly identified commercial grievance as a central theme in eighteenth-century Irish political thought. Commercial grievance can be seen not as an isolated concern but rather as a component of an enlightened political economy that focused on the transformation—or improvement—of Ireland into a prosperous commercial society. Ireland's great economic potential was a truism across the political spectrum; the question was how government could help achieve it. For some United Irishmen, being a democrat entailed pursuing the goals specified by this political economy. Emmet believed in revolutionary political economy, while another leading United Irishman, Arthur O'Connor, forged 'a distinctive Irish language of radical democracy out of the French sources, by fusing them with the local political tradition and Scottish political economy'.[36] O'Connor's *The State of Ireland* (1798) offered the fullest revolutionary elaboration of enlightened political economy. It argued that the growth of commerce and the influence of the press had transformed society and the European mind. Consequently, Europe had reached 'that period in which Hereditary Aristocracy and Representative Democracy cannot exist together'.[37] O'Connor did not envisage a clash of abstract political systems, but rather the triumph of 'the Democracy' (the people) and 'the Representative Democracy' (the people's representatives) in the context of the destruction of all forms of monopoly, political, religious, social, and economic—without which, he argued, even universal suffrage would be meaningless. O'Connor also deployed revolutionary internationalism. The forces of aristocracy were fighting not French principles and French revolution, but European principles and European revolution.[38] The French had abolished monopoly to establish liberty. In doing so, they had inspired peoples everywhere, none more so than the Irish.

---

[34] Cited in Jim Smyth, *The Men of No Property: Irish Radicals and Popular Politics in the Late Eighteenth Century* (revised edn, Houndmills, 1998), 168.

[35] 'The Union Doctrine, or Poor Man's Catechism', *Labour History*, 75 (1998), 33–7.

[36] James Quinn, 'The United Irishmen and Social Reform', *Irish Historical Studies*, 31 (1998), 188; James Livesey, 'Introduction' to Arthur O'Connor, *The State of Ireland*, ed. James Livesey (Dublin, 1998), 2.

[37] Arthur O'Connor, *The State of Ireland* (1798), 128.

[38] Ibid. 113. This passage does not appear in the second edition, the basis of Livesey's modern edition.

CONCLUSION

Radicals, Whigs, and conservatives all agreed that democrats and democratic ideas were an important force in Irish politics and society by the early 1790s, but the meaning and implications of democracy, and who was a democrat, remained highly contested. Examples of democratic government were cited (positively and negatively) from the ancient world, the 1640s, America, and, most often, France, especially once the foundation of the Republic linked France and democracy in many people's minds. Opponents of democracy certainly had France in mind when they denounced its consequences, while for Tone, France provided *the* test of democratic credentials. Conservatives had the clearest vision of what democracy entailed, and they perhaps best understood how from the late 1770s changes in political beliefs and practices—the rise of what was often called the spirit of democracy—were undermining traditional assumptions and feeding the emergence of a democratic model of politics. For them, the term 'democracy' could apply to any political or social reforms that would significantly alter the political, social, or religious order. They therefore had a much more inclusive understanding of what constituted democracy than had democrats themselves. Hence Whigs were denounced as 'democrats' by conservatives and as 'aristocrats' by democrats. The United Irishmen—regarded as 'democrats' by both their opponents and their leaders—sought to meld a wide range of influences—domestic and foreign, historical and contemporary—into a coherent ideology and practical programme that addressed the fundamental political, religious, social, and economic problems of the Irish people. At an ideological level, Irish democracy contained contradictions and compromises, as it did everywhere in the Atlantic world in the age of revolution. Unlike their British cousins, Irish democrats failed not because they lost the argument but because of defeat on the battlefield.

The practical programmes drawn up throughout the 1790s by United Irish leaders who avowed themselves democrats suggest that they associated certain ideas and practices with democracy. Elements of the programmes were fixed (e.g. religious equality, representative government) whereas others were less static (qualifications for the franchise, whether independence required separation from Britain, republicanism, social reforms). From the perspective of practical measures, the *Poor Man's Catechism*, for example, despite never mentioning the word 'democracy', would have been recognized as a democratic document not only by men like Tone, Russell, Emmet, and O'Connor (or by their opponents), but also by its target audience among the lower orders after nearly a decade of newspaper reports, pamphlets, speeches in Parliament, poetry, and song identifying the measures it advocated with democracy. The United Irish leaders' relative lack of conceptual discussions of democracy reflected their focus on practical outcomes and popular politicization, their desire to secure the widest possible support, and the attractiveness of the term 'republican' as a self-description, especially when related to America and France.

The main languages out of which an Irish democratic vision was constructed—claims of right, classical republicanism, Enlightenment toleration and political economy, egalitarianism, and revolutionary internationalism—reflect the extent to which Ireland partook of broader developments in the Atlantic world, but also the unique circumstances of Irish history. Claims of right functioned at the national and the individual level, and inevitably religious equality was central. While only some favoured universal suffrage, the overturning of aristocracy was essential for all democrats. Ireland's geopolitical situation made revolutionary internationalism an integral part of this vision, while the legacy of Volunteering boosted the importance of classical republicanism to the extent that more modern and commercial aspects have often been obscured. While it is tempting to see democratic discourse in this era as simple cover for the selfish interests of various groups within society, the subsequent history of democratic thought and practice—much more accommodating as it proved to sectarian divisions—highlights the fact that the democrats of the age of revolution created a genuinely radical, secular, and novel ideology that seemed to huge numbers of the Irish middle and lower orders, for a short time at least, to offer a path to a better world, and to be a vision worth fighting for.

11

'Democracy' and the Irish People, 1830–48

Laurent Colantonio

Who talked and wrote about 'democracy' in Ireland during the 1830s and 1840s? For what purposes? Why was this particular word used? And who was the expected audience? I propose to examine various expressions of this contested and unstable idea, focusing on common points and divergences, on the discursive strategies at work, on the democratic horizons displayed, and on whether the notion was presented as an aspiration or as a nightmare. This paper investigates the existence of a particular Irish language of democracy around 1840, asking what was—or was not—specifically Irish about use of the term.

Given the scale of the topic, I have chosen to focus on the main, nationalist, discourse on democracy. I go on to contrast this with the views of persons opposed to nationalist demands, and finally with the opinion of those who might be seen as bearers of an alternative language of democracy within the nationalist sphere. The study of other forms of democratic expression, notably by the people as opposed to the elite, can only be touched upon in this short essay. Before exploring the language of democracy in Ireland, I will first move briefly off centre and glance at several non-Irish usages.

FRENCH ACCOUNTS OF 'IRISH DEMOCRACY'

Two considerations encourage a brief detour through the Continent. First, Ireland was not isolated internationally and it is important to think about democracy in Ireland in terms of circulations and appropriations of the word. Second, many European contemporaries evoked an Irish democratic model. They were fascinated by the way popular agitations in Ireland suggested that democratic social relations might operate.

On a European level, French comments were certainly the most surprising. Since France was at that time one of the few nations in Europe where modern democracy had already been experienced as a political regime, it is unexpected to see French people interested in what they called 'the Irish democracy'. And yet many French contemporaries, from Liberal Catholics to Republicans, saw the Irish experience of the 1820s to 1840s both as reflecting a successful process of democratization and as a source of inspiration. They stressed the specificity of the Irish situation—characterized by the precocity of a national and Catholic mass

movement—and the 'universal' dimension of what they described as the appearance of the 'people' in the political sphere, raising questions about their representation and control, at a time when it was still forbidden to assemble in France.
Examining what they emphasized in the Irish experience will bring out the variety
of ways in which French commentators thought about democracy.

French republicans were particularly receptive to the efforts made by the Irish
nationalist movement to arouse the political consciousness of non-voters. Until
1843 the movement's leader, Daniel O'Connell, was presented as the archetypal
popular hero, 'the orator of democracy',[1] the advocate of peoples oppressed by
tyrants and kings, the natural representative of the masses excluded from the
vote—a status to which republicans themselves aspired. In 1835 the insurgents
who had participated in the failed rebellions of the previous year—in Lyon (9–12
April) and Paris (14 April)—were put on trial. On this occasion, French republicans asked O'Connell, a lawyer, to come and defend the cause of republican pris-
oners at the bar, in the name of a shared spirit of democracy in the face of the
assault of despotism. O'Connell, who did not want to be considered a supporter
of their cause, refused to attend.[2] This episode reveals much about the divergence
between the Irishman's beliefs and those attributed to him by republicans such as
Félicité Lamennais, who described him in the same year as 'this gigantic revolutionary.... This O'Connel [*sic*] who, with his vigorous arm, is pushing the old
world into the depths, and proclaiming the advent of a new right—the right of
peoples—and the reign of equality and liberty.'[3]

Gustave de Beaumont, Alexis de Tocqueville's fellow traveller in Ireland in the
1830s, was not a republican. He considered the coming of democracy as something irresistible but troubling and potentially devastating if not brought under
control. In *L'Irlande sociale, politique et religieuse*, a report on his observations, he
wrote that the island showed how a European nation could progressively embrace
'the democratic spirit' (in contrast to the aristocratic one) without destroying the
entire social order. In Beaumont's account, O'Connell appears as the prototype of
the modern politician, the paradigm of the reasonable democrat whose action is
situated 'between submission and revolt'.[4]

DANIEL O'CONNELL OR THE
NATION AND DEMOCRACY

More than that of the republicans, Beaumont's depiction of O'Connell echoed the
latter's own understanding of his role. But how precisely did O'Connell and his
followers use the term 'democracy' and present their own, positive version of it?

---

[1] *Le National* (Paris), 22 June 1835.
[2] Laurent Colantonio, 'Daniel O'Connell: un Irlandais au cœur du discours républicain pendant
la monarchie de Juillet', *Revue d'histoire du XIXᵉ siècle*, 20–21 (2000/1 and 2), 39–53.
[3] *Correspondance générale de Lamennais*, ed. Louis Le Guillou (9 vols, Paris, 1971–81), 6: 495.
[4] Gustave de Beaumont, *Ireland: Social, Political, and Religious*, ed. and trans. William C. Taylor (new
edn, Cambridge, MA, 2006), 230. Originally, *L'Irlande sociale, politique et religieuse* (2 vols, Paris, 1839).

What O'Connell named 'democratic liberty' and the measures he advocated were closely associated with a variety of qualifiers: popular expression, mass participation, 'moral force', liberty, and at the same time moderation, respectability, and property.

O'Connell's main practical contribution to the democratization of Irish politics lies in the way he brought the 'beggars'—the majority of the people—into visibility in the political arena. He advocated mass participation and the empowerment of the people, either by voting (for the minority who had the franchise) or by alternative means (by signing petitions, entering political organizations, or mobilizing in mass meetings) that demonstrated their presence, expressing a national and powerful public opinion—a 'moral force', in contrast to a 'physical force'—that the government could not ignore any longer. As Bill Kissane rightly noted, 'from the 1820s, [O'Connell] was able to construct a political movement that was expansive, rather than restrictive in its attitude towards membership, geared towards politicising the people rather than excluding them'.[5]

O'Connell took great care to emphasize that his legitimacy as a spokesman issued strictly from the will of the people. 'The voice of the people ha[s] sent [me] there', he justified himself as he faced the Commons in May 1829. '[I am] a representative of the people.'[6] Further, almost invariably, public meetings began with a toast to 'the People, the genuine source of legitimate power'. In most of O'Connell's public speeches and addresses, the 'people' was used as a synonym for 'the Irish nation'. As he put it, whenever in history the 'spirit of democracy' developed, the 'nation prospered. [By contrast], without the spirit of democracy, governors are tyrants, and the people are slaves.'[7]

Democracy, here as in much other contemporary discourse, meant primarily 'non-aristocratic' rather than denoting any specific model of government. Hence aristocracy was described as the arch-enemy of 'Irish democracy' and tirelessly denounced in O'Connell's speeches. Those who defended the undue privileges of an oligarchic minority were excluded from the Irish people/nation.[8] The Repeal programme that O'Connell championed during the 1840s echoed demands for male universal suffrage, the secret ballot, and socio-economic claims such as tenant rights or the repeal of the newly established Irish Poor Law. Yet, it is striking that all those promised reforms were subordinated to the great plan of national regeneration. The dozens of speeches pronounced during so-called 'monster meetings' in 1843 were all built on the same pattern. Most of the speaking time was devoted to describing the scandalous British domination in Ireland and to justifying the claim that the repeal of the Union represented the sole remedy for Irish ills. Among the arguments deployed to convince the Irish people of the advantages that would derive from such a political step, O'Connell assured them that once political

[5] Bill Kissane, *Explaining Irish Democracy* (Dublin, 2002), 85.
[6] Hansard, 2nd ser., 21: 1,402 (Commons, 18 May 1829).
[7] O'Connell's speech at the Loyal National Repeal Association (*LNRA*) weekly meeting, *Tuam Herald*, 24 April 1841.
[8] O'Connell's speech at Meath, *Freeman's Journal* (Dublin), 1 April 1837.

autonomy was recovered, then all popular aspirations would soon be satisfied—without explaining exactly why or how the latter would spring from the former.

What has previously been said must be linked with a second aspect of O'Connell's imaginative horizon. He was concerned about the groundswell of public opinion that he had triggered. O'Connell was aiming for a controlled explosion of the masses into public affairs, an experience of popular power in which the passions of the multitude could be safely channelled through a powerful and well-structured organization; the whole tempered by the wisdom of 'representatives duly chosen by all the people'.[9] O'Connell and his leading lieutenants were fundamentally attached to the existing social order.[10] He always stated that he was ready to lead a constitutional revolution but steadily repeated that he 'desire[d] no social revolution, no social change'.[11] O'Connell was open to extending the political sphere to great numbers but believed that the nationalist middle class would remain the rulers within a 'respectable' version of democracy. His capacity to channel the process particularly impressed commentators in Europe. Beaumont shared O'Connell's fears of 'democratic excess' and praised the Irishman's strategy in creating a system which 'does not confer on the people the benefits of a sudden and prosperous revolution, but which also does not expose the country to the awful responsibilities of an unsuccessful insurrection'.[12]

O'Connell's dislike of what he called 'fierce' or 'wild' democracy was informed both by his efforts to master and canalize the emergence of the people into public life and by the way he accused 'wild democrats' of trying to destroy the framework of society and 'individual liberties'. He directed accusations at 'Socialists' especially, as they threatened to undermine 'the grand sentiment on which society is based—namely, the sentiment of property'.[13] English Chartists and French republicans (even though most of them were admirers of O'Connell until 1842–3) were also criticized, being associated with violence—especially the French 'Terror'—and (as O'Connell saw it) with the desire for social revolution. At the beginning of the 1840s, when Chartists tried to develop a foothold in Ireland, O'Connell was instrumental in opposing them.[14]

During his long parliamentary career (1830–47), O'Connell also championed a number of demands which we might term 'democratic' that were not directly connected with the national question. He expressed most of them by means of language that was characteristic of British radicalism, defining himself as a member

[9] O'Connell's speech at the *LNRA* weekly meeting, *Tuam Herald*, 24 April 1841.

[10] See for example W. J. O'Neill Daunt's speech on democracy, at the *LNRA* weekly meeting, *The Nation* (Dublin), 4 September 1843.

[11] Maurice R. O'Connell (ed.), *The Correspondence of Daniel O'Connell*, (8 vols, Dublin, 1972–80), 5: 11.

[12] Beaumont, *Ireland*, 230.

[13] *The Nation* (Dublin), 3 December 1842. This article suggests that during its first months of existence, the organ of Young Ireland shared the main nationalist view on democracy.

[14] O'Connell's stance on French republicans was developed in numerous speeches. See for example *Dublin Evening Post*, 20 July 1843 and 5 August 1843; *Freeman's Journal* (Dublin), 4 October 1843. On his opposition to Chartism in Ireland, see Christine Kinealy, '"Brethren in Bondage": Chartists, O'Connellites, Young Irelanders and the 1848 Uprising', in Fintan Lane and Donal Ó Drisceoil (eds), *Politics and the Irish Working Class, 1830–1945* (Basingstoke, 2005), 87–111.

of the 'small and sacred band of Radical reformers'.[15] He opposed the death penalty, pronounced in favour of a new Upper House with elected peers, and defended propositions for the secret ballot and for the extension of suffrage. He supported the unsuccessful campaign for Jewish emancipation in 1829–30 when the cause was unpopular in Britain.[16] He pronounced in favour of the complete severance of Church and State, rejecting the idea of a state-favoured religion, even if it was Catholic. He developed an international reputation as an influential spokesman for the anti-slavery movement, suffering in consequence a drastic reduction of contributions from anti-abolitionist Irish Americans during the 1840s.[17]

On this account, O'Connell appears to have been simultaneously a subversive figure in a chaotic and unfinished process of popular and national mobilization *and* an agent of social normalization, interested in reconstructing a hierarchical order following mass popular demonstrations. His invocations of 'democracy' were moulded by a continuous tension between these two poles.

At this stage, it seems instructive to compare what has been said here with what historians have previously said on the subject. Sean O'Faoláin wrote in 1938: 'What he [O'Connell] gave us is hard to tell. Much good, much bad, but one thing was priceless—the principle of life as a democracy.'[18] Since then, several historians have followed in O'Faoláin's wake, and have situated 'the birth of Irish democracy' in the first half of the nineteenth century,[19] seeing 'O'Connell as having established the tradition of democracy in Ireland'.[20] But what precisely was democratic about O'Connell's achievements, according to those writers and scholars? Or to put it another way, what do they have in mind when they use the term 'democracy' and associate it with O'Connell?

This is not easy to establish. Although a link between O'Connell and democracy is often asserted, it is rarely clearly demonstrated, nor is the concept of democracy always precisely defined: its meaning is taken as obvious, unproblematic—a given—such that it does not need explanation. A striking case is a 1993 article by Maurice R. O'Connell, historian and great-great-grandson of Daniel O'Connell,[21] in which the words 'democrat' or 'democracy' were neither discussed nor even employed...except in the title: 'Daniel O'Connell. Democrat, Liberal Catholic and Husband'.[22] Other writers have been somewhat more explicit. For example,

---

[15] Hansard, 2nd ser., 23: 793 (House of Commons, 23 March 1830).

[16] *Correspondence of Daniel O'Connell*, 4: 95–7.

[17] In a vast bibliography see for example Christine Kinealy, *Daniel O'Connell and the Anti-Slavery Movement* (London, 2010).

[18] Sean O'Faoláin, *King of the Beggars: A Life of Daniel O'Connell in a Study of the Rise of Modern Irish Democracy* (New York, 1938), 329.

[19] For example Fergus O'Ferrall, *Catholic Emancipation: Daniel O'Connell and the Birth of Irish Democracy, 1820–30* (Dublin, 1985); Donal McCartney, *The Dawning of Democracy: Ireland 1800–1870* (Dublin, 1987).

[20] Maurice R. O'Connell (ed.), *People Power: Proceedings of the Third Annual Daniel O'Connell Workshop* (Dublin, 1993), introduction.

[21] Maurice R. O'Connell (1922–2005) is the author of numerous studies on his ancestor and the editor of the very valuable *Correspondence of Daniel O'Connell*.

[22] Maurice R. O'Connell, 'Daniel O'Connell: Democrat, Liberal Catholic and Husband', *Blackrock Society Proceedings*, 2 (1993–4), 4–17.

Donal McCartney chose as his criterion the fact that O'Connell and his political movement gave birth both to a popular public opinion ('The monster meetings were demonstrations of the massiveness of organised democracy') and to the first modern political structure in Europe ('[the Catholic Association] became an unprecedented organization of democratic power').[23] However, there are problems with this account, even in its own terms. It is true that the popular base was involved and consulted, particularly at the parish level where Repeal wardens were chosen by the inhabitants. But the main political decisions were first taken by the central body of the association, in which O'Connell exercised a considerable influence, as shown by the reports of the Dublin weekly meetings. In fact, few people were really engaged in the process of decision-making, and true dialogue between the masses and their leaders was limited. Moreover, O'Connell was known for his authoritarian tendencies and his difficulties in accepting contradiction and power-sharing. In 1836 Feargus O'Connor—who had been a Repealer MP for County Cork between 1832 and 1835—referred to him as 'a whimsical Dictator';[24] and in the last years of his life O'Connell refused to accommodate the challenge to his authority represented by the Young Ireland movement.

Overall, academic discourse on the democratization of popular politics in Ireland before the famine of 1846–51 has largely echoed O'Connell's own language of democracy without considering what precisely it meant to him. The social dimension has generally been little considered, and historians have tended to underestimate limits and discontinuities when describing the Irish leader and his movement as having initiated a linear process of development. Consider another instance of these limits. In 1829, at the same time that it granted Catholic Emancipation, Parliament increased the amount of property needed to vote in Irish county elections and, consequently, drastically reduced the number of Irish electors from about 300,000 to a mere 37,000. How can this development be situated inside a progressive and linear reading of the democratization process? Historians have seldom interpreted the measure as a democratic retreat. Accepting O'Connell's own justification for a concession he was prepared to endorse, they have instead analyzed it as 'a necessary sacrifice to achieve equal rights across confessions'.[25]

There are reasons to be cautious in hailing O'Connell as one of the founding fathers of Irish democracy. Was he a steadfast democrat? In what sense was the political system that he had in mind democratic? Facilitating continuing popular participation in politics was probably an important issue for him, but was not a priority as against his political/nationalist goals. He used democratic language and practices to achieve goals that his followers were not given much voice in shaping, and it might be more accurate to analyze the mobilization he triggered as a first step towards a popular *Catholic* political culture in Ireland. Overall, the Irish contribution to the democratization of political life and society during the first half of

[23] McCartney, *Dawning of Democracy*, 153, 113.

[24] Feargus O'Connor, *A Series of Letters from Feargus O'Connor to Daniel O'Connell* (London, 1836), 20.

[25] McCartney, *Dawning of Democracy*, 118–19. See also Thomas Bartlett, *The Rise and Fall of the Irish Nation: The Catholic Question, 1690–1830* (Dublin, 1992), 342.

the nineteenth century is to be found far more in democratic practices than in deep reflection on the implications and tendency of these practices.

CONFLICTING VOICES

Alongside the main, O'Connellite, language on democracy, can we identify dissonant voices in Ireland? Consider the case of the 'defenders of the Union',[26] and particularly of the most conservative among them. O'Connell habitually described his political enemies in Ireland as men opposed both to nationalist politics and to democracy.[27] But did being unionist and against nationalist demands during the 1830–1840s necessarily mean opposing democracy? Here, the peculiarity of the Irish context matters in explaining why the two points were actually often linked. After the first few years of the Union, the defence of the institutional status quo became a rallying point for a great majority of Irish Protestants—from members of the Established Church to Ulster Presbyterians, from conservatives through to liberals opposed to Orangeism and the privileges of the 'Ascendancy'. Conversely, the prospect of repealing the Union became a major goal on the nationalist—mainly Catholic—side. As unionists in Ireland were members of the Protestant minority, arithmetically every extension of the suffrage tended to strengthen their political enemies. Their fear of being overwhelmed by a 'Catholic democracy' was certainly a chief reason why unionists in Ireland during the 1830–1840s supported a restricted suffrage.

A survey of unionist discourses on 'democracy' confirms that they used the word negatively, usually of their nationalist opponents. The published proceedings of Protestant conservative societies and journals displayed a general hostility towards 'democratic principles'. *The Belfast News Letter*—a strong Ulster conservative newspaper—described democracy as a threat to 'Protestant ascendancy' in Ireland. Sometimes the argument was even more alarming: as a political system and ideology, democracy was stated to present a peril not only for Ireland but for the whole British constitutional system and society, if not for 'the whole civilized world'.[28] At a meeting of the Brunswick Constitutional Club of Ireland in February 1829, William Saurin, a fierce and long-lasting adversary of Catholic claims, opposed Catholic Emancipation with the assertion that Catholicism was destructive of civil liberty and inconsistent with the very essence of the Protestant constitution of Britain (notably the organic union of Church and State), which might be overthrown as a result of passing the bill. Interestingly, the danger presented by emancipating Catholics was associated by Saurin with the threat of democracy: he stated that Emancipation was 'a measure suggested and argued upon by those who were anxious to seduce people from their allegiance, and to involve them in the conspiracy formed in this country forty years ago [by the United Irishmen]—

---

[26] David George Boyce and Alan O'Day (eds), *Defenders of the Union: A Survey of British and Irish Unionism since 1801* (London, 2001).

[27] e.g. *Correspondence of Daniel O'Connell*, 5: 152–3.   [28] *Belfast News Letter*, 31 December 1830.

under the influence of those principles of democracy which progressed in this country—and that have been from that period shaking our Constitution to its centre. ... The present measure is of revolutionary tendency.' Democracy was all the more dangerous given that it was born of foreign ideas and came from the United States and France, the countries of revolution and republicanism. In Saurin's terms, 'democratical principles' were the basis of 'that Constitution formed in the United States of America; a Constitution founded upon principles the direct opposite to the British Constitution'.[29] It is worth noting that on the O'Connellite side, Irish democracy was equally often justified in the name of the same—non-written—constitution. As the first Secretary of the Catholic Association, Nicholas O'Gorman, declared in 1828, employing language that was characteristic of British radicalism, 'Democracy shall [recover] that influence which was *originally* intended for it by the Constitution.'[30] In this case and others the same references were mobilized by pro- and anti-O'Connell factions to make opposite points.

In 1833 a leader in the *Belfast News Letter* reiterated that 'a democracy is still more intolerable' than aristocracy or oligarchy.[31] Overall, as during the Catholic Emancipation campaign, after 1829 speakers at Conservative meetings in the north-east of Ireland regularly amalgamated within the same notion repeal of the Union, revolution, and 'the shoals and quicksands of anarchy and democracy'.[32] At the beginning of the 1840s the young Isaac Butt, although at that time 'a conditional unionist' with a critical attitude to his political allies,[33] feared that the abrogation of the Union would bring chaos, anarchy, and confusion in Ireland. Contesting O'Connell's arguments in 1843, he declared that 'Repeal was a revolution. ... [T]he proposition was not to return to any state of things that previously existed in Ireland—not to adopt the constitution of any European state—but to enter on an untried and wild system of democracy.'[34] When coupled with nationalist demands, the notion of democracy still served as a terrible *repoussoir*.

To the *Belfast News Letter* in 1840 it seemed that 'It would be manifestly absurd to set persons, who had no property, to rule the destinies of those who had.'[35] In the Irish context, where property was mostly Protestant, this conservative and anti-democratic argument was also a way to wrestle with nationalist claims. The Presbyterian Reverend Henry Cooke, a famous spokesman of the Protestant unionist opposition to O'Connell in the north, and one of the most vehemently

[29] Saurin's speech at the second general meeting of the Brunswick Constitutional Club of Ireland, *Belfast News Letter*, 24 February 1829.
[30] 'Roman Catholic Association—Extracts from Mr O'Gorman's Speech', *Belfast News Letter*, 23 September 1828.
[31] *Belfast News Letter*, 25 January 1833.
[32] 'Irish Metropolitan Conservative Society—Great Anti-Repeal Demonstration', *Belfast News Letter*, 20 June 1843; see also 5 November 1833 and 21 July 1835.
[33] Joseph Spence, 'Isaac Butt, Irish Nationality and the Conditional Defence of the Union, 1833–70', in Boyce and O'Day, *Defenders of the Union*, 65–89.
[34] Isaac Butt, *A Full and Revised Report of the Three Days' Discussion in the Corporation of Dublin on the Repeal of the Union* (1843), p. 84, quoted in Pauline Collombier, *Le discours des leaders du nationalisme constitutionnel irlandais sur l'autonomie de l'Irlande* (2 vols, unpublished Ph.D., University Sorbonne Nouvelle-Paris 3, 2007), 1: 227.
[35] *Belfast News Letter*, 22 December 1840.

anti-democratic Irish orators, condemned in 1841 'that "fierce democracy" that would rob the rich and rifle the industrious, to endow the pauper who will but beg, the lazy that will not work, or the factious and seditious demagogue'.[36] In Cooke's speeches as in O'Connell's (as previously noted) 'fierce democracy' was castigated, with the noteworthy difference that O'Connell was included—as the worst of those 'seditious demagogue[s]'—within the 'fierce democracy' imagined by Henry Cooke!

In a society where sectarianism gained ground every day, the 'democratic' question in Ireland was intrinsically linked with the national/religious question. In the first part of the nineteenth century, as rightly underlined by D. George Boyce, 'If democracy meant playing the game by numbers, then it was a useful game for catholics to play; whether or not they would respect the need to look after the minority in a democratic Ireland remained doubtful.'[37] However, this depiction of democracy as a sectarian tactic must be qualified by the fact that some—including some prominent—members of the nationalist camp came from an Anglican or a Presbyterian background. This was particularly common in the ranks of Young Ireland.

Did those who identified with 'Young Ireland' offer approaches or demands regarding democracy alternative to the main nationalist discourse? When the group first appeared as a branch of the O'Connellite movement around 1841–2, the individual commitment of its members to democracy was far from general. On matters relating to social reform, most of the Young Ireland leaders were as moderate or conservative as those representing 'Old Ireland' within the Repeal Association. Indeed, the political positions of Young Irelanders were sometimes less radical than O'Connell's, especially in relation to slavery and universal male suffrage.

Nevertheless, from the beginning, some of those 'young' men and women were at ease with the idea of democracy, as shown in the following text written in May 1843 in *The Nation* (the weekly newspaper launched by Young Ireland in October 1842). Its subject was the Chartist movement; the article asserted that there is 'no reason why we should not be grateful for the tone and purpose expressed by them [English Chartists] towards us'. No doubt the author had in mind the positioning of the Irish demand for the repeal of the Act of Union in the preamble of the 1842 Charter. In addition, when O'Connell rejected Chartism because he feared that its vision entailed the giving of too much initiative to the uneducated masses, and too much in the way of social levelling, *The Nation* defended Chartism in the name of a common democratic ideal: '*They are the democracy of England*, wronged into trembling madness by the quiet but awful pressure of a bloated aristocracy. Their cause is the cause of work against idleness—of industry against plunder—of the oppressed against the tyrant.'[38] Although isolated, this example provides us with a first indication that the univocality of nationalist discourse on democracy in the 1840s must be qualified. Well before the Repeal Association's split with Young

---

[36] 'Speech of Dr Cooke at the Conservative Meeting', *Belfast News Letter*, 26 January 1841. See also 'Speech of the Rev. Dr. Cooke', *Belfast News Letter*, 21 July 1840.
[37] D. George Boyce, *Ireland 1828–1923: From Ascendancy to Democracy* (Oxford, 1992), 26–7.
[38] *The Nation* (Dublin), 20 May 1843.

Ireland, O'Connell's position on Chartism—and, therefore, on democracy—was open to challenge from among those who supported his cause.

The change towards a wider endorsement of democracy inside the Young Ireland movement was significant from 1846 onwards, following its clash with mainstream O'Connellite nationalism. From that moment, looking elsewhere for support, Young Irelanders sought closer relations with trade unions and Chartism, in both Ireland and Britain. The tightening of Young Ireland's relationship with Chartism was reinforced after the Parisian revolution of February 1848, which radicalized their nationalist discourse. Between March and July 1848, Chartists and Irish Confederates[39] briefly collaborated, posing a joint democratic threat that British authorities took very seriously.[40] During that year, the entire Confederate movement converted to democracy. 'The revolution in France has made me a democrat,' declared, for example, Thomas Francis Meagher on 25 March 1848. A month before, the same man, then still opposed to male universal suffrage, maintained in public: 'No; I am not for a democratic, but I am for a national movement—not for a movement like that of Paris in 1793, but for a movement like that of Brussels in 1830.'[41] The conservative Catholic Young Irelander, Charles Gavan Duffy, declared on 29 April 1848: 'Democracy, I believe, is the destiny of the world. Probably we are contemporary with the last race of Kings.'[42]

For members of the Young Ireland/Irish Confederation to which Meagher and Duffy belonged in 1848, 'democracy' became at this point a badge of identity, clearly associated with the memory of the United Irishmen ('Who fears to speak of Ninety-eight?', *The Nation* had asked rhetorically as early as 1843)[43] and with the French republican model; it defined itself against *both* monarchy and aristocracy. By contrast, O'Connell hoped to see democracy coupled with a constitutional monarchy relieved of the burden of the aristocracy; it was to remain aloof from violence and the murderous chaos he associated with Wolfe Tone and the republican ideal. O'Connell often condemned those 'men of '98' because they took the path of a 'fierce democracy' that led to a bloodbath and to the loss of Irish national sovereignty. 'I honour the pure spirit which animated certain high-souled members of that insurrection,' he wrote in 1841, 'but I denouce their deeds in the strongest terms of which language is capable, for their fatal and short-sighted policy entailed the blighting union of their country.'[44]

In the nationalist Ireland of the late 1840s two distinctive democratic imaginaries confronted each other. By 1846–8 both dynamics had been broken. The O'Connellite movement, already running out of steam, was weakened by the death of its leader in May 1847; while from 1846 onwards, the catastrophe of the Famine damaged all political/national prospects for at least a decade.

---

[39] Young Ireland had been renamed the Irish Confederation in January 1847.

[40] As recently reassessed by Christine Kinealy in Kinealy, *Repeal and Revolution: Ireland in 1848* (Manchester, 2009).

[41] Christine Kinealy, 'Brethren in Bondage', 100; 'Meeting of the Irish Confederation', *The Nation* (Dublin), 12 February 1848.

[42] *The Nation* (Dublin), 29 April 1848.

[43] This is the first phrase of a poem published in *The Nation* (Dublin), 1 April 1843.

[44] *Freeman's Journal* (Dublin), 20 May 1841.

THE LANGUAGE OF THE PEOPLE:
DEMOCRACY WITHOUT WORDS?[45]

One of the main difficulties confronting the present study is that of identifying the 'popular' language—or languages—of democracy, given that historical sources mainly come from sociopolitical elites. Actually, the most notable absentee in this study on the languages of democracy in Ireland is the mass of the people. It is very difficult to find evidence about how they talked about democracy, if indeed they talked about it at all.

By considering public meetings held during the 1840s both as a practice (with rituals and symbols) and as a language (without words), it may be possible to compensate for this absence of words and to rediscover—as far as possible—how people gave meaning to democracy through lived experience. During the second quarter of the nineteenth century, Ireland was the scene of a mass political mobilization. Huge public demonstrations brought together hundreds of thousands of people and had no equivalent in Europe. Why did those 1.5 million Irishmen and women—at the lowest estimate—attend at least one among forty 'monster meetings' organized during the summer of 1843? They left few written traces or testimonies explaining why they took part.[46] As a result, the motivations of those 'silent' actors have often been inferred from the propagandist messages—obviously effective—intended for them. Meetings were highly staged and ritualized in order to show the respectability of the crowd and to represent a non-conflictual and socially unified Irish nation. They have often been analyzed in historiography as expressing people's support for their leaders' call for national sovereignty. Without denying this, it is worth enriching this nationalist scenario to take into account other political, socio-economic, or cultural aspirations that were, more or less, articulated with it, such as the hope of obtaining a lower rent or the attraction of the spectacular or the festive. Moreover, attendance was probably experienced as a founding political act, an alternative and non-conventional way of entering the political arena, a privileged moment when individuals, mostly excluded from the vote, could exchange ideas and emotions, could express their collective desire to become actors of their own history, using a specific (in this case, symbolic) 'language of democracy' and a 'repertoire of collective action' (Charles Tilly) that bypassed the usual forms of access to politics.[47]

La parole populaire also intersected with public debate through other channels, where spoken and written languages joined, for example through sung or printed

---

[45] This subtitle echoes the titles of two important articles: Paul A. Pickering, 'Class without Words: Symbolic Communication in the Chartist Movement', *Past and Present*, 112 (1986), 144–62; Gary Owens, 'Nationalism without Words: Symbolism and Ritual Behaviour in the Repeal "Monster Meetings" of 1843–45', in James S. Donnelly and Kerby A. Miller (eds), *Irish Popular Culture, 1650–1850* (Dublin, 1998).

[46] A difficulty clearly exposed by Maura Cronin, '"Of One Mind?": O'Connellite Crowds in the 1830s and 1840s', in Peter Jupp and Eoin Magennis (eds), *Crowds in Ireland 1790–1920* (Basingstoke, 2000).

[47] A more detailed presentation of these hypotheses can be found in Laurent Colantonio, 'Mobilisation nationale, souveraineté populaire et normalisations en Irlande (années 1820–1840)', *Revue d'histoire du XIXe siècle*, 42 (2011), 53–69.

ballads. Well distributed, they formed a privileged medium by which popular expression might enter the public sphere. According to historian Theodore Hoppen, political texts were numerous amongst those sheets and ballads. Some of them urged voting for a particular candidate; others relayed imaginaries, angers, and hopes, as in the following excerpt: 'And of ministers we will make labourers/each day for our endustry/To earn 4 pence wages to teach them frugality,/.... And we will plant a tree in Erin and the/name it takes is Liberty.'[48] The background is undeniably Irish: blame is concentrated upon Protestant clergymen, and the Catholic nation appears between the lines. However, democratic demands for liberty and social justice are expressed in a more international language, refering to the famous 'trees of liberty' planted in Ireland at the end of the eighteenth century, following the model of the French Revolution.

As we can observe through ballads and mass meetings, the firm and spectacular intrusion of the masses into the political sphere, from which they were otherwise mostly excluded or with which they were unfamiliar, was expressed and carried out in various ways, and was not limited to the act of voting. Such an appropriation of the public arena was seen as potentially subversive and, for that reason, these experiences of popular sovereignty were challenged as illegitimate.

CONCLUSION

The presentation above suggests the need for a nuanced answer to the question of the specificity of the language of democracy in Ireland. In one sense, there is no absolute Irish 'exceptionalism' in relation to democracy during the 1830–1840s, because many Irish discourses on democracy echoed elements of those which appear elsewhere in the United Kingdom, Europe, and the Americas during the same period. Yet within this transnational framework, an important 'Irish touch' may nevertheless be identified: the 'democratic' issue in Ireland was usually expressed in the language of the nation—the relationship between democracy and nationalism was key—and most of the debates and contestations over democracy were intimately connected with, indeed subordinated to, nationalist/unionist politics, relating to the specific problem of relations with Britain (notably the fact that supreme political authority remained outside the territory) and the confessional nature of Irish society.

---

[48] K. Theodore Hoppen, *Elections, Politics and Society in Ireland, 1832–1885* (Oxford, 1984), 424ff, quotation at 426. This ballad, by an unknown author, was called *Poor Erin* (1835).

12

The Limits of Democracy: Ireland 1778–1848

S. J. Connolly

'A LONG DEMOCRATIC TIRADE'

In July 1835 Alexis de Tocqueville, passing through the town of Carlow, dined with the Catholic bishop of Kildare and Leighlin, Edward Nolan, and a group of his fellow prelates:

> The conversation turned on the state of the country and politics. The sentiments expressed were extremely democratic. Contempt and hatred for the great landlords. Love of the people, confidence in them. Bitter memories of past oppression. A certain exultation at present or approaching victory. A profound hatred of the Protestants and, above all, of their clergy. Little apparent impartiality. Clearly as much the heads of a party as the representatives of a church.

A few days later Tocqueville recorded a second dinner, this time at Kilkenny, where a group of Catholic priests and laymen listed appreciatively as the local bishop, William Kinsella, delivered a 'long democratic tirade' against the callous behaviour of Irish landlords.[1]

Tocqueville's belief that what he encountered among the Catholic clergy of mid-1830s Ireland was the spirit of 'democracy' is of particular significance because his journey to Britain and Ireland came just after he had completed the first volume of his celebrated *Democracy in America*. Here he depicted the United States as a society in which the principle of the sovereignty of the people 'has been disengaged from all the fictions with which one has taken care to surround it elsewhere'. Birth had entirely given way to numbers as the basis of political power. Voting was by universal suffrage or something close to it. Representatives were directly elected, often for periods of no longer than a year, 'to keep them more completely under their dependence'.[2] There was also a massive optimism about the future. Just as the Irish bishops had impressed Tocqueville by their confidence in the people, so his American hosts responded robustly to his reservations about the potential way-wardness of the omnipotent majority. 'That the majority can be fooled once, no

[1] *Alexis de Tocqueville's Journey in Ireland, July–August 1835*, ed. Emmet Larkin (Washington DC, 1990), 47, 78.
[2] Alexis de Tocqueville, *Democracy in America*, ed. Harvey C. Mansfield and Delba Winthrop (Chicago, IL, 2000), 55, 165, 576.

one denies, but people think that necessarily in the long run the majority is right, that it is not only the sole legal judge of its interests but also the surest and most infallible judge.'[3]

The reasons why Tocqueville, fresh from these encounters, should write in such extravagant terms about the discovery of a similar spirit of 'democracy' in Ireland are fully explored in two other contributions to this volume. Ultán Gillen (see chapter 10) shows how the Volunteers and then the United Irishmen developed a political vision more radical than anything that had preceded it, accompanied in the case of the United Irishmen by the creation of a formidable mass movement that sought to disseminate ideas of political, religious, and social equality to a wide popular following. Laurent Colantonio (see chapter 11) analyzes the achievement of Daniel O'Connell in creating a new style of agitation based on the promotion of direct mass participation through petitions and public meetings, an enactment of 'democracy without words'. Taken together these three Irish movements represent a significant chapter in the history of late eighteenth- and early nineteenth-century popular politics. O'Connell's campaigns in particular attracted widespread attention. In France they were watched closely, as Colantonio shows, both by radicals and by those, like Tocqueville and his friend Gustave de Beaumont, who looked more warily at what they saw as the irresistible rise of democracy. More striking still is the inspiration that O'Connell's emancipation campaign gave to one of the central institutions in the English campaign for parliamentary reform, Thomas Attwood's Birmingham Political Union. The dependency was teaching political lessons to the metropolitan centre; the de-industrializing periphery provided a model for one of the very heartlands of the British economic miracle to follow.

At the same time that they emphasize the significance of what took place in the 1790s and in the era of O'Connellism, however, both Gillen and Colantonio also acknowledge the extent to which the development within Ireland of the ideas and political practices of democracy was shaped by the local context. In particular they point to the influence of two central issues: the constitutional subordination of Ireland to Great Britain, and the divisions created by the confessional nature of the Irish state. The present chapter seeks to develop these points in greater detail. It will suggest that what Tocqueville saw as a striking instance of the same democracy that he had studied in the United States was in fact something more complex and less clear-cut. A belief in the sovereignty of the people as the basis of legitimacy, and in the direct judgement of the majority as the best guarantor of good government, was only one of several sets of ideas and aspirations at work among those who sought to reshape the Irish political system. In the short term, at a time when 'democracy' had yet to be clearly defined, the distinction between different conceptions of popular action was of limited significance. But in the long term it had important implications for the development of Ireland's political culture.

---

[3] Tocqueville to Louis de Kergorlay, 29 June 1831, in Robert Boesche (ed.), *Alexis de Tocqueville: Selected Letters on Politics and Society* (Berkeley, CA, 1985), 47.

DEMOCRACY IN PRINCIPLE?
PEOPLE, SECT, AND NATION

To appreciate the problems inherent in any attempt to present the political history of late eighteenth- and early nineteenth-century Ireland in terms of a straightforward progress towards democracy, it is only necessary to look briefly at the background to the main developments of the period. The Volunteer movement of 1778–85, as is well known, originated not as a political organization but as a defence force. As such it was a socially exclusive body. Membership was in practice open only to those with the means to equip themselves appropriately, and the economic independence to abandon their place of work for the parade ground or the mock battlefield. When these Volunteers did go on to demand a political voice, they did not do so on the basis of their numbers, but rather of their standing as free citizens of substance mobilized in the defence of their country. They were, in Henry Grattan's famous phrase, the armed property of the nation. It was only in the last phase of the movement, when the propertied classes and the parliamentary patriots had largely withdrawn their support, that a different rhetoric emerged.

The shift in language that then took place is evident in the most striking text to emerge from this last phase of the Volunteer movement, William Drennan's *Letters of Orellana, an Irish Helot* (1785). In particular, Drennan explicitly rejected the traditional notion of a balance between monarchy, aristocracy, and democracy. Those who looked to such mechanisms, he wrote, 'are more conversant in the constitution of a clock than that of a commonwealth'. Instead the only guarantee of freedom was constitutional rights, 'enforced by the controlling energy and momentum of that mighty mass to which those rights belong'. On closer examination, however, Drennan's text also illustrates the difficulty of separating out distinct but closely related political languages. In practice what he was defending was not any specific system of representation, but rather the right of the people, in this case the Volunteers, to assemble and petition Parliament—a right challenged by the Lord Chancellor, who had threatened prosecutions against those involved. This, moreover, was an intervention legitimized by necessity. If 'the dregs of democracy' asserted themselves, it was because 'rich, respectable honourable gentlemen' had withdrawn prematurely from the agitation. Read more closely, in fact, Drennan's *Letters* are by no means an unqualified celebration of popular power. The proceedings of the Volunteers were 'a coarse stone in the arch which juts out a little from the rest but which, notwithstanding, filled up a vacancy when a better was not to be had'. In places, indeed, Drennan's argument was closer to John Locke's notion of an appeal to heaven taking place at a point where the original compact had been unacceptably infringed. If the Irish House of Commons rejected the principle of reform, he argued, 'it becomes the business of the people who first formed that house to deliberate on the means of reforming it'. Elsewhere the argument was that mass support vindicated the claim of the nation to collective freedoms. 'The spirit of a nation able to be free must be a haughty and magnanimous spirit, strenuous, vigilant, vindictive, always impatient, sometimes impetuous, sometimes inexorable.'[4] The appeal here was not to majority rule but to a broader notion of the popular will. If Drennan's language betrays a transatlantic influence, it is less that of the first article of the Declaration of Independence than of Jefferson's famous defence of Shay's rebellion. ('What country can preserve its liberties if their rulers are not warned from time to time that their people preserve the spirit of resistance?') And indeed Drennan too wrote of 'the restorative virtue of revolutions'.[5]

In the event the 'dregs of democracy' failed to achieve their goal against a political establishment, on both sides of the Irish Sea, that had by now recovered its nerve. Just over five years later events in France inspired Drennan and others to revive the cause of reform. The founding declaration of the new Society of United Irishmen, in October 1791, called for 'an equal representation of all the people in parliament'. Once again, however, apparently clear words cannot be taken at face value. Wolfe Tone, author of the declaration, had only a few months earlier announced his belief that the constitution would be improved by disenfranchising the poorest and least independent voters—'the wretched tribe of forty shilling freeholders, whom we see driven to their octennial market by their landlords, as much their property as the sheep or the bullocks which they brand with their names'. A committee of the United Irishmen did eventually confirm that 'an equal representation' meant universal manhood suffrage. But it reached this conclusion only after substantial debate. It is also important to note the sequence of thought in Tone's inaugural resolutions. Its starting point was not the principle of democracy, but rather Ireland's subordinate constitutional status. 'We have no national government; we are ruled by Englishmen and the servants of Englishmen.' It was the scale of this all-pervasive influence, sustained by the massive resources of patronage available to seduce the people's representatives, that made it necessary to introduce the scrutiny of a mass electorate as the only possible counterweight. Democracy, in other words, was less a principle in its own right than a means to the end of national liberation. Indeed Tone's most frequently quoted comment on the subject echoed Drennan in that an appeal to the masses was justified on the basis of necessity rather than principle: 'If the men of property will not support us, they must fall; we can support ourselves by the aid of that numerous and respectable class of the community, the men of no property.'[6]

The other main group who in the 1790s based their political claims in part on an appeal to numbers, the Catholics, did so in a slightly different context. That Ireland's penal laws excluded from civil life three-quarters or more of the population did not initially figure prominently in debates on the legitimacy of that exclusion. Jonathan Swift, addressing his fellow Protestants in 1724 as 'the whole people

    [4] [William Drennan], *The Letters of Orellana, an Irish Helot* (Dublin, 1785), 28–9, 15, 23.
    [5] Thomas Jefferson, *Political Writings*, ed. Joyce Appleby and Terence Ball (Cambridge, 1999), 110; Drennan, *Orellana*, 54.
    [6] 'An argument on behalf of the Catholics of Ireland' (1791), in Thomas Bartlett (ed.), *Life of Theobald Wolfe Tone: Memoirs, Journals and Political Writings* (Dublin, 1998), 293; Declaration and Resolutions of the Society of United Irishmen of Belfast, October 1791, in ibid. 298–9; Tone's Journal, 11 March 1796, in ibid. 494.

of Ireland', did so without irony. 'The people' were those who counted, in the sense that their property and status entitled them to a voice in public affairs. A century later the same broad principle, that property not numbers was what should matter politically, continued to shape debate on the Catholic question. In 1818, for example, the government commissioned a return showing the amounts of capital in Protestant and Catholic hands in every Irish urban centre of note.[7] But it was no longer possible to be quite so insouciant about the huge disparity in numbers between the minority of full citizens and the excluded majority. The Catholic Committee, in 1792, followed the example of the Volunteers a decade earlier by summoning a Convention of elected delegates, whose claims to speak for the nation could be set against those of the unreformed Parliament. The government's response was the Convention Act of 1793, declaring illegal the meeting of any body claiming representative status for the purpose of discussing changes to the constitution. In taking this action the state implicitly acknowledged the increased sensitivity of notions of representation and legitimacy. Where the Catholics themselves were concerned, attitudes were likewise in transition. The summoning of the Convention followed a revolt against the original aristocratic leadership by a more radical faction. Tone, in his memoirs, spoke of 'the triumph of the young democracy', and some of those involved did in fact go on to become United Irishmen.[8] Others, however, responded to the Catholic Relief Act of 1793 with a rapid retreat from radicalism, indicating that their flirtation with representative politics had been a pragmatic tactic, clearly modelled on those of the Protestant reformers of the preceding decade.

The proceedings of the Volunteers, the United Irishmen, and the Catholic Committee thus serve as clear precursors to the mass political mobilization that was later to impress Tocqueville and others. At the same time it is clear that more was involved than a simple progress towards 'democracy'. The appeal to the masses, for both the Volunteers and the United Irishmen, was justified on the grounds of necessity rather than principle. In each case, moreover, the concept of the people overlapped with that of the nation. In the case of the Catholic issue, meanwhile, the language of majority and minority was inextricably tied up with the fears and aspirations created by confessional divisions. In the decades that followed the interplay of this trinity of democracy, nation, and religion was to become more rather than less complex.

Of these three it was religion that was initially to dominate the politics of post-union Ireland. The re-established Catholic Committee attempted in 1811 to revive the tactics of the 1790s, by turning itself into a board of elected delegates from every county. However, a fresh invocation of the Convention Act brought this initiative to a sudden halt. Instead the return to mass agitation came only a decade later, and in response to a new twist in the numbers game. Although the argument that Catholic numbers counted for less than Protestant property had not lost its power, opponents also suggested that the surviving points at issue, admission to

[7] British Library, Liverpool papers, Add. MS 38,368.
[8] *Life of Theobald Wolfe Tone*, 44.

Parliament and to the upper levels of public and legal office, were of no interest to the mass of the population. Instead they had significance only for a self-interested minority of wealthy Catholics, whose claims could thus be set aside. It was in response to this challenge that O'Connell in 1823 launched his celebrated 'Catholic rent'. In the event what began as a public-relations exercise designed to show that there was more to the emancipation campaign than the ambitions of a minority of Dublin-based 'agitators' developed into a hugely successful instrument of popular mobilization, and the basis of an organizational network that could be adapted to other purposes. Even at this point, however, there was no immediate conversion to faith in mass agitation. In 1825 O'Connell was still prepared to agree to the disenfranchisement of the forty-shilling freeholders. His argument was the same as Tone's thirty years earlier, that the economic circumstances of the poorest voters made them irretrievably subject to the electoral dictation of their landlords. It was others, in the face of his open scepticism, who the following year took the initiative in running pro-emancipation candidates against established county interests, and it was only their spectacular success in County Waterford and elsewhere that convinced O'Connell of the potential of the mass electorate.

The new style of popular agitation that so much impressed Tocqueville, then, emerged from pragmatic experimentation, rather than from any dramatic conversion to a new political principle. The outlook of its chief exponent, as Colantonio has shown (see chapter 11), was likewise ambiguous and sometimes contradictory. O'Connell did, it is true, make reasonably frequent use of the term 'democracy'. 'The young mind as well as young blood of the British dominions is strongly tinged with democracy,' he proclaimed in the aftermath of his victory in Clare in 1828. 'The democratic principle is making a silent but steady progress.' But for him 'democracy' generally meant, not a principle of representation, but a spirit of opposition to oligarchy or privilege. The Whig government, he announced in 1834, was 'too democratic' to permit Orangeism to operate unchecked. He also on occasion spoke of 'the democracy', meaning his plebeian supporters as opposed to the middle classes. When he argued the case for the extension of the franchise 'to the people at large' (having earlier been willing to see it further restricted), he did so on pragmatic grounds: that in the absence of the secret ballot numbers were the only means of protecting plebeian voters from landlord intimidation. He wrote of the need for men 'of intellect and information' to lead public opinion. Faced with independent plebeian action, in the shape of the Chartist movement, he was strongly and consistently hostile. Once the Chartists had been crushed by the government, he wrote in 1839, 'we will easily unite a large portion of the middle classes in favour of further reform'.[9]

To say this is not to question the significance of O'Connell's achievement as an innovator in techniques of mass political agitation. His political rhetoric was indeed founded on numbers. But the numbers were those of the mobilized collectivity, rather than of the citizen body. The tactics of the Catholic

[9] Maurice R. O'Connell (ed.), *The Correspondence of Daniel O'Connell* (8 vols, Dublin, 1972–80), 3: 408; 5: 152–3; 4: 197; 6: 237; 7: 236. For 'the democracy' see *The Nation* (Dublin), 22 April 1843.

Emancipation campaign, such as the collection of the 'Catholic rent', or the simultaneous meetings organized in 1,600 of the 2,500 parishes in Ireland on 13 January 1828 to stiffen the will of Lord Goderich's administration, dramatized the protest of a whole people denied its rights. By the 1840s the emphasis had shifted from religion to nation (although O'Connell's critics in Young Ireland argued, with some justification, that his rhetoric failed to draw a clear line between the two). The fifty or so mass meetings held between the spring of 1843 and the autumn of 1845 were a clear attempt to overawe the government by the force of numbers. Nationalist sources regularly reported the attendance in multiples of 100,000, although police reports of 30,000 or fewer are probably closer to the truth. Here again, however, the appeal was not to the legitimacy of majorities, but to the image of a national community demanding justice. Part of the elaborate choreography of the meetings, it has been pointed out, was the dramatized representation of social hierarchy. Labourers, farmers and artisans, middle-class professionals and businessmen, the clergy and civic dignitaries, processed in their allotted places, while the presiding figure of O'Connell drew the different components into one united whole.[10]

In the era of O'Connell, then, as in the 1790s, the rhetoric of political mobilization blurred the distinction between the claims of the people, the nation, and the disenfranchised Catholic majority. Even where the appeal was to the people, moreover, its scope was limited by a second powerful influence. This was the particular style of constitutional argument that the repeal movement inherited from its eighteenth-century patriot predecessors. A succession of Irish political writers, from William Molyneux in 1698 to Henry Grattan and others a century later, had consistently rested their case on the existence of an Irish 'ancient constitution', established in 1171 when the island had accepted Henry II as its king.[11] The attraction of this appeal to historically grounded corporate rights was obvious enough. But it also meant that the case for national rights was firmly located within the framework of the traditional three components of the mixed constitution. Ireland's claim was to be governed by laws enacted by its own Crown, Lords, and Commons. The straitjacket thus created, despite Drennan's dismissal of the balanced constitution in 1785, proved remarkably durable. When the Dublin Society of United Irishmen, in 1794, drew up a plan for electoral reform, they thought it necessary to deny that their proposal for a House of Commons elected by universal suffrage in equal constituencies would mean that 'the monarchy and the aristocracy of the constitution would soon be overborne and destroyed, by the exorbitant power and republican spirit of the democracy'. On the contrary, they maintained, 'pure democracy' in this branch of government would preserve the traditional mixed constitution, by balancing the wide prerogative powers of the monarchy and the great

---

[10] Gary Owens, 'Nationalism without Words: Symbolism and Ritual Behaviour in the Repeal "Monster Meetings" of 1843–5', in J. S. Donnelly and Kerby A. Miller (eds), *Irish Popular Culture 1650–1850* (Dublin, 1998), 255–6.

[11] S. J. Connolly, 'Precedent and Principle: The Patriots and their Critics', in S. J. Connolly (ed.), *Political Ideas in Eighteenth-Century Ireland* (Dublin, 2000).

wealth of the aristocracy.[12] This, of course, was a document prepared for public consumption, and in time the United Irishmen were to move on to the pursuit of a democratic republic modelled on France. After 1800, however, the myth of the restoration of an ancient Irish constitution once again became central to popular politics. The membership card for the revived repeal movement of 1843 deliberately looked back to 1782, and 'the united elements of the old regal, aristocratic and democratic constitution of Ireland, as acknowledged and confirmed in the time of our fathers'.[13] A year later O'Connell's son and political heir rejected claims that an Irish Parliament would be 'too democratic'. Repealers, he conceded, looked for vote by ballot and short parliaments to ensure 'a full and free representation of the people'. But they were devoted to the constitutional monarchy, 'and are far less hostile to a house of peers as a state institution than are the people and middle classes of England'.[14]

Daniel O'Connell was not, of course, the only leader seeking to mobilize the Irish masses. By the 1840s he faced what was eventually to become an explicit challenge from the Young Ireland movement. Here, however, the concept of the people even more clearly took second place to that of the nation. O'Connell's nationalism was that of the eighteenth-century patriots: the nation was a corporate entity whose claim to autonomy rested on specific historical and legal rights. For Young Ireland, inspired by the romantic nationalism of Young Europe, the nation was an organic community whose claim to self-determination took precedence over political forms. Theories of government, the Young Ireland *Nation* newspaper proclaimed in 1846, were of little interest to them. '...the great want and unvarying aim of them all is a *National Government*, no matter what may be its form'. Even those who were 'democrats in abstract principle' would prefer 'an oligarchy of *our own* aristocrats to the most popular forms of rule under foreign institutions and foreign governors'.[15]

If the organic nationalism of the Young Irelanders encouraged a lofty indifference to forms of government, it also placed a premium on unity across divisions of class and creed. Thomas Davis and other leaders looked back enviously to the 1780s, when, as they saw it, the Protestant gentry had placed themselves at the head of an inclusive patriot movement. The main basis of their quarrel with O'Connell was that he had supposedly betrayed the national cause by linking the repeal movement to the sectional interest of the Catholic Church. The same aspirations produced a determined refusal to tie their own advanced nationalism to any programme of either social or political reform. 'We seek union amongst all sects and parties at home,' the *Nation* proclaimed in 1842, 'Protestant as well as Catholic, Presbyterian and Quaker, Conservative and Democrat—all are welcome in our ranks.'[16] For similar reasons the Young Irelanders, despite their hostility to

---

[12] *Address from the Society of United Irishmen of Dublin, to the People of Ireland* (London, 1794), 3–4.
[13] *The Nation* (Dublin), 18 March 1843.
[14] John O'Connell, *An Argument for Ireland* (Dublin, 1844), 27.
[15] *The Nation* (Dublin), 2 January 1847, reprinting a comment from the previous June.
[16] *The Nation* (Dublin), 17 December 1842.

O'Connell's links to the English Whigs, spurned any alliance with English radicalism, instead joining with O'Connell in noisy denunciation of the Chartist movement. It was only in 1848, in response to events in Paris and in Great Britain itself,
that the leaders of the movement thought again. In March, John Mitchel told a
meeting in the Free Trade Hall in Manchester that he and his fellow Young Irelanders retracted every offensive word and claimed an alliance 'with the democracy of
England'. He returned to Dublin to tell an audience there that 'we have been guilty
of sad injustice in our abuse of the English democracy'.[17] Excited talk of a revolutionary alliance continued for a few months, but this belated conversion had no
significant long-term effect on Irish political vocabularies.

DEMOCRACY IN ACTION? POPULAR MOBILIZATION

Why did the Ireland of the late eighteenth and early nineteenth centuries exhibit
this precocious development of mass politics? The influences on the leaders are
clear enough. The Protestant patriots who pioneered new forms of mass agitation
in the 1770s and 1780s were driven to less dangerous extremes than their American counterparts. But they shared with them the sense of being ruled by a metropolitan government indifferent to their concerns, and unresponsive to protest
through traditional channels. The Catholic middle-class leaders who in the 1790s
began a more vigorous campaign for civic equality, and the French-inspired radicals of the United Irish movement, had even more reason to believe that only an
appeal to numbers would outweigh the formidable opposition they faced. Daniel
O'Connell's Catholic Association turned to the masses after it had become clear
that, although a succession of petitions and parliamentary debates had won over
the House of Commons, something more would be required to break down the
resistance of the Crown and the House of Lords. The other half of the equation was
social and cultural change, creating the following that made bolder methods possible. A long wave of economic expansion, driven by rising agricultural exports and
the runaway growth of linen manufacture, began in the 1740s and continued to
the end of the Napoleonic wars. Commercialization accelerated the circulation of
people, information, and ideas. In particular there was a rise in literacy: statistics
collected in 1841 showed that only 35 per cent of males born in the 1820s were
unable to read and write, as compared to 50 per cent of those born in the 1740s
and 1750s. The English language, essential to political participation, likewise
spread rapidly. Only 28 per cent of children born in the 1830s grew up with a
knowledge of Irish. There was also the mobilizing effect of two decades of war,
during which it was been estimated that one in six adult males spent some part of
their lives in uniform, many of them serving outside Ireland.[18]

---

[17] *The Nation* (Dublin), 25 March 1848.
[18] Thomas Bartlett, *The Fall and Rise of the Irish Nation: The Catholic Question, 1690–1830* (Dublin,
1992), 322.

A further crucial part of the background to the explosion of Irish popular politics, in the case of O'Connellism, was the contribution of the Catholic clergy. The 'extremely democratic' sentiments Tocqueville observed were a dramatic new development. Up to the 1820s the great majority of priests and bishops had given unqualified support to the principle of the natural inequality of men in a God-given hierarchical social order. As late as 1822, indeed, James Warren Doyle, noted as one of the most politically outspoken of the Irish bishops, had appealed to the traditional analogy between the gradations of society and the clearly differentiated functions of the human body. 'If your feet, seeing your hands are idle, would refuse to walk—if your hands would undertake to do the duties of the head, how monstrous and absurd would it not appear?'[19] The conversion soon after of Doyle and others to intense political activism was in part at least a result of pressure from their congregations. In this sense hostile claims that mounting political unrest could be attributed entirely to the malign influence of the priests over a credulous and obedient flock can be dismissed out of hand. At the same time this abandonment of the political quietism of earlier generations of clergy was of central importance. Distributed more or less evenly across the country, accustomed both to public speaking and to the dispatch of business, and generally possessed of public confidence, the priests provided a ready-made network of local organizers, compensating for what would otherwise have been the huge disadvantage of the weakness or absence in many areas of a Catholic middle class.

The forces encouraging the emergence of a new style of popular politics did not operate in an ideological vacuum. By the late eighteenth century there was already a well-developed tradition of popular collective action. The appearance of the Whiteboys in Munster in 1761–5 and of the Oakboys or Hearts of Oak in Armagh, Tyrone, and Monaghan during 1763 marked the beginning of what was to be a long series of movements of agrarian protest. Their activities can be attributed not only to the disruptive impact of commercialization on the precarious network of relationships and entitlements that sustained the rural poor, but also to the development of a new capacity for self-assertion. (There had in fact been one earlier movement of agrarian protest, the Connacht Houghers of 1711–13, but these had operated only with the support of a disaffected section of the local gentry.)[20] Nevertheless both these and later movements remained limited and conservative in their aims, generally acting in response to falling prices, the extension of pasture at the expense of tillage, or other threats of disruptive change. They were also, initially, relatively sparing in their use of violence. Protest became more violent after the traumatic 1790s. But its reactive character, and its focus on the defence of existing rights, place it firmly within the pattern of collective action seen elsewhere in pre-industrial Europe.[21]

---

[19] James Warren Doyle, *Pastoral Address...against the Illegal Association of Ribbonmen* (Dublin, 1822), 22–3.

[20] S. J. Connolly, 'The Houghers', in C. H. E. Philpin (ed.), *Nationalism and Popular Protest in Ireland* (Cambridge, 1987).

[21] The large literature on Irish agrarian protest is now conveniently summarized in Maura Cronin, *Agrarian Protest in Ireland 1750–1960* (Dublin, 2012).

A second element in popular political thinking had more complex implications. For at least the first half of the eighteenth century the primary allegiance of the majority of Irish Catholics was to the exiled house of Stuart. Even after the 1740s, when Jacobitism had ceased to be a credible political movement, the theme of the eventual return of the rightful rulers, and the great changes that would follow, remained a staple of popular poetry. Jacobitism, unlike Whiteboyism, provided the basis for a rejection of the entire existing political and social order. As such it has been legitimately cited as evidence of the deep fissures concealed behind the apparent stability and calm of Augustan Ireland, and hence as one explanation of the speed with which that stability crumbled from the 1780s. Attempts to depict a direct line of development from the Jacobitism of the eighteenth century to the popular nationalism of the nineteenth, however, are often curiously blind to the difficulties. In the first place, the Jacobite vision of Catholic Ireland rescued by the re-establishment of the Stuart dynasty took for granted the continued incorporation of Ireland into some kind of British state. Secondly, and more relevant in the present context, Irish Jacobitism was a quintessentially *ancien régime* ideology. The values on which it rested were those of dynastic and hereditary right, combined, in the Irish case, with the vision of a lost golden age when Ireland had been ruled by a native aristocracy.[22]

If either agrarian protest or Jacobitism was to feed into the development of a political culture of democracy, then, it would only be by means of some radical process of transformation. In the 1790s a change of some kind clearly took place, as these conservative indigenous traditions collided with the new ideas arising from the American and French Revolutions. The rise of the Defenders indicates that lower-class Catholics, even without the leadership of middle-class radicals, were capable of moving beyond the defence of existing rights to visions of a transformation of the social and political order. What remains disputed is how far the process of politicization went. Some accounts argue for a complete transformation of values and aspirations. Loyalty to a dispossessed dynasty gave way to a demand for representative government, nostalgia for a vanished aristocracy to a vision of lost lands restored to the people as a whole. France the champion of democratic republicanism replaced France the traditional friend of Catholic Ireland.[23] Others would argue that democratic republicanism was at best superficially grafted on to a disaffection based primarily on long-standing sectarian and economic grievances. Indeed it has been suggested that the insistence of many United Irish leaders that military action should await a French landing was a reflection less of timidity than of a distrust of their own unreliable plebeian allies.[24]

---

[22] It has to be emphasized that the relationship between Jacobitism and later popular movements remains a matter of debate. For the view taken here see S. J. Connolly, 'Jacobites, Whiteboys and Republicans: Varieties of Disaffection in Eighteenth-Century Ireland', *Eighteenth-Century Ireland*, 18 (2003), 63–79. For a direct challenge see Vincent Morley, 'The Continuity of Disaffection in Eighteenth-Century Ireland', *Eighteenth-Century Ireland*, 22 (2007).

[23] Breandán Ó Buachalla, 'From Jacobite to Jacobin', in Thomas Bartlett et al. (eds), *1798: A Bicentenary Perspective* (Dublin, 2003).

[24] Marianne Elliott, *Partners in Revolution: The United Irishmen and France* (New Haven, CT, and London, 1982), xvii, 4, 227, 244.

The clandestine nature of Defenderism makes it difficult to offer a definite answer. For the period from the 1820s to the 1840s the picture is clearer. A range of studies suggest that O'Connellism operated at two levels. Popular enthusiasm for Catholic emancipation and repeal was general throughout the country. Formal involvement in the Catholic Association or the Repeal Association, by contrast, was consistently stronger in the towns than in the countryside, and was heavily concentrated in the more anglicized and commercialized regions of the south and east. Different levels of incorporation into the O'Connellite machine, moreover, were reflected in differences in political outlook. The 'reading farmers' whom O'Connell's lieutenant Thomas Wyse identified as the rank and file of the Liberal Clubs created from 1826 were introduced by their membership to a culture of political activism.[25] In the Irish-language poetry of the period, on the other hand, O'Connell appears, not as the spokesman for an emergent democracy, but as a champion who would strike down the traditional Protestant foe and the bringer of a vaguely imagined societal transformation. Once again the rhetoric of democracy blurred into that of the nation, or of the Catholic people. A ballad overheard in Tipperary in 1843, meanwhile, looked back to one of the most brutal episodes of 1798:

> Were you at Scullabogue barn?
> And did you see the Orangemen roasting?
> Tally heigh ho![26]

Texts of this kind perhaps cast a retrospective light on what had and had not been achieved by the massive effort at politicization undertaken by the United Irishmen in the 1790s, as well as by two decades of subsequent mobilization by O'Connell.

DEMOCRACY REJECTED? PROTESTANT RESPONSES

If Ireland's unusual religious demography encouraged Catholics to emphasize numbers, it did even more to turn the minds of Protestants to questions of majority and minority. Already in the 1790s the eventual commitment of the United Irishmen to a programme of universal male suffrage was achieved only after an intense behind-the-scenes debate. This had seen Protestant members in particular hold out for the retention of some form of property qualification, and also for open voting, in each case clearly hoping to see Catholic numerical superiority

---

[25] Thomas Wyse, *Historical Sketch of the Late Catholic Association on Ireland* (2 vols, London, 1829), 1: 343–4. For a general discussion of the points raised in this paragraph see S. J. Connolly, 'Mass Politics and Sectarian Conflict, 1823–30', in W. E. Vaughan (ed.), *New History of Ireland*: vol. V, *Ireland Under the Union I: 1801–70* (Oxford, 1989), 88–94.

[26] Maura Cronin, 'Memory, Story and Balladry: 1798 and its Place in Popular Memory in Pre-Famine Ireland', in Lawrence Geary (ed.), *Rebellion and Remembrance in Modern Ireland* (Dublin, 2001), 121.

balanced by the greater wealth and status of the Protestant minority.[27] The Act of Union, abolishing at a stroke the majority of the boroughs that had formerly sent members to the Dublin Parliament, gave the issue a greater urgency. As early as 1805 John Foster, former speaker of the Irish Commons, identified the loss of the boroughs and the admission of Catholics to Parliament as representing equally serious threats to Protestant interests.[28] Later, in the 1840s, the concern of Young Ireland with restoring the lost alliance of gentry and people was also a programme to restore Protestant men of property to the leadership they had forfeited to the Catholic middle classes.

The revival of sectarian divisions also had implications for what had been the heartland of 1790s radicalism, the Protestant, or more correctly Presbyterian, north-east. It has long been recognized that Protestant radicalism did not disappear immediately in the disillusioning aftermath of 1798. Some level of clandestine activity continued for a decade or more. Later episodes, such as Belfast's violent riot in support of Queen Caroline in November 1820, revealed a continued support for the politics of opposition. There were likewise demonstrations in support of the Reform Act of 1832. Immediately afterwards the apparent success of this campaign encouraged the leaders of the Belfast radicalism to put forward two candidates on a radical platform including further suffrage extension and the secret ballot. In the event, however, the majority of Protestant voters, including the majority of Presbyterians, voted for the Conservatives, giving them both Belfast seats. At this point, it seems clear, Ulster Protestant radicalism had ceased to be a significant force.

Liberalism, it is true, remained a force in Belfast politics for another four decades. Increasingly, however, its fortunes depended on an alliance between the town's expanding Catholic electorate and a leadership drawn from a small group of mainly affluent Presbyterians. The political outlook of this Presbyterian elite, meanwhile, shifted steadily towards the centre. They were openly hostile both to Repeal and to Young Ireland. Their response during 1848 to events in London and Paris also made clear how far they had moved from the politics of the 1790s. The *Northern Whig*, the main organ of Belfast Liberalism, welcomed the departure of Louis Philippe, but expressed alarm at subsequent developments, attacking the provisional government for pandering to 'the almost lawless democracy', rather than 'leaning upon the intellect and virtues of the middle and more steady class of people'. In so doing it was concerned to make a clear distinction between a representative government, in the form of 'the elected of the people', and the direct exercise of power by 'the men of pick axes and wheelbarrows'. Closer to home the *Whig* gave an enthusiastic welcome to the mass enrolment of special constables

---

[27] Maureen Wall, 'The United Irish Movement', in J. L McCracken (ed.), *Historical Studies V*, (London, 1965), 122–40.

[28] See Foster's speech on the first post-Union Catholic petition: Hansard, 1st ser., 4: 1003–4 (John Foster, Commons, 14 May 1805).

that allowed the government to face down the Chartists, 'the uprising of order and rational loyalty against thieves, marauders and incendiaries'.[29]

THE BIRTH OF IRISH DEMOCRACY?
LONG-TERM PERSPECTIVES

In Ireland the late eighteenth and early nineteenth centuries saw bold experiments with a new style of popular politics. Tocqueville, visiting at the height of O'Connell's success, linked what he saw to the democracy of the United States, and later historians, as Laurent Colantonio shows (see chapter 11), have been free with the same terminology. On closer examination, however, the picture is by no means clear-cut. The appeal of the United Irishmen to 'the men of no property' was driven by a combination of necessity and the mood of exhilaration inspired by events in America and France. The language of democracy, for both the radical Volunteers and their United Irish successors, remained enmeshed with that of the nation. The rhetoric and symbolism of O'Connellism, even more clearly, mixed together the people, the nation, and the Catholic faithful. The Young Irelanders, subordinating all to their version of the doctrines of romantic nationalism circulating in contemporary Europe, moved from open hostility to democracy to a hastily proclaimed and unconsummated alliance.

Against this background it becomes easier to understand why the dramatic popular political mobilization that so impressed Tocqueville and other observers during the 1820s, 1830s, and 1840s was not in fact sustained. Instead the 1850s and 1860s, with the mobilizing issue of self-government in abeyance, and against a background of rising prosperity and reduced social conflict, saw a return to the older style of politics that had been temporarily overthrown by the rise of O'Connellism. In the counties, landlords, deploying a sophisticated blend of clientelism and coercion, once again dominated most elections. In urban constituencies voting was determined by a combination of local issues and hard cash, and a local Protestant elite once again retained a strong presence.[30] In theory, the Famine (1845–9), along with the sustained heavy emigration that followed, should have provided the basis for a more effective popular mobilization. The 'reading farmers' who had provided the core of the O'Connellite machine now became the dominant social group in the Irish countryside, while what had been the more unstable element, the labourers and cottiers, dwindled into a depressed majority. But in practice it was not until the 1870s that the Home Rule movement, riding on the back of a campaign for an amnesty for imprisoned Fenians, once again posed a serious challenge to a political culture characterized by parochialism and deference to proprietorial authority.

The element of 'democracy' in the popular politics of the late eighteenth and early nineteenth centuries thus emerges both as incompletely realized and, in the longer term, as incapable of sustaining itself in the new circumstances of

---

[29] *Northern Whig* (Belfast), 11, 14, 21, 23 March 1848.
[30] K. Theodore Hoppen, *Elections, Politics and Society in Ireland 1832–1885* (Oxford, 1984).

post-Famine Ireland. To say this is in no way to contradict the analysis offered elsewhere in the present volume by Gillen (see chapter 10) and Colantonio (see chapter 11). Between the suggestion that ideas of democracy in Ireland took on what Colantonio neatly defines as 'an Irish touch', and the argument that in Ireland democracy never fully established itself alongside other ways of thinking and acting politically, the division is wafer thin. But an emphasis on the limits to the reception in Ireland of ideas of democracy is nevertheless relevant. The Parnellism of the 1880s dramatically widened the scope for political participation, not just by efficiently mobilizing the new electorate created by the third Reform Act but also by funding the election and maintenance of MPs recruited from outside the traditional political class. Yet it was also a movement controlled by an autocratic Protestant landlord, appealing to a collective will whose weapon was the boycott as well as the ballot box. The Sinn Féin of the period 1917–22 based its success on the same claim to represent, not a sectional interest, but an entire nation. Even after the achievement of Irish independence, Fianna Fáil was likewise to present itself, if not quite so credibly, as a national movement, rather than a mere political party. The ambiguities visible in the rhetoric of O'Connellism thus had a longer-term presence in Irish political culture. There was also the question of what happened when the demands of the nation and the voice of the people, mathematically calculated, no longer coincided. In 1922 Eamon de Valera, confronted with the willingness of a Dáil Éireann elected by universal suffrage to endorse a compromise Anglo-Irish treaty, reportedly proclaimed that 'the people had never a right to do wrong'.[31] In subsequent decades others were to base their actions on the same principle, with equally destructive consequences.

---

[31] Michael Laffan, *The Resurrection of Ireland: The Sinn Féin Party, 1916–1923* (Cambridge, 1999), 218.

SYNERGIES

Synergies

Joanna Innes and Mark Philp

This book has charted the re-imagining of 'democracy' around the North Atlantic region between 1750 and 1850. It has traced the transformation of the word, from being a literate term denoting above all direct government in ancient city states, to diversification in its reference and entry into popular use—increasingly, with reference to modern circumstances. We have organized the book primarily by political unit. Within that context, contributors have focused on language and ideas to provide snapshots of two major moments—around the time of the first French Revolution and the 1848 revolutions—when activists operating on the edge of existing power structures called for major institutional change, and sometimes achieved it. We have focused on particular polities in order to convey a sense of the differing institutional environments and political cultures in which these changes played out.

We have suggested that in the middle of the eighteenth century, across the different polities with which we are concerned, there was an initial stock of ideas about democracy, informed both by knowledge of the ancient world and by standard ways of describing current constitutional forms. According to these notions, republics might be more democratic or more aristocratic, while monarchies might preside over 'mixed constitutions', incorporating aristocratic and democratic elements. Chapters in this book have demonstrated how these common ideas developed under the pressure of local events and through application to local institutions and practices, so that, by the end of our period, there had emerged more diverse understandings of democracy. In 1850 the United States of America claimed to constitute a 'democracy'; France had recently instituted a 'democratic republic' (but would soon abrogate it); the kingdom of Great Britain and Ireland claimed to operate under a mixed government with a democratic element, but decidedly did not claim to be a democracy. Nonetheless, in each of these places, the relationship between the political order and the people had changed significantly. In the middle of the eighteenth-century the Scottish philosopher David Hume claimed that 'it is...on opinion only that government is founded'.[1] This maxim about governments and the basis of their legitimacy had ancient roots; it remained plausible in Hume's time. By the middle of the nineteenth century, it had become more central than ever to the practice of

---

[1] David Hume, 'Of the First Principles of Government', in Eugene Miller (ed.), *Essays, Moral, Political and Literary* (Indianapolis, IN, 1987), 32.

government. States had come to be active across a wide social spectrum, mobilizing and directing opinion, seeking to harness it, and attempting to prevent its ebbs and flows from destabilizing regimes.

This trend of change was not primarily the result of people having demanded 'democracy'. Popular demands certainly played a part in driving change, but the people sought all kinds of things, and only rarely was more voice in politics explicitly one of these (even if it was often an implicit corollary). By the middle of the nineteenth century those who thought that the people should be given more voice in politics often described themselves as 'democrats', yet still they only occasionally demanded 'democracy' *tout court*. For there was as yet no clear consensus as to what this might entail: how democracy could effectively be embodied in a political order. Accordingly, the goal was usually described in other, or in more elaborate terms: as 'equal representation' or 'a democratic republic'. 'Democrat' and 'democracy' were terms whose meanings were in flux—along with 'the people', 'the nation', 'representation', 'popular sovereignty', and 'republic'—as men and women strove to describe, shape, and respond to a changing political world.

We have structured this book so as to emphasize diversity of experience. But across that diversity there were many common themes, and people in one place were often influenced by ideas about what was happening elsewhere. In this final chapter, we explore some of these synergies: some of the ways in which the diverse local experiences that we have charted interacted. We sketch the broader context of intellectual exchange in which these interactions took place, examine some of the mechanisms by which information and ideas were transmitted, and offer some reflections on what people did with what they learned and believed about developments elsewhere. People in all the places this book has considered thought of themselves as acting against the background of a wider common heritage and shared culture. There were multiple interactions, at many levels. Each of the places that we are concerned with came to serve as a reference point, even an icon, to those elsewhere in terms of their experience in giving power to the people. Yet people everywhere interpreted what was happening elsewhere in the light of their own preoccupations, and appropriated from others' experience things that engaged with their own needs.

THE AGE OF ENLIGHTENMENT

Eighteenth-century Europe and the Americas were once commonly represented by historians as having been touched, to varying degrees, by a common intellectual phenomenon: 'the Enlightenment'. Following the publication of Roy Porter and Mikulas Teich's book, *The Enlightenment in National Context*, it became more common to stress diversity.[2] Recently, historians have again emphasized international elements in the set of conversations that we term 'the Enlightenment': the

---

[2] Roy Porter and Mikulas Teich (eds), *The Enlightenment in National Context* (Cambridge, 1981).

international dissemination of books and journals; international correspondence; reputations that transcended national boundaries and people who moved across them.[3] Not only did texts and people move, but also eighteenth-century intellectual endeavour took place against the background of a widely shared culture, in which knowledge of the ancient world and its literary remains formed an important component. Common reference points facilitated international communication, and collaboration in the tasks of extending knowledge, developing new modes of thought, and rethinking values and aspirations.

One strand in this international interchange was spun out of the interest that people took in each other's political and social systems: what was specific to individual polities was among the objects of international enquiry. These were not new concerns, but the eighteenth century saw them systematized for an expanding reading public, enjoying unprecedented access to scholarly and semi-scholarly works in the vernacular. These issues were addressed in treatises and reference books, including atlases, which classified systems of government according to standard taxonomies as well as providing insights into their idiosyncrasies. Montesquieu's *L'Esprit des Lois* (1748) was the most highly theorized example of this kind, much translated and long influential. Young men travelling as part of their education were expected to study and attend to such matters—and their elders often reflected on them too. Travel narratives both attested and catered to this interest, engaging those unable to travel themselves. Books, pamphlets, and newspapers kept the reading public informed of global current events.[4]

Montesquieu described a changeable but nonetheless relatively stable social world, in which, though sudden, willed change was a possibility, the slow mutation of one state and social form into another was more typical. He had no basis for foreseeing the coming age of revolutions, in which what would galvanize interest would be sudden, dramatic changes in the character of states. It was on the causes and implications of these dramatic changes that later eighteenth-century social and political commentators would above all focus.

Britain had experienced revolutionary change—and attracted international notice on that account—in the mid-seventeenth century (during their own Revolution, the French often looked back to this period in Britain's history, to see what could be learnt from that).[5] At the end of the century, the 'Glorious Revolution' was better contained, yet left much in contention. Still, against initial expectations, the British did manage to negotiate their differences and develop their state into a great power, while maintaining a relatively open and participatory form of government and a measure of religious toleration. The expanding print media increasingly presented this as a success story. When during the Seven Years War (1756–63)

---

[3] Jonathan Israel, *Radical Enlightenment: Philosophy and the Making of Modernity* (Oxford, 2001); John Robertson, *The Case for Enlightenment: Scotland and Naples 1680–1760* (Cambridge, 2005).

[4] Daniel R. Headrick, *When Information Came of Age: Technologies of Knowledge in the Age of Reason and Revolution, 1700–1850* (Oxford, 2000); Leopold, Graf von Berchthold, *An Essay to Direct and Extend the Enquiries of Patriotic Travellers* (London, 1789).

[5] Olivier Lutaud, 'Emprunts de la révolution française à la première révolution anglaise. De Stuart à Capet, de Cromwell à Bonaparte', *Revue d'histoire moderne et contemporaine*, 37 (1990), 589–607.

this relatively small state pulled off a series of stunning victories, and significantly expanded its global sway, interest sharpened in how Britain's governors had managed so effectively to harness the spirit of its people—and whether, in the context of growing wealth, that support could be sustained. Later eighteenth-century European intellectuals taking an interest in Britain included Gabriel Bonnot de Mably, Jean Louis De Lolme, Jean-Paul Marat, and Jean-Pierre Brissot de Warville.

Britain's power rested on global territorial acquisitions, and global commerce. From the epoch of her civil wars, she had joined in a game in which the Portuguese, Spanish, and Dutch were already engaged, and into which the French also entered. In the later eighteenth century some began to prophesy that the apparently increasingly successful process of European expansion was in fact heading for cataclysm. In that context, Britain's power might be expected to wane, but more than that, the whole world order faced disruption. The Abbé Raynal's *Histoire philosophique et politique des establishments et du commerce des européens dans les deux Indes*—an influential work with many contributors—identified the Americas as the site in which this unravelling might begin. The Americas' inhabitants currently suffered at European hands, but in fact needed nothing from them. Once Americans started making good their claims to their native liberties, then the states of the Old World were headed for ruin. Ultimately 'Europe', Raynal predicted, 'may . . . find its masters in its children'. Raynal and his contributors were prescient in predicting change (if over-sanguine about its medium-term effects), for Britain's North American colonies rose in revolt between the first and later editions of the *Histoire*.[6]

War between Britain and her revolting colonies became global when France and Spain made common cause with the rebels, hoping to reverse Britain's previous gains. The conflict affected the inhabitants of all these nations, being associated (as wars commonly were) with high taxes and the disruption of commerce. In Britain and Ireland (as the relevant chapters in this volume have noted), these stresses were combined with loss of confidence in the ruling ministry, a crisis whose political effects were far-reaching, the more so because American example suggested dramatic new ways of challenging government. In Britain, petitioning took off as a political tactic. In Ireland, Volunteer forces, formed to defend against French invasion, made political demands while brandishing bayonets. In both countries, conventionism took root: that is, the theory that people might reclaim from governments the trust they had invested in them and draw up the terms of a new compact.[7] These tactics were deployed to pursue local grievances: in Britain, to press for spending cuts, and the reduction of ministerial influence on Parliament; by some, to make the case for a reform in the system of representation. In Ireland, demands focused on the elimination of disadvantageous tariff barriers, and then on 'legislative independence': that is, enhanced autonomy for the Irish Parliament under a shared monarch. However, the shoots of this incipiently revolutionary

---

[6] First published in Paris in 1770 and then translated and published in Edinburgh in 1776. Michael Sonenscher, *Before the Deluge: Public Debt, Inequality, and the Intellectual Origins of the French Revolution* (Cambridge, 2007), chapter 1; 30–1 for the passage cited.

[7] T. M. Parssinen, 'Association, Convention and Anti-Parliament in British Radical Politics, 1771–1848', *English Historical Review*, 88 (1973), 503–44.

challenge withered as the war crisis passed, as the British ministry was reconstituted and certain concessions were made.

The United States' post-war efforts at state and nation-building did not evoke as much interest as their initial struggles: they touched Europe less closely. But there was interest in American constitutions—those of the individual states, most of them first forged during the struggle, then in 1787, the Federal Constitution. Benjamin Franklin—as American plenipotentiary in Paris from 1778 to 1785—persuaded Louis XVI's chief minister Vergennes to allow him to translate and publish a complete set of American constitutions to cater to, and further stimulate, this interest.[8] American constitution-making ran in parallel to increasingly intense debates in France about the need for more adequate ways of representing the French people in, and to, the French government (which Malcolm Crook sketches in chapter 6).

During the American and early French Revolutionary era, several major intellectuals and writers in America, France, and Britain personally interacted in the context of struggling to comprehend and shape these challenging events.[9] The career of Thomas Paine illustrates this. Born and resident in England for the first thirty-seven years of his life, he emigrated to America and became a propagandist for the American Revolution. He returned to Europe in the late 1780s (when he developed an acquaintance with Edmund Burke and other leading Whigs), and then for several years until August 1792 criss-crossed between England and France, mingling in French Revolutionary circles, while also becoming a major contributor to pamphlet debates and the growing reform movements in Britain.[10] In Paris in 1788 and 1789, Paine spent time with Thomas Jefferson (then American representative in Paris), Lafayette (who had led French troops in America), the Marquis de Condorcet and others discussing the proposed American Federal Constitution, the French fiscal crisis, and plans to convoke the Estates General.[11]

One focus of their discussion was a pamphlet by John Stevens defending Federal constitutional proposals and distinguishing the American from the British model; this had been sent to Jefferson by a friend in America.[12] Jefferson and his French friends saw it as strikingly germane to French debates, and arranged to have it translated and published—with some two hundred pages of additional notes,

---

[8] *Constitutions des treize États-Unis de l'Amerique* (Philadelphia and Paris, 1783).

[9] For the broader debate, Durand Echeverria, *Mirage in the West: A History of the French Image of American Society to 1815* (Princeton, NJ, 1957); Arthur Sheps, 'The American Revolution and the Transformation of English Republicanism', *Historical Reflections*, 2 (1975), 3–28; Colin Bonwick, *English Radicals and the American Revolution* (Chapel Hill, NC, 1977); Nadia Urbinati, *Representative Democracy: Principles and Genealogy* (Chicago, IL, 2006).

[10] Alfred Owen Aldridge, *Man of Reason* (London, 1959); John Keane, *Thomas Paine: A Political Life* (London, 1995).

[11] Mark Philp, 'Revolutionaries in Paris: Paine, Jefferson and Democracy', in Simon Newman and Peter Onuf (eds), *Paine and Jefferson in the Age of Revolutions* (Charlottesville, VA, 2013).

[12] John Stevens, *Observations on Government, including some Animadversions on Mr Adams's Defence* (New York, 1787); see also Joyce Appleby, 'America as a Model for the Radical French Reformers of 1789', *William and Mary Quarterly*, 3rd Ser., 28 (1971), 267–86.

underlining its relevance.[13] A number of innovations in Paine's thinking at this time stem from these discussions with American and French associates and prepared the ground for his *Rights of Man* (1791 and 1792), which responded to Edmund Burke's strikingly negative take on French developments in his *Reflections on the Revolution in France* (1790).

These discussions played a part in the formation of a platform for constitutional reform in France which self-consciously rejected the British model of mixed government. The alternative, American-influenced model gave the nobility no independent power, aiming instead to establish a constitutional monarchy dominated by a single-chambered representative legislature. Clermont-Tonnerre, who was elected president of the French National Assembly in mid-August 1789, was horrified by the groundswell against the English model that had for many years been lauded. As he saw it: 'One cannot pretend to do better than that nation (Britain). Not long ago, on the credit of several writers, people professed the most exaggerated admiration for the British constitution. Today they affect to despise it, following the opinion of an American writer who is full of contradictions.'[14] The American writer may have been Paine or Stevens; both were pressing a similar case against the bestowal of independent power on the nobility.

Paine was in Paris in July 1791 and assisted in the lurch towards republicanism that followed Louis XVI's flight to Varennes. Returning to Britain shortly afterwards, Paine played an important role in the resurgence of one of the reforming societies that had been created during the American war: the Society for Constitutional Information. His attempt (with the SCI's aid) to flood Britain with copies of the republican Part II of his *Rights of Man* provoked the ministry to prosecute him for sedition. He then returned to Paris, where he was elected to the Convention in time to take part in debates on the French king's fate. His attempt to defend Louis' life almost led him to the guillotine. In 1795, after his release from prison, Paine pressed for the new, post-Terror Constitution to include universal manhood suffrage—something of whose merits he had only recently become convinced.[15] He also became intimate with leaders of the Irish reform movement then in Paris, such as Wolfe Tone, and supported plans in 1796 and 1797 for a French invasion to assist an Irish uprising; later he sought to influence Napoleon's British invasion plans.

Unsurprisingly, Paine proclaimed himself a citizen of the world and thought of his ideas as of international scope and relevance. Citizen of an already freed republic, he was not chiefly concerned to recruit external aid for his own nation, seeking rather to disseminate principles that he took to be of universal validity across all those regions where he had influence.

The implosion from 1789 of continental Europe's most populous, wealthy, and civilized state, France, inevitably aroused extraordinary international interest, far

---

[13] *Examen du gouvernement d'Angleterre comparé aux constitutions des états unis* (Paris, 1787).

[14] Quoted in Norman Hampson, *Prelude to Terror* (Oxford, 1988), 73.

[15] His first defence of the principle was in his *Letter Addressed to the Addressers* (London, 1792), written after the second part of *Rights of Man*. He returned to the theme in his discussion of the French Constitution of 1795, *Dissertation on First Principles of Government* (London, 1795).

outstripping the attention that had been given in preceding years to events on North America's Atlantic seaboard. Europe's place in the world ensured that revolution in France would have global impact, which soon became evident as a dramatically escalating series of revolts ignited in France's pre-eminent Caribbean colony, Saint Domingue/Haiti.[16] The French Revolution magnetized attention as it unfolded, and for several generations afterwards. It provided a new source of hope for dissidents elsewhere, suggested new ways of framing aspirations, and new strategies for effecting change. It also prompted fear and horror among many, especially as revolution gave way to Revolutionary Terror. Both in France and elsewhere, the unfolding of the Revolution stimulated new thinking about how to contain or avoid such catastrophes.[17]

How exportable was the French model? In the early years of the Republic, French Revolutionary actors and international supporters were keen to represent the new France as a model that other peoples should institute in their own territories. Direct appeals to the peoples of other states presented a highly provocative challenge to their rulers. French diplomatic representatives abroad became suspect. Yet (true to the populist ideology of the venture) most of the responsibility for propagating international fraternity devolved onto less traditional structures: above all, onto political clubs. Political clubs in Britain, Ireland, and America gained new significance for both their members and their antagonists once cast as interlocutors between peoples.[18] The spread of the club idea can be used to illustrate both the power of the French model and its limits, and illuminate differences in the ways in which new impulses played out around the North Atlantic region.

French Jacobin clubs, as they developed under the Republic, came to differ sharply from the 'corresponding', 'democratic', and kindred societies of the English-speaking world. In the early years of the Revolution, clubs had sprung up spontaneously, as sites for discussion, formation of groups of the like-minded, and—increasingly—places in which Revolutionary leaders sought to cultivate and hold the loyalty of supporters. But after the establishment of the Republic, as the Revolution became more intolerant, monarchical societies and Girondin clubs were destroyed, and provincial Jacobin clubs became quasi-official organs of government: it was directed that there should be one Jacobin club in every *département*, whose responsibilities included education and propaganda for the Revolutionary government.[19] The new Republic's effort to align French government and people

---

[16] C. A. Bayly, *The Birth of the Modern World, 1780–1914: Global Connections and Comparisons* (Oxford, 2004); David Armitage and Sanjay Subhramanyam (eds), *The Age of Revolutions in Global Context, c.1760–1840* (Basingstoke, 2010).

[17] William Doyle and Haydn Trevor Mason (eds), *The Impact of the French Revolution on European Consciousness* (Gloucester, 1989); Joseph Klaits and Michael H. Haltzel, *The Global Ramifications of the French Revolution* (Washington DC, 1994).

[18] Albert Goodwin, *Friends of Liberty: The English Democratic Movement in the Age of the French Revolution* (London, 1979); Nancy J. Curtin, *The United Irishmen: Popular Politics in Ulster and Dublin, 1791–1798* (Oxford, 1994); Philip S. Foner, *The Democratic-Republican Societies, 1790–1800* (Westport, CN, 1976); Seth Cotlar, *The Rise and Fall of Transatlantic Radicalism in the Early Republic* (Charlottesville, VA, 2011).

[19] Michael L Kennedy, *The Jacobin Clubs in the French Revolution: The First Years* (Princeton, NJ, 1982) and *The Jacobin Clubs in the French Revolution, 1793–1795* (New York, 2000).

through the clubs aimed to discipline both. Yet attempting this courted the risk that one might become hostage to the other: on the one hand, government might be forced to identify with what the people did; on the other, people might be forbidden to dissent from government. In practice, both possibilities were realized. After Thermidor, clubs were banned, amidst other efforts to re-establish a distinction between state and society.

By contrast, in Britain, Ireland, and the United States the would-be reforming political clubs that sprang up on the 1790s never became organs of government. On the contrary, in Britain, the organization that came closest to replicating the privileged position of the Jacobin clubs was the counter-revolutionary Association for the Protection of Liberty and Property against Republicans and Levellers, founded in 1792. This was not officially sanctioned—indeed, Pitt's government did its best to keep it at arm's length. But it was instigated by people closely connected with government, and by Members of Parliament. The Association's object was to rally community leaders, and behind them local communities, to promote the objects of a May 1792 Royal Proclamation against Seditious Writings and Publications.[20]

In Britain, Ireland, and America, the combination of official reaction and the mobilization of loyalism in response to the rise of reforming clubs in the early 1790s did much to destroy them. Britons, Irish, and Americans for whom French ideals still resonated even as the Revolution continued to radicalize found themselves ostracized and persecuted, hard pressed to defend the legitimacy of their commitments. Nonetheless, a hard core persisted. They did so with most success in the United States, where (as Seth Cotlar explains in chapter 1) by the late 1790s even those of their compatriots who did not share their radicalism came to see the need to appropriate their democratic language. Thomas Jefferson's victory in the 1800 presidential election subsequently did its bit to make the United States a relatively safe home for democrats.

In Britain, by contrast, government hostility was unrelenting, and was backed by widespread social disapproval—though it was possible for government to overstep the mark. When leading English radicals were tried on (tenuous) charges of treason in 1794, the jury acquitted them, and in 1795 when new restrictive legislation against treasonable and seditious practices was proposed, there was widespread (though unsuccessful) counter-petitioning. English radicals on trial for treason did not lose their nerve, though they focused on challenging the government that was charging them, rather than on elucidating their own intentions. In Scotland, radicals (who fared substantially worse) protested their peaceful intentions, claiming that they had never intended to exceed what was sanctioned by their fellow citizens.[21] Widespread rallying in the cause of national defence in the late 1790s

---

[20] Eugene Charlton Black, *The Association: British Extraparliamentary Political Organization, 1769–1793* (Cambridge, MA, 1963), chapter 7; Michael Duffy, 'William Pitt and the Origins of the Loyalist Association Movement of 1792', *Historical Journal*, 39 (1996), 943–62.

[21] John Barrell, *Imagining the King's Death* (Oxford, 2000).

created a context for some reintegration of British reformers. But some had by this point despaired to the point of believing the only way forwards to lie in insurrection. The existence of this element kept other reformers under pressure.[22] Not until reformers succeeded in re-inventing themselves as patriots in the new century would the British political climate significantly change.

In Ireland, conversion to an insurrectionary strategy was more rapid and much more pervasive, notably among discontented smallholders in both the Presbyterian north and the Catholic south, some of whom already had experience of direct action addressing agrarian or sectarian grievances. Irish rebel leaders were astonishingly forthright in avowing revolutionary intent, buoyed up both by their conviction that their cause was the cause of justice and national improvement, and by confidence that they commanded the support of large swathes of the population.[23]

These were evidently very different contexts, with different effects both on how those who wished to give more power to the people conceived of what they might achieve, and on their readiness to articulate their intentions.

If British, American, and French models of government all provided bases for thinking about how power might be given to the people, yet it was the French experience that had most impact on invocations of 'democracy': giving the word and its cognates both new currency and new connotations around the North Atlantic and beyond. In preparing the ground for his study of *The Age of Democratic Revolutions* (1959, 1964), R. R. Palmer published a still-valuable piece defending his use of the adjective and identifying a range of uses across Europe and North America, often negative in tone but also sometimes positive.[24] Knowledge of these patterns has developed since he wrote; some of the fruits of new scholarship are set out in this book.

Quite why the French Revolution promoted new international uses of this cluster of terms remains puzzling. The name 'democrat' was used in France by 1789 to designate those sympathetic to political reform, and this usage was no doubt encouraged by the movement against privilege that crystallized early in the Revolution, and the concomitant demonization of 'aristocrats'. Yet it was far from obvious what if anything 'democrats' distinctively stood for, particularly in constitutional terms (although some members of the Cordeliers Club, influenced by the English republican past, tried to envisage appropriate institutional forms).[25] Moreover, though these terms acquired new currency, they were by no means central to the discourse of the French Revolution: they rarely figure, for example, in the record

[22] Roger Wells, *Insurrection: The British Experience 1795–1803* (Gloucester, 1983).

[23] Thomas Addis Emmet, *Memoire; or, Detailed Statement of the Origin and Progress of the Irish Union: delivered to the Irish Government, by Messrs. Emmett, O'Connor, and M'Nevin; Together with the Examinations of these Gentlemen before the Secret Committees of the Houses of Lords and Commons, in the Summer of 1798* ([Dublin?], 1800).

[24] R. R. Palmer, 'Notes on the Use of the Word "Democracy" 1789–99', *Political Science Quarterly*, 68 (1953), 203–26.

[25] Rachel Hammersley, *French Revolutionaries and English Republicans: The Cordeliers Club, 1790–1794* (Woodbridge, 2005).

of debates in the National Assembly. Yet in Britain, Ireland, and America, the language of 'democracy' rapidly established itself as central to the discussion of developments in France. Mark Philp points in chapter 7 to the possibly crucial role of Edmund Burke's widely reproduced and influential diatribe, *Reflections on the Revolution in France*. Burke seized on the language of democracy—associated as that was with the corruption of Greek city states and fall of the Roman Republic—to help him suggest what was wrong with the emergent French political order, why it was likely to destroy itself, and possibly other states in the process. But how crucial a role did Burke play in crystallizing these as key terms? Did he merely articulate what was anyway an emergent usage?

That the term 'democracy' was ambiguous in its connotations helped it to acquire prominence, by making it available for appropriation by both critics and friends of the Revolution. In the United States, and for a few years in France, it also helped that representative institutions were coming to be identified as potential means for instantiating modern democracy. Indeed, 'representative democracy' was the form of government that the post-Terror French regime, the Directory, sought to promote, both in France and abroad.

Among the nations that we are concerned with here, only in the United States did democracy enjoy a fairly continuous upward trend in approval from this point (complicated only by the term's arrogation by the Democratic Party). In Britain and Ireland, it acquired new connotations: it came to suggest not just disorderly popular assertiveness but seditious radicalism. This made it very much *not* the term of choice to describe officially sanctioned ways in which government sought to relate to people (except insofar as democracy could be firmly anchored in the traditional mixed-monarchy model). In France under the Empire, the term remained useful for characterizing recent events, but lost current application. In the new century, surviving French republicans mostly characterized their political ideal as 'the sovereignty of the people'. As Michael Drolet tells us in chapter 5, under the Restoration and July monarchies, the term 'democracy' was normally employed to characterize not any polity, actual or wished for, but instead the character of modern society.

AFTER NAPOLEON

The concept of 'the Enlightenment', endlessly contested though it has been, has stimulated a body of research that has illuminated not only the content but also the forms and material underpinnings of eighteenth-century intellectual and cultural life. No such unifying concept organizes work on mid-nineteenth-century Europe and America. In consequence we lack a broadly conceived account, comparable to the many that have been devoted to 'the enlightenment world', exploring how intellectual and cultural practices functioned and interacted on the national and international stage. The sketch of developments in thinking and in the circulation of ideas that we next offer is therefore highly provisional.

Through the middle decades of the nineteenth century, questions about the political ordering of states certainly continued to attract interest, sometimes abstract or academic, sometimes more empirical or practical in nature—shading into reportage and travellers' narratives, which could be read for instruction or amusement. The English legal and constitutional theorist Jeremy Bentham—who was born in the middle of the eighteenth century, but lived until 1832—stands out as someone who considered such issues at a high level of abstraction, and accordingly felt qualified to advise political actors across Europe and the Americas how best to frame constitutions and legal systems so as to advance the 'happiness' of their populations. This agenda echoed core themes from the Enlightenment. Bentham's memory was treasured into the next generation, but his heirs shifted focus. Within Britain, the next generation of 'Benthamites' concerned themselves with the design and implementation of particular strands of policy. John Stuart Mill, who grew up in Bentham's shadow, retained an interest in constitutional questions. He was the most distinguished and influential of Bentham's heirs—but he was only an heir up to a point, because he rethought the approach, questioning the possibility of determining from first principles what was likely to make any given individual happy, and, on this basis, stressing the importance of designing polities to allow their denizens to pursue individual and collective experiments in living.[26]

More commonly, early nineteenth-century writers developed a different strand of enlightenment thought: a broadly Montesquieuian agenda. That is to say, they built on the notion that states developed in interaction with the societies that they governed. This idea was susceptible to development in many different directions. The nineteenth century saw the crafting of impressive, historically and sociologically informed analyses of the legal systems of particular political cultures. It also saw the emergence of constitutional history: of histories which traced the way in which forms of government and society had interacted through time. Sismondi's widely translated *Histoire des républiques italiennes du moyen age*, the first volumes of which appeared in 1807, provides an early example in this vein; François Guizot's *Histoire des origines du gouvernement representative* (1821–2; English translation 1852) addressed a European canvas. The first self-proclaimed 'Constitutional History of England', by the Whig writer Henry Hallam, was published in 1827. Other writings, more contemporary in focus, stressed the shaping of political options by social and economic circumstance, 'national character', and the kindred and increasingly popular category of the 'race'.[27]

These emphases did not preclude searches for pattern, or the belief that something of value could be learned from others' experiences and practices. One standard lesson

---

[26] John Dinwiddy, *Bentham* (Oxford, 1989), includes a brief account of Benthamism and Benthamites; Philip Schofield, *Utility and Democracy: The Political Thought of Jeremy Bentham* (Oxford, 2006); Fred Rosen, 'The Method of Reform: J. S. Mill's Encounter with Bentham and Coleridge', in Nadia Urbinati and Alex Zakaras, *J. S. Mill: A Bicentennial Reassessment* (Cambridge, 2007), also his forthcoming *Mill*.

[27] Roberto Romani, *National Character and Public Spirit in Britain and France 1750–1914* (Cambridge, 2002); Paul Stock, ' "Almost a Separate Race": Racial Thought and the Idea of Europe in British Encyclopedias and Histories, 1771–1830', *Modern Intellectual History*, 8 (2011), 3–29.

drawn from history was that forms of government—constitutions in the loose sense—changed over time. Change was commonly conceived as, in large part, a matter of adapting to changing circumstances. In so far as modern states operated in the *same* changing environment, it was easy to conclude that they might benefit from observing the effects of each other's attempts to adapt: some elements of what was involved in becoming a successful modern state could plausibly be supposed to be generic.

Yet emphasis on local, historically formed particularities, and on the constraining power of circumstance, also made it easy to argue for limits to the relevance of others' experience. Some conservative British writers, building on Edmund Burke's conviction that healthy political development took place through a process of local adjustment, in which local problems were addressed with the aid of local resources, argued that all imitation was misguided and must fail. The French Revolution—for them, the greatest catastrophe of modern times—had (they said) arisen because the French had misguidedly tried to imitate the Americans. Conservative Europeans continued throughout the first half of the nineteenth century to assert the sharply limited relevance of American example (until the outbreak of Civil War in any case tarnished the United States' image among liberals and radicals).

Yet such arguments could also be used in support of innovation. Thus, it could be argued that, though the French had failed during the 1790s and again in 1848 to establish a convincing version of democracy, yet that failure was chiefly due to faults in their national character. By contrast, the pragmatic English, representatives of the same Anglo-Saxon race that had made a go of things in the United States, could reasonably hope to strengthen the democratic part of *their* Constitution without encountering similar difficulties.[28]

In 1835 a young Englishman in Paris, Henry Reeve, told his mother that a work had just appeared that was 'perhaps the most important treatise on the Science of States...since Montesquieu'.[29] This was the first volume of Alexis de Tocqueville's *De la démocratie en Amérique*, which Reeve translated into English that same summer. (A second part appeared in French in 1840, and was also promptly translated by Reeve.) Tocqueville's study was at one level just one more addition to the already well-established genre of American travel narratives. Once the end of the Napoleonic Wars had removed barriers to Atlantic travel, first-hand accounts of conditions in the United States had proliferated. These were widely cited for the light they shed on this notable experiment in popular self-government—or 'democracy' as it was also standardly termed, following Americans' own usage. Tocqueville's travels had been undertaken under the auspices of the French government, their ostensible object being to determine what might be learned from American practices of prison government. It was Tocqueville himself who decided to develop his wider observations and reflections for publication.[30]

---

[28] David Paul Crook, *American Democracy in English Politics* (Oxford, 1965), 116–19; James Bryce, 'The Historical Aspect of Democracy', in *Essays on Reform* (London, 1867).
[29] Crook, *American Democracy*, 186–7.
[30] James T. Schleifer, *The Making of Tocqueville's Democracy in America* (Chapel Hill, NC, 1980).

What lifted Tocqueville's text above the level of others was, first, the balance that he struck between abstraction and observation: his account was analytically driven to an exceptional degree. Second, the power and subtlety of his analysis. And third, the fact that this very subtlety made the text available for a wide variety of readings and appropriations: most readers could find in Tocqueville something to agree with, as well as something to disagree with.

By 'democracy' Tocqueville understood, above all, in the standard French style, 'equality of condition': a state of legal equality, coupled with wide diffusion of wealth and broadly egalitarian manners—though he also sometimes used the term to refer to participatory and representative political institutions (and sometimes to refer to the mass of the people: 'the democracy' of America). Like many travellers, he took the United States to display both generic and particular features: generic because the trend to abolish formal social distinctions and towards egalitarian values was, as he saw it, a general and irresistible feature of modern times; particular because the United States was a relatively young, settler society, whose general prosperity and expanding frontier offered its population a wealth of opportunities. There had never been an American titled nobility: in that sense egalitarian manners had deep local roots. Moreover, English tradition, together with the local institutions that the settler society had developed for itself, afforded opportunities to participate at a local level. The federal character of the national government, and limited ambition and practical weakness of even the several states' central institutions, determined that much scope for initiative lay at this local level.

This mix of the generic and the particular, in Tocqueville's eyes, made the American case fascinating and suggestive. The American case illuminated aspects of what—for better or worse—might be expected to be Europe's future. But, taking into account different circumstances prevailing in Europe, it also suggested ways in which Europe's future might be different—for better and for worse. Better, insofar as the legacy of European aristocratic culture might make it possible to moderate the vulgarity and conformism that (as Tocqueville reported) ran unchecked in America. Worse—particularly in France—if traditions of centralization proved to have weakened citizens' practical political skills to such a point that they would happily, time after time, surrender power to a despot claiming to rule in the name of the people, if by doing this they could free themselves to pursue their private projects.[31]

Tocqueville's darker themes—themes of democratic cultural tyranny, and the possible collapse of democracy into outright despotism—had classical roots, and had figured in previous commentaries on the United States. Some commentators indeed had prophesied that a Caesar-figure might arise there; Andrew Jackson was identified as a possible candidate for this role even before his election to the presidency in 1828. But Tocqueville located these themes within an overall account that

---

[31] For context and reception, Annalien de Dijn, *French Political Thought from Montesquieu to Tocqueville: Liberty in a Levelled Society* (Cambridge, 2008), chapter 6; Crook, *American Democracy*, chapter 5; Oliver Zunz, 'Tocqueville and the Americans: *Democracy in America* as Read in America', in Cheryl B. Welch (ed.), *The Cambridge Companion to Tocqueville* (Cambridge, 2006).

was intriguingly ambivalent: for he found much to praise, and many grounds for hope, in America's democratic experience. Democracy, he thought, had a great deal to offer the many, and was in any case inevitable. The challenge for the few was to make the best of it.

Tocqueville's account resonated particularly powerfully with French and British literati, professionals, public-spirited landowners, and businessmen, people who were often already politically engaged in one or another way. Such people already experienced themselves as easing into the role of governors, leaders, and opinion-formers in an ever more democratic society. Tocqueville's ambivalence mirrored their ambivalence towards the masses. It is in this light that we might set John Stuart Mill's initial enthusiasm for Tocqueville's study. Mill responded partly to the intellectual quality of Tocqueville's analysis, and to the seriousness of his engagement with the issues. (Tocqueville would continue to explore these themes subsequently, in travels to Britain and Ireland and elsewhere, and in reading and correspondence.) But, emerging into print a few years after the passage of the British Great Reform Act and subsequent changes in local government, Tocqueville's book could be read by a British reader who was generally positive about the direction of change as a summary of the challenges facing a new generation of political leaders.[32]

Philosophical studies of states, their development and contemporary condition, and the travel narratives with which such accounts cross-fertilized, were well-established genres, though they underwent changes in form and content. A newer form of writing was the empirical or polemical account of 'social conditions' (a phrase that came into use in both English and French from the 1820s). British parliamentary inquiries into poverty, crime, and working conditions, and associated pamphlet literature, played an important part in putting information and opinions about these matters into the public sphere. Elsewhere in Europe, and in cities of the United States, British reports were sometimes read as warnings of what might lie in their future. In France, in the immediate aftermath of Napoleon's defeat at the battle of Waterloo in 1815, some commentators were happy to seize on such material as evidence that their victorious rival faced imminent catastrophe. But soon the same lens was turned on France. By mid-century, accounts of popular suffering in Paris, London, and more generally of the poorer classes in modern society increasingly formed a backdrop against which proposals for political change were evaluated.[33]

In this context, popular demands for political rights could be reinterpreted by the sceptical as effectively cries of despair from suffering people who were incapable of grasping the true causes of their suffering. In parallel, proponents of democracy

---

[32] *London Review*, October 1835.

[33] Emma Rothschild, 'The English *Kopf*' and Gareth Stedman Jones, 'National Bankruptcy and Social Revolution: European Observers on Britain, 1831–44', both in Donald Winch and Patrick K. O'Brien (eds), *The Political Economy of British Historical Experience, 1688–1914* (Oxford, 2003); Andrew Lees, *Cities Perceived: Urban Society in European and American Thought, 1820–1940* (Manchester, 1985), Part I. Eugène Sue, *Les Mystères de Paris* was originally published serially 1842–3; G. W. M. Reynolds' imitative *Mysteries of London* began publication in 1844.

increasingly argued that, though an extension of political rights was essential, the democratic programme might need further development—might need to be accompanied by a specifically social programme—to meet these challenges. The rise of socialism partly registered a sense that merely political agendas failed to address some deep problems. It took shape partly as a response to challenging conditions: city growth, intensified competition, boom-bust economic cycles, and changes in production technologies. But it also represented a response to new *representations* of key challenges: representations that were often international in reference, and increasingly shaped by international debate.[34]

Eighteenth-century developments had given Britain, America, and France each in their own way iconic status in debates about possibilities and dangers inherent in attempts to extend the power of the people. Each retained that status during the nineteenth century—though established images were subject to revision as each underwent change. Britain continued to command attention because it retained a mixed form of government, with monarchical and aristocratic elements, and yet allowed the role both of the democratic component of the Constitution and of the people in the raw to grow, in the context of relatively broad freedoms of assembly, association, publishing, and speech. Britain's stability even under these conditions made her an attractive model for cautious innovators. A complication was that, throughout the first half of the nineteenth century, that stability was moot. Tocqueville in the mid-1830s, Marx and Engels in the 1840s all thought that more serious upheaval might be imminent. What was demonstrated by the example of the United States was that representative democracy of a quite radical kind was a possible regime for a large, modern—if admittedly a distinctively placed—state. As America developed, economically and culturally, it provided increasingly intriguing food for thought about the characteristics of a *modern* democracy. France retained iconic status as the site of the first great democratic revolution—itself subject to re-imagining from the 1820s as it was subjected to retrospective recollection and became the subject of documentary history. In 1830 and again in 1848 the French displayed their willingness and capacity to restage revolution, and to touch off revolutions elsewhere in Europe.[35]

Alongside these established icons, Ireland gained new importance as a reference point, not because of the 1798 rebellion—whose impact beyond the British Isles was muffled by the variety of upheavals taking place at that tumultuous moment—but rather because of a post-war development: Daniel O'Connell's extraordinary

---

[34] For other approaches to the social question, Mary Poovey, *Making a Social Body: British Cultural Formation, 1830–1864* (Chicago, IL, 1995); Michael Drolet, *Tocqueville, Democracy and Social Reform* (Basingstoke, 2003); Albert S. Lindemann, *A History of European Socialism* (New Haven, CT, 1983).

[35] De Dijn, *Aristocratic Liberalism*, esp. chapters 3–4; Alexis de Tocqueville, *Journeys to England and Ireland*, ed. Seymour Drescher (London, 1958); Crook, *American Democracy*; Marc Lahmer, *La Constitution Américaine dans le débat français, 1795–1848* (Paris, 2001); Sergio Luzzatto, 'European Visions of the French Revolution', in Isser Woloch (ed.), *Revolution and the Meanings of Freedom in the Nineteenth Century* (Stanford, CA, 1996); Fabrice Bensimon, *Les Britanniques face à la revolution française de 1848* (Paris, 2000); Guy P. C. Thomson, *The European Revolutions of 1848 and the Americas* (London, 2002). See also the Guide to Further Reading under 'Synergies—Nineteenth Century' for other relevant works.

mobilization of a largely Catholic peasantry, initially in the cause of Catholic
Emancipation, subsequently (somewhat less resonantly) behind his campaign to
repeal the 1800 act that had united the governments of Britain and Ireland. Irish
example showed that it was possible to mobilize even rural populations. Also, that
such mobilizations, though pressing and relentless, might be orderly and peaceful,
and—contrary to any impression that might have been left by the events of the
first French Revolution—might advance the interests of the Catholic Church,
and accept leadership from pious Catholic priests. Though—as Innes, Philp, and
Saunders show in chapter 8—Irish example played an important part in stoking
negativity about democracy in early nineteenth-century Britain, these features
made a much more positive impression in some Catholic milieux, including on
some whose preoccupations were more religious than political.[36]

An effect of possessing iconic status was that each of these countries played a
symbolic role in other countries' political culture and debates. People elsewhere
evoked or repudiated American, French, British, or Irish examples as a means of
defining their own identities, and conducting local battles. That this was so makes
the power of example intrinsically difficult to assess.

Though much cited through the nineteenth century, during these years North
Atlantic states were by no means the only or even the most interesting sites of
change. The effects of the French Revolution had unsettled Europe more generally,
as well as the Caribbean and, more indirectly, Latin America. Across all these regions, these effects had interacted with existing local controversies and animosities,
often exacerbating them but also transmuting them. Post-Napoleonic attempts at
'restoration' reworked but did little to resolve these tensions. In the 1820s, discontent with the Restoration political order stirred in Britain and France, but flared in
Spain, Spanish America, and Italy. Greek expatriates helped to engineer what
proved to be an exhausting and bloody national rising against Ottoman rule, while
revolutionary zeal momentarily gripped some Russian army officers. When, charging that the monarch and his government were breaching the terms of the political
settlement, the French resorted to revolution again in 1830, their example helped
to touch off significant indigenous uprisings in Belgium and Poland, and more
abortive demonstrations and confrontations elsewhere; 1848 brought general con-
flagration; ministries and even thrones toppled across Europe. In this context, for
those in Britain or France interested in according the people more power, what was
happening beyond the North Atlantic region—in southern, central, or eastern
Europe, or in South America—sometimes seemed more promising and significant
than what was happening at home or near at hand. This diffuse pattern of unrest
could be seen as demonstrating the sheer scale of forces making for change. More
pragmatically, for would-be reformers at home, focusing attention on and mobilizing support for protest movements elsewhere, offered means of keeping the pot

---

[36] Colantonio above, chapter 11, also Henri Rollett, 'The Influence of O'Connell's Example on
French Liberal Catholicism' in Donal McCartney (ed.), *The World of Daniel O'Connell* (Dublin, 1980);
T. D. Williams, 'O'Connell's Impact on Europe', in Kevin B. Nowlan and Maurice R. O'Connell
(eds), *Daniel O'Connell: Portrait of a Radical* (Belfast, 1984).

bubbling. When an explicitly 'democratic' international movement first took shape in the 1840s, London and Paris (both prominent refugee destinations) were important sites for its operation, but its geographical range was much wider, and if anything its centre of gravity lay amidst other nationalities, especially Germans, Italians, and Poles.[37]

In the decades following the end of the Napoleonic wars, forms of government in the United States, the kingdom of Great Britain and Ireland, and France all underwent changes. In the United States and in Britain and Ireland these changes were achieved by legal means and were broadly democratizing. In the United States, they involved changes in state constitutions. From 1820, some states new to the Union identified the offer of universal (manhood) suffrage as a possible means of attracting settlers. Some old states followed suit. Though there were no significant amendments to the Federal Constitution, Andrew Jackson did what he could to emphasize the president's status and power as an independent representative of the people. In Britain and Ireland, rationalization and extension of the parliamentary franchise in 1832 (by three separate acts, dealing with England and Wales, Scotland and Ireland) was followed by (similarly parallel) measures of local government reform, designed especially to make urban governing bodies elective and accountable. In France, change was effected by a variety of more and less extra-legal devices, and there was no clear direction of travel. The Restoration saw the monarch (under pressure from the Allies) grant a written Constitution (drafted for him by the imperial Senate as its last significant act). This enshrined a bicameral representative assembly, as well as assurances that civil liberties would be broadly respected. France remained a constitutional monarchy for the next thirty-three years; for the next five, under republican auspices, it continued to operate a mixed government, in which the power of the executive was counterweighted by the power of an elected assembly. But following that, Louis Napoleon reinstated what was effectively a plebiscitary dictatorship.[38]

At times of change in forms of government, it was always possible to advert to practice elsewhere, as a way of generating options or assessing alternatives. American, British, and French examples, which were all widely known and well documented, were often (though by no means always accurately) cited. The French broadly followed British example when they instituted constitutional monarchies in 1814/15 and in 1830 (though they also repeatedly noted ways in which they differed and wished to differ from Britain). Following the revolution

---

[37] Maurizio Isabella, *Risorgimento in Exile: Italian Emigrés and the Liberal International in the Post-Napoleonic Era* (Oxford, 2009), Part I; Clive H. Church, *Europe in 1830: Revolution and Political Change* (London, 1983); Jonathan Sperber, *The European Revolutions, 1848–1851* (Cambridge, 1994); Salvo Mastellone, 'Mazzini's International League and the Politics of the London Democratic Manifestos, 1837–50', in C. A. Bayly and Eugenio F. Biagini (eds), *Giuseppe Mazzini and the Globalisation of Democratic Nationalism 1830–1920* (Oxford, 2008).

[38] Morton Keller, *America's Three Regimes: A New Political History* (Oxford, 2007); Philip Harling, *The Modern British State: An Historical Introduction* (Cambridge, 2001); André Jardin and André-Jean Tudesq, *Restoration and Reaction 1815–1848*, trans. Elborg Forster (Cambridge, 1983) for outline accounts.

of 1848, American example was much invoked, especially by advocates of a two-chamber legislature—though it was ultimately decided that a single-chamber legislature better expressed the unity of the French people. The establishment of the post of President of the Republic broadly followed American example, though suggestions that popular election be in some way institutionally mediated (as under the Federal Constitution) were rejected. Britons cited American example—sometimes positively, sometimes negatively—when they wanted to think about how a broader electorate might behave, and how it might be managed. American experience was cited mainly against the secret ballot (which Parliament in 1840 decided not to adopt).[39]

John Markoff, in his book *Waves of Democracy*, argues that what we now recognize as standard technologies of democratic practice had multiple origins; they have developed by a cumulative process of selective imitation over time.[40] Arguably something like that process of mutual inspection and selection, giving rise to convergence, was in train in this period. The French, for example, both helped to shape, and themselves participated in, a trend favouring Anglo-American-style direct against their own tradition of indirect voting—such that when manhood suffrage was reinstated under the Second Republic voting was direct. Nonetheless, underlying expectations, institutional design, and political practice remained multiform, as they do today. Knowledge or belief about practice elsewhere generated ideas about options, but local considerations shaped choice. Invocation of examples is often best analysed as a rhetorical strategy.

What made possible such synergies as we can discern? The case of Alexis de Tocqueville illustrates some of the ways in which international interactions were maintained at high social levels. Tocqueville read widely. In Paris, he attended some of the salons at which visiting foreigners were especially welcomed, and thus internationalized his social circle. He travelled internationally, and was introduced to people who shared his interests on these travels (the more so once publication of the first volume of *De la démocratie en Amérique* earned him renown). He maintained correspondence with some of the people he met, and sought out or was sought out by others keen to exchange information and ideas on themes of mutual interest. His books were translated into other languages, and thus were able to reach non-French-speaking audiences; they were also widely reviewed, and thus came to the notice of many who did not read them. Having made his name as an author, Tocqueville was elected a deputy, and was later given ministerial office, further extending his opportunities to gain information (if also complicating his relationship to that information).[41]

---

[39] Benoit Agnès, 'L'Inspiration britannique au miroir du *National* et du *Journal des Débats* (1830–2)', in Patrick Harismendy (ed.), *La France des années 1830 et l'esprit de réforme* (Rennes, 2006); Lahmer, *La Constitution américaine*; Crook, *American Democracy*.

[40] John Markoff, *Waves of Democracy: Social Movements and Political Change* (Thousand Oaks, CA, 1996), and see also his 'Where and When Was Democracy Invented?', *Comparative Studies in Society and History*, 41 (1999), 660–90.

[41] Hugh Brogan, *Alexis de Tocqueville: A Biography* (London, 2006); Alexis de Tocqueville, *Correspondance anglaise* (3 vols, Paris, 1954), *Correspondance étrangère d'Alexis de Tocqueville: Amérique, Europe continentale* (Paris, 1986). For discussion of Tocqueville in the Chartist press, see e.g. *NS*, 2 January 1841.

At lower social levels, popular enlightenment—that is, shifts that increased popular access to, and engagement with, literate culture, including the development of more demotic sections of the newspaper press—helped to broaden the social range of those who could engage with confidence in political controversy.[42] Both international news reporting and movement of people aided the development of mutual awareness across borders. Some awareness of developments in France had penetrated deeply into populations during the first revolution. But as popular political awareness spread, gained more information content, and was complicated by a swirling range of ideological currents, popular engagement with wider developments and their local implications probably also developed in scale and complexity.

Political exile was very much a minority experience in this period, but it did affect many thousands of people. Some French republicans fled to Britain—for example, following the foiling of Carbonari plotting in the early 1820s, or in the wake of the failed risings of the early 1830s; many more made their way to London following the collapse of the second republic. But until that point, most political refugees came to Paris or London from other parts of Europe, or Latin America. Political refugees added to the mix of influences *within* French and British cultures, but exile was of minor significance in terms of interchange between them.[43]

Though distance reduced the attractions of the United States for European political exiles who wanted to keep a close eye on affairs at home and preserve the possibility of intervening quickly, it had other attractions. Financial support might be recruited there—a reason why Daniel O'Connell travelled there in the 1840s, targeting especially, but not only, the expatriate Irish community.[44] To Anglophone proselytizers—such as the followers of Robert Owen—the United States offered a new arena in which to spread the word.[45] For republicans and democrats quitting their native shores in disgust, and not primarily concerned to maintain old connections, it had attractions as a democratic polity, one where land and work were reputed to plentiful, taxes light, and wages good. British Jacobins and United Irishmen headed there in the 1790s; French republicans at the

---

[42] Broad surveys of developments in popular culture in the nineteenth century are also lacking. For particular places, see: David Vincent, *Literacy and Popular Culture: England 1750–1914* (Cambridge, 1989); Niall O Ciosáin, *Print and Popular Culture in Ireland, 1750–1850* (Basingstoke, 1997); Mary Jo Maynes, *Taking the Hard Road: Life Course in French and German Worker's Autobiographies in the Era of Industrialization* (Chapel Hill, NC, 1995). Hannah Barker and Simon Burrows (eds), *Press, Politics and the Public Sphere in Europe and North America 1760–1820* (Cambridge, 2002); Richard D. Brown, *Knowledge is Power: The Diffusion of Information in Early America, 1700–1865* (New York, 1989).

[43] Sylvie Aprile, *Le siècle des exilés: bannis et proscrits de 1789 à la Commune* (Paris, 2010); Lloyd S. Kramer, *Threshold of a New World: Intellectuals and the Exile Experience in Paris 1830–48* (Ithaca, NY, 1988); Sabine Freitag (ed.), *Exiles from European Revolutions: Refugees in Mid-Victorian England* (New York, 2003).

[44] Huston Gilmore, 'Radicalism, Romanticism and Repeal: The Repeal Movement in the Context of Irish Nationalist Culture between Catholic Emancipation and the 1848 Rising' (unpublished D.Phil. thesis, Oxford, 2010), chapter 5.

[45] J. F. C. Harrison, *Robert Owen and the Owenites in Britain and America: The Quest for the New Moral World* (London, 1969).

Restoration; later disillusioned Chartists—though for the discontented from Britain and Ireland, increasingly Australia offered an alternative.[46]

Politically motivated movement was a minor eddy over the surface of deeper currents of short- and long-term movement, all forms of which were on the rise in these decades.[47] The distinction, though, should not be too sharply drawn. People often moved from place to place for more than one reason. The young wine merchant and Bentham associate John Bowring crossed to and fro between London and Paris on business trips in the late 1810s and early 1820s—but he took advantage of these trips to make and maintain contacts with French radicals and republicans.[48] People who moved in the hope of making a better living elsewhere may nonetheless have had well-defined political opinions, which may indeed have framed how they thought about the need to move. Reflection on their past and present experiences from their new home, perhaps under new political influence, led some to write privately or to the press or otherwise in print, providing a political gloss on the contrast. As emigration from Britain to America and elsewhere in the empire rose from the 1820s, and Irish emigration to Britain, the United States, and the empire likewise, the odds grew that people attracted to popular movements in Britain or Ireland would have relatives or friends abroad. Knowledge of why they had gone, and news communicated by those who had ventured abroad, in person or in writing, sometimes played a part in shaping the self-understanding of those who remained.[49]

FINAL THOUGHTS

Synergistic interactions apart, ideas and practices of democracy underwent certain common changes in all the places that this book has considered. In moving towards a conclusion, we will sketch two of these.

First, the period saw a shift in the way in which 'the people' figured in debate. In the later eighteenth century (to schematize), the issue confronting those whom we might very broadly term democrats in the United States, France, Britain, and Ireland had been how to make government more accountable to the people—'the people' themselves often being quite vaguely conceived. During the first third of the nineteenth century, in the countries we are surveying, significant ground was

---

[46] Michael Durey, *Transatlantic Radicals and the Early American Republic* (Lawrence, KS, 1997); David A. Wilson, *United Irishmen, United States: Immigrant Radicals in the Early Republic* (Dublin, 1998); Ray Boston, *British Chartists in America 1839–1900* (Manchester, 1971); Paul Pickering, '"A Wider Field in a New Country": Chartism in Colonial Australia', in Marian Sawer (ed.), *Elections Full, Free and Fair* (Leichhardt, 1991).

[47] Leslie Page Moch, *Moving Europeans: Migration in Western Europe since 1650* (Bloomington, IN, 1992); Dirk Hoerder (ed.), *Labour Migration in the Atlantic Economies: The European and North American Working-Classes during the Period of Industrialization* (Westport, CT, 1985); Alan Atkinson, *The Europeans in Australia: Vol. 2: Democracy* (Oxford, 2004).

[48] Gerald Stone, 'Bowring, Sir John (1792–1872)', *Oxford Dictionary of National Biography* (eds) H. C. G. Matthew and Brian Harrison (Oxford, 2004).

[49] David A. Gerber, *Authors of their Lives: The Personal Correspondence of British Immigrants to North America in the Nineteenth Century* (New York, 2006); David Fitzpatrick, *Oceans of Consolation: Personal Accounts of Irish Migration to Australia* (Cork, 1994).

gained in this regard. The principle that there should be a significant measure of public accountability came to be broadly accepted; to some extent it was formalized in new institutions; more broadly it affected conduct. In this context, a new question came to the fore: accountable to whom exactly? Differences in the ways in which polities and societies were structured produced different forms of marginalization or exclusion and therefore different forms of contention in different places. In Britain, France, and urban America, class was increasingly the characteristic in contention. Were working men to have the vote? If (as in many American states) significant numbers of them had the vote, how could they translate votes into real power? In Ireland, the religious issue was more prominent: the right to vote had been extended to those Catholics who met property or other qualifications in the 1790s (when it had been deemed wise to try in this way to rally them to the existing order), yet Protestant hegemony persisted. In the United States more widely, race was an emergent issue. Extension of the franchise was commonly associated with the formal limitation of voting rights to 'white' men (previously a formal principle only in a few southern states). This in itself was not immediately controversial, but the rise of anti-slavery organization and militancy and fierce debates about the character of America's commitment to freedom staked out ground for future controversy. The question of whether women should have the vote was nowhere central to public controversy, but in Britain it was raised in parliamentary debate leading to the passage of the 1832 Reform Act (which for the first time explicitly confined voting rights to men). In the United States, revisions to several state constitutions explicitly barred women from voting; critics of the Democratic regime noted its insouciance about the rights of women as one symptom of its limitations. In contrast, across southern Europe, where the issue was still how to make government accountable to the people, such refined probing of who precisely the people were as yet barely figured.[50]

Second, the period saw a shift in how issues of equality were conceptualized. Democracy was at this time strongly associated with equality—above all (as Michael Drolet notes in chapter 5) in France, where it came to connote *primarily* the post-privilege or levelled society, but equality was among the things that it connoted everywhere. France had previously had the most significant and powerful regime of privilege (helping to explain the issue's special resonance there). In Britain, certain forms of privilege—noble privilege, in the form of membership of the House of Lords, and religious privilege, arising from the 'established' position of the Church of England—survived through the nineteenth century and indeed survive in reduced form in the twenty-first century, though some other forms of privilege and 'monopoly' (such as privileges associated with membership of urban corporations) were dismantled by the Whig Reform ministry. However, neither in France, nor Britain or Ireland did the legal changes that took place secure agreement that 'equality' now reigned. On the contrary, the problem of inequality was increasingly reinterpreted, not as a question of legal privilege or formal exclusion, but instead as arising from uneven access to social resources. Social justice rose up the agenda. It was plain to all

---

[50] See chapters above.

that this was the next frontier, however much observers differed about possible modes and consequences of breaching it. In France in 1848, there was general agreement (among those elected to the Constituent Assembly) about the merits of establishing a 'democratic republic' (even if it was intentionally left unclear precisely what that entailed). But much more ink (and blood) was spilt over the proposition that what should be called into being was a 'democratic and social republic'.

By the mid-nineteenth century, modern democracy was often contrasted with ancient democracy. Sometimes comparison was held to show the superiority of the modern form, in that the developing practice of representative government had moderated ancient democracy's worst features. Sometimes modern democracy was represented as worse: usually because wanting in public spirit. Modern democracy was said to be deeply coloured by individualism and materialistic competition. Though such contrasts were often drawn, yet it is striking how much ancient tropes continued to shape perceptions of democracy's potential. The ancient pairing of democracy and tyranny continued to shape mid-nineteenth century discourse. Democracy was still commonly represented as tending to bring in its train the tyranny of the masses, whether exercised through intimidation and force or (as Tocqueville suggested) in the relatively benign, though still regrettable, form of pressure to conform to the debased values of mass culture. Equally, observers often continued to fear—and mid-nineteenth-century French experience suggested that there was still reason to fear—that democracy would prove hard to stabilize, tending to give way to monocratic tyranny.[51]

One way out of this determinist fix was to reconsider the ancient record. It could be suggested that the potential of democracy was *not* best demonstrated by the fate of the Roman Republic, but rather by the glory that was Greece: and above all by the achievements of bustling, commercial yet intellectually distinguished Athens. Several proponents of democracy in the nineteenth century saw this as a fruitful line of thought to develop. The Greek insurrection against Ottoman rule— crowned by the establishment of an independent (if geographically highly restricted) modern Greek state, given international recognition in 1830—encouraged fresh interest in the ancient Greek example.[52] By the 1840s, English Chartists paid tribute not only to French Revolutionaries but also to ancient Greek political leaders as their forebears.

It is interesting to observe our forebears rethinking their past in order to open up scope for rethinking their present—but this serves too as a reminder that, though the study of history promises to increase our understanding of human possibility and the forces that shape its realization, there is always some tension between our natural desire to do this in ways that are empowering for us, and what we stand to lose by reshaping the past to fit our own preferences. If we do not discipline this impulse, we risk compromising the very enhancement of understanding that we seek.

---

[51] Bryce, 'Historical Aspect'.

[52] Kyriacos N. Demetriou, *George Grote on Plato and Athenian Democracy: A Study in Classical Reception* (New York, 1999); Caroline Winterer, *The Culture of Classicism: Ancient Greece and Rome in American Intellectual Life, 1780–1810* (Baltimore, MD, 2002).

Guide to Further Reading

* indicates that an item pays special attention to contemporary use of the word 'democracy' and its cognates

US AND EUROPE—GENERAL

*Christophersen, Jens Andreas, *The Meaning of 'Democracy' as Used in European Ideologies from the French to the Russian Revolution: An Historical Study in Political Language* (Oslo, 1966).

Dunn, John, *Setting the People Free: The Story of Democracy* (London, 2005).

Gauchet, Marcel, *L'Avènement de la démocratie.* vol. 1 *La Révolution moderne* (Paris, 2007).

Israel, Jonathan, *A Revolution of the Mind: Radical Enlightenment and the Intellectual Origins of Modern Democracy* (Princeton, NJ, 2010).

Keane, John, *The Life and Death of Democracy* (London, 2009).

Manin, Bernard, *The Principles of Representative Government* (Cambridge, 1997).

Markoff, John, *Waves of Democracy: Social Movements and Political Change* (Thousand Oaks, CA, 1996).

Millar, Fergus, *The Roman Republic in Political Thought* (Hanover, NH, 2002).

Palmer, R. R., *The Age of the Democratic Revolution: A Political History of Europe and America, 1760–1800* (2 vols, Princeton, NJ, 1959–64).

*Palmer, R. R., 'Notes on the Use of the Word "Democracy" 1789–1799', *Political Science Quarterly*, 68 (1953), 203–26.

Roberts, Jennifer Tolbert, *Athens on Trial: The Antidemocratic Tradition in Western Thought* (Princeton, NJ, 1994).

Tilly, Charles, *Democracy* (Cambridge, 2007).

AMERICA

Sources for the study of language and concepts
Eighteenth century (Cotlar)

The research for this chapter was conducted primarily in the Early American Newspaper Database, the Evans Early American Imprint Series, and Madison's Notes on the Constitutional Convention (online at http://avalon.law.yale.edu/subject_menus/debcont.asp).

Nineteenth century (Smith)

The most useful primary sources for examining political language in nineteenth-century America are newspapers, now increasingly available via databases like Readex's American Historical Newspapers and on the Library of Congress's Chronicling America website. Speeches in Congress for this period are available in the Congressional Globe. Political speeches were often reprinted as pamphlets.

General

Horwitz, Morton, *The Transformation of American Law, 1780–1860* (Cambridge, MA, 1977).

Jacobs, Meg, Novak, William J., and Zelizer, Julian E. (eds), *The Democratic Experiment: New Directions in American Political History* (Princeton, NJ, 2003).

Kramer, Larry D., *The People Themselves: Popular Constitutionalism and Judicial Review* (New York, 2004).

*Laniel, Bertlinde, *Le Mot 'democracy' et son histoire aux États-Unis de 1780 à 1856* (Saint-Etienne, 1995).

Tomlins, Christopher L., *Law, Labor, and Ideology in the Early American Republic* (Cambridge, 1993).

Eighteenth century

Adams, Willi Paul, *The First American Constitutions: Republican Ideology and the Making of the State Constitution in the Revolutionary Era* (Landham, MD, 2001).

Bouton, Terry, *Taming Democracy: 'The People,' the Founders, and the Troubled Ending of the American Revolution* (New York, 2007).

Brown, Richard, *Middle-Class Democracy and the Revolution in Massachusetts, 1691–1780* (Ithaca, NY, 1955).

Cotlar, Seth, *Tom Paine's America: The Rise and Fall of Transatlantic Radicalism in the Early Republic* (Charlottesville, VA, 2011).

Freeman, Joanne B., *Affairs of Honor: National Politics in the New Republic* (New Haven, CT, 2001).

Frey, Sylvia, *Water from the Rock: Black Resistance in a Revolutionary Age* (Princeton, NJ, 1991).

Holton, Woody, *Forced Founders: Indians, Debtors, Slaves, and the Making of the American Revolution in Virginia* (Chapel Hill, NC, 1999).

Holton, Woody, *Unruly Americans and the Origins of the Constitution* (New York, 2007).

*Jensen, Merrill, 'Democracy and the American Revolution', *The Huntington Library Quarterly*, 20 (1957), 321–41.

Kars, Marjolcine, *Breaking Loose Together: The Regulator Rebellion in Pre-Revolutionary North Carolina* (Chapel Hill, NC, 2002).

Kerber, Linda K., *Women of the Republic: Intellect and Ideology in Revolutionary America* (Chapel Hill, NC, 1980).

Kulikoff, Allan, *The Agrarian Origins of American Capitalism* (Charlottesville, VA, 1992).

McDonnell, Michael, *The Politics of War: Race, Class, and Conflict in Revolutionary Virginia* (Williamsburg, VA, 2010).

Nash, Gary B., *The Unknown American Revolution: The Unruly Birth of Democracy and the Struggle to Create America* (New York and London, 2005).

Norton, Mary Beth, *Liberty's Daughters: The Revolutionary Experience of American Women, 1750–1800* (Boston, MA, 1980).

Rakove, Jack, *Original Meanings: Politics and Ideas in the Making of the Constitution* (New York, 1996).

Smith-Rosenberg, Carol, 'Dis-Covering the Subject of the "Great Constitutional Discussion", 1786–1789', *Journal of American History*, 79 (1992), 841–73.

Wilf, Steven, *Law's Imagined Republic: Popular Politics and Criminal Justice in Revolutionary America* (New York, 2010).

*Wood, Gordon S., *The Creation of the American Republic, 1776–1787* (Chapel Hill, NC, 1969).

Wood, Gordon S., *The Radicalism of the American Revolution* (New York, 1992).

Wulf, Naomi, 'République ou démocratie? Évolution du système politique américain de la révolution à la présidence de Jefferson (1775–1800)', in Philippe Bourdin and Jean-Luc

Chappey (eds), *Révoltes et révolutions en Europe et aux Amériques, 1773–1802* (Nantes, 2004).

Young, Alfred F. (ed.), *Beyond the American Revolution: Explorations in the History of American Radicalism* (DeKalb, IL, 1993).

Zagarri, Rosemarie, *Revolutionary Backlash: Women and Politics in the Early American Republic* (Philadelphia, PA, 2007).

Nineteenth century

Ashworth, John, *'Agrarians' and 'Aristocrats': Party Political Ideology in the United States, 1837–1846* (Cambridge, 1983).

Baker, Jean H., *Affairs of Party: The Political Culture of Northern Democrats in the Mid-Nineteenth Century* (Ithaca, NY, 1983).

Boydston, Jeanne, *Home and Work: Housework, Wages, and the Ideology of Labor in the Early Republic* (New York, 1990).

Edwards, Laura F., *The People and their Peace: Legal Culture and the Transformation of Inequality in the Post-Revolutionary South* (Chapel Hill, NC, 2009).

Ford, Lacy K., *Deliver Us from Evil: The Slavery Question in the Old South* (New York, 2009).

Hanson, Russell L., *The Democratic Imagination in America* (Princeton, NJ, 1985).

Howe, Daniel Walker, *The Political Culture of the American Whigs* (Chicago, IL, 1979).

Huston, Reeve, *Land and Freedom: Rural Society, Popular Protest, and Party Politics in Antebellum New York* (New York, 2000).

Kohl, Lawrence Frederick, *The Politics of Individualism: Parties and the American Character in the Jacksonian Era* (New York, 1989).

McCurry, Stephanie, *Masters of Small Worlds: Yeoman Households, Gender Relations, and the Political Culture of the Antebellum South Carolina Low Country* (New York, 1995).

Novak, William J., *The People's Welfare: Law and Regulation in Nineteenth-Century America* (Chapel Hill, NC, 1996).

Ryan, Mary P., *Civic Wars: Democracy and Public Life in the American City during the Nineteenth Century* (Berkeley, CA, 1997).

Saxton, Alexander, *The Rise and Fall of the White Republic: Class, Politics, and Mass Culture in Nineteenth-Century America* (London, 1990).

Stanley, Amy Dru, *From Bondage to Contract: Wage Labor, Marriage, and the Market in the Age of Slave Emancipation* (Cambridge, 1998).

Welke, Barbara Young, *Law and the Borders of Belonging in the Long Nineteenth Century United States* (New York and Cambridge, 2010).

Wilentz, Sean, *The Rise of American Democracy: Jefferson to Lincoln* (New York, 2005).

Wilson, Major L., 'The "Country" versus the "Court": A Republican Consensus and Party Debate in the Bank War', *Journal of the Early Republic*, 15 (1995), 619–47.

Slavery—cross period

Genovese, Eugene D., *Roll, Jordan, Roll: The World the Slaves Made* (New York, 1976).

Hahn, Steven, *A Nation Under Our Feet: Black Political Struggles in the Rural South from Slavery to the Great Migration* (Cambridge, MA, 2003).

Harris, Leslie M., *In the Shadow of Slavery: African Americans in New York City, 1626–1863* (Chicago, IL, 2003).

Klein, Rachel N., *Unification of a Slave State: The Rise of the Planter Class in the South Carolina Backcountry, 1760–1808* (Chapel Hill, NC, 1990).

Tomlins, Christopher L., *Freedom Bound: Law, Labor, and Civic Identity in Colonizing English America, 1580–1865* (New York, 2010).

Young, Jeffrey Robert, *Domesticating Slavery: The Master Class in Georgia and South Carolina, 1670–1837* (Chapel Hill, NC, 1999).

FRANCE

Sources for the study of language and concepts
Eighteenth century (Scurr)
There is a rich historiography on these themes, so this chapter is able to exploit both primary and secondary sources. Among primary sources, it draws especially on the rich accounts of some of the more reflective participants and contemporary commentators, thus:

Chateaubriand— *Essai sur les révolutions; Genie du Christianisme* (Paris, 2008).
Condorcet—*Condorcet: Selected Writings*, ed. K. M. Baker (Indianapolis, IN, 1976).
Constant—*Constant: Political Writings*, ed. B. Fontana (Cambridge, 1988).
Robespierre—Maximilian Robespierre, *Oeuvres complètes*, ed. E. Hamel (10 vols, Paris, 1910–67).
Rœderer—*Oeuvres du comte P.-L. Rœderer*, ed. A.-M. Rœderer (8 vols, Paris, 1853–9), and *The Spirit of the Revolution of 1789 and Other Writings of the Revolutionary Epoch [1789–1815]*, ed. M. Forsyth (Aldershot, 1989).
Sieyes—Fauré, C., *Des Manuscrits de Sieyès, 1773–1799, sous la direction de Christine Fauré, avec la collaboration de Jacques Guilhaumou et Jacques Valier* (Paris, 1999).

Nineteenth century (Drolet)
The research for this chapter was conducted primarily in the Bibliothèque Nationale de France and the British Library. The BNF's Gallica website offers a rich source of published material from the nineteenth century (online at http://gallica.bnf.fr/).

General
*Dijn, Annelien de, *French Political Thought from Montesquieu to Tocqueville: Liberty in a Levelled Society?* (Cambridge, 2008).
Godechot, Jacques, *Les Constitutions de la France* (Paris, 1970).
Jennings, Jeremy, *Revolution and the Republic: A History of Political Thought in France since the Eighteenth Century* (Oxford, 2011).
Pertué, Michel (ed.), *Suffrage, citoyenneté et révolutions* (Paris, 2002).
*Rosanvallon, Pierre, *La Démocratie inachevée: histoire de la souveraineté du peuple en France* (Paris, 2000).
Rosanvallon, Pierre, *Le Peuple introuvable: histoire de la représentation démocratique en France* (Paris, 1998).
*Rosanvallon, Pierre, 'The History of the Word "Democracy" in France', *Journal of Democracy*, 6 (1995), 140–54.

Eighteenth century (to 1815)
Aulard, F., *Histoire politique de la Révolution française: Origines et développement de la démocratie et de la République (1789–1804)* (Paris, 1901).
*Baczko, Bronislaw, 'Democratie rationelle et enthousiasme', *Melanges de l'Ecole Française de Rome. Italie et Mediterranee*, 108 (1996), 583–99.
Baker, Keith Michael et al. (eds), *The French Revolution and the Creation of Modern Political Culture* (4 vols, Oxford, 1987–94).

Baker, Keith Michael, *Condorcet: From Natural Philosophy to Social Mathematics* (Chicago, IL, 1975).

Berenson, Edward et al. (eds), *The French Republic: History, Values, Debates* (Ithaca, NY, 2011).

Cobban, Alfred, 'The Fundamental Ideas of Robespierre', in Alfred Cobban, *Aspects of the French Revolution* (London, 1971).

Coppolani, Jean-Yves, *Les Elections en France à l'époque napoléonienne* (Paris, 1980).

Crook, Malcolm, *Elections in the French Revolution: An Apprenticeship in Democracy, 1789–1799* (Cambridge, 1996).

Doyle, William, *Aristocracy and its Enemies in the Age of Revolution* (Oxford, 2009).

*Fabre, Michel Henri, 'Les Mots "nation" et "peuple" dans la langage politique de la revolution francaise', in *Nation et république: les eléments d'un débat* (Aix-en-Provence, 1995).

Fitzsimmons, Michael, *The Night the Old Regime Ended: August 4 1789, and the French Revolution* (University Park, PA, 2003).

Gainot, Bernard, 'Du Néo-jacobinisme de 1799 au libéralisme de 1815: Les impasses d'une opposition démocratique', *The European Legacy: Toward New Paradigms*, 1 (1996), 78–83.

Gauchet, Marcel, *La Révolution des pouvoirs: la souveraineté, le peuple et la représentation 1789–1799* (Paris, 1995).

Gueniffey, Patrice, *Le Nombre et la raison: La Révolution française et les élections* (Paris, 1993).

Hazareesingh, Sudhir, *Intellectual Founders of the Republic: Five Studies in Nineteenth-Century French Republican Political Thought* (Oxford, 2001).

Hufton, Olwen H., *Women and the Limits of Citizenship in the French Revolution* (Toronto, 1992).

Jainchill, Andrew, *Reimagining Politics after the Terror: The Republican Origins of French Liberalism* (Ithaca, NY, 2008).

Jaume, Lucien, *Le Discours jacobin et la démocratie* (Paris, 1989).

Jaume, Lucien, *La Liberté et la loi: les origines philosophiques du libéralisme* (Paris, 2000).

Jones, P. M., *Reform and Revolution in France: The Politics of Transition, 1774–1791* (Cambridge, 1995).

Livesey, James, *Making Democracy in the French Revolution* (Cambridge, MA, 2001).

*Monnier, Raymonde, 'Démocratie et révolution française', *Mots*, 59 (1999), 47–68.

Monnier, Raymonde, '"Démocratie représentative" ou "république démocratique": de la querelle des mots (République) à la querelle des anciens et des modernes', *Annales historiques de la Révolution française*, 325 (2001), 1–21.

Monnier, Raymonde (ed.), *Citoyens et citoyenneté sous la Révolution française* (Paris, 2006).

Pasquino, Pasquale, *Sieyès et l'invention de la constitution en France* (Paris, 1998).

Roels, Jean, *Le Concept de représentation politique au dix-huitième siècle français* (Louvain, 1969).

Sonenscher, Michael, *Before the Deluge: Public Debt, Inequality and the Intellectual Origins of the French Revolution* (Princeton, NJ, 2007).

Sonenscher, Michael, *Sans-Culottes: An Eighteenth-Century Emblem in the French Revolution* (Princeton, NJ, 2008).

Woloch, Isser, *Jacobin Legacy: The Democratic Movement under the Directory* (Princeton, NJ, 1970).

Zizek, Slavoj, 'Introduction', in Maximilien Robespierre and Slavoj Zizek, *Virtue and Terror* (London, 2007).

Nineteenth century

Amann, Peter, *Revolution and Mass Democracy: The Paris Club Movement of 1848* (Princeton, NJ, 1975).

Aprile, Sylvie, *La Révolution inachevée, 1815 à 1870* (Paris, 2010).

Armenteros, Carolina, *The French Idea of History: Joseph de Maistre and his Heirs, 1794–1854* (Ithaca, NY, 2011).

Azouvi, François, *Maine de Biran, la science de l'homme* (Paris, 1995).

Beecher, Jonathan, *Charles Fourier: The Visionary and his World* (Berkeley, CA, 1986).

Drolet, Michael, 'Carrying the Banner of the Bourgeoisie: Democracy, Self and the Philosophical Foundations to François Guizot's Historical and Political Thought', *History of Political Thought*, 32 (2011), 645–90.

Garrigou, Alain, *Histoire sociale du suffrage universel en France 1848–2000* (Paris, 2002).

Goldstein, Jan, *The Post-Revolutionary Self: Politics and Psyche in France, 1750–1850* (Cambridge, MA, 2005).

Guionnet, Christine, *L'Apprentissage de la politique moderne: Les élections municipales sous la Monarchie de Juillet* (Paris, 1997).

Huard, Raymond, *Le Suffrage universel en France, 1848–1946* (Paris, 1991).

Jaume, Lucien, *L'Individu effacé ou le paradoxe du libéralisme français* (Paris, 1997).

Kelly, George Armstrong, *The Humane Comedy: Constant, Tocqueville, and French Liberalism* (Cambridge, 1992).

Klinck, David, *The French Counterrevolutionary Theorist Louis de Bonald (1754–1840)* (New York, 1996).

Lebrun, Richard, *Throne and Altar: The Political and Religious Thought of Joseph de Maistre* (Ottawa, 1965).

Lovell, D. W., 'Early French Socialism and Class Struggle', *History of Political Thought*, 9 (1988), 327–48.

Luchaire, François, *Naissance d'une constitution: 1848* (Paris, 1998).

Manent, Pierre, *An Intellectual History of Liberalism*, trans. Rebecca Balinski (Princeton, NJ, 1994).

Pilbeam, Pamela M., *Republicanism in Nineteenth-Century France, 1814–1871* (London, 1995).

*Richter, Melvin, 'Tocqueville and Guizot on Democracy: From a Type of Society to a Type of Political Regime', *History of European Ideas*, 30 (2004), 61–82.

Rosanvallon, Pierre, *Le Sacre du citoyen: histoire du suffrage universel en France* (Paris, 1992).

Rosanvallon, Pierre, *La Monarchie impossible: les chartes de 1814 et de 1830* (Paris, 1994).

Whatmore, Richard, 'Democrats and Republicans in Restoration France', *European Journal of Political Theory*, 3 (2004), 37–51.

BRITAIN

Sources for the study of language and concepts
Eighteenth century (Philp)

Research for this chapter began with a search of electronic databases for eighteenth- and nineteenth-century newspapers in the British Library; pamphlets and books in Eighteenth Century Collections Online (ECCO) and The Making of the Modern World; also in the British Museum Print Collection (http://www.britishmuseum.org/research/search_the_collection_database.aspx). Locating instances of usage in private papers and correspondence has inevitably been more serendipitous, drawing on various collections (and following the advice of colleagues).

Nineteenth century (Innes, Philp, and Saunders)

This chapter draws on a variety of electronic databases, as well as on some reading in printed primary sources. We have surveyed Hansard with the aid of the Millbank online version: http://hansard.millbanksystems.com/. The British Library's Nineteenth-Century British Newspaper database has been invaluable. It includes for this period the Tory *Morning Post* and Whig *Morning Chronicle*, a variety of local papers, John and Leigh Hunt's radical *Examiner* (1808–81), Cobbett's *Political Register* (1802–36), the radical *Poor Man's Guardian* (1831–5), and several Chartist papers, including the long-running and best-selling *Northern Star* (1838–52). We have dipped into other periodicals and books with the aid of ProQuest's British Periodicals Platform, the Making of the Modern World database (comprising social and economic pamphlets from the Goldsmith's and Kress collections), and Google Books. We would have liked to be able to spend more time exploring local electioneering and other political material. Coverage of the provincial press in the Nineteenth-Century British Newspaper database is not ideal from this point of view: geographical range has been prioritized over political diversity. Hannah Barker and David Vincent (eds), *Language, Print and Electoral Politics, 1790–1832: Newcastle-under-Lyme Broadsides* (Woodbridge, 2001), currently stands alone of its kind. When the History of Parliament's 1832–68 section comes online (at http://www.historyofparliamentonline.org/), that should assist future researchers in exploring this level of political activity.

General

Burns, Arthur and Innes, Joanna (eds), *Rethinking the Age of Reform, Britain, 1780–1850* (Cambridge, 2003).

Cannon, John, *Parliamentary Reform, 1640–1832* (Cambridge, 1972).

Clark, Anna, *The Struggle for the Breeches: Gender and the Making of the British Working Class* (Berkeley, CA, 1995).

Dinwiddy, J. R., *Radicalism and Reform in Britain, 1780–1850* (London, 1992).

Drescher, Seymour, *Capitalism and Antislavery: British Mobilization in Comparative Perspective* (Basingstoke, 1986).

Gleadle, Kathryn and Richardson, Sarah (eds), *Women in British Politics, 1760–1860: The Power of the Petticoat* (Basingstoke, 2000).

Innes, Joanna, 'Legislation and Public Participation, 1760–1830', in David Lemmings (ed.), *The British and their Laws in the Eighteenth Century* (Woodbridge, 2005), 102–32.

Innes, Joanna and Rogers, Nicholas, 'Politics and Government, 1700–1840', in Peter Clark (ed.), *The Cambridge Urban History of Britain, vol. 2: 1540–1840* (Cambridge, 2000), 529–74.

Knights, Mark, 'Participation and Representation before Democracy: Petitions and Addresses in Pre-Modern Britain', in Ian Shapiro et al. (eds), *Political Representation* (Cambridge, 2009).

Leys, Colin, 'Petitioning in the Nineteenth and Twentieth Centuries', *Political Studies*, 3 (1955), 45–64.

McCalman, Iain, *Radical Underworld: Prophets, Revolutionaries and Pornographers in London, 1795–1840* (Cambridge, 1988).

McCormack, Matthew, *The Independent Man: Citizenship and Gender Politics in Georgian England* (Manchester, 2005).

Navickas, Katrina, *Loyalism and Radicalism in Lancashire, 1798–1815* (Oxford, 2009).

O'Gorman, Frank, *Voters, Patrons and Parties: The Unreformed Electoral System of Hanoverian England, 1734–1832* (Oxford, 1989).

Poole, Steve, *The Politics of Regicide in England, 1760–1850* (Manchester, 2000).

Randall, Adrian, *Riotous Assemblies: Popular Protest in Hanoverian England* (Oxford, 2006).

Stevenson, John (ed.), *London in the Age of Reform* (Oxford, 1977).

Thompson, E. P., *The Making of the English Working Class* (rev. edn, Harmondsworth, 1968).

Vickery, Amanda (ed.), *Women, Privilege and Power: British Politics, 1750 to the Present* (Stanford, CA, 2001).

Eighteenth century

Barker, Hannah, *Newspapers, Politics, and Public Opinion in Late Eighteenth-Century England* (Oxford, 1998).

Black, Eugene Charlton, *The Association: British Extraparliamentary Political Organization, 1769–1793* (Cambridge, MA, 1963).

Bradley, James E., *Popular Politics and the American Revolution in England: Petitions, the Crown and Public Opinion* (Macon, GA, 1986).

Brewer, John, *Party Ideology and Popular Politics at the Accession of George III* (Cambridge, 1976).

Butterfield, H., *George III, Lord North and the People, 1779–80* (London, 1949).

Clark, Peter, *British Clubs and Societies, 1580–1800: The Origins of an Associational World* (Oxford, 2001).

Corfield, Penelope J. and Evans, Chris (eds), *Youth and Revolution in the 1790s: Letters of William Pattisson, Thomas Amyot and Henry Crabb Robinson* (Stroud, 1996).

Dickinson, H. T., *The Politics of the People in Eighteenth-Century Britain* (Basingstoke, 1996).

*Early Modern Research Group, 'Commonwealth: The Social, Cultural, and Conceptual Contexts of an Early Modern Keyword', *The Historical Journal*, 54 (2011), 659–87.

Goodwin, Albert, *The Friends of Liberty: The English Democratic Movement in the Age of the French Revolution* (London, 1979).

*Hampsher-Monk, Iain, 'The Conceptual Formation of Democracy', in Mauro Lenci and Carmelo Calabrò (eds), *Viaggio nelle democrazia: Il cammino dell'idea democratica nella storia del pensiero politico* (Pisa, 2010).

Harris, Bob, *The Scottish People and the French Revolution* (London, 2008).

Haywood, Ian and Seed, John (eds), *The Gordon Riots: Politics, Culture and Insurrection in Late Eighteenth-Century Britain* (Cambridge, 2012).

Hellmuth, Eckhart (ed.), *The Transformation of Political Culture: England and Germany in the Late Eighteenth Century* (Oxford, 1990).

*Ihalainen, Pasi, *Agents of the People: Democracy and Popular Sovereignty in British and Swedish Parliamentary and Public Debates, 1734–1800* (Leiden, 2010).

Innes, Joanna, 'Des Tisserands au Parlement: la légitimité de la politique du people (Angleterre, 1799–1800)', *Revue d'histoire du XIXᵉ siècle*, 42 (2011), 85–100.

Knights, Mark, *Representation and Misrepresentation in Late Stuart Britain: Partisanship and Political Culture* (Oxford, 2004).

*Philp, Mark, 'Reaching for Democracy in Britain 1760–1830', in Mauro Lenci and Carmelo Calabrò (eds), *Viaggio nelle democrazia: Il cammino dell'idea democratica nella storia del pensiero politico* (Pisa, 2010).

Philp, Mark (ed.), *The French Revolution and British Popular Politics* (Cambridge, 1991).

Rogers, Nicholas, *Whigs and Cities: Popular Politics in the Age of Walpole and Pitt* (Oxford, 1989).

Rogers, Nicholas, *Crowds, Culture and Politics in Georgian Britain* (Oxford, 1998).

Sainsbury, John, *Disaffected Patriots: London Supporters of Revolutionary America, 1769–1782* (Gloucester, 1987).

Thale, Mary, 'London Debating Societies in the 1790s', *Historical Journal*, 32 (1989), 57–86.

Thale, Mary (ed.), *Selections from the Papers of the London Corresponding Society, 1792–1799* (Cambridge, 1983).

Wells, Roger, *Insurrection: The British Experience, 1795–1803* (Gloucester, 1983).

Wilson, Kathleen, *The Sense of the People: Politics, Culture and Imperialism in England 1715–85* (Cambridge, 1995).

Nineteenth century

Belchem, John, *Popular Radicalism in Nineteenth-Century Britain* (Basingstoke, 1996).

Belchem, John. *'Orator' Hunt: Henry Hunt and English Working-Class Radicalism* (Oxford, 1985).

Brock, Michael, *The Great Reform Act* (London, 1973).

Chase, Malcolm, *Chartism: A New History* (Manchester, 2007).

Cookson, J. E., *The Friends of Peace: Anti-War Liberalism in England, 1793–1815* (Cambridge, 1982).

Epstein, James, *Radical Expression: Political Language, Ritual, and Symbol in England, 1790–1850* (New York, 1994).

Fisher, D. R. (ed.), *The History of Parliament: The House of Commons, 1820–1832* (7 vols, Oxford, 2009).

Fraser, Derek, *Urban Politics in Victorian England: The Structure of Politics in Victorian Cities* (Leicester, 1976).

Harling, Philip, *The Waning of 'Old Corruption': The Politics of Economical Reform in Britain, 1779–1846* (Oxford, 1996).

Haywood, Ian, *The Revolution in Popular Literature: Print, Politics and the People, 1790–1860* (Cambridge, 2004).

Hollis, Patricia, *The Pauper Press: A Study in Working-Class Radicalism of the 1830s* (Oxford, 1970).

Hollis, Patricia (ed.), *Pressure from Without in Early Victorian England* (London, 1974).

Pentland, Gordon, *Radicalism, Reform and National Identity in Scotland, 1820–1833* (Woodbridge, 2008).

Pentland, Gordon, *The Spirit of the Union: Popular Politics in Scotland, 1815–1820* (London, 2011).

Pickering, Paul A., '"And Your Petitioners &c": Chartist Petitioning in Popular Politics 1838–48', *English Historical Review*, 116 (2001), 368–88.

Prothero, Iorwerth, *Artisans and Politics in Early Nineteenth-Century London: John Gast and His Times* (London, 1979).

Rogers, Helen, *Women and the People: Authority, Authorship and the Radical Tradition in Nineteenth-Century England* (Aldershot, 2000).

Salmon, Philip, *Electoral Reform at Work: Local Politics and National Parties, 1832–1841* (Woodbridge, 2002).

Salmon, Philip, '"Reform should Begin at Home: English Municipal and Parliamentary Reform, 1818–32', in Clyve Jones et al. (eds), *Partisan Politics, Principle and Reform in Parliament and the Constituencies, 1689–1880* (Edinburgh, 2005).

*Saunders, Robert, *Democracy and the Vote in British Politics, 1848–1867: The Making of the Second Reform Act* (Farnham, 2011).

*Saunders, Robert, 'Democracy', in David Craig and James Thompson (eds), *Languages of Politics in Modern British History* (Basingstoke, 2013).

Thomas, William, *The Philosophic Radicals: Nine Studies in Theory and Practice, 1817–1841* (Oxford, 1979).

Vincent, David, *Bread, Knowledge and Freedom: A Study of Nineteenth-Century Working Class Autobiography* (London, 1981).

IRELAND

Sources for the study of language and concepts
Eighteenth century (Gillen)

I have drawn primarily upon Ireland's very active print culture when writing this essay, privileging pamphlets over newspapers as they tended to offer the most in-depth discussions of the concepts associated with democracy. In addition to the propaganda of the United Irishmen, I have relied on published editions of the papers and correspondence of their leaders, as this is where they were freest about avowing themselves democrats. The extensive 1798 Rebellion Papers in the National Archives of Ireland contain many references to democracy but they tend to be along the lines of complaints that the lower orders in an area have become democrats without much discussion of what that means ideologically. These references do, however, provide indications of what concrete changes were expected from democracy among the lower orders, and I have silently drawn on the Rebellion Papers (and the historiography) when discussing this issue. Almost all the pamphlets used are easily accessible through *Eighteenth Century Collections Online* or Google Books. The best place for Irish newspapers is the National Library of Ireland, but the British Library is also excellent, while the Bodleian and Liverpool University Library hold microfilms of the *Northern Star*. Liverpool also holds the Rebellion Papers on microfilm.

Nineteenth century (Colantonio)

In search of the uses of the word 'democracy' in Ireland (1830–1840s), I went through newspapers, where I found interesting leading articles and where public meetings were widely reported and political speeches (e.g. O'Connell, H. Cooke, W. Saurin) often reproduced at length. I examined mainly the nationalist press—local (*Tuam Herald*) and national (*Freeman's Journal, Dublin Evening Post, The Nation*)—as well as the unionist *Belfast News Letter*. My task was facilitated by the digitization of those titles (*Irish Newspaper Archives:* http://www.irishnewsarchive.com; *The British Newspaper Archive:* http://www.british newspaperarchive.co.uk), which allows research by keywords. A number of nineteenth-century French titles, briefly mentioned in my paper, are also accessible online via the *Gallica* website (http://gallica.bnf.fr). To explore more specifically O'Connell's language of democracy, *Hansard's Parliamentary Debates* is useful, as are other collections of his speeches and public letters (for example M. F. Cusacks, *The Speeches and Public Letters of the Liberator*, 1875, 2 vols), and of course his voluminous correspondence, edited by M. R. O'Connell (8 vols, 1972–80), now accessible online: http://www.irishmanuscripts. ie/digital. Lastly, among contemporaneous foreign comments on 'Irish democracy', Gustave de Beaumont's *Ireland: Social, Political, and Religious* is certainly one of the most thoroughgoing.

General

Bartlett, Thomas, *The Fall and Rise of the Irish Nation: The Catholic Question 1690–1830* (Dublin, 1992).

Blackstock, Alan, *Loyalism in Ireland 1789–1829* (Woodbridge, 2007).

Hall, Gerard R., *Ulster Liberalism 1778–1876: The Middle Path* (Dublin, 2011).

Hill, Jacqueline, *From Patriots to Unionists: Dublin Civic Politics and Irish Protestant Patriotism, 1660–1840* (Oxford, 1997).

Whelan, Kevin, *The Tree of Liberty: Radicalism, Catholicism and the Construction of Irish Identity, 1760–1830* (Cork, 1996).

Eighteenth century

Bartlett, Thomas, Dickson, David, Keogh, Dáire, and Whelan, Kevin (eds), *1798: A Bicentenary History* (Dublin, 2003).

Connolly, S. J., *Divided Kingdom: Ireland 1630–1800* (Oxford, 2008).

Connolly, S. J. (ed.), *Political Ideas in Eighteenth-Century Ireland* (Dublin, 2000).

Curtin, Nancy J., *The United Irishmen: Popular Politics in Ulster and Dublin, 1791–1798* (Oxford, 1994).

Elliott, Marianne, *Partners in Revolution: The United Irishmen and France* (New Haven, CT, 1982).

Higgins, Padhraig, *A Nation of Politicians: Gender, Patriotism and Political Culture in Late Eighteenth-Century Ireland* (Madison, WI, 2010).

McBride, Ian, *Eighteenth-Century Ireland: The Isle of Slaves* (Dublin, 2009).

Morley, Vincent, *Irish Opinion and the American Revolution, 1760–1783* (Cambridge, 2002).

Ó Ciardha, Eamonn, *Ireland and the Jacobite Cause 1685–1766: A Fatal Attachment* (Dublin, 2002).

O'Connell, Maurice R., *Irish Politics and Social Conflict in the Age of the American Revolution* (Philadelphia, PA, 1965).

Quinn, James, 'The United Irishmen and Social Reform', *Irish Historical Studies*, 31 (1998), 188–201.

Ryder, Sean, 'Young Ireland and the 1798 Rebellion', in Lawrence M. Geary (ed.), *Rebellion and Remembrance in Modern Ireland* (Dublin, 2001).

Small, Stephen, *Political Thought in Ireland, 1776–1798: Republicanism, Patriotism and Radicalism* (Oxford, 2002).

Smyth, Jim, *The Men of No Property: Irish Radicals and Popular Politics in the Late Eighteenth Century* (revised edn, Basingstoke, 1998).

Nineteenth century

Colantonio, Laurent, 'Mobilisation nationale, souveraineté populaire et normalisations en Irlande (années 1820–1840)', *Revue d'histoire du XIXᵉ siècle*, 42 (2011), 53–69.

Connolly, S. J., 'Mass Politics and Sectarian Conflict 1823–30', in W. E. Vaughan (ed.), *A New History of Ireland*: vol. V, *Ireland under the Union, I: 1801–70* (Oxford, 1989).

Cronin, Maura, ' "Of one mind?": O'Connellite Crowds in the 1830s and 1840s', in Peter Jupp and Eoin Magennis (eds), *Crowds in Ireland c. 1720–1920* (Basingstoke, 2000).

Davis, Richard, *The Young Ireland Movement* (Dublin, 1987).

Hoppen, K. Theodore, *Elections, Politics and Society in Ireland 1832–1885* (Oxford, 1984).

Hoppen, K. Theodore, 'Riding a Tiger: Daniel O'Connell, Reform, and Popular Politics in Ireland, 1800–1847', in T. C. W. Blanning and Peter Wende (eds), *Reform in Great Britain and Germany, 1750–1850* (Oxford, 1999).

Kinealy, Christine, '"Brethren in Bondage": Chartists, O'Connellites, Young Irelanders and the 1848 Uprising', in Fintan Lane and Donal Ó Drisceoil (eds), *Politics and the Irish Working Class, 1830–1945* (Basingstoke, 2005).

MacDonagh, Oliver, *The Life of Daniel O'Connell, 1775–1847* (Dublin, 1991).

O'Ferrall, Fergus, *Catholic Emancipation: Daniel O'Connell and the Birth of Irish Democracy, 1820–30* (Dublin, 1985).

Owens, Gary, 'Nationalism without Words: Symbolism and Ritual Behaviour in the Repeal Monster Meetings of 1843–45', in James S. Donnelly and Kerby A. Miller, *Irish Popular Culture, 1650–1850* (Dublin, 1998).

Philpin, C. E. H (ed.), *Nationalism and Popular Protest in Ireland* (Cambridge, 1987).

Ridden, Jennifer, 'Irish Reform between the 1798 Rebellion and the Great Famine', in Arthur Burns and Joanna Innes (eds), *Re-Thinking the Age of Reform: Britain, 1780–1850* (Cambridge, 2003).

SYNERGIES

Cross-period

Aprile, Sylvie, *Le siècle des exilés: bannis et proscrits de 1789 à la Commune* (Paris, 2010).

Blamires, Cyprian, *The French Revolution and the Creation of Benthamism* (Basingstoke, 2008).

Champs, Emmanelle de and Cléro, Jean-Pierre (eds), *Bentham et la France: fortune et infortunes de l'utilitarisme* (Oxford, 2009).

Claeys, Gregory, 'The Example of America a Warning to England? The Transformation of America in British Radicalism and Socialism, 1790–1850', in Ian Dyck and Malcolm Chase (eds), *Living and Learning: Essays in Honour of J. F. C. Harrison* (Aldershot, 1996).

Durey, Michael, *Transatlantic Radicals and the Early American Republic* (Lawrence, KS, 1997).

Echeverria, Durand, *Mirage in the West: A History of the French Image of American Society to 1815* (Princeton, NJ, 1957).

Kramer, Lloyd, *Lafayette in Two Worlds: Public Cultures and Personal Identities in an Age of Revolutions* (Chapel Hill, NC, 1999).

Lahmer, Marc, *La Constitution américaine dans le débat français, 1795–1848* (Paris, 2001)

Rogers, Alan, 'American Democracy: The View from Scotland, 1776–1832', *Albion*, 6 (1974), 63–71.

Twomey, Richard J, *Jacobins and Jeffersonians: Anglo-American Radicalism in the United States, 1790–1820* (New York, 1989).

Eighteenth century

Appleby, Joyce, 'America as a Model for the Radical French Reformers of 1789', *William and Mary Quarterly* 3rd Ser., 28 (1971), 267–86.

*Bourke, Richard, 'Enlightenment, Revolution and Democracy', *Constellations*, 15 (2008), 10–32.

Claeys, Gregory, *The French Revolution Debate in Britain: The Origins of Modern Politics* (Basingstoke, 2007).

Cotlar, Seth, *Tom Paine's America: The Rise and Fall of Transatlantic Radicalism in the Early Republic* (Charlottesville, VA, 2011).

Darnton, Robert, 'The Craze for America: Condorcet and Brissot', in Darnton (ed.), *George Washington's False Teeth* (New York, 2003).

Dippel, Horst, 'Condorcet et la discussion des constitutions américaines en France avant 1789', in Anne-Marie Chouillet and Pierre Crepel (eds), *Condorcet: Homme des lumières et de la révolution* (Fontenay-aux-Roses, 1997).

Elliott, Marianne, *Partners in Revolution: The United Irishmen and France* (New Haven, CT, 1982).

Hammersley, Rachel, *French Revolutionaries and English Republicans: The Cordeliers Club, 1790–1794* (Woodbridge, 2005).

Harris, Bob, *The Scottish People and the French Revolution* (London, 2008).

Lutaud, Olivier, 'Emprunts de la révolution française à la première révolution anglaise. De Stuart à Capet, de Cromwell à Bonaparte', *Revue d'histoire moderne et contemporaine*, 37 (1990), 589–607.

Morgan, Edmund S., *Inventing the People: The Rise of Popular Sovereignty in England and America* (New York, 1988).

Morley, Vincent, *Irish Opinion and the American Revolution, 1760–1783* (Cambridge, 2002).

O'Connell, Maurice R., *Irish Politics and Social Conflict in the Age of the American Revolution* (Philadelphia, PA, 1965).

Philp, Mark (ed.), *The French Revolution and British Popular Politics* (Cambridge, 1991).

Sheps, Arthur, 'The American Revolution and the Transformation of English Republicanism', *Historical Reflections*, 2 (1975), 3–28.

Urbinati, Nadia, *Representative Democracy: Principles and Genealogy* (Chicago, IL, 2006).

Whatmore, Richard, 'Etienne Dumont, the British Constitution and the French Revolution', *Historical Journal*, 50 (2007), 23-47.

Nineteenth century

Agnès, Benoît, 'L'Appel au pouvoir. Essai sur le petitionnement auprès des chambres législatives et électives en France et au Royaume Uni entre 1814 et 1848' (unpublished doctoral thesis, Paris I, 2009).

Agnès, Benoît, 'L'inspiration britannique au miroir du *National* et du *Journal des Débats* (1830–2), in Patrick Harismendy (ed.), *La France des années 1830 et l'esprit de réforme* (Rennes, 2006).

Bayly, C. A. and Biagini, Eugenio F. (eds), *Giuseppe Mazzini and the Globalisation of Democratic Nationalism 1830–1920* (Oxford, 2008).

Bensimon, Fabrice, *Les Britanniques face à la revolution française de 1848* (Paris, 2000).

Bertier de Sauvigny, Guillaume de, *La Révolution parisienne de 1848, vue par les Américains* (Paris, 1984).

Boston, Ray, *British Chartists in America 1839–1900* (Manchester, 1971).

Claeys, Gregory, 'The Example of America a Warning to England? The Transformation of America in British Radicalism and Socialism, 1790–1850', in Ian Dyck and Malcolm Chase (eds), *Living and Learning: Essays in Honour of J. F. C. Harrison* (Aldershot, 1996).

Crook, David Paul, *American Democracy in English Politics: 1815–50* (Oxford, 1965).

Dinwiddy, J. R., 'English Radicals and the French Revolution, 1800–50', in Dinwiddy, *Radicalism and Reform in Britain, 1780–1850* (London, 1992).

Dowe, Dieter (ed.), *Europe in 1848: Revolution and Reform* (Oxford, 2001).

*Dupuis Déri, François, 'The Political Power of Words: The Birth of Pro-Democratic Discourse in the Nineteenth Century in the United States and France', *Political Studies*, 52 (2004), 118–34.

Finn, Margot, *After Chartism: Class and Nation in English Radical Politics 1848–74* (Cambridge, 1993).

Freitag, Sabine (ed.), *Exiles from European Revolutions: Refugees in Mid-Victorian England* (New York, 2003).

Gilmore, Huston, 'Radicalism, Romanticism and Repeal: The Repeal Movement in the Context of Irish Nationalist Culture between Catholic Emancipation and the 1848 Rising' (unpublished doctoral thesis, Oxford, 2010), chapters 4–5 on the Repeal movement in Britain and the United States.

Gray, Walter Dennis, *Interpreting American Democracy in France: The Career of Édouard Laboulaye, 1811–1883* (London, 1994).

Haynes, Sam W., *Unfinished Revolution: The Early American Republic in a British World* (Charlottesville, VA, 2010).

Kinealy, Christine, '"Brethren in Bondage": Chartists, O'Connellites, Young Irelanders and the 1848 Uprising', in Fintan Lane and Donal Ó Drisceoil (eds), *Politics and the Irish Working Class, 1830–1945* (Basingstoke, 2005).

Kramer, Lloyd S., *Threshold of a New World: Intellectuals and the Exile Experience in Paris 1830–48* (Ithaca, NY, 1988).

Lillibridge, George D., *Beacon of Freedom: the Impact of American Democracy upon Great Britain, 1830–1870* (Philadelphia, PA, 1955).

Luzzatto, Sergio, 'European Visions of the French Revolution', in Isser Woloch (ed.), *Revolution and the Meanings of Freedom in the Nineteenth Century* (Stanford, CA, 1996).

Pickering, Paul, 'Repeal and the Suffrage: Feargus O'Connor's Irish "Mission" 1849–50', in Owen R. Ashton, Robert Fyson, and Stephen Roberts (eds), *The Chartist Legacy* (Rendlesham, 1999).

Prothero, Iorwerth, *Radical Artisans in England and France 1830–70* (Cambridge, 1997).

Rémond, René, *Les Etats-Unis devant l'opinion française 1815–52* (2 vols, Paris, 1962).

Rollett, Henri, 'The Influence of O'Connell's Example on French Liberal Catholicism', in Donal McCartney (ed.), *The World of Daniel O'Connell* (Dublin, 1980), 150–62.

Sperber, Jonathan, *The European Revolutions, 1848–1851* (2nd edn, Cambridge, 2005).

Thistlethwaite, Frank, *The Anglo-American Connection in the Early Nineteenth Century* (Philadelphia, PA, 1959).

Thomson, Guy P. C., *The European Revolutions of 1848 and the Americas* (London, 2002).

Weisser, Henry, *British Working-Class Movements and Europe 1815–48* (Manchester, 1975).

Williams, T. D., 'O'Connell's Impact on Europe', in Kevin B. Nowlan and Maurice R. O'Connell (eds), *Daniel O'Connell: Portrait of a Radical* (Belfast, 1984), 100–6.

Wilson, David A, *United Irishmen, United States: Immigrant Radicals in the Early Republic* (Dublin, 1998).

Index

Printed and bound by CPI Group (UK) Ltd, Croydon, CR0 4YY